Mental Toughness in Sport

The pursuit of excellence in sport depends on four key facets of performance, namely physical, technical, tactical and mental skills. However, when physical, technical and tactical skills are evenly matched, a common occurrence at elite level, it is the performer with greater levels of mental toughness that seems to prevail most often.

This book brings together the world's leading researchers and practitioners working on mental toughness to discuss this vital ingredient of performance excellence in sport, to survey the latest research and to present cutting-edge developments in theory and professional practice. It explores key conceptual, methodological and practical issues including:

- what mental toughness is and is not
- how to measure mental toughness in sport
- how to develop mental toughness in sport
- mental toughness in other human performance settings, from business to coping and life skills.

Also highlighting important avenues for future research, *Mental Toughness in Sport* is essential reading for all advanced students, researchers and practitioners with an interest in sport psychology or performance sport.

Daniel F. Gucciardi is a Postdoctoral Research Fellow in the School of Human Movement Studies, The University of Queensland, Australia.

Sandy Gordon is a Professor in the School of Sport Science, Exercise and Health, The University of Western Australia, Australia.

Routledge Research in Sport and Exercise Science

The *Routledge Research in Sport and Exercise Science* series is a showcase for cutting-edge research from across the sport and exercise sciences, including physiology, psychology, biomechanics, motor control, physical activity and health, and every core subdiscipline. Featuring the work of established and emerging scientists and practitioners from around the world, and covering the theoretical, investigative and applied dimensions of sport and exercise, this series is an important channel for new and ground-breaking research in the human movement sciences.

Also available in this series:

Paediatric Biomechanics and Motor Control
Theory and Application
Mark De Ste Croix and Thomas Korff

Mental Toughness in Sport

Developments in theory and research

Edited by Daniel F. Gucciardi and Sandy Gordon

Routledge
Taylor & Francis Group

LONDON AND NEW YORK

First published 2011
by Routledge
2 Park Square, Milton Park, Abingdon, Oxon OX14 4RN

Simultaneously published in the USA and Canada
by Routledge
711 Third Avenue, New York, NY 10017

Routledge is an imprint of the Taylor & Francis Group, an informa business

First issued in paperback 2013

British Library Cataloguing in Publication Data
A catalogue record for this book is available from the British Library

Library of Congress Cataloging in Publication Data
Mental toughness in sport : developments in theory and research / edited by Daniel Gucciardi and Sandy Gordon.
    p. cm.
    1. Sports – Psychological aspects. 2. Athletes – Mental health.
    I. Gucciardi, Daniel. II. Gordon, Sandy, 1951–
    GV706.4.M46 2011
    796.01–dc22   2011001664

ISBN: 978-0-415-57298-9 (hbk)
ISBN: 978-0-415-85781-9 (pbk)
ISBN: 978-0-203-85577-5 (ebk)

Typeset in Times New Roman
by HWA Text and Data Management, London

Contents

Figures

Tables

Contributors

Mark B. Andersen Victoria University, Melbourne, Australia

Joanne Butt Centre for Sport and Exercise Science, Sheffield Hallam University, UK

Sarah Carson James Madison University, USA

Declan Connaughton University of Wales Institute, Cardiff, UK

Tristan J. Coulter School of Human Movement Studies, The University of Queensland, Australia

Tom Fawcett University of Salford, UK

Sandy Gordon School of Sport Science, Exercise and Health, The University of Western Australia, Australia

Daniel Gould Michigan State University, USA

Katherine Griffes Michigan State University, USA

Daniel F. Gucciardi School of Human Movement Studies, The University of Queensland, Australia

Stephanie J. Hanrahan School of Human Movement Studies and School of Psychology, The University of Queensland, Australia

Sheldon Hanton University of Wales Institute, Cardiff, UK

Robert J. Harmison Department of Graduate Psychology, James Madison University, USA

Clifford J. Mallett School of Human Movement Studies, The University of Queensland, Australia

Herb W. Marsh University of Western Sydney, Australia

Andrew J. Martin University of Sydney, Australia

S. Cory Middleton University of Western Sydney, Australia

Adam R. Nicholls Department of Psychology, The University of Hull, UK

Richard Thelwell University of Portsmouth, UK

Robert Weinberg School of Education, Health & Society, Miami University, USA

Acknowledgements

As co-editors we are indebted to several people whose efforts, expertise and guidance we would like to recognize. First, all chapter authors and co-authors, some of whom also served as reviewers, who evidenced exemplary professionalism both in meeting response deadlines and in producing state-of-the-art contributions. Second, all reviewers who also demonstrated similar discipline in performing their important roles, which included providing constructive and encouraging feedback to all contributors. Finally, the Routledge team who commissioned this book, and in particular Joshua Wells and Simon Whitmore who helped us navigate through the entire editorial process.

Sincere thanks to you all.

Daniel F. Gucciardi
Sandy Gordon

Introduction

1 An introduction to mental toughness in sport

Developments in research and theory

Sandy Gordon and Daniel F. Gucciardi

Introduction

We welcome readers to the most up-to-date and comprehensive collection of articles that examine *mental toughness in sport* to appear in one book. Mental toughness has caught the attention of both the academic community and the general public. For example, a Google search for 'mental toughness' reveals 350,000+ hits. Compare this finding to 'positive psychology' which reveals over 588,000 hits (performed on 12 December 2010). Moreover, at the time of writing, the number of peer-reviewed articles focusing on mental toughness has nearly reached 50. Thus, given the recent interest in this 'thing called mental toughness', and the incidence of empirical examinations and theoretical contributions to a burgeoning literature, as co-editors we felt that the time was ripe for a seminal text devoted specifically to the topic.

Attention on our intention

The main intention of this book is to focus on optimal functioning under stress, both positively and negatively construed forms, which we believe general sport and exercise psychology approaches have not always been good at. So we ask questions related to furthering our understanding of mental toughness and how best to operationalize it, such as 'Is mental toughness an outcome or a process of positive adaptation to stress?' As an outcome, when we describe athletes as being mentally tough, we are probably talking about maintenance of functionality and overt competent behaviours despite the interference of emotionality. But does that mean winning? Are only winners mentally tough? Many might think so; we don't think it is that simple. Or does it mean that mentally tough individuals have highly developed social competencies and mentally healthy perspectives? Again, we don't necessarily think so because psychological well-being alone may provide a misleading impression. For example, we know athletes described as hi-copers who deal with stress best, often show higher levels of emotional stress compared to lo-copers (Gould et al., 1993, 2002). As a process, we ask *why* people are mentally tough and choose to adapt positively to stress and bounce back, not just *how* they do what they do. Clearly, to prevent unhealthy experiences we need to remove or avoid factors implicated in problematic outcomes, but at the same time we want to build skills or capacities to deal with adversity and failure that act as protective processes. Such processes already exist and are informing resilience interventions in cancer survival (Hasse, 2004; Kupst, 2004) and resisting bullying (Luthar, 2006; Masten, 2007).

Another intention of this book, which we wish to clarify from the outset, is to investigate responses to significant challenges, stresses, threats and *not* typical everyday reactions to demands that athletes face regularly. In the same way that muscle physiology distinguishes between tonic activity (baseline electrical activity when muscles are idle) and phasic activity (the burst of electrical activity that occurs when muscles are challenged and contract), contributions in this book attempt to explain when, why and how 'mentally tough' individuals rise to the occasion and appear to thrive under pressure. Tonic measures and studies of typical behaviour can predict phasic action to some extent, but most applied practitioners would admit that they fail to explain individual differences and, specifically, what is exceptional about some performers under fire but not everyone. Furthermore, contributors to this book understand that phasic traits require different research approaches and strategies than investigations of tonic traits. They also understand that, besides some work on resilience, general psychology has failed to account for how certain individuals respond the way they do when their typical (tonic) responses are challenged.

We also intend to describe the lineage of mental toughness research and provide some common language in terms of definitions. The contributors have drawn on different psychological traditions that have examined optimal human functioning, and while these research trajectories have typically been diverse, and will likely remain so, some sort of conceptual integration, which we discuss in more detail in the final chapter, appears possible. Finally, we deliberately intend to situate our focus exclusively on the individual. While mental toughness is relevant for groups, teams, tribes, federations, organizations, communities and societies, contributions to this book will only address the individual as the level of analysis and application.

Planning

In planning this book our general aims were twofold. First, we wanted to draw together the existing expertise of international specialists on mental toughness. We invited every colleague who had ever written anything on the topic, or a related area, to consider how best they could contribute to the book. Second, because we wanted to create a resource for practitioners as well as advanced students and researchers, we invited contributions dedicated to applied issues as well as empirical, methodological and conceptual matters. Courtesy of the professionalism, discipline and competence of both our international reviewers (n = 20) and authors (n = 20) we believe we have delivered what we initially planned to produce, and we hope you agree.

Peer-review process

Unlike existing books on mental toughness, contributions to this text were subjected to a rigorous peer-review process in which at least two anonymous scholars as well as ourselves reviewed manuscripts against standard criteria for publication in academic journals. We felt that this process was important, as did our contributors, and that this scientific approach distinguishes this book from all others. Specifically, each chapter was first reviewed by us as co-editors and then by at least two independent scholars. However, rather than have only publication standards in mind, reviewers were asked to present their comments as suggestions on how to improve each manuscript. Subsequently, authors were encouraged to discuss and debate reviewers' comments in their revised submissions so as to facilitate the conceptual evolution of this construct.

Organization of the book

From the contributions we received three themes were identifiable and, subsequently, the ten chapters were grouped into three sections on understanding, measuring and developing mental toughness.

Part 1, 'Understanding mental toughness', is comprised of four chapters. First, Tom Fawcett introduces a phenomenological perspective and presents case studies illustrating the usefulness of this particular qualitative approach. Next, Adam Nicholls critiques research supporting a relationship between mental toughness and coping, and concludes with recommendations on how to develop mental toughness as well as future research directions for examining these two separate constructs. Robert Harmison investigates the utility of a social-cognitive model of personality functioning, namely the Cognitive-Affective Processing System (Mischel and Shoda, 1995; Shoda and Mischel, 1996) for understanding and developing mental toughness. And finally, Mark Andersen adopts a sceptic's view and questions whether or not mental toughness as a distinct psychological construct actually exists, and if it isn't simply a reified popular phrase.

Part 2 has two chapters on 'Measuring mental toughness'. Using a construct validation approach Cory Middleton, Andrew Martin and Herb Marsh review key findings from their own research and then present a general mental toughness in sport measure. In the other chapter, Cliff Mallett and Stephanie Hanrahan join us in reviewing and assessing the extant literature on mental toughness measurement, and offering recommendations specifically related to measurement research issues for the future.

Part 3, 'Developing mental toughness', has four chapters. First, in addition to reviewing the literature on the development and maintenance of mental toughness, Declan Connaughton, Richard Thelwell and Sheldon Hanton report recent investigations of the themes, experiences and strategies that appear critical to the development and maintenance of mental toughness. Next, Dan Gould and his colleagues present an overview of general life skills theory and research, and discuss potential links and applications to the development of mental toughness in sport. Cliff Mallett and Tristan Coulter review several important attributes for success that appear in the literature, and isolate 'will to win' as central both to understanding and developing mental toughness. Finally, Bob Weinberg and Joanne Butt identify facilitative considerations such as phases of development and the importance of significant others. They also provide an overview of both physical and mental strategies to build 'pillars' of mental toughness.

In the final chapter we draw together some of the key findings and issues from contributions in this book and elsewhere, and attempt to summarize past and present approaches as well as offer some suggestions for the future. Our ideas on future research and theorizing are not presented as answers but rather are held up for scrutiny and consideration by others, including you the reader.

References

Gould, D., Dieffenbach, K., and Moffett, A. (2002) 'Psychological characteristics and their development in Olympic champions', *Journal of Applied Sport Psychology*, 14, 172–204.

Gould, D., Eklund, R., and Jackson, S. (1993) 'Coping strategies used by U.S. Olympic wrestlers', *Research Quarterly for Exercise and Sport*, 64, 83–93.

Haase, J. E. (2004) 'The adolescent resilience model as a guide to interventions', *Journal of Pediatric Oncology Nursing*, 21, 289–99.

Kupst, M. J. (2004) 'The adolescent resilience model and interventions to promote resilience critique', *Journal of Pediatric Oncology Nursing*, 21, 302–4.

Luthar, S. S. (2006) 'Resilience in development: A synthesis of research across five decades', in D. Cicchetti and D. J. Cohen (eds), *Developmental Psychopathology*, vol. 3, *Risk, Disorder, and Adaptation* (2nd edn), Hoboken, NJ: Wiley, pp. 739–95.

Masten, A. S. (2007) 'Resilience in developing systems: Progress and promise as the fourth wave rises', *Developmental Psychopathology*, 19, 921–30.

Mischel, W., and Shoda, Y. (1995) 'A cognitive-affective system theory of personality: Reconceptualizing situations, dispositions, dynamics, and invariance in personality structure', *Psychological Review*, 102, 246–68.

Shoda, Y., and Mischel, W. (1996) 'Toward a unified, intra-individual dynamic conception of personality', *Journal of Research in Personality*, 30, 414–28.

Part I
Understanding mental toughness

2 Mental toughness

A phenomenological perspective

Tom Fawcett

The interest in and attention towards understanding mental toughness over the past decade has gathered academic momentum. Academics have investigated this construct from different perspectives initiated by the fundamental question, 'What is this thing called mental toughness?' (Jones et al., 2002). More recent efforts have sought to explore the construct at a deeper level through conceptual, developmental and psychometric examinations. There is little need to assess this body of knowledge here, as comprehensive reviews exist both within this volume and elsewhere (e.g. Connaughton et al., 2008; Crust, 2008; Gucciardi et al., 2009). Nevertheless, this chapter returns to the fundamental question 'What is mental toughness?' and the contention that academics seem to have adopted a fairly myopic approach to the application of suitable research methodologies.

In attempting to understand what mental toughness is researchers initially focused on obtaining the perspectives of participants from different sporting disciplines (e.g. Jones et al., 2002, 2007). Other researchers have looked at more specific sporting disciplines, such as cricket (Bull et al., 2005; Gucciardi and Gordon, 2009), soccer (Coulter et al., 2010; Thelwell et al., 2005) and Australian football (Gucciardi et al., 2008). A key issue with these qualitative investigations is that mental toughness is open to fairly diverse individual interpretation and there needs to be a more cautious approach to assuming a general research consensus, which is becoming a dominant approach to conceptualizing mental toughness. Specifically, it is argued in this chapter that the lack of conceptual consistency in the area may be related to idiosyncratic differences in interpretation. Put simply, different people explain mental toughness differently depending on their personal experience and interactions within their own social world. Thus the term 'mental toughness' may mean something different to different people (depending on age groups, gender, cultures) and is arguably interpreted differently within different situational circumstances (e.g. sports performance, dealing with adversity such as career-ending injury, being disabled or suffering bereavement). The general purpose of this chapter is to introduce the application of the phenomenological approach to understanding mental toughness. Case studies are presented to illustrate the usefulness of this methodological approach for data generation and interpretation.

Phenomenology

Phenomenological inquiry is about attempting to explore the 'insider's perspective' (Conrad, 1987). It is a branch of philosophy and a research method that provides an opportunity to gain an understanding of the meaning of a phenomenon as it really is. The term is derived from two Greek words: *phainomenon*, meaning 'appearance', and *logos*, meaning 'reason' (Seymour and Clark, 1998). Phenomenology was initiated by a German philosopher named Edmund Husserl at the start of the 20th century in an attempt to provide a perspective on how objects and events appeared to consciousness. That is, how people experience objects or events requires conscious interpretation and active processing, although Giorgi and Giorgi (2004: 25) state 'consciousness should not be limited to awareness, but in a much broader sense it would include pre-conscious and subconscious processes'. The primary focus of a phenomenological investigation is on how individuals articulate the world they exist in and describe experiences of the world that surrounds them (Nesti, 2004). Of particular interest is a detailed exploration of the individual's 'lifeworld', the environmental setting and subjective perception or account of an event rather than an objective statement of that event. Few studies have attempted to adopt phenomenological inquiry within sports psychology since the pioneering work of Dale (1996). Within mental toughness research this methodological approach has not yet been explored. Interested readers are referred elsewhere for a more detailed discussion of phenomenology (e.g. Giorgi and Giorgi, 2004; Nesti, 2004).

Exploring mental toughness from a phenomenological perspective is about attempting to get at the essence of what this construct is, how people describe it and experience it, what it means to participants and how it forms part of their daily existence (i.e. 'lived experience'). It is not really about consideration of a collection of group responses from generic or sport-specific samples as portrayed in much of the existing published literature (Bull et al., 2005; Gucciardi et al., 2008; Jones et al., 2002, 2007; Thelwell et al., 2005), but rather is primarily concerned with the individual's interpretation of mental toughness within their own personal and social environment. If mental toughness is an accepted psychological construct, as has been reported over the past 10 years, then by adopting a phenomenological perspective the researcher would focus solely on the present experience. It is about real direct experiences and encounters with the immediate environment. Central to phenomenology is the process of 'bracketing' where a person investigating must attempt to reduce his or her biases by suspending belief in everything that is not actually experienced. If this process is achieved then it is meant to allow for a more direct focus on the 'what' of the experience itself (Nesti, 2004). In summarizing phenomenology, Nesti (2004: 42) concludes that the aim is to 'describe, as far as possible, the intentional experience as uncontaminated by foreknowledge, bias and explanation'.

Interpretative phenomenological analysis (IPA) is a relatively new phenomenological approach (Smith and Osborn, 2004) that attempts to explore in detail how participants make sense of their personal and social world within different contexts, and the main currency is the specific meaning that particular experiences and events hold for participants. IPA was deemed to be ideally suited as an appropriate research method to fit in with the study design, as it offers an alternative approach to how 'sense' is made of people's interpretations of their own personal and social worlds, and views research as a dynamic process, with the researcher being actively engaged in the interpretation of the data. Rather than suspending belief the researcher attempts to make sense of the participant's meaning through interpretative activity.

Research overview

The current research attempted to locate what mental toughness meant to different people in different sporting and outdoor/adventure contexts. By adopting IPA, the primary objective was to explore individual meaning and diversity through the idiosyncratic nature of mental toughness from within the world of each participant.

Sample

As advocated (Patton, 1990), elite athletes ($n = 37$) and coaches ($n = 33$), together with 21 experienced adventurer/explorers ($n = 21$), were purposefully sampled, based on strict inclusion/exclusion criteria. For example, all athletes and coaches had to have medalled or coached medallists at a major international event (Olympic or Commonwealth Games), which at the time of the study data collection (2001) was unique to mental toughness research. A wide range of sporting disciplines were included, such as field hockey, badminton, cycling, track and field athletics, swimming, basketball, equestrian, sailing and windsurfing, rugby, bobsleigh, and canoe slalom. The complementary adventurer/explorer sample consisted of seven Everest climbers (six had successfully ascended the world's highest mountain). The remaining climbers were peer-recognized elite mountaineers who for the past 50 years have regularly climbed the world's highest peaks in the Himalayas, the Karakoram, the Alps and the Andes. The adventurer/explorer cohort included sailors who had successfully crossed the Atlantic, successful polar explorers, expeditioners who had explored remote regions of the world such as the Arka Tagh, the great Australian outback, Patagonia, Amazonia, the Andes and the Galapagos.

As previous research has provided detailed accounts of athlete experiences of how mental toughness may be interpreted (e.g. Coulter et al., 2010; Gucciardi et al., 2008; Jones et al., 2002, 2007; Thelwell et al., 2005), this chapter will focus on alternative interpretations through two case studies of an elite coach and an outdoor adventurer/explorer to demonstrate the value of a phenomenological approach.

Method

In order to phenomenologically explore personal experience and 'get inside the mind' of each individual, an interpretative phenomenological interview method based on IPA was adopted (Smith and Osborn, 2004). This method explored the essence of what mental toughness was by employing more 'in-depth' as opposed to semi-structured interviews, which examined personal accounts of direct experience within sporting and adventure environments. In order to achieve the methodological goal, participants described situations in which they had firsthand experience, thereby allowing them to describe in detail what exactly took place, the thoughts, feelings and emotions which they experienced at that very moment. The aim was to stay faithful to the phenomenon and the context in which it appeared in the world of the participant (Giorgi and Giorgi, 2004). Given that the research was directed at understanding the essence of what mental toughness is all about, the phenomenological method allows individuals to describe their experiences in rich detail, and provides researchers and applied practitioners with information that might be impossible to access in any other way (Nesti, 2004).

Within the interview process a general open-ended question 'What does mental toughness mean to you?' was used to begin the interview. This question was followed by 'based on your direct experience could you please offer a detailed account of one experience where you personally demonstrated or witnessed what you accept as mental toughness?' Follow-up questions requesting the participant to offer elaborations to support their responses were applied. Procedures advocated within interpretative phenomenological method were followed (Smith and Osborn, 2004). The use of open-ended questions with elaboration, together with the rule of *epochè* ('attempt to reduce their personal biases via a suspension of their belief in everything that is not actually experienced': Nesti, 2004: 41), in allowing data to emerge spontaneously were considered essential to the research process. The challenge for a researcher is to allow the voices of subjectivity to emerge authentically in coming to an understanding of what essentially the research respondents mean in their personal accounts expressed through the data collection devices. This rule of *epochè* obligates researchers to separate any past knowledge or experience they might have had in their other positions (e.g. an experienced applied sport psychologist) but then to legitimize that experience by connecting it interpretatively to the meanings of the respondents. Such a connected relationship was only made possible by the concepts of *epochè* and bracketing. Interviews were transcribed verbatim and member-checked for credibility and trustworthiness of emergent themes; researcher interpretations of the participants' discourse reached a 90 per cent success rate.

Data analysis

In accordance with IPA, data collection and analysis involved a dynamic process with the active engagement of the researcher throughout the entire process. Taking an 'insider's perspective' may be complicated by the researcher's own conceptions and acknowledgement of these is required to make sense of a participant's personal world through the process of interpretative activity (Smith and Osborn, 2004). The researcher, being a sport psychologist, has his own opinions and conceptualization of what mental toughness is and how it may be best explained, due to applied experience, extensive reading and his academic responsibility to teach the subject area. Such beliefs must remain suspended in order to reduce the influence of expectations, personal bias and preconceived views. A two-stage interpretation process is involved (i.e. a double hermeneutic): (i) the participant is attempting to make sense of their own world whilst (ii) the researcher simultaneously also attempts to make sense of the participant's construal processes. IPA is basically concerned with what the phenomenon is like from the participant perspective; that is what mental toughness is all about, how it is explained, displayed and demonstrated. Also, IPA demands critical insight and combines empathic hermeneutics with questioning hermeneutics (Smith and Osborn, 2004). IPA encourages researchers to understand the phenomenon from the participant's perspective (adventurer/elite coach/elite athlete); to 'stand in their shoes' and take their side in empathic communication, but distance themselves from their own set of personal beliefs and opinions. Simultaneously, the researcher in this study asked critical questions of the texts from participants such as the following: Is something being expressed that the participants are unaware of? What is the person attempting to convey, given their direct experience? Or, is something else emerging which was not intended? Smith and Osborn (2004: 52) state:

> The word 'understanding' usefully captures the two aspects of interpretation-understanding in the sense of identifying or empathizing with and understanding as trying to make sense of. Allowing for both aspects in the inquiry is likely to lead to a richer analysis and to do greater justice to the totality of the person 'warts and all'.

IPA has a theoretical commitment to a person as a cognitive, linguistic, affective and physical being and for this reason it was suited to the mental toughness investigation. IPA is directed towards making sense of meaning and it has a cognitive analytical concern and combines cognitive and social cognition approaches.

The content and complexity of meaning, as opposed to the assessment of frequency of responses, is central to analysis within IPA. A stepped approach was adopted for the study, as advocated by Smith and Osborn (2004). The stepped approach consisted of searching for initial raw data themes (stage 1), and developing thematic connections and clusters (stage 2). Within such thematic emergence, data which provide the essence of the quality of the emergent theme are explored and extracted. When additional participants are added to the sample the process is replicated, and although the researcher may well locate convergences/divergences in the subsequent data, they seek to recognize ways in which accounts from participants may be similar but also differ (Smith and

Osborn, 2004). The interested reader is guided to the author's doctoral thesis for a detailed explanation of the IPA process when applied to mental toughness investigation (Fawcett, 2006). The reader is referred elsewhere for comprehensive accounts of the phenomenological research process (Nesti, 2004; Smith, 2004), and journal papers which demonstrate the use of phenomenology within sport (Dale, 1996), rehabilitation (Arvinen-Barrow et al., 2009) and health behaviour settings (Willig, 2008).

When adopting the phenomenological approach, the researcher is more interested in the 'person' than the group or shared opinion, since it is argued the person is unique and meaning is more of an idiographic representation, and not something which is comparable between individuals or groups (i.e. nomothetic). However, it is not uncommon for phenomenologists to offer general statements based on commonalities that emerge from their idiographic analysis (Nesti, 2004). It was the intention of the researcher to explore the unique individual experience of each participant, to have them describe their singular and combined set of personal meanings attached to what 'mental toughness' meant to them and have them describe it in rich detail via personal descriptive accounts. This approach provided a different perspective on how mental toughness has been explained in previous work.

Overview of research findings

Interpretations of mental toughness registered massive variation and individual differences existed within and across all samples. There were striking differences on an individual level within each sample (i.e. athletes, coaches, adventurers/explorers) as to how participants interpreted mental toughness, as well as between groups (e.g. the emergent mental toughness interpretations for sporting cohorts differed considerably to the adventure/exploration sample). For example, major emergent constructs such as safety and survival, knowing oneself, coping with success and failure, coping with stress and undivided attention, reflected different interpretations of what mental toughness means to people in different contexts. Put simply, when in an extreme risk environment and performance is a matter of life and death, one's perceptions of what is 'mentally tough' differs from those individuals performing in less risky environments. These emergent themes are unique to the adventure/ exploration sample and reflect the contention that mental toughness may well be individually driven by personal interpretation and possible situational influence (such as the high-risk environment). The interested reader is referred to Fawcett (2006) for a detailed discussion of the overall findings of the research project.

For the purpose of this chapter the findings of the research project will be presented as short case studies containing themes with related discussion and direct quotations to explicate thematic interpretation. This approach is deemed necessary to illuminate the idiosyncratic nature of the data which emerged from the study. At the beginning of each case study a brief vignette will outline the background and situational context of the participant. The case studies will attempt to reflect the diversity of individual interpretation of mental toughness perceptions based on direct experience to support the phenomenological method.

Given that previous work has illuminated the nature of elite athlete mental toughness interpretations, this chapter will focus on alternative perspectives of an elite coach and an experienced adventurer/explorer. To ensure anonymity the names of participants have been changed.

Case study 1 – adventurer/explorer (Alex)

Alex is a high-level mountaineer with over 30 years' climbing experience. He has regularly climbed the world's highest peaks in the Himalayas, the Karakoram and the Alps, and has successfully climbed all 14 of the world's 8,000-metre peaks. Alex has faced many adverse situations whilst climbing, such as surviving in the death zone, losing climbing colleagues in fatal accidents, and suffered numerous major setbacks during his career when experiencing repeated failure on expeditions, through either worsening weather conditions or serious injury. He is an international mountain guide and continues to climb.

With regard to the key facets of mental toughness, the major themes which emerged for Alex were ensuring safety and survival, knowing oneself, having physical coping ability, dealing with stress and anxiety in critical moments, coping with success and failure, and having undivided attention. When asked what mental toughness meant to him Alex explained that the phrase meant different things at different times during high level-expeditions:

> I would have different answers for different times, at the start, in the middle and perhaps right at the very end of an expedition, than what I have now when I've been in civilization for a while and I think about things, but ultimately it is based on your own safety and survival.

Safety and survival

Maybe, as Alex implies, mental toughness may well be interpreted differently depending on the task being performed, either in preparation, application or evaluation/reflection of performance. Within this theme planning and goal setting were considered essential components of mental toughness due to the important factors he identified:

> I would say preparation, attention to detail, accurate risk assessment, the need to be realistic, seeing the bigger picture and having a sense of perspective and being adaptable.

Such characteristics are rarely quoted in previous research conducted with elite athletes, but in a high-risk activity are considered important components of mental toughness. Alex further stated:

> Even getting a trip together is tough with all the planning, sponsorship, getting in to the mountain, uncertainty of the weather, without even considering the

climb itself, which is why I do it. High level climbs [such as K2] are very difficult on certain peaks due to their unpredictable nature.

He emphasized that mental toughness is about having a 'correct response in the "moment" it happens'. Emphasizing the importance of accurate decision-making when high up on K2 close to the summit, Alex explained, 'I had to make the decision to turn around and go back and wait another year for another crack at it.' Accurate risk assessment and making a series of logical judgements related to the challenge were considered central for safety and survival. Alex stated that, 'I'm pushing my envelope but being realistic. Mental toughness is not much more than having made an assessment of the situation and knowing what the real dangers are.'

When asked about 'pushing his envelope' he explained that 'when engaged in the climb essential decision-making is critical to mental toughness' and it becomes 'seriously influenced by altitude and it is mentally demanding', in what Alex termed the need for 'keeping a lid on things'. He explained:

> Everything becomes difficult really when high up in the death zone and it comes down to weighing the situation up, make your judgements and carrying on or turning back. You need to keep your emotions in check, stay composed and stay calm.

Being mentally tough when engaged in high-level climbing requires parallel and simultaneous processing and is dependent on the nature of the direct situation. When faced with a potentially fatal situation, effectively coping with the stress and anxiety whilst making essential decisions and maintaining emotional control are considered by Alex to be prerequisites for safety and survival, and what mental toughness is really all about when securing one's survival. He explained:

> I have fallen through into a crevasse on Kangchenjunga when a snow bridge collapsed and suffered a broken arm, then suffered chest infections which forced a second aborted attempt. I have suffered a slipped disc from a bizarre sneezing incident on Nanga Parbat. I managed to summit K2 but lost a climbing friend with five others on a final attempt.

Effective decision-making also emerged as a dominant theme, which included making correct decisions under pressure, and having patience when making decisions, whilst maintaining emotional control. Alex offered the following quotation:

> Sometimes the right decision is to turn back … to have the mental toughness that says 'I am going to go on under whatever circumstances' can lead so easily to disaster. So it is actually steering the right course and that is not necessarily attaining the objective at all costs. Not letting emotions rule the

quality of your decisions is what a large part of being mentally tough is all about high up in the death zone.

For Alex 'steering the right course' is making accurate and emotionally considered decisions irrespective of the outcome and is more attuned to the process of engagement rather than the final result. He was well aware of the dangers of being consumed by what he termed 'summit fever' and highlighted many climbers who had perished as a consequence of 'getting it all wrong'. This theme is related to how people deal with success and failure experiences.

Coping with success and failure

Alex highlighted that mental toughness is about having the ability and courage to accept failure at the expense of personal achievement or ego satisfaction. He offered the following example to describe his thoughts on this issue:

> People get carried away with their own egos and the need to summit takes control over more logical judgements. People 'lose it' and many people have unfortunately lost their lives because of their obsession to get to the top. I have seen it and witnessed it on both Everest and K2. They gamble and forfeit their lives in the quest for absolute success and the need to avoid failure.

Alex explained that 'ego control' is a central factor in adventure/mountaineering and it does unfortunately cost people their lives. When in life-threatening situations 'ego balance' and the need to make 'logical judgements' are somehow displaced by the desire for outcome achievement and reward. Alex commented that many climbers have a great deal of personal investment in the experience. They have 'limited opportunity to possibly summit on a major peak' and thereby gain public recognition and peer status by 'making their name by bagging the peak', and along with not wanting to be 'thought of as a failure', these are all important factors which fuel one's ego. 'Being mentally tough enough to deal with such matters and deciding that survival is the most important thing and keeping it in perspective when on expedition and living the moment' he described as the thing that requires a high degree of mental toughness. In existing mental toughness research 'ego control' and 'decision-making' remain largely ignored, which is interesting given that most research has focused on elite sports people who can be ego driven and are required to make accurate decisions.

Knowing oneself

Alex discussed this theme as a central mental toughness characteristic in times of high stress and adversity. He described knowing oneself as a 'combination of having absolute honesty with oneself in relation to one's personal competency, skill level and judgement in relation to dealing with a risk situation'. The following quotation describes the real threat of potential death whilst descending K2 and combines numerous aspects of mental toughness:

> I was making a summit bid [on K2] in good weather with three other people. Six people were supposed to be descending from the summit as I went up and I only saw three coming down. Three had fallen off to their deaths in perfect weather, in daylight. So there I was, nearly dark on top of K2 on my own, and I did actually remember thinking 'I'm going to have to pull myself together here and stay in control.

Alex explained that such a difficult situation required him to 'immediately collect his thoughts whilst in isolation'. Mental toughness was needed in his moment of extreme danger whilst dealing with the fatalities on the mountain around him and attempting to pull himself together and to 'stay in control'. He commented that being in the death zone it is 'easy to lose mental function due to high altitude cerebral edema (HACE)' and 'one needs to be very aware of its symptoms due to the rapidity of onset'. Due to his knowledge, experience and awareness that typical symptoms of being extremely fatigued and confused, the presence of a drunken stagger (ataxia), vomiting and hallucinations, he described the moment on top as 'euphoric but concerning and very dangerous'. His account of the lived experience was:

> Not that you don't feel anything sometimes on the top, it's because you're not out of danger, when you're on the top of big mountain like ... it's not over. It's not over until you're back down. I think I tried to force myself to say it's not even half way so I've always got a lot of energy and mental toughness left over to get down. I think the reason a lot of people get killed is that they don't think of the top as half way, they think of it as most of the way. Or they even forget and think 'well I know I can get to the top' and, that's all they focus on rather than thinking, 'I know I can get to the top and back down'. I need to believe I've still got something left at least when on top. I'm sure people push 120 per cent for the top sometimes too early, and pay the price.

The only treatment for HACE is immediate descent, and when performed alone is extremely dangerous as one requires help and support. If descending alone and suffering from HACE then the likely outcome is fatality. Within events that combine high emotion, the need for accurate decision-making and honest risk assessment/appraisal – 'knowing oneself' – Alex regards highly as being a prerequisite of a mentally tough performer.

Connecting themes

Within the IPA it is possible to explore emergent themes which are connected, and previous literature fails to acknowledge that characteristics of mental toughness are related and happen in combination as opposed to being demonstrated in isolation in performance settings. The following quotation highlights how Alex interprets mental toughness in climbing in a way that combines aspects of attentional control, dealing with extreme pressure (life threat), drawing on experience and physical coping ability in explaining how he managed to cope with his adversity whilst surviving in the death zone:

> You have to draw on all the skill level you've developed over more than 20 years of climbing in Scotland and the Alps. I pulled myself together and made sure I kept my feet well apart as I was going down on the easy bits as it's where you can switch off. I'm facing out on the snow slip so I don't catch my crampons, trip and go the full 12,000ft. I could have slid but I kept myself together completely until I got down safely, not far from the tent at 8,000m. It was on the high shoulder up on top of K2. It was more easily angled and even if I fell over I wouldn't go anywhere, it was almost flat. I could hardly walk at that point; I could only do 20 steps and then collapse in the snow. I was absolutely knackered. Once I'd got past the dangerous bit, you know, burnt out, I crawled into the tent virtually on my hands and knees. But you've got no option if you're talking about mental toughness; you have to be mentally tough there. It's really not an option in that situation as if you are not mentally tough you die – simple as that really!

The situation required immense physical, mental and emotional toughness to survive and it is rarely reported that mental toughness might best be considered as a holistic concept as opposed to being described as an isolated factor of attention control, the ability to withstand pain, or having self-belief (see Gucciardi et al., 2009 for an exception). Based on these findings, it appears that mental toughness is displayed as a combination of psychological, emotional and physical responses when challenged rather than any single aspect alone.

When prompted to explain what 'holding himself together' meant, Alex described it as keeping his attention 'on the moment', 'keeping things simple' and 'minimizing risk completely'. It meant drawing 'confidence and self-belief … from experience' developed over 20 years to be able to 'manage the situation moment by moment without being distracted'. Being in the death zone, he was extremely fatigued in a state of what he termed 'burnt out', which he explained was 'mentally, emotionally and physically exhausted' as a result of fighting for his life on a treacherous part of the mountain. Alex stated bluntly, 'it's really not an option in that situation as if you are not mentally tough you die', thereby suggesting that at certain levels mental toughness may well be a contributing factor to life or death experience in the death zone. However, he also stated: 'I know of several very tough mountaineers who have died and this was not because they lacked mental toughness! I also know many climbers who continually fail and they are extremely mentally tough characters.' This point is important as previous mental toughness literature has yet to associate failure with being mentally tough. It is assumed that the winners and the elite have the monopoly on what constitutes being mentally tough. Perhaps most importantly, there are other important reasons for suffering failure which are outside of individual control (e.g. illness, changing weather conditions, injury).

The findings reinforce the need to know oneself in times of real danger as a central component of mental toughness, together with self-belief. Alex explained that having self-confidence in one's ability influences self-sufficiency and reduces the element of self-doubt when making important decisions. The following example demonstrates this theme as he explains his descent on K2:

> I had seen the other party had been through the day before; there were some tracks there and I'd been through the icefalls several times, so I felt confident and I knew where all the crevasses were in order to jump over them. I knew which snow bridges were weak and the ones which were strong enough. But the problem being there are hidden crevasses. You could be walking across a flat snowfield and you could just go into a hole. So I had to pull myself together for that. But that was a calculated risk. I thought, 'I need to go down to base camp', so I went down. I think that is mental toughness, being able to suffer that anxiety and that stress level, and having the confidence to deal with all that, and being able to recover from it.

As shown here, Alex described mental toughness as being able to suffer and manage anxiety in the moment without getting 'phased by it all' and 'staying on top of it', essentially by having the confidence to be able to deal with the situation which was presented to him without considering potential failure. He also describes taking a 'calculated risk' and, when prompted for further elaboration, he explained it as the need to 'weigh up and correctly assess the situation in terms of risk management', as he was fairly confident that he knew the mountain and the geography of the terrain on the lower slopes. Alex explained that the risk was calculated in his favour and he carefully considered the decision to descend, fully understanding that many climbers suffer fatalities on such parts of the mountain when they 'switch off', get complacent and stop doing what has kept them alive until that point. He explained that even experienced mountaineers can make errors of judgement and he places himself on 'mental alert' during such challenges.

Mental toughness was interpreted as the need to be able to handle both success and failure in relation to desired outcomes. Interestingly, not all failure was related to lacking mental toughness and there was evidence in his discourse that such constructs are related to aspects of one's personality and attribution style. For him, it represented the ability to accept failure and embrace the fact that you have been seriously challenged, and survived to have the opportunity for another attempt:

> Your failures are going to be times when you actually get to the top of a mountain and not actually reach your limit. You can have a lot of you left [resources and physical effort] but so often when you have taken it to the limit and failed you have actually taken it to your very limit. So often your failures are illustrations that you have gone to your limit. Whereas reaching the summit and being successful you have not have had the option. Mental toughness is accepting that and realizing it.

This outlines a paradoxical situation where success is an indication that one has not been fully challenged, whereas failure means that one can be pushed further and there remains a challenge to strive for. Being successful, according to Alex, is merely an indicator that one has not been truly tested to the ultimate limit. This perception implies that failing may well be more mentally demanding than achieving success and requires additional mental toughness. The notion that accepting failure is a characteristic of mental toughness is fairly unique, and there is an obvious link to the sporting situation when the need to consider failure in performance is important to how athletes demonstrate toughness (see Jones et al., 2007). Alex perceived failure to be tougher to deal with in the decision-making process:

> Yes mental toughness can make the difference between succeeding and failing. But you can fail and still be extremely mentally tough. In some ways it might be tougher to make the decision to go down rather than to carry on. Acceptance of failure is more difficult to handle when emotions are running high and success is within your grasp.

When prompted to explain why it would be tougher to go down rather than carry on Alex explained that acceptance of failure needed to be balanced with securing safety and survival against the temptation for the pursuit of self-satisfaction and external reward. He explained many climbers are obsessed with social recognition, gaining external credit and what he calls 'bagging the peak'. He described occasions when he turned back on major expeditions and one when within touching distance of the summit, which was possibly the toughest he has ever considered himself in his climbing career:

> I was within touching distance of the top of K2, it was late and the weather was coming in. It is not the place to be stuck in the death zone. I have tried for the past three years. The first time [year] I turned back not far from the summit of K2 because I helped somebody down. The second time [year] the weather broke and I turned back within hours of the summit. For 10 days I was above 22,500 feet and went up to 27,000 feet. Then I finally managed to summit K2 in [year], but it was a terrible experience that resulted in me losing a close friend on the mountain.

It seems perceptions of mental toughness in success and failure experiences are in need of further examination, particularly in how experience of failure is ultimately dealt with and explained. Phenomenological evidence suggests that it is not only required, but can be essential to becoming mentally tougher within an adventure environment.

Mental toughness is not all about outcomes, but more about the mental processes which guide and determine human behaviour (Gucciardi et al., 2009). The phenomenological method revealed the paradox of the perception of failure to be rewarding. To many people not achieving one's ultimate goal is perceived failure, but to adventurers/explorers who value personal challenge and self-fulfillment as the most important motivation, having given their all and not succeeded is immensely satisfying and can be perceived as a relative success. This rather contradictory viewpoint has not been previously reported in mental toughness literature. Dealing with failure is extremely difficult, but through Alex's discourse it appears that it can paradoxically also be satisfying, as he succinctly offered:

> We experience failure occasionally and it just reminds you how wonderful it is to succeed. It is impossible to succeed every time, if you set out your objectives wrongly. Failures are inner rewarding and not external like reaching a summit. I climb to live, not to die. The summit is optional, but returning is mandatory.

It may be that those people who have developed the ability to handle failure and place it in perspective refuse to accept that failure is all negative. They recognize it has much to offer for one's self-development and can be very rewarding if interpreted differently, and used for a positive purpose. They may well be the mentally tough individuals, whilst others wrestle with handling failure as it provides a blow to one's ego. Alex continued:

> Well failure is always present in adventure experiences, and it is very hard to put up with it. I have experienced numerous failures and it has made me a stronger and more mentally resilient person in the long run, even though it was incredibly difficult to handle at the time. The big thing is having a sense of perspective and that requires a lot of mental toughness.

Such examples demonstrate that for some people succeeding is actually viewed as a sign of not being tested to one's true limits. Phenomenological interpretation would suggest that mental toughness in dealing with failure means different things to different people and it is down to how one interprets failure and success that needs to be considered more closely. Mental toughness has multiple meanings attached to it within the adventure context of high-altitude mountaineering. There is no single interpretation which dominates the participant's account.

This case study highlights numerous emergent themes from a single participant from the adventurer/explorer sample. It demonstrates the diversity of possible interpretations of how a person may explain mental toughness. Such interpretations seem not to happen in isolation but in combinations of psychological, emotional and behavioural responses to any given situation. Profiles from other participants registered as much diversity in personal interpretation of what mental toughness is and how it is best explained through direct experience (see Fawcett, 2006). It is hoped that the case-study interpretation provides a fresh insight into what mental toughness means to one participant from within a sample of 21 adventurer/explorers, all of whom offered idiographic representations of what they perceived mental toughness to be.

The focus will now switch to consideration of a female international hockey coach. Mental toughness had not previously been investigated within elite coaching and the study was an attempt to provide fresh insight into complementary perceptions of the concept (Fawcett, 2006).

Case study 2 – elite field hockey coach (Ann)

Ann is an international hockey coach with over five years' elite coaching experience and a past World Cup winner. Previously an elite athlete, having been involved in the sport since she was 6 years old, she made the successful transition to coaching and took her team to fifth ranked in the world, before experiencing a setback in qualification with her squad in the preparation for an Olympics. Around this time she also suffered from personal adversity and retired from the sport just after the Olympics.

When asked what mental toughness meant to her and if she accepted the term within her sport, Ann responded:

> The term mental toughness is one that I'm familiar with and one that is thrown around a fair bit in this sport. I prefer to use the term mental resilience. I think that has a different connotation to it. Also, being mentally resilient as a coach may be different than being mentally resilient as an athlete and I have experienced both. They have different roles and responsibilities and different demands. As an athlete you train and compete, as a coach you help and support athletes to train and compete.

When prompted to elaborate on the difference between the two terms Ann replied:

> I think the word tough sometimes makes you think of absolute strength and it gives a picture of someone who wanders around and looks strong. Whereas I think the term mental resilience is about the ability to cope with lots of things and the ability to keep going and to bounce back. It needs to consider more than just strength such as mental endurance, game intelligence and being able to deal with setbacks and I think that gives me a more preferable picture of what is required at top level, than the term mental toughness. Hockey is not all about strength it is about skill, technique, strategy and being in a team, whilst having an insatiable desire to win through and having the stomach to face and take on adversity.

Ann makes a valid point in challenging the synonymous terms and one which has not been adequately addressed in published literature over the past 10 years, despite the two terms being used interchangeably. Her point which challenged the need to consider contextually different interpretations for what mental toughness may be is also worthy of further critical review. That is, mental toughness from a coach perspective, in performing a coaching role with a unique set of situational demands, is quite different than what athletes may face and this deserves research attention.

When prompted to explain 'lots of things' she responded: 'Issues such as injury, being deselected, poor form, travel and being away from home, suffering defeat and enduring a hard training programme are vitally important performance aspects that require mental resilience.' She did also state that mental strength was important but 'merely looking at mentally tough in terms of a physical image was not a guarantee of actual mental resilience', based on her experiences as a coach. From a coaching perspective, Ann stated:

> Mental resilience has to be quite differently demonstrated in terms of management of athletes, dealing with entire squad issues, collective responsibility, management and organization, media representation, national pressure, pressure of results and organizing training schedules for starters. I do not see the term being easily transferable between the two disciplines.

Ann clearly interpreted the fundamental question of 'what is mental toughness' from dual perspectives and the contextual differences must be acknowledged as an important factor in determining possible interpretations of the concept. To date, there is a dearth of research which attempts to understand what mental toughness in coaching incorporates.

Mental toughness has largely been explained as a response to adversity or a threat, but Ann offers a proactive interpretation:

> I think resilience is also about being proactive and how you prepare to face particular things that are going to be difficult. I tend to work on a philosophy which is very process-oriented. If you can control as many things as you can and set contingency plans or at least be aware of what you are going to do in a particular situation, then you become more resilient. You have either rehearsed it before or you have considered it before, or it is something that's been part of your practice in practical sense.

This proactive interpretation of mental toughness echoes recent research involving Australian football coaches (Gucciardi et al., 2008). Ann strongly reinforced the belief that she considered mental resilience to be multidimensional and not based on any singular characteristic which makes or breaks athletes or coaches. The message that mental toughness is considered to be multidimensional and emerges in many different ways indicates that it is best suited to not being too narrowly defined or reported. Ann preferred to offer examples of combined characteristics as she considered them to be more related to 'reality situations'. Whereas subthemes were used to guide the discussion of Alex's perspectives on mental toughness in the previous example, such headings are not included with Ann to stay true to her viewpoint.

During the interview Ann interpreted mental toughness as being centrally linked to self-confidence and belief, the will to win, hard work ethic, assuming personal responsibility, knowing oneself as an athlete, self-determination and having the courage to operate outside of a comfort zone in training and competition. The majority of these characteristics support existing conceptualizations from within mental toughness research of what elite athletes require to be successful (Jones et al., 2002, 2007). She stated that in many ways coaches also require some of the same characteristics when performing their coaching roles, but there are important additional factors when operating within a coaching capacity. She also made a pertinent point on the relationship between mental toughness and self-confidence:

> I don't see self-confidence and mental toughness/resilience as two separate things. I think part of resilience is if you know yourself well as a person and you have a strong sense of identity, and you know that you can cope, you tend to have the self-confidence within you. It all comes from knowing yourself, recognizing situations and knowing that you have been there before. Then, being able to react, knowing that you can react appropriately and cope with it all effectively.

Self-confidence is consistently supported within existing literature as a mental toughness prerequisite (e.g. Gucciardi et al., 2008; Jones et al., 2002, 2007), but Ann also links it into having a strong personal identity together with having effective coping skills and previous experience. As in the previous case study it may well be that having a strong sense of personal identity, knowing oneself and having a sense of maturity and experience is at the core of mental toughness, plus having the suitable coping skills to effectively respond to situations of pressure and adversity. She stated: 'Self-confidence is very important, but it is vulnerable and open to fairly immediate change', so it may be that being strong in multiple mental and emotional areas of performance enables an athlete to sustain their toughness over a period of time.

Ann identified that athletes who demonstrate self-determination, assume personal responsibility and have a consistent work ethic are more likely to be mentally resilient than athletes who lack these qualities within a squad set-up.

> Even at the top level, what you need is self-starters and athletes who are self-determined and who don't constantly need to be driven. They are prepared to take responsibility for their actions, work consistently hard week in week out; they are driven to want to keep competing and facing the challenge and putting themselves on the line, and also they are committed to improving in their twilight years, they just have this amazing ability just to keep going. I have a couple of senior athletes in the programme who constantly display an incredible level of determination, commitment and resilience in the most difficult of situations.

The coach's comments highlight the importance of intrinsic motivation, personal responsibility and inner drive/determination. When questioned if she believed it is possible to identify mentally tough athletes by their specific behaviour and the way they approach their sport, she offered:

It is the people who work incredibly hard and don't cut corners. They are quite often the ones that when things get incredibly tough are the ones that are never going to back down from the contest. They don't try and run away, because it's almost like they make such a huge investment in everything they do. I think that's part of it, because I think there are people in life that look to do difficult things and look to constantly challenge themselves or to raise the bar.

Ann was challenged to explain what 'raising the bar' would include within her sport and she explained that 'it was those athletes who explore life outside of their comfort zone … deal with difficult situations and they are unflappable. The way they rise to the occasion when the most pressure is on makes them stand out above the rest.'

In the above discussion, Ann is linking mental toughness with some form of adversity situation. She explained being 'unflappable' as remaining 'calm under intense pressure and consistent with it'. Being unflappable, she maintained, means 'being resistant to change' and when under pressure that is what you require in your players in times of difficulty. As a coach she explained that athletes who are 'not easily upset and can handle setbacks well' are the ones who demonstrate mental toughness.

Dealing with performance setbacks was a particularly important mental toughness aspect identified by Ann as an athlete and a coach. The squad she was coaching was initially successful, but fairly inconsistent and she recognized that athletes display mental toughness by the way they deal with performance setbacks. She explains:

> I think everybody accepts that there probably are going to be setbacks, I think, it would be a very naïve approach to say 'oh I am going to get there and I am never going to have any setbacks on the way'. The ability to deal with the setbacks when they come along and recover from them quickly is definitely a sign of mental resilience.

Ann explained that 'recognizing and rationalizing a temporary setback with performance feedback and modifying performance to demonstrate that one has learnt from the experience, may in the short term make athletes mentally stronger'. Recovering from a serious setback, however, demands varying degrees of mental toughness and depends on the severity of the setback: 'It requires a sense of resilience and dogged determination to succeed and learn from a setback if it happens within a major tournament and the next one is a number of years away.' She continued:

> I think that mentally resilient people turn setbacks on their head and say – well whatever the reason was they try to figure it out, deal with it and then go forward. I don't think it does any athlete any harm to suffer a setback early in their career. If they are tough/resilient enough to come back they will do it. That's what makes them tough and I think it is critical because people will

always lose form in every sport, you will never find anybody who hasn't at some stage.

Ann believes that observing the approach/avoidance behaviour in the way athletes deal with setbacks indicates the degree of mental toughness they hold. When exploring her quotations it seems that mentally tough athletes respond better than others. They do not dwell on failure, they deal with it and move on to the next task, almost immediately if required. Reflection time is minimal but effective enough to learn and take note of what is needed to improve. Ann also included a sense of optimism and patience within mentally tough performers. She offered:

When they lose they are much more devastated but stronger, and that allows them to come back much quicker. They are stronger and they think after a setback, 'OK, I'll be strong and think OK, there's another day so what's next, let's set another goal, there will be another day that will allow me to come through.'

Ann conveyed her comments very passionately and emphasized the meaning and the importance of being able to deal with temporary setbacks (performance mistakes) and more serious setbacks (e.g. serious injury, prolonged loss of form, deselection, tournament failure). In many ways it is possibly one of the few measures that allow a coach to assess athletes on mental toughness whilst working alongside them. She continued:

What I would say even when you lose games there are people who fight to the death and they are the ones who are the most devastated. They are the ones who then can step back and reflect and be the most realistic and honest in their assessment of failure. They can point the finger at themselves if need be, and they are the ones with the true mental resilience.

This short case study finishes with a set of detailed quotations from Ann which summarized her thoughts on how important dealing with a setback is to an elite athlete and places it all in perspective in relation to wider life events:

Regardless of whether you are super successful, whether you struggle as an individual or you struggle within a team then there are always going to be situations when you have setbacks. I was part of a very successful programme across two Olympic campaigns but you had athletes who had serious career-threatening injuries, you had athletes who were so close to Olympic selection yet just missed out and yet came back and the next time won gold medals in the next campaign. You had players who walked away and then came back. You had inconsistencies in performance and in some phases of preparation and yet both individuals and the team showed abilities when it counted and when the pressure was really on, to perform and produce and win through they did it.

Conclusion

It is important to register that each individual case chronicles its own unique idiographic profile of how participants attempt to explain mental toughness within their own specific domain. Their interpretations were highly idiosyncratic and such differences were echoed within the remaining members of each sample group. It is within each of the individual profiles that diversity of mental toughness interpretation exists.

The findings offer new insights to some previously neglected psychological, emotional and behavioural characteristics within mental toughness research (e.g. safety and survival, knowing oneself), thereby supporting the notion that it is open to much broader interpretation than currently exists in published literature. This interpretation may be due to a lack of focused research into more specific sporting disciplines as opposed to generic samples, or more importantly due to the lack of methodological diversity, not having used phenomenological inquiry as reported in this chapter. The findings also underscore the importance of differentiating mental toughness and resilience, if possible, and that both may well be contextually driven. Broad views of mental toughness based on generic samples have failed to detail individual differences located within samples and to date mental toughness literature has largely reported group responses. This approach in itself does not convey the potential individual variation of how people purport to fully explain the phenomenon based on important factors such as age, gender, sporting discipline, sporting level or cultural background. Given the application of more varied methodological approaches, diversity of mental toughness interpretations will flourish.

In conclusion, it appears that mental toughness remains unexplained from an individual differences perspective and, given the potential variations possible, due to variables outlined above, together with a distinct lack of idiographic research focus it will continue to confound academics and practitioners in years to come. The main message from the current phenomenological research is that being mentally tough means different things to different people at different times of their life cycle; it possibly changes due to gender, age, level of maturity and cultural background, not to mention the sporting discipline being performed. When one considers life outside of sport the potential diversity of interpretation is amplified. Considering other professions, how people continue to survive in adversity and seriously challenging environments is another interesting question.

References

Arvinen-Barrow, M., Penny, P., Hemmings, B., and Corr, S. (2009) 'UK chartered physiotherapists' personal experiences in using psychological interventions with injured athletes: An interpretative phenomenological analysis', *Psychology of Sport and Exercise*, 11, 58–66.

Bull, S. J., Shambrook, C. J., James, W., and Brooks, J. E. (2005) 'Towards an understanding of mental toughness in elite English cricketers', *Journal of Applied Sport Psychology*, 17, 209–27.

Connaughton, D., Wadey, R., Hanton, S., and Jones, G. (2008) 'The development and maintenance of mental toughness: Perceptions of elite performers', *Journal of Sports Sciences*, 26, 83–95.

Conrad, P. (1987) 'The experience of illness: Recent review and new directions', *Research in the Sociology of Health Care*, 6, 1–31.

Coulter, T. J., Mallett, C. J., and Gucciardi, D. F. (2010) 'Understanding mental toughness in Australian soccer: Perceptions of players, parents, and coaches', *Journal of Sports Sciences,* 28, 699–716.

Crust, L. (2008) 'A review and conceptual re-examination of mental toughness: Implications for future researchers', *Personality and Individual Differences*, 45, 576–83.

Dale, G. (1996) 'Existential phenomenology: Emphasizing the experience of the athlete in sport psychology research', *The Sports Psychologist*, 10, 307–21.

Fawcett, T. (2006) 'An investigation into the perceptions of mental toughness of adventurers/explorers, elite athletes, and elite coaches', unpublished doctoral thesis, University of Northumbria at Newcastle, UK.

Giorgi, A., and Giorgi, B. (2004) 'Phenomenology', in J. A. Smith (ed.), *Qualitative Psychology: A Practical Guide to Research Methods,* Thousand Oaks, CA: Sage, pp. 25–50.

Gucciardi, D. F., and Gordon, S. (2009) 'Development and preliminary validation of the Cricket Mental Toughness Inventory', *Journal of Sports Sciences*, 27, 1293–1310.

Gucciardi, D. F., Gordon, S., and Dimmock, J. A. (2008) 'Towards an understanding of mental toughness in Australian football', *Journal of Applied Sport Psychology*, 20, 261–81.

Gucciardi, D. F., Gordon, S., and Dimmock, J. A. (2009) 'Advancing mental toughness research and theory using personal construct psychology', *International Review of Sport and Exercise Psychology*, 2, 54–72.

Jones, G., Hanton, S., and Connaughton, D. (2002) 'What is this thing called mental toughness? An investigation of elite sport performers', *Journal of Applied Sport Psychology*, 14, 205–18.

Jones, G., Hanton, S., and Connaughton, D. (2007) 'A framework of mental toughness in the world's best performers', *The Sport Psychologist*, 21, 243–64.

Nesti, M. (2004) *Existential Psychology and Sport: Implications for Research and Practice,* London: Routledge.

Patton, M. Q. (1990) *Qualitative Evaluation Methods* (2nd edn), Newbury Park, CA: Sage.

Seymour, J., and Clark, D. (1998) 'Phenomenological approaches to palliative care research', *Palliative Medicine*, 12, 127–31.

Smith, J. (2004) *Qualitative Psychology: A Practical Guide to Research Methods,* Thousand Oaks, CA: Sage.

Smith, J. A., and Osborn, M. (2004) 'Interpretative phenomenological analysis', in J. A. Smith (ed.), *Qualitative Psychology: A Practical Guide to Research Methods,* Thousand Oaks, CA: Sage, pp. 51–80.

Thelwell, R., Weston, N., and Greenlees, I. (2005) 'Defining and understanding mental toughness in soccer', *Journal of Applied Sport Psychology*, 17, 326–32.

Willig, C. (2008) 'A phenomenological investigation of the experience of taking part in "extreme sports"', *Journal of Health Psychology*, 13, 690–702.

3 Mental toughness and coping in sport

Adam R. Nicholls

Introduction

> I think fear sometimes comes from a lack of focus or concentration, especially in sports. If I had stood at the free-throw line and thought about 10 million people watching me on the other side of the camera lens, I couldn't have made a thing. So I mentally tried to put myself in a familiar place. I thought about all those times I shot free throws in practice and went through the same motion, the same technique that I had used thousands of times. You forget about the outcome. You know you are doing the right things. So you relax and perform. After that you can't control anything anyway. It's out of your hands, so don't worry about it. (Jordan, 1994: 11)

In this quotation Michael Jordan reveals the coping strategies he used to manage the stressor of taking a free throw shot knowing that millions of people were watching him live on television. Participating in sport, at all levels, can be a stressful experience (Nicholls et al., 2009b). Failing to cope with stress can result in a variety of undesirable consequences, including decreased performance (Haney and Long, 1995), increased risk of injury (Smith et al., 1992), decreased well-being (Nicholls et al., 2009b), and burnout (Smith, 1986). It is therefore important that athletes cope with the stress they experience.

Both qualitative and quantitative research has revealed that coping is related to the construct of mental toughness (for a review, see Connaughton et al., 2008a). It has been suggested that mental toughness is one of the most important psychological attributes that determines athletic success (Gucciardi et al., 2008, 2009a). Thus, understanding more about mental toughness and the variables that may shape it is important for developing theory-guided mental toughness interventions, which could include enhancing this desirable construct. Several interventions have been developed to enhance mental toughness, but these interventions do not appear to have included any coping training (e.g. Gucciardi et al., 2009b). This finding is surprising given the conceptual relatedness of these two constructs and research supporting the usefulness of coping interventions for positively impacting the ability of athletes to manage stress more effectively (e.g. Nicholls, 2007a; Reeves et al., in press). Thus, the purpose of this chapter is to critically evaluate the literature regarding the relationship between coping and mental toughness.

Mental toughness: a brief overview

Comprehensive reviews of the mental toughness literature are available elsewhere (e.g. Crust, 2008; Gucciardi et al., 2009a). Nevertheless, this brief overview will feature studies that have given rise to a specific exploration of the relationship between mental toughness and coping in sport. Although not a study on mental toughness per se, Gould et al. (1987) were among the first to report a relationship between mental toughness and coping. In this study 126 intercollegiate wrestling coaches completed a survey in which they ranked the importance of 21 psychological techniques or skills. Mental toughness was rated as the most important construct that determines success in wrestling. The coaches in this study also believed mental toughness was reflected in an athlete's ability to cope with stress and the resultant emotions. Gould et al. (1987) did not state how they defined mental toughness or the exact terminology that the coaches responded to when they were ranking the importance of mental toughness in the list of 21 psychological techniques or skills – thereby representing a major methodological limitation to their study.

Building upon this study, Jones et al. (2002) explored the attributes associated with mental toughness. Ten international sports performers participated in either a focus group or semi-structured interviews. Among the 12 attributes reported as being associated with mental toughness were accepting anxiety and knowing that one could cope with it. The centrality of coping to their conceptualization of mental toughness was reflected in their construct definition.

> Mental toughness is having the natural or developed psychological edge that enables you to: generally, cope better than your opponents with the many demands (competition, training, lifestyle) that sport places on a performer; specifically, be more consistent and better than your opponents in remaining determined, focused, confident, and in control under pressure.
>
> (Jones et al., 2002: 209)

Other research has also revealed a link between mental toughness and coping. Thelwell et al. (2005) interviewed six professional soccer players regarding their own understanding of mental toughness. Jones et al. (2002) had suggested that mentally tough athletes 'generally' cope better than their opponents, whereas the players in the Thelwell et al. (2005) paper reported that mentally tough soccer players should 'always' cope better than their opponents. In a study that included 12 international cricketers, it was reported that the most mentally tough players were able to 'cope with pressure'[1] (Bull et al., 2005). More recent research concerning the development of mental toughness found that mentally tough athletes became aware, through experience, that they needed to cope in order to succeed in sport (Connaughton et al., 2008b), although the processes by which coping changed through experience or the strategies employed were not discussed.

Collectively, the results of these studies support the idea that mentally tough athletes are able to cope with the stress they encounter during sport. Nevertheless, there is no evidence from the coping literature to suggest that athletes always cope effectively. Rather, research concerning coping effectiveness has revealed that athletes have both effective and ineffective coping experiences (e.g. Nicholls, 2007b; Nicholls et al., 2005a, 2009b). Perhaps most importantly, the aforementioned research provides little evidence to support the idea that mentally tough athletes cope more effectively than less mentally tough athletes (Nicholls et al., 2008). Despite the reported link between mental toughness and coping, these researchers have failed to illustrate *how* mental toughness is related to coping, and therefore whether athletes having differing levels of this desirable construct: (a) use different coping strategies, (b) cope more effectively, and (c) have higher levels of coping self-efficacy, as is inferred. Before evaluating subsequent research that has attempted to address these gaps in the literature, a brief review of the coping literature is provided to familiarize the reader. For a more comprehensive review of the coping literature, please see recent articles by Nicholls and Polman (2007) or Hoar et al. (2006).

Coping conceptualized

Coping has been defined as 'constantly changing cognitive and behavioural efforts to manage specific external and/or internal demands that are appraised as taxing or exceeding the resources of the person' (Lazarus and Folkman, 1984: 141). This definition and conceptualization of coping has been adopted by over 80 per cent of the coping research articles published in the sport psychology literature (Nicholls and Polman, 2007). However, this definition of coping requires some additional clarification, due to the ongoing debates regarding coping that are taking place in the mainstream psychology literature. According to Lazarus and Folkman, coping is a conscious process that consists of thoughts and actions that are directed towards reducing or eliminating stress. Other researchers (e.g. Coyne and Gottlieb, 1996; Skinner, 1995) have argued that *all* responses to relieve stress should be classified as coping, regardless of whether they are voluntary or involuntary acts. In contrast, Nicholls and Thelwell (2010) argued that only coping strategies that are voluntary acts directed towards reducing stress should be deemed as coping. According to Nicholls and Thelwell, including involuntary responses would involve practically everything that an individual does in response to stress, thereby making it difficult to define and measure (Lazarus, 1999; Lazarus and Folkman, 1984). Furthermore, athletes experience volitional and involuntary responses differently and have the ability to differentiate between behaviours and thoughts that are under control, but less so involuntary responses to stress (Skinner, 1995). Therefore, it would seem highly appropriate to differentiate intentional stress responses as coping, with involitional responses to stress not considered as coping.

Aldwin (2007) also suggested that management skills should not be classified as coping strategies. A management skill is somewhat similar to coping in that the action is either a thought or a behaviour that is learned to cope with stress. However, the key difference between 'managing' and 'coping' is that a management skill is performed without stress. Therefore, the same behaviour such as visualization can be a management skill and a coping strategy at different times for the same individual, depending on whether stress is present. For example, a golfer may use visualization to see the flight of her ball path on the third hole of a round whilst not experiencing any stress and also use visualization to manage the stress she experiences caused by the threat appraisal of hitting her ball out of bounds on the tenth hole. In this example, visualization was a management skill on the third hole and coping strategy on the tenth hole. In determining whether a cognition or behaviour is a coping strategy, one has to determine whether stress is present and whether the individual directs their behaviour and cognitions at reducing the stress they are experiencing.

Classifying coping in sport

Within the sport literature, coping is frequently classified using one of two classifications. First, there is problem- or emotion-focused coping, with some researchers adding a third dimension called avoidance coping (e.g. Holt and Hogg, 2002). Second, researchers have also classified coping as task-, disengagement- and distraction-oriented coping (e.g. Gaudreau and Blondin, 2002).

Problem- and emotion-focused coping

Problem-focused coping refers to strategies that are directed towards the problem that evokes a stress response (Lazarus and Folkman, 1984). There are numerous coping strategies within the sport psychology literature that have been classified as problem-focused coping. These include: increased effort (e.g. Reeves et al., 2009), remained on task (e.g. Anshel, 2001), time management (e.g. Gould et al., 1993b), problem-solving (e.g. Holt and Hogg, 2002) and goal setting (e.g. Thelwell et al., 2007). Emotion-focused coping refers to strategies that regulate the emotional responses to stress, such as anxiety, guilt, or shame. Coping strategies that have been classified within the emotion-focused dimension include: seeking support from others (e.g. Poczwardowski and Conroy, 2002), humour (e.g. Crocker and Graham, 1995), prayer (Gould et al., 1993a) and thought control (e.g. Holt and Mandigo, 2004).

Avoidance coping

Based upon the recommendations of Kowalski and Crocker (2001), researchers have added a third dimension to the two-dimensional classification of coping, called avoidance coping. Avoidance coping refers to strategies that consist of cognitive and behavioural attempts to disengage from a stressful encounter (Krohne, 1993). Strategies that have been cited as avoidance coping include: blocking negative thoughts (e.g. Nicholls, 2007b), walking away (e.g. Nicholls et al., 2009b) and ignoring other people (e.g. Nicholls et al., 2005b).

Task-, distraction-, and disengagement-oriented coping

An alternative approach to classifying coping within the sport psychology literature has been the task-, distraction-, and disengagement-oriented coping dimensions (e.g. Amiot et al., 2004; Gaudreau and Antl, 2008; Gaudreau and Blondin, 2002; Gaudreau et al., 2010). Task-oriented coping includes coping strategies that are aimed at managing the stressful situation and resulting thoughts and emotions (e.g. thought control, mental imagery and relaxation; Gaudreau and Blondin, 2002). Distraction-oriented coping refers to strategies that result in the athlete focusing on either internal or external stimuli that are completely unrelated to the stressful situation, such as where an athlete might be going on vacation. Strategies that are classified within this dimension include distancing and mental distraction (Gaudreau and Blondin, 2002). Finally, disengagement-oriented coping refers to withdrawal strategies from actively trying to achieve desirable outcomes or goals. Strategies such as disengagement and venting of unpleasant emotions have been classified as disengagement-oriented coping (Gaudreau and Blondin, 2002).

Coping effectiveness

Based upon Lazarus's (1999) conceptualization of coping effectiveness, Nicholls (2010: 264) defined coping effectiveness as the 'degree in which a coping strategy or combination of strategies is or are successful in alleviating stress'. Folkman and Moskowitz (2004) suggested that the underlying reason for researching coping is that some forms of coping will be more effective than others and that identifying the most effective forms of coping is vital for developing coping interventions. However, determining coping effectiveness is one of the most perplexing issues in coping research (Somerfield and McRae, 2000). The difficulty in establishing coping effectiveness is because a coping strategy could be rated as being effective at reducing stress during the outset of a stressful encounter, but as the event unfolds the same coping strategy could become ineffective as it no longer reduces the stress a person experiences (Folkman and Moskowitz, 2004).

Scholars from the mainstream psychology literature have debated whether coping strategies can be inherently effective or ineffective. Lazarus (e.g. Lazarus, 1999; Lazarus and Folkman, 1984), for instance, has argued that coping strategies are neither inherently effective nor ineffective. He also stated that a coping strategy could be effective in one situation, but not another. Conversely, Carver et al. (1989) suggested that coping strategies are either predominantly effective or ineffective in nature and this can vary across individuals, although a coping strategy will not be effective or ineffective all of the time.

Within a sporting context, Nicholls (2007b) provided some support for the changing nature of coping effectiveness (Lazarus, 1999), but strategies on the whole are inherently effective or ineffective (Carver et al., 1989). In his longitudinal diary study with five Scottish international adolescent golfers, Nicholls found that certain coping strategies were both effective in managing a stressor during one round and ineffective during the same round or on a different day in managing the same stressor. For instance, to cope with opponent stressors, blocking (e.g. when the golfers stopped any negative thoughts) was cited as an effective coping strategy five times and an ineffective coping strategy on three occasions by the golfers. However, certain strategies such as increasing focus, taking more time and maintaining a routine were only cited as effective coping strategies, whereas making technical adjustments and remembering previous shots were only cited as ineffective coping strategies. The notion that coping strategies are inherently effective or ineffective has been supported by Nicholls et al. (2005a) who examined coping effectiveness among a sample of 18 international youth golfers. In this study there were clear differences between effective (e.g. positive self-talk and seeking on-course social support) and ineffective (e.g. trying too hard and speeding up) coping strategies. Coping effectiveness appears to be an important concept within sporting domains because athletes who cope more effectively maintain performance standards during periods of stress (Haney and Long, 1995) and perhaps more importantly, experience greater emotional well-being during periods of intense stress (Lazarus, 1999) than athletes who cope less effectively.

Coping self-efficacy

Self-efficacy refers to an individual's belief in his or her ability to execute a specific task (Bandura, 1997). Self-efficacy is thought to be an important attribute within sport. For example, a review by Moritz et al. (2000) reported a 'positive' and 'moderate' relationship between sport-specific skill-based self-efficacy and performance in a variety of sports ($r = .38$). It has been proposed that individuals may have a number of efficacy-related beliefs that can be different in nature and can vary greatly from person to person (Feltz et al., 2008; Forsyth and Carey, 1998). One type of efficacy belief refers to a person's ability to cope with stress, which is referred to as coping self-efficacy (Chesney et al., 2006). Coping self-efficacy refers to a person's belief in his or her ability to deploy strategies that will assist in coping with diverse threats or stressors (Perraud et al., 2006). Scholars (e.g. Bandura, 1997; Feltz et al., 2008; Scorniaenchi and Feltz, 2010) have argued that, regardless of the coping strategy an athlete may deploy, coping self-efficacy is one of the most important constructs that shapes coping in sport.

There is an emerging body of research that has explored coping self-efficacy among sporting populations. Nicholls et al. (2010b) explored the mediating role of coping in the relationship between coping self-efficacy and coping effectiveness. Three hundred and fifty-three athletes (male $n = 206$, female $n = 147$) completed the Coping Self-Efficacy Scale (Chesney et al., 2006) the night before an event, with the Inventaire des Stratégies de Coping en Compétition Sportive (ISCCS, Coping Strategies in Sport Competition Inventory: Gaudreau and Blondin, 2002) and the coping effectiveness scale (Gottlieb and Rooney, 2004) completed immediately after competition. Higher coping self-efficacy scores were associated with coping effectiveness ($r = .33$; $p < .01$), which were partially mediated by task- and disengagement-oriented coping. Nicholls et al. (2010a) explored the relationship between coping self-efficacy, pre-competitive anxiety and subjective performance among a sample of 307 athletes (male $n = 252$, female $n = 55$). Pre-competitive anxiety was measured using the Competitive State Anxiety Inventory-2R (CSAI-2R: Cox et al., 2003) and subjective performance was measured using a Likert-type scale (e.g. Biddle et al., 2001). Participants completed the Coping Self-Efficacy Scale and the CSAI-2R before competition and the subjective performance Likert-type scale after competition. There was a positive relationship between coping self-efficacy and performance ($r = .22$; $p < .01$), but a negative relationship between coping self-efficacy and both cognitive ($r = -.15$; $p < .01$) and somatic anxiety ($r = -.17$; $p < .01$).

Mental toughness, coping, coping effectiveness and coping self-efficacy

In an attempt to address the ambiguity between the constructs of mental toughness and coping stemming from qualitative research, a number of studies have quantitatively explored the relationship between mental toughness and variations in coping. The first study that directly explored the relationship between mental toughness and coping was conducted by Nicholls et al. (2008). This study contained 677 (male $n = 454$; female $n = 223$) athletes, who competed at international ($n = 60$), national ($n = 99$), county ($n = 198$), club/university ($n = 289$) and beginner ($n = 31$) levels. All participants completed measures of mental toughness and coping, namely the Mental Toughness Questionnaire 48 (MTQ48: Clough et al., 2002), the ISCCS (Gaudreau and Blondin, 2002). Mental toughness scores correlated with eight of the ten coping strategies on the ISCCS. These correlations ranged from -.28 to .30. Specifically, higher mental toughness scores were associated with a variety of task-oriented coping strategies such as mental imagery, effort expenditure, thought control, relaxation and logical analysis. However, there was also an inverse relationship between mental toughness scores and a number of coping strategies, such as distancing, mental distraction, resignation. That is, the most mentally tough athletes used less of these coping strategies.

Nicholls et al. (2008) also revealed the relationship between the different subcomponents of mental toughness and coping. For example, the highest positive correlation between challenge, commitment, life control, ability confidence, interpersonal confidence and coping was with logical analysis, whereas the highest negative correlation with these five subcomponents of mental toughness and coping was with resignation. Effort expenditure was the coping strategy that had the strongest positive correlation with the emotional control component of mental toughness. Mental distraction and venting emotions had the highest negative correlation with emotional control. The study by Nicholls et al. confirmed that there is an association between mental toughness and coping. More specifically, it provided information regarding the coping strategies used by the most mentally tough athletes, which had not previously been established.

Kaiseler et al. (2009) explored the relationship between mental toughness, stressor appraisal, coping and coping effectiveness among a sample of 482 athletes (male $n = 305$, female $n = 177$). The athletes in Kaiseler et al. (2009)

competed at international (n = 15), national (n = 60), county (n = 220) and club/ university (n = 175) levels. After completing the MTQ48 (Clough et al., 2002), participants wrote down the most intense stressor that they had experienced within the previous 14 days. Participants then indicated how they appraised this stressor by dissecting two 10 centimetre bipolar lines. One bipolar line was anchored with statement 'not at all stressful' versus 'extremely stressful' and the other bipolar line was anchored with the statement 'no control at all' versus 'full control'. The participants then completed a modified MCOPE (Crocker and Graham, 1995), with a five-point Likert-type scale added to measure coping effectiveness. Higher mental toughness scores were associated with more problem-focused coping strategies, but less emotion-focused and avoidance coping strategies. The highest positive correlations between the subcomponents challenge, commitment, emotional control, life control, interpersonal confidence and coping were with the coping strategy increased effort. This study extended the research by Nicholls et al. (2008) to include an association between mental toughness and coping effectiveness, which aligns with previous qualitative research (e.g. Bull et al., 2005; Jones et al., 2002, 2007; Thelwell et al., 2005).

Despite these encouraging findings, Kaiseler et al. (2009) did not assess overall coping effectiveness, so could not ascertain if mentally tough athletes are able to cope more effectively (e.g. Bull et al., 2005; Jones et al., 2002, 2007; Thelwell et al., 2005). Nevertheless, the problem-focused strategies that correlated with higher mental toughness scores (e.g. seeking informational social support, planning, suppression of competing activities and increasing effort) were rated effectively. Another limitation refers to the retrospective recall of the coping strategies used to manage the self-selected stressor, as participants recalled a stressor that had occurred within the previous 14 days. With the passage of time, people cannot accurately recall the coping strategies they deployed. Some individuals may forget the coping strategies they used, whereas others tend to over-report the coping strategies that they used in a stressful incident (Ptacek et al., 1994; Smith et al., 1999). Additionally, recalling coping can be distorted by whether an individual was successful in coping (Brown and Harris, 1978) and the results of a stressful situation in sport (Brewer et al., 1991).

Previous qualitative research supports a relationship between mental toughness and coping self-efficacy (e.g. Jones et al., 2007), and with coping effectiveness (e.g. Bull et al., 2005; Thelwell et al., 2005). Taking a quantitative approach, Nicholls et al. (2010) examined the relationship between mental toughness and coping self-efficacy, and the relationship between mental toughness and coping effectiveness. Their sample comprised of 206 athletes (male n = 182, female n = 24) who competed at international/national (n = 55), county (n = 24), club/ university (n = 119) or beginner (n = 8) level. Participants completed the MTQ48 (Clough et al., 2002) and the Coping Self-Efficacy Scale (Chesney et al., 2006) prior to competing, and the Coping Effectiveness Scale (Gottlieb and Rooney, 2004) within 30 minutes of their competition ending. A stepwise linear regression analysis revealed that mental toughness predicted 3 per cent additional variance in coping effectiveness beyond that explained by coping self-efficacy. This finding provides partial support for the notion that mentally tough athletes, overall, cope more effectively than less mentally tough athletes (e.g. Bull et al., 2005; Jones et al., 2002, 2007; Thelwell et al., 2005). However, it should be noted that Nicholls et al. (in press) did not examine whether the most mentally tough athletes always coped effectively or always coped more effectively than their opponents. Longitudinal research would be required to address this research question. Furthermore, the findings from Nicholls et al. also provide support for Jones et al.'s (2007) assertion that the most mentally tough athletes believe they will be able to cope effectively, as there was a significant relationship between mental toughness and coping self-efficacy ($r = .35$; $p < .01$). A limitation of Nicholls et al. (in press) is the low internal reliability of the coping effectiveness scale (.56) and the influence of social desirability from measuring mental toughness using only self-reported data.

The results from the papers by Nicholls and colleagues (e.g. Kaiseler et al., 2009; Nicholls et al., 2008, in press) provide more quantitative support for a relationship between coping and mental toughness than was initially obtained using qualitative methodologies (e.g. Bull et al., 2005; Jones et al., 2002; Thelwell et al., 2005). However, it should be noted that Nicholls and colleagues used the MTQ48 (Clough et al., 2002) to measure mental toughness. The MTQ48 has been heavily criticized, with some authors even advising 'against its use in future mental toughness investigations' (e.g. Connaughton et al., 2008a: 198), in part, due to a lack of information on the factor structure and the internal reliability for the scale. Although there are limitations of this scale, which will be outlined later in this chapter, it could be argued that the comments by Connaughton et al. (2008a) are somewhat premature and ill-informed because there is evidence to support the construct validity and psychometric properties of the MTQ48. Horn (2002: 39) stated that 'construct validity is demonstrated by an accumulation of evidence that the construct the inventory purports to measure is related to the other constructs with theoretical predictions'. As described above, there is now an accumulation of research that has used the MTQ48 as the measure of mental toughness as related to coping (Nicholls et al., 2008), coping effectiveness (Kaiseler et al., 2009) and both coping self-efficacy and overall coping effectiveness (Nicholls et al., in press). Furthermore, Clough et al. (2002) reported that mentally tough athletes see situations, such as sport, as challenging, which mitigates how an individual perceives potentially stressful situations. This finding has been supported by Kaiseler et al. (2009), who found that the most mentally tough athletes reported stressors as being less intense. Based upon the criteria outlined by Horn (2002), there is comprehensible evidence that the MTQ48 has construct validity.

The psychometric structure of the MTQ48 has also received support. Horsburgh et al. (2009) conducted an exploratory and factor analysis using data from 152 pairs of monozygotic and 67 pairs of dizygotic adult twins, with a twin from each pair randomly assigned the label of Twin 1 and Twin 2, so that independent tests could be carried out. The analysis procedures conducted by Horsburgh et al. (2009) indicate that the MTQ48 had acceptable psychometric properties, although there are limitations of this study pertaining to how the data were reported.

Specifically, Horsburgh et al. could have provided more statistical information regarding the model fit. Despite the limitations of the Horsburgh et al. study, it is still somewhat surprising that Connaughton et al. (2008a) have advised mental toughness scholars not to use a questionnaire that appears to have acceptable psychometric predictive validity and construct validity. Based upon the criteria outlined by Horn (2002), it appears that the MTQ48 should be accepted in the sport psychology literature as it is in the mainstream psychology literature as an established measure of mental toughness (e.g. Marchant et al., 2009; Nicholls et al., 2009c).

Despite there being evidence to suggest that the MTQ48 (Clough et al., 2002) has both predictive and construct validity (e.g. Nicholls et al., 2008), in addition to having acceptable psychometric properties (e.g. Horsburgh et al., 2009), there are a still a number of conceptual issues that should be considered. For instance, the MTQ48 was based upon Kobasa's (1979) conceptualization of hardiness, with the addition of confidence. Therefore, it could be argued that the MTQ48 does not capture all aspects of mental toughness as perceived by other scholars (e.g. Gucciardi et al., 2008; Jones et al., 2002). Additional research is required to further assess the construct validity of the MTQ48 in relation to psychological variables that are thought to be related to mental toughness, other than coping, coping effectiveness, coping self-efficacy or optimism. These analyses should include variables such as motivation, attitude, sport intelligence, resilience and recovery rates from injury (e.g. Gucciardi et al., 2008, 2009a), but most important is 'hardiness'.

Conceptual implications

The evidence from the available literature indicates that there is a relationship between mental toughness and coping. In particular, it would appear that the most mentally tough individuals are likely to use coping strategies such as effort expenditure and thought control, but deploy less avoidance coping strategies (Kaiseler et al., 2009; Nicholls et al., 2008). Furthermore, it appears that the most mentally tough athletes cope effectively and are confident about their ability to successfully deploy coping strategies (e.g. Nicholls et al., in press). It should be noted, however, that coping effectiveness was only examined on one occasion by Nicholls et al. (in press), so it would be incorrect to assume that the most mentally tough athletes always cope effectively. Furthermore, the aforementioned studies by Nicholls and colleagues have been cross-sectional, so this research cannot infer causality. It is therefore impossible to determine if mental toughness is caused by coping, if coping is caused by mental toughness or if mental toughness and coping are caused by other variables.

In order for the mental toughness literature to evolve, researchers could consider integrating coping within their research by adapting or developing new psychometric measurements of mental toughness. Future psychometric measurements of mental toughness could include elements that reflect coping, coping effectiveness or indeed coping self-efficacy, given that these are possibly important components of mental toughness. At the present time, questionnaires such as the MTQ48 (Clough et al., 2002) or the Cricket Mental Toughness Inventory (CMTI: Gucciardi and Gordon, 2009) include a variety of components associated with mental toughness, but do not include questions directly related to coping, coping effectiveness or coping self-efficacy.

Limitations and future research directions

In order to clarify our understanding of the relationship between mental toughness and coping, future research could address some of the limitations of the extant research, such as the cross-sectional nature of coping and mental toughness research. Although the research by Nicholls and colleagues (e.g. Kaiseler et al., 2009; Nicholls et al., 2008, in press) cannot infer causality, it has been argued that cross-sectional research is required when little is known about the relationship between different constructs (Crocker et al., 2010) to guide experimental research. Future research could build upon the existing literature and explore the relationship between mental toughness and coping, using experimental research designs so that causality can be inferred.

Another limitation of the research by Nicholls and colleagues is the participant sampling. Despite large sample sizes, only athletes from the United Kingdom have been sampled. Given that there appear to be cultural differences in coping (for a review, see Anshel, 2010), one might expect there to be cultural differences in mental toughness, due to the association between mental toughness and coping. However, research is required to test this assertion by sampling athletes from a variety of different cultures.

Researchers have generally relied upon athletes self-reporting either their mental toughness or coping, via interviews, questionnaires or diaries. Researchers could use other techniques to rate mental toughness, such as using both coach and peer ratings of mental toughness in addition to self-ratings of mental toughness (e.g. Gucciardi et al., 2009b, 2009c). However, moving away from self-reports is a little more difficult in examining coping or coping effectiveness because coping is a subjective experience; that is, one cannot infer what a person has done from observing them or the outcome of what they are doing (i.e. whether a golfer holes a putt or a striker scores a penalty). It has been suggested that coping effectiveness could be assessed by measuring the outcome of a situation (e.g. Folkman, 1984), such as whether an athlete is successful. However, 'if an athlete is failing, it does not follow that he or she is not coping' (Crocker et al., 1998: 150). Crocker et al. (1998) suggested that there could be a number of reasons why an athlete may fail, despite coping effectively, such as poor technical skills, fatigue, tiredness or an opponent playing well. Instead of using outcomes to assess coping, researchers could perhaps use physiological markers of stress such as heart-rate, blood pressure or cortisol levels to determine the effectiveness of coping strategies deployed. However, these markers would not indicate *how* an athlete has coped. Therefore, self-reports of coping are required to address how people cope with stress.

Coping is a process that changes across the lifespan (Lazarus and Lazarus, 2006) so it could be fruitful to explore whether any changes in coping are associated with mental toughness. For instance, Nicholls et al. (2009d) revealed that athletes of different pubertal status and chronological age used different coping strategies. It would be interesting to monitor mental toughness in individuals through adolescence (12 to 18 years of age), given that this is a time when coping changes the most (e.g. Compas et al., 2001). Researchers could then explore whether changes occur in mental toughness as coping changes. It is accepted that this type of study would be labour-intensive and would take several years of data collection, but it has the potential to shed light on the mental toughness and coping relationship.

Concluding remarks

It is apparent from both qualitative (e.g. Bull et al., 2005; Jones et al., 2002; Thelwell et al., 2005) and the quantitative research (e.g. Kaiseler et al., 2009; Nicholls et al., 2008) that there is an association between mental toughness and coping. Furthermore, elements of coping such as coping effectiveness and coping self-efficacy are also related to mental toughness. At the present time, however, causality has not been established to explain these relationships, which could be resolved by employing experimental research designs. In mind of the present findings, sport psychology researchers and applied practitioners who develop mental toughness could include coping training in any interventions.

Note

1 The term 'cope with pressure' is a somewhat redundant statement, given that coping can only be classified as coping if it is directed towards stress (Lazarus, 1999; Nicholls and Thelwell, 2010).

References

Aldwin, C. M. (2007) *Stress, Coping and Development: An Integrative Perspective* (2nd edn), New York: Guilford Press.

Amiot, C. E., Gaudreau, P., and Blanchard, C. M. (2004) 'Self-determination, coping, and goal attainment in sport', *Journal of Sport and Exercise Psychology*, 26, 396–411.

Anshel, M. H. (2001) 'Qualitative validation of a model for coping with acute stress in sport', *Journal of Sport Behavior*, 24, 223–46.

Anshel, M. H. (2010) 'Cultural differences in coping with stress in sport: Theory and practice', in A. R. Nicholls (ed.), *Coping in Sport: Theory, Methods, and Related Constructs,* New York: Nova Science Inc., pp. 119–38.

Bandura, A. (1997) *Self-Efficacy: The Exercise of Control,* New York: W. H. Freeman.

Biddle, S. J. H., Hanrahan, S. J., and Sellars, C. N. (2001) 'Attributions: Past, present, and future', in R. N. Singer, H. A. Hausenblaus, and C. M. Janelle (eds), *Handbook of Sport Psychology,* Chichester: Wiley, pp. 444–71.

Brewer, B. W., Van Raalte, J. L., Linder, D. E., and Van Raalte, N. S. (1991) 'Peak performance and the perils of retrospective introspection', *Journal of Sport and Exercise Psychology*, 8, 227–38.

Brown, G. W., and Harris, T. (1978) *The Social Origins of Depression: A Study of Psychiatric Disorder in Women,* New York: Free Press.

Bull, S. J., Shambrook, C. J., James, W., and Brooks, J. E. (2005) 'Towards an understanding of mental toughness in elite English cricketers', *Journal of Applied Sport Psychology,* 17, 209–27.

Carver, C. S., Scheier, M. F., and Weintraub, J. K. (1989) 'Assessing coping strategies: A theoretically based approach', *Journal of Personality and Social Psychology,* 56, 267–83.

Chesney, M.A., Neilands, T. B., Chambers, D. B., Taylor, J. M., and Folkman, S. (2006) 'A validity and reliability study of the coping self-efficacy scale', *British Journal of Health Psychology,* 11, 421–37.

Clough, P., Earle, K., and Sewell, D. (2002) 'Mental toughness: The concept and its measurement', in I. Cockerill (ed.), *Solutions in Sport Psychology,* London: Thomson, pp. 32–45.

Compas, B. E., Connor-Smith, J. K., Saltzman, H., Harding Thomsen, A., and Wadsworth, M. E. (2001) 'Coping with stress during childhood and adolescence: Problems, progress, and potential in theory and research', *Psychological Bulletin,* 12, 87–127.

Connaughton, D., Hanton, S., Jones, G., and Wadey, R. (2008a) 'Mental toughness research: Key issues in this area', *International Journal of Sport Psychology,* 39, 192–204.

Connaughton, D., Wadey, R., Hanton, S., and Jones, G. (2008b) 'The development and maintenance of mental toughness: Perceptions of elite performers', *Journal of Sports Sciences,* 26, 83–95.

Cox, R. H., Martens, M. P., and Russell, W. D. (2003) 'Measuring anxiety in athletics: The revised Competitive State Anxiety Inventory-2', *Journal of Sport and Exercise Psychology,* 25, 519–33.

Coyne, J. C., and Gottlieb, B. H. (1996) 'The mismeasure of coping by checklist', *Journal of Personality,* 64, 959–91.

Crocker, P. R. E., and Graham, T. R. (1995) 'Coping with competitive athletes with performance stress: Gender differences and relationships with affect', *The Sport Psychologist,* 9, 325–38.

Crocker, P. R. E., Kowalski, K. C., and Graham, T. R. (1998) 'Measurement of coping strategies in sport', in J. L. Duda (ed.), *Advances in Sport and Exercise Psychology Measurement,* Morgantown, WV: Fitness Information Technology, pp. 149–61.

Crocker, P. R. E., Mosewich, A. D., Kowalski, K., C., and Besenski, L. J. (2010) 'Coping: Research design and analysis issues', in A. R. Nicholls (ed.), *Coping in Sport: Theory, Methods, and Related Constructs,* New York: Nova Science Inc., pp. 53–76.

Crust, L. (2008) 'A review and conceptual re-examination of mental toughness: Implications for future researchers', *Personality and Individual Differences,* 45, 576–83.

Feltz, D. L., Short, S. E., and Sullivan, P. J. (2008) *Self-Efficacy in Sport: Research and Strategies for Working with Athletes, Teams, and Coaches,* Champaign, IL: Human Kinetics.

Folkman, S. (1984) 'Personal control and stress and coping processes: A theoretical analysis', *Journal of Personality and Social Psychology,* 46, 839–52.

Folkman, S., and Moskowitz, J. T. (2004) 'Coping: Pitfalls and promise', *Annual Review of Psychology,* 55, 745–74.

Forsyth, A. D., and Carey, M. P. (1998) 'Measuring self-efficacy in the context of HIV risk reduction: Research challenges and recommendations', *Health Psychology,* 17, 559–68.

Gaudreau, P., and Antl, S. (2008) 'Athletes' broad dimensions of dispositional perfectionism: Examining changes in life satisfaction and the mediating role of sport-related motivation and coping', *Journal of Sport and Exercise Psychology*, 30, 356–82.

Gaudreau, P., and Blondin, J.-P. (2002) 'Development of a questionnaire for the assessment of coping strategies employed by athletes in competitive sport settings', *Psychology of Sport and Exercise*, 3, 1–34.

Gaudreau, P., Nicholls, A. R., and Levy, A. R. (2010) 'The ups and downs of sports performance: An episodic process analysis of within-person associations', *Journal of Sport and Exercise Psychology*, 32, 298–311.

Gottlieb, B. H., and Rooney, J. A. (2004) 'Coping effectiveness: determinants and relevance of the mental health and affect of family caregivers of persons with dementia', *Aging and Mental Health*, 8, 364–73.

Gould, D., Eklund, R. C., and Jackson, S. A. (1993a) 'Coping strategies used by US Olympic wrestlers', *Research Quarterly for Exercise and Sport*, 64, 83–93.

Gould, D., Finch, L. M., and Jackson, S. A. (1993b) 'Coping strategies used by national champion figure skaters', *Research Quarterly for Exercise and Sport*, 64, 453–68.

Gould, D., Hodge, K., Peterson, K., and Petlichkoff, L. (1987) 'Psychological foundations of coaching: similarities and differences among intercollegiate wrestling coaches', *The Sport Psychologist*, 1, 293–308.

Gucciardi, D. F., and Gordon, S. (2009) 'Development and preliminary validation of the Cricket Mental Toughness Inventory', *Journal of Sports Sciences*, 27, 1293–1310.

Gucciardi, D. F., Gordon, S., and Dimmock, J. A. (2008) 'Towards an understanding of mental toughness in Australian football', *Journal of Applied Sport Psychology*, 20, 261–81.

Gucciardi, D. F., Gordon, S., and Dimmock, J. A. (2009a) 'Advancing mental toughness research and theory using personal construct psychology', *International Review of Sport and Exercise Psychology*, 2, 54–72.

Gucciardi, D. F., Gordon, S., and Dimmock, J. A. (2009b) 'Evaluation of a mental toughness training program for youth aged Australian footballers: I. A quantitative analysis', *Journal of Applied Sport Psychology*, 21, 307–23.

Gucciardi, D. F., Gordon, S., and Dimmock, J. A. (2009c) 'Evaluation of a mental toughness training program for youth aged Australian footballers: II. A qualitative analysis', *Journal of Applied Sport Psychology*, 21, 324–39.

Haney, C. J., and Long, B. C. (1995) 'Coping effectiveness: A path analysis of self-efficacy, control, coping and performance in sport competitions', *Journal of Applied Social Psychology*, 25, 1726–46.

Hoar, S. D., Kowalski, K. C., Gaudreau, P., and Crocker, P. R. E. (2006) 'A review of coping in sport', in S. Hanton and S. Mellalieu (eds), *Literature Reviews in Sport Psychology*, Hauppauge, NY: Nova Science Publishers, pp. 47–90.

Holt, N. L., and Hogg, J. M. (2002) 'Perceptions of stress and coping during preparations for the 1999 women's soccer world cup finals', *The Sport Psychologist*, 16, 251–71.

Holt, N. L., and Mandigo, J. L. (2004) 'Coping with performance worries among male youth cricket players', *Journal of Sport Behavior*, 27, 39–57.

Horn, T. S. (2002) *Advances in Sport Psychology*, Champaign, IL: Human Kinetics.

Horsburgh, V. A., Schermer, J. A., Veselka, L., and Veron, P. A. (2009) 'A behavioural genetic study of mental toughness and personality', *Personality and Individual Differences*, 46, 100–5.

Jones, G., Hanton, S., and Connaughton, D. (2002) 'What is this thing called mental toughness? An investigation of elite performers', *Journal of Applied Sport Psychology*, 14, 205–18.

Jones, G., Hanton, S., and Connaughton, D. (2007) 'A framework of mental toughness in the world's best performers', *The Sport Psychologist*, 21, 243–64.

Jordan, M. (1994) *I Can't Accept Not Trying,* San Francisco, CA: Harper.

Kaiseler, M. H., Polman, R. C. J., and Nicholls, A. R. (2009) 'Mental toughness, stress, stress appraisal, coping, and coping effectiveness in sport', *Personality and Individual Differences,* 47, 728–33.

Kobasa, S. C. (1979) 'Stressful life events, personality, and health: An inquiry into hardiness', *Journal of Personality and Social Psychology*, 37, 1–11.

Kowalski, K. C., and Crocker, P. R. (2001) 'Development and validation of the Coping Function Questionnaire for adolescents in sport', *Journal of Sport and Exercise Psychology*, 23, 136–55.

Krohne, H. W. (1993) 'Vigilance and cognitive avoidance as concepts in coping research', in H.W. Krohne (ed.), *Attention and Avoidance: Strategies in Coping with Aversiveness*, Seattle, WA: Hogrefe & Huber, pp. 19–50.

Lazarus, R. S. (1999) *Stress and Emotion: A New Synthesis,* New York: Springer.

Lazarus, R. S., and Folkman, S. (1984) *Stress, Appraisal and Coping,* New York: Springer.

Lazarus, R. S., and Lazarus, B. N. (2006) *Coping with Aging,* New York: Oxford University Press.

Marchant, D. C., Polman, R. C. J., Clough, P. J., Jackson, J. G., Levy, A. R., and Nicholls, A. R. (2009) 'Mental toughness in the work place: Managerial and age differences', *Journal of Managerial Psychology*, 24, 428–37.

Moritz, S. E., Feltz, D. L., Fahrbach, K. R., and Mack, D. E. (2000) 'The relation of self-efficacy measures to sport performance: A meta-analytic review', *Research Quarterly for Exercise and Sport*, 71, 280–94.

Nicholls, A. R. (2007a) 'Can an athlete be taught to cope more effectively? The experiences of an international level adolescent golfer during a training program for coping', *Perceptual and Motor Skills*, 104, 494–500.

Nicholls, A. R. (2007b) 'A longitudinal phenomenological analysis of coping effectiveness among Scottish international adolescent golfers', *European Journal of Sport Science*, 7, 169–78.

Nicholls, A. R. (2010) 'Effective versus ineffective coping', in A. R. Nicholls (ed.), *Coping in Sport: Theory, Methods, and Related Constructs*, New York: Nova Science Inc., pp. 263–76.

Nicholls, A. R., and Polman, R. C. J. (2007) 'Coping in sport: A systematic review', *Journal of Sport Sciences*, 25, 11–31.

Nicholls, A. R., and Thelwell, R. (2010) 'Coping conceptualized and unraveled', in A. R. Nicholls (ed.), *Coping in Sport: Theory, Methods, and Related Constructs*, New York: Nova Science Inc., pp. 3–14.

Nicholls, A. R., Holt, N. L., and Polman, R. C. J. (2005a) 'A phenomenological analysis of coping effectiveness in golf', *The Sport Psychologist*, 19, 111–30.

Nicholls, A. R., Holt, N. L., Polman, R. C. J., and James, D. W. G. (2005b) 'Stress and coping among international adolescent golfers', *Journal of Applied Sport Psychology*, 17, 333–40.

Nicholls, A. R., Polman, R. C. J., Levy, A. R., and Backhouse, S. H. (2008) 'Mental toughness, optimism, pessimism, and coping among athletes', *Personality and Individual Differences*, 44, 1182–92.

Nicholls, A. R., Backhouse, S. H., Polman, R.C. J., and McKenna, J. (2009a) 'Stressors and affective states among professional rugby union players', *Scandinavian Journal of Medicine and Science in Sports*, 19, 121–8.

Nicholls, A.R., Jones, C. R., Polman, R. C. J., and Borkoles, E. (2009b) 'Stressors, coping, and emotion among professional rugby union players during training and matches', *Scandinavian Journal of Medicine and Science in Sports*, 19, 113–20.

Nicholls, A. R., Polman, R. C. J., Levy, A. R., Backhouse, S. H. (2009c) 'Mental toughness in sport: Achievement level, gender, age, experience, and sport type differences', *Personality and Individual Differences*, 47, 73–5.

Nicholls, A. R., Polman, R. C. J., Morley, D., and Taylor, N. (2009d) 'Coping and coping effectiveness in relation to a competitive sport event: Pubertal status, chronological age, and gender among adolescent athletes', *Journal of Sport and Exercise Psychology*, 31, 299–317.

Nicholls, A. R., Polman, R. C. J., and Levy, A. R. (2010a) 'Coping self-efficacy, pre-competitive anxiety, and subjective performance among athletes', *European Journal of Sport Science*, 10, 97–102.

Nicholls, A. R., Polman, R. C. J., Levy, A. R., and Borkoles, E. (2010b) 'The mediating role of coping: A cross-sectional analysis of the relationship between coping self-efficacy and coping effectiveness among athletes', *International Journal of Stress Management*, 17, 181–92.

Nicholls, A. R., Levy, A. R., Polman, R. C. J., and Crust, L. (in press 2011) 'Mental toughness, coping self-efficacy, and coping effectiveness among athletes', *International Journal of Sport Psychology*.

Perraud, S., Fogg, L., Kopytko, E., and Gross, D. (2006) 'Predictive validity of the Depression Coping Self-efficacy Scale (DCSES)', *Research in Nursing and Health*, 29, 147–60.

Ptacek, J. T., Smith, R. E., Espe, K., and Raffety, B. (1994) 'Limited correspondence between daily coping reports and retrospective coping recall', *Psychological Assessment*, 6, 41–8.

Poczwardowski, A., and Conroy, D. E. (2002) 'Coping responses to failure and success among elite athletes and performing artists', *Journal of Applied Sport Psychology*, 14, 313–29.

Reeves, C., Nicholls, A. R., and McKenna, J. (2009) 'Stress and coping among academy footballers: Age-related differences', *Journal of Applied Sport Psychology*, 21, 31–48.

Reeves, C. W., Nicholls, A. R., and McKenna, J. (in press) 'The effects of a coping intervention on coping self-efficacy, coping effectiveness, and subjective performance among adolescent soccer players', *International Journal of Sport and Exercise Psychology*.

Scorniaenchi, J. A., and Feltz, D. L. (2010) 'Coping self-efficacy in sport', in A. R. Nicholls (ed.), *Coping in Sport: Theory, Methods, and Related Constructs*, New York: Nova Science Inc., pp. 279–92.

Skinner, E. A. (1995) *Perceived Control, Motivation, and Coping*, Thousand Oaks, CA: Sage.

Smith, R. E. (1986) 'Toward a cognitive-affective model of athletic burnout', *Journal of Sport Psychology*, 8, 36–50.

Smith, R. E., Leffingwell, T. R., and Ptacek, J. T. (1999) 'Can people remember how they coped? Factors associated with discordance between same-day and retrospective reports', *Journal of Personality and Social Psychology*, 76, 1050–61.

Smith, R. E., Ptacek, J. T., and Smoll, F. L. (1992) 'Sensation seeking, stress, and adolescent injuries: A test of stress buffering, risk-taking, and coping skills hypotheses', *Journal of Personality and Social Psychology*, 62, 1016–24.

Somerfield, M. R., and McCrae, R. R. (2000) 'Stress and coping research: Methodological challenges, theoretical advances, and clinical applications', *American Psychologist*, 55, 620–5.

Thelwell, R., Weston, N., and Greenlees, I. (2005) 'Defining and understanding mental toughness in soccer', *Journal of Applied Sport Psychology*, 17, 326–32.

Thelwell, R. C., Weston, N. J. V., and Greenlees, I. A. (2007) 'Batting on a sticky wicket: Identifying sources of stress and associated coping strategies for professional cricket batsmen', *Psychology of Sport and Exercise*, 8, 219–232.

4 A social-cognitive framework for understanding and developing mental toughness in sport

Robert J. Harmison

What is this thing called mental toughness? A simple question really, yet one that was posed by Jones et al. (2002) less than a decade ago, sparking a series of invigorating theoretical and empirical attempts to understand the mental toughness construct in sport. Whereas mental toughness as a term to describe athletes is a very popular and valued label in the world of sport, as an academic construct it historically has been defined in a number of different ways with relatively little conceptual clarity or usefulness (Connaughton and Hanton, 2009; Crust, 2007). Vince Lombardi, the legendary coach of the National Football League's Green Bay Packers, best known for his 'winning is the only thing' quote, probably put it best when he also said that 'mental toughness is many things and rather difficult to explain' (Lombardi, 2001: 120).

In his review of the emerging definitions and conceptualizations of mental toughness in sport, Crust (2007) noted that one point of contention in the literature has been related to whether mental toughness is conceptualized as an inherited, innate personality characteristic or if the acquisition of mental toughness is believed to be due more to environmental factors and learning. On one side of the argument is a group of early researchers (e.g. Cattell, 1957; Tutko and Richards, 1972) who examined various personality characteristics encompassed by the current conceptualization of the mental toughness construct and claimed that these variables were an important dimension of personality and a necessary trait or quality for successful performance. On the other hand, the work of more recent researchers (e.g. Bull et al., 2005; Thelwell et al., 2005) and the experiences of a number of practitioners (e.g. Goldberg, 1998; Loehr, 1995) have suggested that mental toughness can be learned as well. If unresolved, this apparent dichotomy to understanding mental toughness in sport surely will continue to add confusion and lessen the conceptual clarity regarding a construct deemed by coaches, athletes, the media, and researchers and practitioners to be an important component related to athletic success. Fortunately, Smith (2006) suggested that the application of social-cognitive models of understanding behavior in sport has substantial potential for advancing theoretical, empirical and practical knowledge of constructs such as mental toughness. More specifically, Smith (2006) proposed that a comprehensive social-cognitive model of personality functioning (Mischel and Shoda, 1995; Shoda and Mischel, 1996) can serve as a valuable framework within which to incorporate and expand the current understanding of mental toughness in sport.

The purpose of this chapter is to elaborate on the application of a social-cognitive framework for understanding and developing mental toughness in sport as initially suggested by Smith (2006). It is hoped that this elaboration will provide researchers and practitioners with additional insights and a valuable heuristic from which they can base their attempts to better describe, explain and predict mental toughness in sport along with its relationship to performance. First, a selected review of the mental toughness literature will be presented to provide a historical perspective on previous attempts to conceptualize mental toughness in sport, highlighting the need for the use of a theoretical framework to guide research in this area. Next, the case will be made to view mental toughness in sport as a social-cognitive personality construct. Then, a social-cognitive approach to understanding personality will be presented, applied to mental toughness in sport, and illustrated via a sport example. Finally, implications for future research on mental toughness in sport will be provided.

Selected review of developments in mental toughness theory and research

The historical name most synonymous with mental toughness in sport belongs to James Loehr (1982, 1986, 1995), who wrote extensively on what he called the new toughness training for sport that focused on mental, emotional and physical conditioning for sport success. Based on his years of experience working with world-class athletes, Loehr (1995: 5) defined toughness as the 'ability to consistently perform toward the upper range of your talent and skills regardless of competitive circumstances'. In addition, Loehr (1982, 1986) developed a model of seven specific mental skills required for someone to be a mentally tough athlete (e.g. self-confidence, negative energy control, motivation). In addition, Loehr (1986) created the Psychological Performance Inventory (PPI) to measure an athlete's level of mental toughness, and a number of researchers have utilized the PPI to assess mental toughness and investigate its relationship to performance (e.g. Golby et al., 2003). Loehr's conceptualization of mental toughness has a certain amount of intuitive appeal, and the PPI appears to have some utility when working with athletes. However, Loehr's conceptualization of mental toughness and creation of the PPI are void of any underlying research evidence or sound theoretical foundation, resulting in questions being raised about the validity of Loehr's model of mental toughness and the use of the PPI as a measure of mental toughness in sport (e.g. Connaughton and Hanton, 2009; Crust, 2007).

Attempting to fill the theoretical void in the literature, Clough et al. (2002) suggested that hardiness could be a robust construct in which the understanding of mental toughness in sport could be rooted. A key concept within the field of health psychology, hardiness is conceptualized as a personality trait that acts as a buffer to influence how a person copes with stressful life events (Kobasa, 1979). Applying the hardiness construct to sport, Clough et al. conceptualized mental toughness as four distinct, yet interrelated attitudes in which mentally tough athletes respond to stressful situations (e.g. control: feeling and acting as if they are influential rather than helpless; commitment: involving rather than alienating themselves). Based on this conceptualization, Clough et al. developed the Mental Toughness 48 (MT48), which often has been utilized to examine the relationship between mental toughness and hypothesized key correlates such as coping (Chapter 3, above). Despite bridging the gap between mental toughness theory and applied practice, Clough et al. have been criticized for failing to adequately justify the transferring of the health psychology construct of hardiness into a more sport-specific setting, basing their conceptualization of mental toughness on hypothetical rather than research-related constructs, and minimally reporting the necessary statistical procedures related to how the MT48 was developed and validated (Crust, 2007; Gucciardi et al., 2009a).

A pioneering study conducted by Fourie and Potgieter (2001) ushered in a new era in the understanding of the nature of mental toughness in sport. These investigators asked expert coaches and elite athletes across an array of sports to list and rank the characteristics of an athlete who is mentally tough, and the results of their analysis revealed a number of components of mental toughness (e.g. motivational level, confidence maintenance, discipline and goal-directedness, competitiveness, psychological hardiness). Although this was a promising initial step to filling the dearth of research studies on mental toughness in sport, Fourie and Potgieter's approach to understanding mental toughness in sport, as well as the discussion of their results and conclusions, was not grounded in any existing theory of behavior in sport. In addition, questions have been raised regarding the elite-level nature of the sample, confusion over the wording and meanings of the components identified, and use of a methodology that limited the sufficient probing of the participants' responses (Connaughton and Hanton, 2009; Gucciardi et al., 2009a).

Credited with being the first to utilize a more rigorous, scientific approach (Crust, 2007), Jones et al. (2002) attempted to add greater conceptual clarity to the mental toughness construct through a series of one-to-one and focus-group interviews with a group of elite, international-level athletes who were asked to define what mental toughness is and to describe the attributes of an ideally mentally tough performer. The results of their analysis revealed that these athletes define mental toughness as a natural or learned psychological edge that allows athletes to better cope with the many demands of sport and be more determined, focused, confident, and in control under pressure. In addition, the athletes identified a number of characteristics of the ideally mentally tough performer, which Jones et al. grouped into several general categories (e.g. self-belief, desire/motivation, performance-related focus). Subsequent research has provided support for Jones et al.'s definition and conceptualization of mental toughness in sport (e.g. Bull et al., 2005; Jones et al., 2007; Thelwell et al., 2005). However, Crust (2007) levied some criticism regarding the methodology utilized by Jones et al. (i.e. small number of athletes in the initial focus group) while also noting that their definition describes what mental toughness allows athletes to do (e.g.

remain more determined, focused, confident) as opposed to what it actually is. Of particular note was the lack of integration of existing theory for understanding their results (Crust, 2007).

In direct response to the inadequate theoretical conceptualizations in the literature, Gucciardi and colleagues recently have applied a personal construct psychology framework (Kelly, 1991) to advance the current understanding of mental toughness in sport. In sum, personal construct psychology is a theory that endeavours to understand how one's attempts to make sense of the world influence one's anticipations and predictions about the world and how these meanings ultimately impact one's behaviors. Gucciardi and colleagues (Coulter et al., 2010; Gucciardi et al., 2008) applied the basic tenets of personal construct psychology to their interview protocol as they attempted to identify key characteristics in mentally tough athletes. Gucciardi et al. interviewed expert male Australian-rules football coaches while Coulter et al. questioned expert male soccer coaches, along with a small group of elite male soccer players and their parents, and the results of their separate analyses revealed a similar set of defining characteristics of mental toughness (e.g. self-belief, work ethic, tough attitude, coping under pressure). In addition, Coulter et al. identified a variety of cognitions (e.g. hopeful outlook) and affects (e.g. love for sport) that were employed by mentally tough athletes, and both Gucciardi et al. and Coulter et al. found that mental toughness was marked by a number of general and competition-specific behaviors (e.g. perform at a high level, do the 'little things') and was needed in both negatively (e.g. adversity) and positively (e.g. challenge) construed situations. Based on these findings, Gucciardi and colleagues offered the following construct definition of mental toughness that provides a useful summary of the key findings to date and captures the conceptual complexity of the mental toughness construct:

> the presence of some or the entire collection of experientially developed and inherent values, attitudes, emotions, cognitions, and behaviors that influence the way in which an individual approaches, responds to, and appraises both negatively and positively construed pressures, challenges, and adversities to consistently achieve his or her goals.
>
> (Coulter et al., 2010: 715)

Mental toughness as a social-cognitive personality construct

As highlighted in the previous section, there have been a number of theoretical and empirical advances regarding the mental toughness construct. However, it remains true that there is a need for the continual development of useful theoretical frameworks to guide research and practice in the area of mental toughness in sport. With that in mind, the argument presented in this chapter is that mental toughness in sport can best be understood as a complex, relatively stable social-cognitive personality construct that can be modified over time if new learning, development, or biochemical changes take place within the athlete. It is important to keep in mind that a social-cognitive view of personality differs from the long-standing tradition of conceptualizing personality in terms of traits that predispose individuals to behave in consistent ways across situations. It also differs from the alternative perspective that situational factors in one's environment account for most of the differences in personality and resulting behaviors. Rather, a social-cognitive view of personality conceptualizes one's personality as a system of internal, mediating processes that interact with each other and one's environment and manifest themselves in predictable patterns of situation–behavior relationships (Mischel and Shoda, 1995). This view of mental toughness in sport has three important implications for researchers and practitioners attempting to better understand and develop mental toughness in athletes.

Implication 1: mental toughness is multidimensional

Conceptualizing mental toughness as a social-cognitive personality construct punctuates the reality that understanding and developing mental toughness in sport is not a simple endeavour. Rather, mental toughness is a multidimensional and dynamic psychological construct of athletes that requires a comprehensive approach to understanding it accurately and developing it effectively. Initial writings on mental toughness (e.g. Goldberg, 1998; Loehr, 1982) typically described the construct in relatively simplistic terms, often at times depicting mental toughness as a singular trait (e.g. resilience) and focusing primarily on the athletes' use of psychological skills (e.g. goal setting, visualization, positive thinking). Over the past decade, a number of investigations have revealed a more accurate definition of mental toughness in sport along with a clearer picture of the characteristics of mentally tough athletes (for reviews, see Connaughton and Hanton, 2009; Gucciardi et al., 2009a). Collectively, the existing research (e.g. Fourie and Potgieter, 2001; Gucciardi et al., 2008; Jones et al., 2002) supports a view of mental toughness in sport as a multidimensional construct that encompasses a number of common psychological attributes possessed by athletes that appear to not vary much from sport to sport. These common attributes, along with a brief description and a sporting example for each, are summarized in Table 4.1.

Implication 2: aspects of mental toughness are inherited

If one operates on the premise that mental toughness in sport is a social-cognitive personality construct, then the same factors that impact the development of any aspect of personality will hold true related to an athlete's level of mental toughness. More specifically, genetic background, biological history, cultural-social influences and social learning history are believed to impact the development of one's personality. For any given personality trait, the consensus is that the average heritability estimate is roughly 50 per cent (Plomin et al., 1990), meaning that genetic background and biological precursors account for approximately half of the individual differences in personality. People differ in various biochemical-genetic factors that act as biological precursors and either directly or indirectly

Table 4.1 Common attributes possessed by mentally tough athletes

Mental Toughness Attribute	Description of Attribute	Sporting Example
Being confident	Believing in one's ability to achieve goals; having faith in ability to reach one's potential; revealing one's competence; wanting to be the person that makes the difference	In the lead up to a competition against an opponent he has never encountered before, John believes without a doubt that he has what it takes to be victorious over his opponent.
Summoning motivation and desire	Possessing an insatiable, internal desire to succeed; having a disciplined, goal-directed orientation; being competitive with self and others; owning a determined, 'go the extra mile' work ethic	Although winning a gold medal is an important goal she wants to achieve, Dawn's unquenchable desire to be the very best athlete she can be is her most powerful motivator to train hard every day.
Effectively dealing with adversity and failure	Bouncing back from set-backs with a greater determination to succeed; persevering in the face of obstacles; remaining positive in response to difficult situations; learning from failure and being more determined as a result	Despite getting off to a slow start during the first half of play, Michael continues to dwell on aspects of his performance that can improve and expects to start performing well in just a matter of time.
Overcoming physical and/ or emotional pain and hardship	Stretching one's perceived physical and psychological limits; challenging self to exert as much effort as physically and emotionally possible; pushing one's body through extreme exhaustion, fatigue, etc.; coping with physical or emotional pain	As she nears the end of the gruelling race Paula copes with her feelings of exhaustion, fatigue, and physical pain by perceiving it as a challenge and maintaining her form and technique.
Successfully managing anxiety, pressure, and other emotions	Accepting competitive anxiety and knowing that one can cope with it; enjoying and thriving on the pressure of competition; accurately understanding one's emotions; channelling negative emotions and using them to one's advantage	Moments before the most important competition in his life Curtis has doubts about his performance, feels jittery and nervous, but knows these are signs that he is mentally and emotionally ready to compete.
Staying focused	Thinking clearly and in the present moment; concentrating on the task at hand; ignoring internal and external distractions; regaining mental control following unexpected, uncontrollable events	Whereas her competitors seem unsettled by the difficult weather-related conditions, Kelly remains committed to her plan and chooses to concentrate on aspects of her performance that she can control.
Finding balance and keeping perspective	Switching one's focus on and off sport as needed or required; showing emotional and psychological well-being; taking responsibility and demonstrating independence on and off the field; devoting time to important aspects of one's life other than sport	After an intense, month-long training camp away from home, Jeff spent the next several weeks being apart from his sport, reconnecting with his loved ones, and pursuing some of his other life interests.

influence personal qualities such as sensory and psychomotor development, skills and competencies, temperament, chronic mood and emotional states (Mischel and Shoda, 1999). Likewise, these biological precursors significantly impact personality and subsequent behavioral expressions by creating individual differences in people's sensory, perceptual, cognitive and affective systems, secretion of hormones, presence of various neurotransmitters, etc. (e.g. Plomin et al., 1997).

Research that has investigated the relationship between genetic make-up and personality in sport in general and mental toughness in particular is a relatively untapped area. Horsburgh et al. (2009) recently attempted to estimate the contribution of genetic and environmental factors to individual differences in mental toughness in the general population. Utilizing twin study methodology, the MT48, and a Big Five personality measure (NEO-PI-R; Costa and McCrae, 1992), Horsburgh et al. found individual differences in overall mental toughness as measured by the MT48 to be attributed primarily to genetic and non-shared environmental factors ($r = .52$). Their results also revealed that heritability estimates for specific aspects of mental toughness (e.g. challenge, commitment) ranged from .36 to .56, suggesting that some aspects may possess a lower level of heritability than overall mental toughness. In addition, heritability estimates in this same sample for the Big Five personality factors were found to range from .47 to .56, which is consistent with the typical pattern of results for the Big Five. These findings led Horsburgh et al. to conclude that mental toughness behaves in a similar way to just about every other personality trait that has been studied to determine the extent to which genetics or environmental factors determine individual differences. Despite some notable limitations to this study (e.g. issues with the use of the MT48 to measure mental toughness discussed earlier in this chapter), the results provide support for the idea of strengthening certain aspects of mental toughness that are more influenced by learning than other components as opposed to attempting to develop an athlete's overall level of mental toughness. Thus, a view of mental toughness in sport that implies that some, but not all aspects, of mental toughness are inherited and potentially resistant to change as a result would seem to be a useful framework for researchers and practitioners as they try to understand and develop mental toughness in athletes.

Implication 3: aspects of mental toughness can be learned

Despite the complex, genetic nature of the mental toughness construct, the final implication asserts that an athlete's level of mental toughness is something that can be cultivated and developed. Viewing mental toughness in sport as a social-cognitive personality construct also allows for the possibility that its development can be influenced by environmental factors and acquired by athletes based on their learning experiences. Very few studies have examined how psychological factors in general develop within athletes over time, and even fewer investigations have looked at the mental toughness developmental and learning process in athletes. Notable exceptions of mental toughness development do exist, and these studies are comprehensively reviewed in Part 3 of this volume. Collectively, the available research supports the notion that mental toughness development requires a longitudinal perspective, and involves a number of interacting personal and environmental influences and progresses in a stage-like fashion over the course of an athlete's participation in sport.

A social-cognitive view of personality

The remainder of this chapter is dedicated to exploring the usefulness of applying Mischel and Shoda's (1995) social-cognitive view of personality to assist in understanding mental toughness and its development. Until the 1960s the prevailing thinking among most personality psychologists was that an individual's personality served as a major internal determinant of behavior. However, Mischel (1968) reviewed the existing evidence and concluded that people actually were more inconsistent than they were consistent in their behavior from one situation to the next, giving credence to the argument that perhaps personality was determined more by the environment and the situations that surrounded people. Mischel's controversial conclusions about the nature of personality sparked the 'person versus the situation debate' that dominated the academic fields of personality and social psychology for the next 15 years. As part of this debate, Mischel (1973) presented a social-cognitive reconceptualization of personality in which he argued that the goal of personality psychology should be to understand the dynamic way in which situations and individuals reciprocally influence one another as opposed to trying to answer the unsolvable dilemma regarding which is more important – the person or the situation – in determining one's behavior.

The personality system

Mischel's (1973) social-cognitive personality theory conceptualizes personality according to how a person encodes or perceives particular types of situations, the beliefs, expectations and values that become activated, and the emotional responses and self-regulation skills that are available to the person. How these person variables interact with one another in relation to the particular type of situation then determines the nature of one's personality and the behavior that follows. Eventually, an enduring network of connections among these person variables within one's personality system emerges to form the stable dispositional qualities of the person. However, as people happen upon different situations, their stable personality systems are required to process the information about the situations and, as a result, their behavior is likely to vary from one situation to the next. This behavioral variation reflects important individual differences in the structure and organization of individuals' personality systems, and specifically how they process and respond to the psychologically active features of each situation (i.e. the external and intrapsychic situational variables that have acquired meaning based on the person's prior experiences with those variables). The end result is a personality style that is marked by relatively stable situation–behavior profiles that reflect individualized, characteristic ways in which a person interacts with different features of the situation.

Application of the social-cognitive view of personality to mental toughness in sport

Mischel's (1973) initial social-cognitive reconceptualization of personality eventually led to the formation of the Cognitive-Affective Processing System (CAPS: Mischel and Shoda, 1995) approach to understanding personality and behavior. Mischel and Shoda proposed the CAPS as a meta-theory for personality science as their answer to best understand the stable differences between people and their differing characteristic behaviors along with people's stable profiles of variability in their behavior from one situation to the next. As a model of personality the CAPS approach is consistent with and informed by advancements in information-processing, connectionist and neural-network models in the areas of perception, social cognition and cognitive neuroscience (e.g. Read and Miller, 1998; Rumelhart and McClelland, 1986). These models focus on understanding the organization of the relationships among the various units within the system as the means for determining how complex, coherent organization of behavior is formed (Shoda and Mischel, 1996). As such, the CAPS approach is based on two fundamental assumptions with regard to individual differences in personality. In addition, the CAPS approach identifies a set of person variables, referred to as cognitive-affective processing units, and elaborates on how these person variables interact with one's environment to generate behaviors associated with one's personality. Each of these aspects of the CAPS approach as applied to understanding mental toughness in sport is described next.

Basic assumptions of the CAPS approach

Assumption 1

Individual differences in personality exist in the ease in which a person is able to activate various cognitive-affective representations available to them (Mischel and Shoda, 1999). According to the CAPS approach, the personality system consists of a set of person variables, referred to as cognitive-affective processing units. Mischel and Shoda (1995) proposed the personality system to be comprised of five types of cognitive-affective units, namely encodings, expectancies and beliefs, affects, goals and values, and self-regulation skills. These units are conceptualized as dynamic, interacting components of one's personality whose organization forms the core of the personality structure and generates the behavior of the person (Mischel and Shoda, 1999).

Applying this assumption to sport, some inexperienced athletes competing for the first time in a game away from the comforts of their home stadium may perceive the loud, hostile crowd as a negative stressor. These athletes may even pay a great deal of attention to the media hype, or even the excitement of a well-intentioned family member, in the build-up to the game. However, other inexperienced athletes will remain relatively oblivious to the crowd and hostile environment and not perceive it to be a negative stressor. These athletes may even participate in multiple media interviews without the hype appearing to affect them, and they might not pay any attention to what their family is saying about the upcoming game. In other words, the exact same competitive situation does not activate the same cognitions and affects in every athlete due to the individual differences in the chronic accessibility of these internal mental representations.

Assumption 2

Individual differences also exist in the stable organization of the relationships between a person's cognitions and affects that are a part of his/her personality (Mischel and Shoda, 1999). According to the CAPS approach, a person will perceive and encode particular features of a given situation that will then activate certain cognitions and affects. Over time the person's cognitive-affective units become distinctly interconnected and follow a characteristic pattern once activated. As various cognitions and affects become activated (or inhibited), the personality system eventually will generate behaviors in a continuous and dynamic way that will reciprocally interact with and influence the social world around the person (Mischel and Shoda, 1999).

To illustrate, consider the different organization of the cognitions and affects of two hypothetical soccer players competing in an important international match. In response to this competitive situation, assume that both competitors perceive the importance of this big game in a similar manner, have comparable high self-expectations about how they should perform and experience the same amount of pressure to meet the expectations of their coaches and fans. As a result of the acquired meaning of these situational features and the player's prior experiences with those features, the first soccer player (see Figure 4.1) feels a sense of excitement about playing in the game. He is optimistic and hopeful about how he will play despite some of the doubts and worries he is having. He also is motivated by feelings of pride and accomplishment that he anticipates receiving from his coaches and fans should he meet the challenge in front of him. As for his behavior, he appears loose and confident to his teammates, competes with poise, makes good on-field decisions and plays error-free. On the other hand, based on the acquired meaning of these same situational features and his prior experiences with those features, the second soccer player (see Figure 4.2) feels extremely nervous and anxious about playing in the game. His doubts and worries leave him apprehensive and feeling fearful of making mistakes. In turn he is focused on avoiding feelings of shame related to disappointing his coaches and is motivated by his desire to not embarrass himself by playing poorly in front of a world-wide audience. As for his behavior, he appears tight and overwhelmed to his teammates, competes with little composure, rushes his decision-making on the field, and commits several costly errors. Thus, despite these two competitors perceiving the upcoming game in a similar manner and experiencing some of the same cognitions and affects in response to the competitive situation, it was the manner in which their cognitive-affective units were organized within their respective personality systems that resulted in the generation of different behavior on the field.

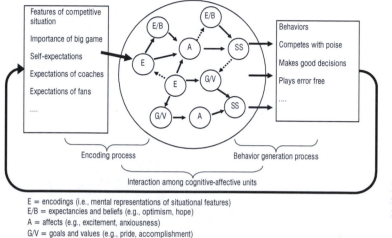

E = encodings (i.e., mental representations of situational features)
E/B = expectancies and beliefs (e.g., optimism, hope)
A = affects (e.g., excitement, anxiousness)
G/V = goals and values (e.g., pride, accomplishment)
SS = self-regulation skills (e.g., positive self-talk)

Figure 4.1 Schematic organization of the personality system of a hypothetical soccer player who displays mentally tough behaviors (adapted with permission from Shoda & Smith, 2006)

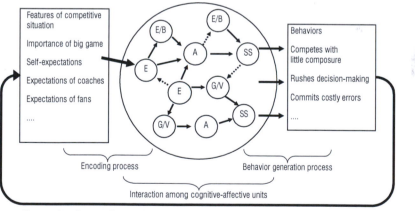

E = encodings (i.e., mental representations of situational features)
E/B = expectancies and beliefs (e.g., apprehension, doubt)
A = affects (e.g., fear , nervousness)
G/V = goals and values (e.g., shame, embarrassment)
SS = self-regulation skills (e.g., negative self-talk)

Figure 4.2 Schematic organization of the personality system of a hypothetical soccer player who displays mentally weak behaviors (adapted with permission from Shoda & Smith, 2006)

Mental toughness as an organized network of cognitions and affects

Based on these two assumptions of the CAPS approach, it should be clear that a key to understanding and developing mental toughness in sport is to view athletes' level of mental toughness as a function of their dynamic personality systems that are comprised of organized networks of interconnected and interacting cognitive-affective processing units. This assertion is in stark contrast to seeing mental toughness in sport as simply how much confidence, motivation, positive emotions, etc. an athlete possesses. What is most important from this perspective is knowing what cognitions and affects comprise an athlete's mentally tough personality, along with how these person variables are interconnected to generate the athlete's mentally tough behaviors. As alluded to previously, Mischel and Shoda (1995) identified and described five major classes of the cognitive-affective components of personality, and each is described below.

Encodings

This component of personality deals with the process of recognizing, identifying and interpreting the situation that exists around us. This aspect of personality involves selectively attending to certain features of the situation and assigning internal meaning to the situational variables. Through this process both internal and external stimuli become mental representations that ultimately form a set of personal constructs for the self, other people, events that happen and situations (Mischel and Shoda, 1995; Smith, 2006).

All athletes have a collection of personal constructs about themselves and the world that consists of their self-attitudes and their perceptions regarding the environments in which they compete. For example, some athletes will look at themselves in a mirror following a hard-fought but close defeat to a highly ranked opponent and see failure. Despite the fact that they played above their typical level, they cannot help but encode or process game information (e.g. a critical turnover, a blown defensive assignment) that serves to provide them with feedback that they have insufficient ability. On the other hand, other athletes can play relatively poorly, yet dominate their opponent, and see themselves as successful by failing to encode mistakes they made, as well as overlooking the deficiencies in their opponent.

Expectancies and beliefs

This component of personality deals with a person's belief system about the self and the world, expectations of outcomes for behavior in particular situations, and self-efficacy. This aspect of personality includes situation-specific beliefs as well as global expectations regarding 'what leads to what' and 'how things are'. People's expectations and beliefs help them to bestow meaning on events that happen in addition to assisting in setting goals, planning behavior and understanding oneself and others (Mischel and Shoda, 1995; Smith, 2006).

Athletes' beliefs and expectancies related to themselves and the competitive environment play an important role in determining how they will ultimately perform. One example of a belief that can affect athletes' performance on the field is whether they believe their ability is innate or can be dramatically improved with hard work (Dweck and Molden, 2005). In addition, confident athletes tend to believe that they are in control of themselves and expect to produce results when their team needs them the most. In contrast, overly anxious athletes typically doubt themselves and worry about being able to perform at a high level when it counts. As a result, they often expect to fail and likely have a long history of doing so in competitive situations.

Affects

This component of personality deals with the feelings and emotions that one experiences in response to situations or events. This aspect of personality includes psychological responses (e.g. worry, doubt) as well as physiological reactions (e.g. increased heart-rate, muscle tension). In addition, certain responses by people to situations or events, such as fear and passion, are thought to occur quickly, impulsively, and reflexively and are considered to operate on a 'hot' emotional 'go' system. On the other hand, other responses to situations or events can be emotionally neutral and more controlled and are believed to occur more slowly, rationally and reflectively as part of a 'cool' cognitive 'know' system (Mischel and Shoda, 1995; Smith, 2006).

Emotion is believed by many sport psychologists to play an important role in determining the outcome of competition (for a review, see Hanin, 2000). Coaches frequently attribute their teams' competitive fire and emotional intensity (or lack thereof) as reasons for their teams' successes (or failures). Failure to effectively manage emotional expression on the court or field can result in undesirable consequences as well, as evidenced in tennis player Serena Williams's profanity-laced tirade that resulted in her losing her semi-final match at the 2009 US Open and receiving a record fine (Clarke, 2009).

Goals and values

This component of personality deals with the short- and long-term desired and undesired outcomes related to one's behavior. This aspect of one's personality includes the importance that one places on achieving goals, and consists of one's values concerning what is significant, moral, and good. In this regard a person's values or motives play a foundational role in guiding the goals that one may seek, the manner in which one perceives and encodes internal and external stimuli, the outcomes one might approach or avoid, and one's emotional responses to situations and events (Mischel and Shoda, 1995; Smith, 2006).

Setting and striving to achieve goals is considered to be standard practice and an important ingredient for success by most athletes and coaches (Weinberg et al., 2005). Nevertheless, athletes vary quite considerably in terms of the goals or motives for their behavior (Burton and Weiss, 2008). For example, some athletes are motivated to seek out challenging goals, yet others are not. Some athletes have a strong desire to avoid failure and possess motives to not feel shamed or embarrassed in front of others based on their performances. Other athletes are more motivated to achieve success and are fuelled by a desire to experience a sense of pride and accomplishment from performing well.

Self-regulation skills

This component of personality deals with the potential plans, strategies and actions in which individuals can engage to manage their own behavior and internal states. This aspect of personality includes a person's abilities to exert control over one's thoughts, feelings and actions by using both psychological (e.g. self-talk or visualization) and physical strategies (e.g. breathing and relaxation techniques). In addition, self-regulation skills involve the use of self-monitoring, self-instruction, self-evaluation and self-reinforcement competencies to effectively organize actions and influence behavioral outcomes (Mischel and Shoda, 1995; Smith, 2006).

The ability to self-regulate is considered to be extremely important to the success of an athlete, and the enhancement of self-regulations skills often is the focus of traditional psychological skills training programmes. Both qualitative and quantitative reviews of the literature provide support for the use of cognitive-behavioral skills as forms of self-regulation to enhance athletic performance (e.g. Meyers et al., 1996; Vealey, 2007). Although the ability to self-regulate is an important aspect of personality as it relates to mental toughness in sport, self-regulation skills should not be the only person variable for researchers and practitioners attempting to understand and develop mental toughness in athletes.

Mental toughness as a behavioral signature

The five person variables described above constitute important pieces of the puzzle to understanding and developing mental toughness in sport. However, the CAPS approach emphasizes that it is the dynamic relationship between these person variables, along with their interaction with the person's environment, that produces the behavioral expression of one's personality. The CAPS approach provides a useful concept referred to as the behavioral signature to clarify the nature of the relationship among and between the person and situational variables related to one's personality.

According to Mischel and Shoda (1995), a person's personality is expressed behaviorally as a set of *if ... then ...* situation–behavior contingencies. In fact, Shoda (1999) argued that one's personality is best represented as a bundle of these *if ... then ...* contingencies that are both internal and external to the individual. Simply put, viewing the behavioral expression of one's personality in this manner suggests that *if* certain situational variables are present, *then* a person is likely to behave in a predictable manner. It also implies that *if* the encoding or perception of these situational variables triggers certain cognitions within the person, *then* it is likely that predictable affects will be activated as well, which may trigger additional cognitions, affects encodings, etc. As the internal *if ...*

then ... cognitive-affective contingencies continuously interact with the external situation–behavior contingencies, what results is a person's distinctive patterns of behavior, otherwise known as the person's behavioral signatures. Over time, these behavioral signatures become relatively stable and define what is observed and known as the person's personality.

Since the consistent display of mentally tough behaviors in competitive situations would seem to be desired by athletes and coaches, conceptualizing the display of mental toughness in sport as a behavioral signature that is the result of a series of internal and external *if ... then ...* situation–behavior contingencies would appear useful. The concept of the behavioral signature suggests that, to fully understand and develop mental toughness in athletes, researchers and practitioners need to take into account both the person (e.g. encodings, affect) and the situation (i.e. psychologically active features such as previous experience) variables and to address questions related to the interconnectedness and interaction among and between these two sets of factors. For example, what are the active features in the competitive situation that activate the desired cognitions and affects in some athletes but not others? How do mentally tough athletes encode and interpret these situational features differently than mentally weak athletes? How do these interpretations influence athletes' expectations regarding their performance in that situation? What feelings and emotions are generated as a result of athletes' encodings and beliefs about their competitive situation? What specific mentally tough behaviors are produced from these desired cognitions and affects?

Mental toughness in sport and the CAPS approach: an illustration

As an aid to explaining how the CAPS approach can be applied in a sport setting to better understand and develop mental toughness in athletes, consider the following illustration of 'Tammy', a female volleyball player for an elite, national-level team. Tammy is a skilled and accomplished outside hitter and is among the best players at her position in the region in which her team competes. Her coach considers her to be a confident and motivated competitor who possesses a strong desire to win, but also a player who does not consistently stay focused nor in control of herself, especially in stressful or high-pressure competitive situations. In a recent match, Tammy showed her mental toughness following an attack error she committed that resulted in her team losing the first set of the match by effectively dealing with this failure and playing well over the next three tightly contested sets. However, during the fifth and deciding set, Tammy became overly anxious and played tentatively, making a series of costly mistakes – a passing error, a service error, a blocking error and an attack error – which significantly contributed to her team losing the set and the match. So, is it correct to say that Tammy lacks mental toughness because she choked under pressure and failed to deliver when her team needed her the most? If so, how does one explain Tammy's apparent display of mental toughness by effectively managing her thoughts and emotions and refocusing herself following her costly mistake early in the match? Is it possible to conclude that Tammy displayed both mental toughness and mental weakness and is capable of being either mentally tough or mentally weak depending on the competitive situation she is in? And can Tammy's mental toughness be developed so that she displays mentally tough behaviors in both situations in the future?

Applying the CAPS concepts of cognitive-affective processing units and the behavioral signature in the illustration described above allows for a better understanding of this athlete's level of mental toughness and offers a direction for developing her mental toughness as well. For the sake of this example, assume that Tammy perceives herself to be one of the best players and leaders on her team (encodings), and this self-attitude triggers her belief in her ability to respond successfully when she makes a mistake, especially early in a match (expectancies and beliefs). Within her personality system, this self-belief is connected to the importance Tammy places on her grit and determination in such situations as well as the enjoyment she feels when mastering such a challenge (goals and values). In addition to believing in her ability to respond to this initial failure and valuing her grit and determination, Tammy is able to feel confident in her ability to be successful (affects) despite costing her team the first set with her mistake, because she possesses the psychological skills to remain optimistic and hopeful despite the setback (self-regulation skills). Most probably would agree that this profile is representative of a mentally tough athlete and the type of player that would be welcomed and coveted on any team.

Continuing with this illustration, further assume that Tammy has a history of choking under pressure during crunch time in matches. As a result, Tammy perceives herself to be an athlete who is not capable of delivering the goods when her team needs it the most (encodings). This self-attitude, in combination with making an early service error followed by an attack error in the pivotal fifth set, triggers memories of times when she has choked in the past, leading Tammy to think to herself, 'Oh no, here we go again!' (expectancies and beliefs). Connected to these thoughts and beliefs are feelings of anxiety and panic (affects), and Tammy attempts to manage these negative feelings by overthinking the execution of her technique (self-regulation skills). As a result of her failed attempts to effectively regulate her cognitions and affects, Tammy continues to make technical errors with her footwork when passing and blocking due to excessive muscle tension in her body and the inability to attend to the necessary cues in her environment. Eventually, Tammy convinces herself that she is helpless, loses her fight, and simply rides out the remainder of the match (goals and values). Quite a different picture than the mentally tough player painted in the preceding paragraph.

It should be apparent that the above illustration of the volleyball player suggests that to truly understand an athlete's level of mental toughness what is needed is further analysis into the relationship between an athlete's cognitions and affects and how these interact with the situations in which the athlete competes. In Tammy's case the first situation was related to her making a costly mistake early in the match whereas the second situation involved a series of mistakes in the pivotal fifth set. On the surface both competitive situations look relatively similar, with Tammy experiencing failure and setbacks in the form of costly errors that required her to deal with some adversity, manage her feelings of anxiety and pressure, and stay focused on the task at hand. However, the psychologically active features in the fifth set (e.g. history of choking under pressure, end-of-match urgency, physical and mental fatigue, multiple errors) are different from those that likely were present in the first set (e.g. history of responding successfully to early mistakes, beginning-of-match excitement, physical and mental energy, single error). In the illustration provided, the features of the competition situation in the first set triggered the activation of a very different combination of interacting cognitions and affects compared to the fifth set, resulting in the athlete displaying mentally tough behaviors in the former and mentally weak behaviors in the latter.

Thus, knowing the specific cognitions and affects that comprise an athlete's mentally tough personality system and determining how these interact with the psychologically active features of the competitive situation are important tasks for the researcher or practitioner when attempting to understand and develop mental toughness in athletes. Determining the types of cognitions and affects experienced by mentally tough athletes and how they are organized within an athlete's personality system will help researchers to better describe, predict and explain mental toughness in sport. In addition, an understanding of the manner in which athletes' cognitive-affective processing units are interconnected and interact with features of the competitive situations will provide practitioners with a better ability to implement intervention programmes to develop athletes' mental toughness and address deficiencies in their display of mentally tough behaviors as well.

Implications for future research

The social-cognitive framework for understanding and developing mental toughness in sport presented in this chapter provides a number of implications for researchers interested in this area. Specifically, viewing mental toughness as a social-cognitive personality construct stands to enhance attempts by researchers to conceptually and theoretically identify, assess and develop mental toughness in athletes.

Identification of the mentally tough personality

The bulk of the research that has examined the mental toughness construct has focused on identifying and describing the psychological attributes associated with mental toughness and less so on the cognitions, affects and behaviors of mentally tough athletes (e.g. Fourie and Potgieter, 2001; Jones et al., 2002; Thelwell et al., 2005). Recent exceptions do exist, however (Coulter et al., 2010; Gucciardi et al., 2008). The social-cognitive framework presented argues for greater attention needing to be paid to the specific cognitions, affects and behaviors of mentally tough athletes when attempting to accurately understand mental toughness in sport. Viewing mental toughness as a social-cognitive personality construct provides a frame through which researchers can further explore the constellation of cognitions and affects that underlie each of the common mental toughness attributes and the mentally tough behaviors that are subsequently generated. For example, when exploring how mentally tough athletes successfully manage their feelings of anxiety and pressure, researchers can ask probing questions, such as 'how do you perceive pressure situations?' (encodings), 'what do you expect from yourself when under pressure?' (expectancies/beliefs), 'how do you experience feelings of pressure to meet others' expectations of you?' (affects), and 'what on-field behaviors result from these specific perceptions, expectations and feelings about pressure situations?' (behaviors). This level of exploration will provide researchers with a richer description of each athlete's idiographic pattern of interacting cognitive-affective-behavioral processes, allowing them draw stronger conclusions regarding the person variables and behaviors associated with the mentally tough personality.

Assessment of the mentally tough personality

The valid and reliable assessment of mental toughness in sport remains an unresolved issue in the current literature. Prior attempts (e.g. PPI, MT48), and even more recent ones (i.e. Gucciardi et al., 2009b; Sheard et al., 2009), to develop measures of the mental toughness construct have been hindered by a number of conceptual, theoretical and/or psychometric issues (Connaughton and Hanton, 2009; Crust, 2007). However, the social-cognitive framework presented in this chapter provides a theoretical foundation upon which a valid, reliable and comprehensive measure of the mental toughness construct can be built. Applying this framework would ground the development of a mental toughness questionnaire in a social-cognitive view of personality that would allow for items to be designed to address the set of common mental toughness attributes across sports and to tap into the specific cognitions and affects that comprise the various components of the mentally tough personality. Preliminary results (Harmison et al., 2008) based on the author's attempts to apply the CAPS approach to personality functioning to the development of a mental toughness questionnaire suggest that the social-cognitive framework has some utility in this regard and warrants further investigation.

In addition, previous research (Coulter et al., 2010; Gucciardi et al., 2008) has indicated that mentally tough athletes display a number of general and competition-specific behaviors (e.g. repeatable high performances, doing the 'little things'). The social-cognitive framework presented conceptualizes mental toughness as a set of cognitive-affective processing units that interact with one another and an athlete's environment to generate the display of mentally tough behaviors. Thus, a key link to understanding mental toughness in sport is the one between athletes' cognitions and affects and the behaviors that are subsequently generated. A need exists, however, to develop valid and reliable ways to assess the display of mentally tough behaviors. One possible avenue is the development of sport- and competition-specific measures of mentally tough behaviors that code how often athletes do the 'little things' associated with their sport (e.g. diving on the floor for a loose basketball). Behavioral assessments of this nature will allow researchers to better quantify the display of mentally tough behaviors and examine the relationship between mentally tough behaviors and mentally tough cognitions and affects.

Development of the mentally tough personality

The scant literature (e.g. Connaughton and Hanton, 2009; Horsburgh et al., 2009) that has addressed the development of mental toughness suggests that it is both an inherited and a learned aspect of an athlete's personality. However, given that these investigations were more or less exploratory by design, the methods used to uncover the developmental aspects of mental toughness as well as the discussion of the ensuing results largely were atheoretical in nature. The social-cognitive framework presented in this chapter establishes the foundation that genetic background, biological history, environmental influences and social learning history contribute to the development of an athlete's mental toughness attributes and constellation of mentally tough cognitions, affects and behaviors. Thus, future research should attempt to identify the bio-genetic and social-environmental factors that affect the acquisition of mentally tough attributes, cognitions, affects and behaviors. In addition, researchers should attempt to determine which cognitions and affects are more influenced by bio-genetic factors and which are more readily shaped by social-learning experiences. Also, it would seem useful for researchers to explore the features of a list of common competitive situations that require mental toughness and have the most impact on activating the desired and undesired cognitions, affects and behaviors.

It should be noted that the knowledge gained about the development of mental toughness from these previous investigations is limited by the use of cross-sectional research designs that relied primarily on retrospective recall of the athletes' developmental history or the use of inadequate psychometric measures of the mental toughness construct. Future research should incorporate longitudinal designs in which the acquisition of the common mental toughness attributes and constellation of key mentally tough cognitions, affects and behaviors are ideographically and nomothetically measured by conceptually and psychometrically sound instruments and tracked over time. Gucciardi et al.'s (2009a) process model of mental toughness and Côté et al.'s (2007) developmental model of sport participation provide potentially useful frames when designing such investigations. Applying these theoretical guides has the potential for illuminating how an athlete's social-cognitive mentally tough personality influences and is shaped by the manner in which the athlete approaches, appraises and responds to competitive situations and how the various trajectories of athlete talent development (e.g. early specialization) and various social influences (e.g. coaches, parents) impact the development of an athlete's mentally tough personality within the context of the developmental, motivational and psychosocial aspects of human performance.

Conclusion

In this chapter the case was made to view this thing called mental toughness in sport as a multidimensional and relatively stable social-cognitive personality construct that can be modified over time if new learning, development or biochemical changes take place within the athlete. A social-cognitive framework of personality, and specifically the CAPS approach, was presented, described and applied to sport to provide a template to incorporate and expand the current understanding of mental toughness in sport. In addition, specific directions for future research based on the application of the social-cognitive framework for understanding and developing mental toughness in athletes were provided to increase theoretically guided investigations in this area. It is hoped that the perspectives and knowledge contained in this chapter will offer researchers and practitioners a useful theoretical foundation to advance future empirical attempts to better understand and develop mental toughness in sport.

References

Bull, S. J., Shambrook, C. J., James, W., and Brooks, J. E. (2005) 'Towards an understanding of mental toughness in elite English cricketers', *Journal of Applied Sport Psychology*, 17, 209–27.

Burton, D., and Weiss, C. (2008) 'The fundamental goal concept: The path to process and performance success', in T. S. Horn (ed.), *Advances in Sport Psychology*, Champaign, IL: Human Kinetics, pp. 339–75.

Cattell, R. B. (1957) *Personality and Motivation Structure and Measurement*, New York: Harcourt, Brace & World.

Clarke, L. (2009) 'S. Williams is fined $82,500'. Retrieved Dec. 2009 from http://www.washingtonpost.com/wpdyn/content/article/2009/11/30/AR2009113002988.html.

Clough, P., Earle, K., and Sewell, D. (2002) 'Mental toughness: The concept and its measurement', in I. Cockerill (ed.), *Solutions in Sport Psychology*, London: Thomson, pp. 32–45.

Connaughton, D., and Hanton, S. (2009) 'Mental toughness in sport: Conceptual and practical issues', in S. D. Mellalieu and S. Hanton (eds), *Advances in Applied Sport Psychology: A Review*, London: Routledge, pp. 317–46.

Costa, P. and McCrae, R. (1992) *The Revised NEO Personality Inventory (NEO-PI-R) and the NEO Five-Factor Inventory (NEO-FFI) Professional Manual*, Odessa, FL: Psychological Assessment Resources.

Côté, J., Baker, J., and Abernathy, B. (2007) 'Practice and play in the development of sport expertise', in G. Tenenbaum and R. C. Eklund (eds), *Handbook of Sport Psychology*, Hoboken, NJ: John Wiley & Sons, pp. 184–202.

Coulter, T. J., Mallet, C. J., and Gucciardi, D. F. (2010) 'Understanding mental toughness in Australian soccer: Perceptions of players, parents, and coaches', *Journal of Sports Sciences*, 28, 699–716.

Crust, L. (2007) 'Mental toughness in sport: A review', *International Journal of Sport and Exercise Psychology*, 5, 270–90.

Dweck, C. S., and Molden, D. C. (2005) 'Self-theories: Their impact on competence motivation and acquisition', in A. J. Elliot and C. S. Dweck (eds), *Handbook of Competence and Motivation*, New York: Guilford Press, pp. 122–40.

Fourie, S., and Potgieter, J. R. (2001) 'The nature of mental toughness in sport', *South African Journal for Research in Sport, Physical Education, and Recreation*, 23, 63–72.

Golby, J., Sheard, M., and Lavallee, D. (2003) 'A cognitive behavioural analysis of mental toughness in national rugby league football teams', *Perceptual and Motor Skills*, 96, 455–62.

Goldberg, A. S. (1998) *Sports Slump Busting: 10 Steps to Mental Toughness and Peak Performance*, Champaign, IL: Human Kinetics.

Gucciardi, D. F., Gordon, S., and Dimmock, J. A. (2008) 'Towards an understanding of mental toughness in Australian football', *Journal of Applied Sport Psychology*, 20, 261–81.

Gucciardi, D. F., Gordon, S., and Dimmock, J. A. (2009a) 'Advancing mental toughness research and theory using personal construct psychology', *International Review of Sport and Exercise Psychology*, 2, 54–72.

Gucciardi, D. F., Gordon, S. D., and Dimmock, J. A. (2009b) 'Development and preliminary validation of a mental toughness inventory for Australian football', *Psychology of Sport and Exercise*, 10, 201–9.

Hanin, Y. L. (2000) *Emotions in Sport*, Champaign, IL: Human Kinetics.

Harmison, R. J., Sims, N. C., and Virden, T. (2008) 'An exploratory factor analysis of the Mental Toughness Questionnaire', paper presented at the 23rd annual meeting of the Association for Applied Sport Psychology, St Louis, MO, Sept.

Horsburgh, V. A., Schermer, J. A., Veselka, L., and Vernon, P. A. (2009) 'A behavioural genetic study of mental toughness and personality', *Personality and Individual Differences*, 46, 100–5.

Jones, G., Hanton, S., and Connaughton, D. (2002) 'What is this thing called mental toughness? An investigation of elite sport performers', *Journal of Applied Sport Psychology*, 14, 205–18.

Jones, G., Hanton, S., and Connaughton, D. (2007) 'A framework of mental toughness in the world's best performers', *The Sport Psychologist*, 21, 243–64.

Kelly, G. A. (1991) *The Psychology of Personal Constructs: A Theory of Personality*, vol. 1, London: Routledge (original work publ. 1955).

Kobasa, S. C. (1979) 'Stressful life events, personality, and health: An inquiry into hardiness', *Journal of Personality and Social Psychology*, 37, 1–11.

Loehr, J. E. (1982) *Athletic Excellence: Mental Toughness Training for Sports*, New York: Plume.

Loehr, J. E. (1986) *Mental Toughness Training for Sports: Achieving Athletic Excellence*, Lexington, MA: Stephen Greene Press.

Loehr, J. E. (1995) *The New Mental Toughness Training for Sports*, New York: Plume.

Lombardi, V. (2001) *What is Takes to be #1: Vince Lombardi on Leadership*, New York: McGraw-Hill.

Meyers, A. W., Whelan, J. P., and Murphy, S. M. (1996) 'Cognitive behavioural strategies in athletic performance enhancement', in M. Hersen, R. M. Eisler, and P. M. Miller (eds), *Progress in Behaviour Modification*, Pacific Grove, CA: Brooks/Cole, pp. 137–64.

Mischel, W. (1968) *Personality and Assessment*, New York: Wiley.

Mischel, W. (1973) 'Toward a cognitive social learning reconceptualization of personality', *Psychological Review*, 80, 252–83.

Mischel, W., and Shoda, Y. (1995) 'A cognitive-affective system theory of personality: Reconceptualizing situations, dispositions, dynamics, and invariance in personality structure', *Psychological Review*, 102, 246–68.

Mischel, W., and Shoda, Y. (1999) 'Integrating dispositions and processing dynamics within a unified theory or personality: The cognitive-affective personality system', in L.A. Pervin and O. P. John (eds), *Handbook of Personality: Theory and Research,* New York: Guilford Press, pp. 197–218.

Plomin, R., DeFries, J. C., and McClearn, G. E. (1990) *Behaviour Genetics: A Premier,* New York: Freeman.

Plomin, R., DeFries, J. C., McClearn, G. E., and Rutter, M. (1997) *Behavioural Genetics,* New York: W. H. Freeman.

Read, S. J., and Miller, L. C. (eds) (1998) *Connectionist and PDP Models of Social Reasoning and Social Behaviour,* Hillsdale, NJ: Erlbaum.

Rumelhart, D. E., and McClelland, J. L. (1986) *Parallel Distributed Processing: Explorations in the Microstructure of Cognition*, vols. 1 and 2, Cambridge, MA: MIT Press.

Sheard, M., Golby, J., and van Wersch, A. (2009) 'Progress toward construct validation of the Sports Mental Toughness Questionnaire (SMTQ)', *European Journal of Psychological Assessment,* 25, 186–93.

Shoda, Y. (1999) 'Behavioural expressions of a personality system: Generation and perception of behavioural signatures', in D. Cervone and Y. Shoda (eds), *The Coherence of Personality: Social-Cognitive Bases of Consistency, Variability, and Organization,* New York: Guilford Press, pp. 155–81.

Shoda, Y., and Mischel, W. (1996) 'Toward a unified, intra-individual dynamic conception of personality', *Journal of Research in Personality*, 30, 414–28.

Shoda, Y., and Smith, R. E. (2006) 'Conceptualizing personality as a cognitive-affective processing system: A framework for models of maladaptive behaviour patterns and change', *Behaviour Therapy*, 35, 147–65.

Smith, R. E. (2006) 'Understanding sport behaviour: A cognitive-affective processing systems approach', *Journal of Applied Sport Psychology*, 18, 1–27.

Thelwell, R., Weston, N., and Greenlees, I. (2005) 'Defining and understanding mental toughness within soccer', *Journal of Applied Sport Psychology*, 17, 326–32.

Tutko, T. A., and Richards, J. W. (1972) *Coach's Practical Guide to Athletic Motivation,* Boston, MA: Allyn & Bacon.

Vealey, R. S. (2007) 'Mental skills training in sport', in G. Tenenbaum and R. C. Eklund (eds), *Handbook of Sport Psychology,* Hoboken, NJ: John Wiley & Sons, pp. 287–309.

Weinberg, R. S., Harmison, R. J., Rosenkranz, R., and Hookom, S. (2005) 'Goal setting', in J. Taylor and G. Wilson (eds), *Applying Sport Psychology: Four Perspectives,* Champaign, IL: Human Kinetics, pp. 101–16.

5   Who's mental, who's tough and who's both?

Mutton constructs dressed up as lamb

Mark B. Andersen

In Australia, we use the phrase 'mutton dressed up as lamb' to describe an older man or woman who acts and dresses as if they were younger, newer and fresher than they actually are. Much of the mental toughness literature, and some in particular (e.g. Clough et al., 2002), appears to contain ideas and constructs (e.g. hardiness, resilience) that have been around for decades but are now repackaged or re-dressed into something that, on the surface, looks new but is probably not as fresh as its champions suggest. The 'mental toughness movement', if one can call it that, shares similarities with the re-emergence of 'positive psychology'. It would be impolite to call Gordon Allport, Carl Rogers, Abraham Maslow and Rollo May 'mutton', but the positive psychology activists seem to have done a lot of dressing them up as lamb. Perhaps something similar has happened with mental toughness.

Many coaches, athletes, sports administrators, researchers and sport psychologists use the term *mental toughness*, but what do all these stakeholders mean when they say, 'Man, that athlete is mentally tough!'? A variety of definitions have appeared in the literature, but consensus about what the popular phrase means does not appear to be on any academic horizon (yet). The term has been used so much, and has so many advocates, that it has taken on a near corporeality. Many sport psychologists believe that there is something (some traits, or some constellation of characteristics) that can be called mental toughness. Problems with the construct of mental toughness abound, not the least of which is the language. 'Tough' and 'toughness' reek of the macho, masculine and pathogenic culture of sport. If one is not mentally tough, then one is weak, soft and a sissy. Organized sport and physical education are environments that can do as much damage (or more) as they can help foster positive experiences (see Leahy, in press). For example, for a young American male hand–eye motor moron, physical education classes can be a daily dose of humiliation. If he cannot get his body to do anything halfway acceptable in the manly sports of football or basketball, he'll hear, 'What a klutz!' 'You throw like a girl!' 'What a sissy!' 'You're worthless!' The word 'toughness' reverberates with much of what is questionable in sport. It carries a macho swagger when it enters the room. Its other names are, 'No pain, no gain', 'it's heroic to play injured', 'silence your emotions', 'don't be a girl' and 'suck it up'. It is the language of patriarchal hierarchy, machismo (including homophobia) and intolerance of human frailty. When we use the word 'tough' what are we communicating? We don't really know, but the receivers of our toughness talks and interventions are already primed to interpret that word in ways that reinforce much of what might be called the 'dark side' of sport. On the other hand, many coaches and athletes have internalized the 'toughness' values of sport, and toughness may be exactly what they want.

In the past, being mentally tough has been associated with overcoming adversity or being better than opponents or having long successful careers (e.g. Jones et al., 2002) – post-hoc judgements that have all of the problems of making judgements about people after the fact. Newer definitions have avoided such descriptions, but are problematic in other ways. The general purpose of this chapter is to explore the issues related to reifying popular phraseology into suspect psychological constructs and the questionable psychometrics used to substantiate what has probably been established, in other terms, years ago. The chapter moves through primarily three stages: the conceptualization of mental toughness and its various definitions, measuring mental toughness and how mental toughness might be developed. Criticisms of the literature in each of the stages are presented. For example, as I look at the mental toughness literature, the construct seems so Gargantuan or Everestian that I am not sure we can successfully tackle that giant or climb that mountain (pick a metaphor), or that we even need to try. This devil's advocate chapter ends with a section on some of the positive contributions and trends in the mental toughness research literature, along with an example of a complex, messy and flawed athlete who, no matter what criteria one uses, would have to be considered mentally tough.

The Gargantuan Everest: conceptualizing and defining mental toughness

Here is a list of attributes, characteristics, behaviors, constructs, cognitions and emotions that researchers (e.g. Connaughton et al., 2008; Crust, 2008; Gucciardi et al., 2009a) have come up with to describe, measure and develop mental toughness: self-belief, work ethic, determination, perseverance, having goals, meticulous preparation, time management, being inspirational, personal values, honesty, pride in performance, accountability, self-motivation, high self-esteem, competitive desire, desire to achieve, team success, vision, tough attitudes, tough character, tough thinking, discipline, commitment, control, challenge, positivity, professionalism, accepting sacrifices, concentration and focus, resilience, handling pressure, overriding negative thoughts, emotional intelligence (awareness of one's own emotions, awareness of others' emotions, controlling emotions, handling others' emotions well, empathy), self-awareness, sport intelligence, team role responsibility, understanding the game, physical toughness, attentional control, generally coping better than opponents, being more consistent than opponents, accepting and embracing challenge, thriving through pressure and challenge, overcoming adversity and pressure, using long-term goals as sources of motivation, controlling the environment, pushing oneself to the limit, regulation of performance, handling failure, handling success, having unshakable beliefs, having insatiable desires, pushing back boundaries of physical and emotional pain, regaining psychological control after unexpected events, having influential parents, childhood background predisposition to be mentally tough, opportunities to survive early setbacks, needing to earn success, independence, being self-reflective, competitiveness with self, exploiting learning opportunities, never-say-die mindset, go-the-extra-mile mindset, belief in making a difference, willing to take risks, robust self-confidence, positive coach–athlete relationships, coaching philosophy conducive to developing mental toughness, intrinsically motivated, internal locus of control, superior decision-making and conducive training environments. This list, of course, has many overlaps and redundancies. It is also incomplete. There's more.

If we are to talk about conceptualizing mental toughness, then we also need to discuss what its opposite, mental weakness for a lack of a better term, would be. If we took the polar opposites of the huge list above, we would have a pathetic, miserable, abused and probably suicidal individual. Given the huge number of possible combinations of positive attributes of mental toughness and their corresponding opposite attributes, it is questionable whether mental toughness and mental weakness are 'conceptualizable' in any coherent and understandable way. There have been, however, some attempts to explore the opposites of mental toughness (Coulter et al., 2010; Gucciardi et al., 2008), but the sheer number of attributes or characteristics covered is rather overwhelming. For example, Gucciardi et al. (2008) described over 30 characteristics (and their 30+ opposites) of mental toughness, and the construct started to appear nearly global. Maybe we need to look at mental toughness as a variety of transient, fluctuating and mercurial states of being and seek ways to increase the probability of those states occurring (e.g. using mindfulness meditation) rather than trying to define or encompass them with words and constructs. Such an approach is closely related to Gardner and Moore's (2007) work on mindfulness, acceptance and commitment in sport.

As a thought experiment, consider the following question: 'If we eliminate the polar opposites of all these variables (or in terms of personal construct psychology (Kelly, 1991), the contrast poles; see Gucciardi et al., 2009a), then what else in an athlete's internal and external worlds is *not* mental toughness?' One personality dimension that comes to mind is introversion–extroversion, and it doesn't seem like we need to worry about that dimension, or do we? Clough et al. (2002: 38) suggested, 'Mentally tough individuals tend to be sociable and outgoing', and those characteristics are common in extroverts. It is unclear how and why Clough et al. came to such a conclusion, but there it is. Also, highly introverted people are often too much inside their heads and are easily overstimulated by external stimuli, which often interfere with functioning. Highly extroverted people may be quite distractible or have high sensation-seeking drives that lead them to risk taking and poor judgements (see Zuckerman, 1983). There may be an optimal level of extroversion to be mentally tough, so why not throw introversion and extroversion into the mental toughness kitchen sink?

Concentration and focus come up in the various lists of mental toughness attributes and abilities, but they seem to be described as effortful and even combative (e.g. eliminating negative thoughts, refocusing, pushing external distracters out of the way). Mindfulness, which is intimately connected to concentration and focus, is all the rage in clinical and counselling psychology these days. In general, mindfulness involves purposefully paying attention to what is happening right now, accepting what is occurring and remaining non-judgemental (Kabat-Zinn, 2005). Being mindful and staying in the present moment would seem to be part of being mentally tough (maybe even one of the major features), so maybe we should include 'mindfulness' as part of mental toughness.

From what has been presented in the literature to date it appears mental toughness could be just about anything in sport. One last question: can one be both clinically depressed and mentally tough? The cognitive, emotional and behavioral signs and symptoms of major depressive disorders would seem nearly antithetical to the signs and symptoms of being mentally tough. There is doubt, self-loathing, incapacitation, suicidal ideation, anhedonia, confusion and agitation (American Psychiatric Association, 2000), everything mental toughness is not. So what about Petria Thomas (Australian Olympic swimmer and gold medallist)? She experienced debilitating depression through some of her career (even taking a drug overdose; see Shea, 2005). In the depths of depression, she would haul herself out of bed, put in a workout and come home and fall into a heap of worthlessness. If one goes back to some early descriptions of mental toughness that include the ability 'to overcome adversity', then Petria Thomas could be classified as a mentally tough athlete. Maybe she had 'state' mental toughness and not 'trait' (there's a whole other issue, see Bull et al., 2005). In recent years, many top-level, apparently mentally tough athletes in Australia have come out of the depression closet with public and heartfelt statements about their struggles. Considering the never-ending list of attributes which have been associated with several athletes who have also experienced mental illness, mental toughness as a construct becomes blurrier and blurrier. Dark clouds on Everest descending.

Other-dependent mental toughness definitions

There is another definition of mental toughness in the literature that also strikes me as odd:

> Mental toughness is having the natural or developed psychological edge that enables you to, generally, cope better than your opponents with the many demands (competition, training, lifestyle) that sport places on a performer and, specifically, be more consistent and better than your components in remaining determined, focused, confident, and in control under pressure.
> (Jones et al., 2002: 209)

In this case, my mental toughness is dependent on my opponents. In other words, if I have a lot of mental toughness attributes, but my opponents are, generally, super mentally tough and better players than I am, then I can't be considered mentally tough. Or if I am only semi-mentally tough, and most of my opponents are semi-demi-mentally tough, and I win more, then I am mentally tough. How can one's mental toughness be tied to opponents? As another example, a top junior player wins a lot, plays in present time and little seems to faze her. By any definition she would be mentally tough. In her first year as a senior she is still playing as solidly as she did as a junior (in present time, generally unfazed), but she is up against more mature athletes with even greater mental and physical skills than she has. She loses a lot to superior players. Is she still mentally tough or is she now not mentally tough because of her opponents? Saying that to be mentally tough one has to generally be better than one's opponents takes one's mental toughness out of one's control and houses it in the opponents' control. This concept came out of fantasy-oriented research and priming participants that this definition was what mental toughness was.

Fantasies and absolute language

Several researchers have tried to get at 'this thing called mental toughness'. One tactic used often to explore what mental toughness is has been to ask experts (e.g. coaches, elite athletes) how they would describe an *ideal* mentally tough athlete (e.g. Jones et al., 2002). Initially this approach does not sound like a bad idea, but what task are the researchers really asking the experts to do? They are asking them to construct fantasies (socially constructed cultural ideals), and then they come up with definitions and attributes that stem from those fantasies. And this is where the problem of absolute language comes in. For example, some descriptions of mental toughness contain the words 'unshakable belief', 'insatiable desire', 'fully focused' and so forth. That's the problem when you ask 'ideal' sorts of questions. You get an ideal (not real, not human) result. Absolute fantasy language is not the language of science; it may be the language of imagination, but it is not science. A good rule of thumb when it comes to absolute language (e.g. nothing, always, never, fully, completely, totally) is to say, with a touch of irony, 'Don't use absolute language; it is *always* false.' There are exceptions such as in physics (*nothing* we have observed moves faster than light), but sport psychology isn't physics. Also, when absolute language such as 'unshakable belief' and 'insatiable desire' are used, mental toughness begins to sound pathological. An unshakable belief would be one that, literally, could not be modified or changed, even in light of disconfirming information. The inability to shake a belief, or to modify it, would seem to be, in many cases, maladaptive and move into the realm of fantasy, fantasies that may lead to unwise choices (e.g. continuing to play after four concussions in one year). Rigidity (unshakableness) is rarely an adaptive trait. An insatiable desire sounds like the realm of the hungry ghosts in Buddhism where creatures constantly thirst and desire things but can never be filled. Insatiable desire makes me think of overtraining syndrome, perfectionism and obsessive-compulsive personality disorders. Such words in the mental toughness literature are problematic because they stem from fantasies, not realities. Even the

Gucciardi et al. (2008) definition for Australian football mental toughness, one of the best of the lot, still has the problem of absolute language.

> Mental toughness in Australian Football is a collection of values, attitudes, behaviors, and emotions that enable you to persevere and overcome *any* obstacle, adversity, or pressure experienced, but also to maintain concentration and motivation when things are going well to consistently achieve your goals. (p. 278, italics added)

Only a superman or superwoman could overcome *any* obstacle, adversity or pressure, but even Superman can't overcome kryptonite. In a later article, Coulter et al. (2010) revised the above definition and got rid of some of the absolute language, but they took a strange path:

> Mental toughness is the presence of some or the entire collection of experientially developed and inherent values, attitudes, emotions, cognitions, and behaviors that influence the way in which an individual approaches, responds to, and appraises both negatively and positively construed pressures, challenges, and adversities to consistently achieve his or her goals. (p. 715)

I would like to break this statement down to its components and what they might mean. The first thing that strikes me is the word 'entire', and that word is an absolute. The authors also hedge their definition by saying 'some or the entire'. The next interesting word is 'inherent'. That adjective means 'innate', 'born with' and 'existing in someone or something as a permanent and inseparable element, quality, or attribute'. As the definition is constructed, the words 'experientially developed and inherent' modify the five nouns that follow. Just how 'values, attitudes, emotions, cognitions, and behaviors' can be inherent (in a mental toughness context) is a mystery. It would seem that almost all values, attitudes, cognitions, emotions and behaviors connected to being mentally tough would have to be acquired through experience. They certainly weren't selected for by evolution, and I am sure we can't find them in the human genome. Such imprecise and incorrect use of language does not give one much faith in this definition of the construct. Construct definitions in psychology tend to be relatively general and abstract, but this definition takes generality to the extreme. It essentially says that 'mental toughness is anything and everything that people have and use to meet the challenges in their lives and consistently reach their goals'. That definition really doesn't say much at all.

This definition is also anchored to 'pressures, challenges, and adversities (both positive and negative)' and how people approach and respond to them. It seems that evidence for mental toughness can only emerge when pressures, challenges and adversities are present. Could one still be mentally tough when there are no pressures, challenges or adversities? There is an illogic operating here. Can I not still be mentally tough when I am competing against an opponent who poses no threat or challenge whatsoever? Can I not use all the same mental skills, emotional control and so forth when I am competing against a strong opponent as I do when faced with someone whom I can beat handily? Am I mentally tough in the former condition and not mentally tough in the latter? That just doesn't make sense.

Finally, why is 'consistently achieving goals' a necessary component? I do not see how an outcome (goal achievement) needs to be tied to something like mental toughness. Given all the problems with this construct definition, I am not sure that Coulter et al. (2010) have made any improvement over Gucciardi et al.'s (2008) formulation. Given the problems with other-dependent definitions, fantasies, absolute language and overly general and vague conceptualizations, it seems that any broad consensus on what mental toughness is remains elusive. Maybe mental toughness is sport jargon that can't be (or shouldn't be) conceptualized or operationalized.

Mental toughness measurement

Table 5.1 shows six mental toughness inventories and their subscales. Discussions on their psychometric rigour can be found in Part 2 of this book and elsewhere (e.g. Gordon and Gucciardi, in press). The point being made here is how wide-ranging they are. The Australian Football Mental Toughness Inventory (AfMTI: Gucciardi et al., 2009b) and the Cricket Mental Toughness Inventory (CMTI: Gucciardi and Gordon, 2009) are interesting to compare. Is mental toughness in

Table 5.1 Six mental toughness inventories and their subscales

Psychological Performance Inventory (Loehr, 1986)	*Psychological Performance Inventory–A (Golby et al., 2007)*	*Sport Mental Toughness Questionnaire (Sheard et al., 2009)*	*Australian Football Mental Toughness Inventory (Gucciardi et al., 2009b)*	*Cricket Mental Toughness Inventory (Gucciardi & Gordon, 2009)*	*Mental Toughness Questionnaire-48 (Clough et al., 2002)*
Self-confidence	Determination	Confidence	Thrive through challenge	Affective intelligence	Challenge
Negative energy	Self-belief	Constancy	Sport awareness	Attentional control	Commitment
Attention control	Positive cognitions	Control	Tough attitude	Resilience	Emotional control
Visual and imagery control	Visualization		Desire success	Self-belief	Life control
Motivation level				Desire to achieve	Confidence in abilities
Positive energy					Interpersonal confidence
Attitude control					

football and cricket so different that we need two different scales that appear to have only low to moderate overlap? Also, these scales have been validated primarily with male athletes. Will we need different scales for females? Given all the sports that are played around the world, just how many inventories will we need? We may need a bucket load. The mental (and physical) demands of performing well in the 100 metre sprint would seem, in many ways, quite different from what is needed to play five sets at a tennis grand slam tournament or 72 holes of golf. It appears that the AfMTI and the CMTI are measuring the levels of mental demands of specific sports. Those demands obviously change from sport to sport, but if mental toughness is a robust construct, then one would expect to find some commonality or core characteristics that cross most sports. In looking at the many tests, that commonality, at present, seems tenuous.

A major point about these tests is that all the subscales on the various mental toughness inventories are arbitrary metrics (see Andersen et al., 2007; Kazdin, 2006). In describing arbitrary metrics, Blanton and Jaccard (2006: 28) wrote:

> We define a metric as arbitrary when it is not known where a given score locates an individual on the underlying psychological dimension or how a one-unit change on the observed score reflects the magnitude of change on the underlying dimension. This definition of metric arbitrariness makes explicit that an individual's observed score on a response metric provides only an indirect assessment of his or her position on the unobserved, hypothetical psychological construct.

There is plenty of evidence that the arbitrary metrics of mental toughness inventories are related to other arbitrary metrics (see Part 2 of this volume). Arbitrary metrics are tremendously useful in model testing and theory building. One can compare mental toughness metrics to other psychosocial metrics to help determine the realm of mental toughness. Also, if some facets of mental toughness appear strongly related to other psychological constructs (e.g. resilience) then at least some of the subscales on mental toughness inventories should substantially correlate with other established scales (convergent validity). If they do not, then there may be something wrong with the model, the measurement or both.

Still, we don't know what scores mean on any of the mental toughness arbitrary metrics. All the mental toughness scales are ordinal-level measurements, so if person A has a 'total mental toughness' score of 56 and person B has a score of 28, we certainly cannot say that person A has twice the mental toughness of person B. We can say that it appears that person A has more mental toughness than person B. But, and I am not trying to be flippant, the question becomes, 'So what?' Unless the mental toughness psychometrics are calibrated against some real-world behaviors, we cannot really say much about what they might mean. Some researchers have suggested that mental toughness research is in its infancy, and that may be the reason why we haven't made solid connections between mental toughness and actual real-world performance. There have been mental toughness training programmes around for quite some time, but we still do not have any solid behavioral evidence that mental toughness training can change people (e.g. to perform better or more consistently) or that mental toughness measures are associated with the dependent variable of interest to coaches and athletes (i.e. performance in real-world competitive situations). Maybe, however, what some coaches and athletes want are some words or slogans that capture characteristics of an ideal athlete. 'Mental toughness' would fit the bill, just as older descriptors have in the past (e.g. 'intestinal fortitude').

Research with mental toughness inventories

In an evaluation of a mental toughness training programme for young male Australian football players, Gucciardi et al. (2009c) measured mental toughness, resilience and flow pre- and post-interventions for three groups: a psychological skills training group (PST), a mental toughness training group (MTT) and a control group. They found that the two intervention groups generally improved their scores on the variables, whereas the control group did not. The coaches and parents also rated the players in the PST and MTT groups as more mentally tough, more resilient and flowier than the control group athletes post-intervention. In the real world of practice, convincing a coach that a programme is helpful is probably the biggest hurdle. This study showed that coaches perceived their athletes to be in better mental shape after the interventions. If coaches believe something is effective, then they (or the administrators) may be willing to pay for it. And the big question in service delivery is: is the service worth paying for? This study is evidence that psychological interventions can help change scores on arbitrary metrics (and coach and parent perceptions), and it is probably a good start. The results, however, are still a few steps away from the acid test of intervention effectiveness – have athletes improved their on-field play? We are still missing the behavioral real-world variable of performance. I think the most important part in this article is:

> But in terms of talent development within a sporting context it is essential that psychological improvements are associated with performance improvements and, due to the subjective nature of the data, we were unable to gauge possible links with improved performance. Although self-report questionnaire data can predict performance … and behavior, … there is some evidence to suggest that this may not always be the case. … Therefore, future researchers should obtain both subjective and objective data when assessing the effectiveness of psychological interventions. (p. 321)

Gucciardi et al.'s suggestion should become law in mental toughness research. Otherwise, we are left with 'So what?'

Where's the beef?

Sheard and Golby (2006) measured positive psychological development (possible aspects of mental toughness) before and after a seven-week psychological skills training programme. They also recorded best competitive times for 36 adolescent swimmers pre- and post-intervention. They concluded that 'adolescent athletes, in addition to developing better coping skills ... benefit also from exposure to PST in terms of their sport performance' (2006: 165). The authors have no basis for this conclusion. There was no control group or attentional-control group. Adolescents, like anyone else, get better at something if they train. Adolescents are also people who are growing while training. This study is hardly any evidence for the effectiveness of PST, but it is just about the only one I could find that used a real-world variable that was directly related to what coaches and athletes are interested in: performance.

In other studies of mental toughness and behavior, the dependent variables are rather divorced from meaningful real-world performance. Clough et al. (2002) first committed the cardinal statistical sin of dichotomizing a continuous variable (classifying participants as either high or low on mental toughness). That datacidal act is enough to question their results. They found that the high mental toughness participants scored consistently on a cognitive planning task regardless of positive or negative feedback, whereas the low mental toughness group scored significantly lower on the cognitive planning task following negative feedback. This finding is a useful one in that it shows some people are more sensitive to negative feedback and that negative feedback, for some, can have deleterious effects on performance. Athletes, however, do not compete in the real world on cognitive planning tasks. With the dichotomization of mental toughness and a dependent variable substantially distant from real competitive performance, one must question the meaningfulness of this study.

In another behavioral study, Crust and Clough (2005) had 41 participants hold 1.5 per cent of their body weight load suspended from their outstretched dominant arms. Their endurance times were correlated with overall mental toughness ($r = .34$), control ($r = .37$) and confidence ($r = .29$), but not with challenge or commitment on the Mental Toughness Questionnaire-48 (MTQ48: Clough et al., 2002). So, scores on some mental toughness subscales account for between 8 and 14 per cent of variance in a task that no athlete ever does in competition (or in training for that matter). At least they didn't dichotomize a continuous variable. The above behavioral studies do not really provide any solid evidence that mental toughness, however it is measured, is related to real-world competitive behavior.

A possible behavioral measure of mental toughness

The problem is to find a real-world competitive behavior or behaviors and measure them and then calibrate them against various indices of mental toughness. What would such a real-world behavioral measure look like? Winning and losing might be one measure, but that variable is all tied in with things beyond the researcher's control, such as the quality of the opponents. Mental toughness researchers might want to develop checklists of behaviors that would be indicators of mental toughness. I am not sure what behaviors those would be, but it would be a good start. Such checklists would probably have to be developed for each sport examined. For example, in tennis, one might compare the percentage of 'first serves in' during the times a player is ahead in serve versus the times a player is behind in serves. If those percentages were similar (or if the first-serve-in percentage were better during times a player is behind) then those performance measures might be behavioral evidence for mental toughness. A similar design could be used for volleyball (percentage of serves in when ahead versus behind) or basketball (free-throw percentage when the team is ahead versus behind) by taking a whole season of statistics and then correlating them with scores on mental toughness inventories.

Here's another design I would like to see someone do. If we believe that 'consistency' of performance is one aspect of mental toughness (just a piece of it, but we have to start somewhere: see Gucciardi et al., 2008), then why not correlate consistency of competitive behavior with mental toughness measures? For example, one could recruit 50 masters aged swimmers (or young swimmers or track athletes, just as long as they all compete in the same event) who have the 100-metre freestyle as one of their main competitive events. One could collect all the times for their 100-metre freestyle competitions over a year. Then one could calculate intra-individual standard deviations for each athlete. Those standard deviations could then be correlated with scores on mental toughness inventories. One would hope for a nice fat negative correlation with low standard deviations (high consistency) related to high mental toughness scores, and high standard deviations (low consistency) correlated with low mental toughness scores. It is not the greatest design, being only correlational, but if the results come out like we would hope, then we would have some meaningful, real-world and understandable research (not laboratory cognitive or endurance tasks) to show coaches and athletes that mental toughness is associated with consistency of performance.

In regards to research on mental toughness training or interventions (maybe we should call it 'mental toughness therapy'), investigators might want to consider whether to take an efficacy or an effectiveness approach (see Seligman, 1995). Efficacy research has, as its gold standard, randomized controlled trials with intervention and control groups. Interventions are standardized and of a set duration. Efficacy research is highly controlled and has high internal validity. Effectiveness research involves examining interventions, therapies and outcomes out there in the real world of practice and has high external validity. If researchers are investigating the outcomes of a set package of mental toughness training, then they would be doing efficacy studies. If they are exploring the real-world practices and outcomes of sport psychology treatment as it happens *in situ* then they would be doing effectiveness research. Many prominent psychologists (e.g. Seligman) have aligned themselves on the side of effectiveness research. Mental toughness researchers might want to carefully consider whether internal or external validity is the most important criterion for their purposes.

Mental toughness development

The term *mental toughness* has been in the sport psychology literature for almost 30 years (see Loehr, 1982), but research and serious test development in mental toughness sprang into prominence only in the last 10 years. In some ways the current mental toughness area reminds me of the emotional intelligence boom that started in the 1990s. Although the topic of emotional intelligence (EI) appeared in Darwin's (1872) work on the survival value of emotional expression, the modern interest in EI, arguably, began with Salovey and Mayer (1990) and then exploded with Goleman's (1995) book. The debate on EI has raged since that time. The debate, on the negative side, has concerned the issues of unsound theories (there are a few different models of EI) and the unsound psychometrics (there are different tests) based on those models. Like EI, the mental toughness literature has different models and different psychometrics that supposedly tap into the models' constructs. The practical (and practice) upshot of the EI field is that EI was taken up by many organizational psychologists and marketed to businesses, in a similar fashion as the Myers-Briggs Type Indicator (more dodgy psychometrics based on dodgy theory; see Boyle, 1995).

The mental toughness development market

Emotional intelligence, personality types, and mental toughness all sound good, and when they are used, many people feel like they can grasp the concepts, and say, for example, 'yes, mental toughness would be nice to have' even though the construct is actually rather vague. The goal of marketing a product or service is to create a need or desire by convincing people they lack something and then informing people that 'we have the product (or service) that will fill your needs' (e.g. a mental toughness development package). The EI and Myers-Briggs advocates have done their marketing jobs brilliantly. Mental toughness marketers are not far behind.

One problem sincere researchers and practitioners face in trying to measure and develop mental toughness, and to help coaches and athletes, is that the mental toughness bandwagon has already taken off. One has only to Google 'mental toughness test' and up will pop dozens of sites for mental toughness testing and development training for sport, business, education (e.g. mental toughness for taking university entrance exams), and so forth. After trawling through many of these sites one day, I began to feel uncomfortable. In the American Psychological Association's (2002) *Ethical Principles of Psychologists and Code of Conduct*, there are these two items under '9.02 Use of Assessments':

(a) Psychologists administer, adapt, score, interpret, or use assessment techniques, interviews, tests, or instruments in a manner and for purposes that are appropriate in light of the research on or evidence of the usefulness and proper application of the techniques.

(b) Psychologists use assessment instruments whose validity and reliability have been established for use with members of the population tested. When such validity or reliability has not been established, psychologists describe the strengths and limitations of test results and interpretation.

I would seriously doubt that most of the mental toughness inventories scattered across the web have been validated on the populations being targeted. It is also questionable whether mental toughness development training programmes have been rigorously evaluated. As a licensed psychologist in the US and a registered psychologist in Australia, I am bound by these principles of test use. Mental toughness inventories may meet the criteria of validity and reliability, but given the wide variety of scales and subscales across the tests, the huge constellation of characteristics that are associated with mental toughness, and (keeping with the astronomy metaphor) the general nebulosity of the construct, I don't think we can be confident that the inventories are measuring mental toughness. They are measuring something, but I am not sure we know what that something is. In item 9.02(a), the words 'for purposes that are appropriate in light of the research on or evidence of the usefulness and proper application of the techniques' strike me as important for consideration. What is the 'usefulness' of a mental toughness inventory (besides getting it published and meeting university productivity quotas)? Ostensibly, one would think its usefulness would be in identifying the mentally tough and the mentally weak because we believe the mentally tough will perform better in the real world of competitive sport than the mentally weak. We have no solid evidence that that is the case. Also, the usefulness of the inventory might be to identify the mentally weak in order to do something (intervene in some way with a mental toughness development programme) to make them tougher and help them perform better. Not much evidence for that one either. In the real world of applied sport psychology practice, mental toughness inventories might be useful as a way to start conversations with athletes about themselves and their performance concerns (a personality inventory would also serve the same purpose), but beyond that, the psychometric and ethical ground becomes shaky. I am not sure that mental toughness inventories are a way forward. Such inventories reduce people to scores on subscales. I am not sure that such information advances our knowledge on mental toughness. What may prove more fruitful are studies that delve into life histories of sports people who appear to have developed the characteristics of being mentally tough. Future investigators might examine works such as Runyan's (1984) *Life Histories and Psychobiography: Explorations in Theory and Method* or Schultz's (2005) *Handbook of Psychobiography* for research methods and paradigms for studying individuals' lives. Maybe I am suggesting that mental toughness development research (and practice) need a more human face than what inventories can supply.

The dark side of mental toughness development

Being mentally tough is desirable (at least many of us think so). But can one be so mentally tough that this constellation of variables might set one at risk? Levy et al. (2006: 252) suggested that:

Despite the benefits of being mentally tough with respect to pain and threat appraisals, there is the possibility that this characteristic may have a negative influence upon rehabilitation adherence and recovery outcomes. This may be due to high mentally tough individuals appraising their injury to be less severe and less susceptible to reoccur and thereby perceive compliance to clinic based activity to be less important.

Crust (2008: 582) also added some words of caution:

Future researchers might consider testing whether mental toughness is associated with playing on while injured, and injury reoccurrence ... is mental toughness about playing on while injured, risking long-term damage, and potentially reducing team efficiency; or is it taking the difficult decision to stop training and competing, seeking medical support, focusing on adhering to a program of rehabilitation and returning to action as soon as possible? With the 'no pain, no gain' philosophy that apparently pervades elite sport, this would appear to be an important question to answer.

Levy et al. and Crust are concerned with physical health and how it may be compromised if one is highly mentally tough, and I think their concerns should be investigated. I have worries that some aspects of what is called mental toughness may be associated with psychological damage and distress. What might be the psychological costs to an athlete who tries to put on the mentally tough face, who keeps vulnerability in the closet, who does not seek help because that is a sign of weakness, who cries alone and whose 'insatiable' desire to make it to the pros compromises his or her loving relationships? I think when we sell mental toughness we need to be mindful that, for some predisposed athletes, we may be selling shackles. Mental toughness fits hand-in-glove with the masculine 'tough' environment of sport, and when coaches (and sport psychologists) champion mental toughness and praise athletes who demonstrate that toughness, and neglect (or abuse) athletes who don't, then mental toughness may become part of the problem. A 'we-all-need-to-be-mentally-tough' atmosphere may help silence athletes who are struggling. Also, what happens to an athlete who gets labelled as 'mentally weak'? I have heard way too many coaches say, 'he is soft' or 'she is mentally weak', and then that label becomes almost a self-fulfilling prophecy. Once an athlete is labelled as weak, then poor performances can be blamed on the athlete, and not on poor, inadequate or neglectful coaching.

Mental toughness development training or positive relationships?

Gucciardi et al. (2009c) showed that a mental toughness training (MTT) programme led to improved scores on various psychometrics, and more important, perceptions of parents and coaches that their athletes were more mentally tough. I am sure some of the variance in the improvements noticed by parents and coaches could be accounted for by athletes learning the content of the MTT and PST programmes. Research such as Gucciardi et al., however, is practitioner evacuated. The interventions are foregrounded in the research, and the personalities and interpersonal skills of the practitioner are nowhere to be seen except in the briefly mentioned consultant effectiveness data. Some of the changes found in Gucciardi et al. might be accounted for by Gucciardi himself and the relationships he formed with the boys in the study. All the consultant effectiveness data had ceiling effects, indicating that the boys really liked their sport psychology consultant. Also, the psychological skills training group and the mental toughness training group were roughly the same in terms of improvement over the control group. What did those two groups have in common besides some overlap in training content? The sport psychology consultant! Gucciardi et al. did not correlate the consultant effectiveness scores with any of the changes in the mental toughness variables, mainly because that was not the research question. A reanalysis of the data might reveal that consultant effectiveness scales also account for changes in mental toughness scores.

We know in counselling and psychotherapy that the one variable consistently associated with outcomes is the quality of the therapeutic relationship or the working alliance between client and practitioner (see Sexton and Whiston, 1994). Good relationships lead to positive outcomes; poor relationships lead to no change or negative outcomes. It almost doesn't really matter what sort of therapy is being conducted (e.g. CBT, psychodynamic, narrative). As long as the relationship is strong, caring and mutually respectful, then the likelihood of positive outcome is increased. What we don't examine much in sport psychology, or in the mental toughness training literature, is the quality of the relationships between practitioners and clients.

How do relationships work?

An athlete starts seeing a sport psychologist, and we hope the practitioner is caring, loving, interested, compassionate, non-judgemental, accepting and knowledgeable and has the best interests of the athlete at heart, and also has no major agenda except the athlete's health and happiness. For the athlete, the sport psychologist may be the only haven in a world of contingent agendas (e.g. coaches' agendas, parents' agendas). The relationship is special; it is confidential and personal. What's not to love?

Positive relationships may develop quickly, or they may take a great deal of time if the athlete has a personal history of being abused by parents or coaches. Trust in the psychologist, and investment in the treatment process, usually need to be carefully nurtured. Ideally, in time, the psychologist becomes (we hope) a model for the athlete of self- and other-acceptance, a model for rational thought and a model for how to be in the world. The psychologist has the ability to 'hold' (not control) the athlete's anger, anxiety and sadness and not become overwhelmed by them, even though the athlete may feel overwhelmed and discombobulated at times. This 'holding' environment (see Winnicott, 1971) and the personality of the psychologist are part of what fuels change for the better (Epstein, 1996). All the mechanisms by which change is made are too complex to describe here, but the one most relevant for the mental toughness discussion is the internalization of the psychologist. Athletes often take the qualities of the psychologist and make internal representations of how the psychologist acts, thinks, feels and behaves. These internal representations act as guides for the athlete to change or alter his or her thinking, emotional reactions and behaviors. When athletes say to their sport psychologists, 'I was at the tournament and getting nervous, and then I heard your voice in my head … .' we know that the internalization of the psychologist is on its merry and helpful way.

We all know relationships fuel change for better and for worse. The evidence is overwhelming. One has only to look at the quality of the relationships between athletes and coaches. Gucciardi et al. (2009d) have suggested that relationships (parent–child, coach–athlete) may be central to developing mental toughness, and they are probably on to something, but relationships have not received the attention they deserve in the mental toughness area. One reason for this lacuna in the research may be because many investigators believe mental toughness is housed within the athlete, and that individualistic, and decidedly Western point of view, may bias the questions asked. Mental toughness (resilience, staying in the present moment or however one wishes to define it) may be a product of psychosocial and cultural variables and the quality of relationship histories of athletes' whole lives. Looking at mental toughness through past ontogenetic and current relationship histories leads to substantially different questions being asked than the ones we currently find in the research. Fabulous relationships can help athletes grow, gain confidence, love life, and probably become more mentally tough. Abusive relationships often lead to anxiety, despair and erratic performance. From years of working with athletes, I am convinced that we need to focus more on relationship histories (loving ones, abusive ones) and relationship building than we do any particular interventions (e.g. mental toughness training) if we want to help athletes change for the better and become happier, and maybe more mentally tough.

Some positives

Despite all my protests about mental toughness, I do see some positive aspects of some of the research. First is the work of Gucciardi and colleagues (e.g. Coulter et al., 2010; Gucciardi et al., 2008, 2009a) on looking at mental toughness through the lens of personal construct psychology (Kelly, 1991). In the history of sport psychology research and theory development there have been tendencies to argue that sport is unique, and we need to have sport-specific theories. I don't want to have a discussion on the merits and flaws in the arguments about the uniqueness of sport, but it is good to see sport psychology researchers taking well-established and respected theoretical approaches from mainstream psychology and exploring how they might be useful in understanding different phenomena in sport. We don't have to reinvent wheels. There are plenty of old wheels out there that are still damn good.

I also see the trend to examining sport environments, and how they may help or hinder the development of mental toughness, as encouraging. It would seem that a nurturing, compassionate, even loving sport environment would probably go a lot further than teaching mental skills when it comes to the development of mentally tough players. In their study of mental toughness in elite English cricketers, Bull et al. (2005: 226) noted:

> It is also interesting to note that very little of the output [results of their study] relates to mental skills training ... . The development of mental skills is obviously still an important outcome. However, it appears that the sport psychology consultant should be considering how best to integrate these skills into an appropriate environment, rather than simply focusing upon the delivery of isolated programs of mental skills training, as has been the historical approach.

Mental toughness and other pertinent constructs (e.g. overtraining) and issues (e.g. eating disorders) are not housed just within the athlete. They occur within a sociocultural context, and the quality of that context exerts a powerful influence on the fostering of salubrious or maladaptive characteristics within athletes (see Richardson et al., 2008, for a discussion of the sociocultural influences that encourage healthy training and those that may foster dangerous overtraining behaviors). All the mental training in the world may not result in positive change if the athlete returns day after day to a hostile, threatening and abusive environment.

As architects of the sport environment, it is also encouraging to see that researchers have begun to explore the role of coaches in the development (or not) of mental toughness. Gucciardi et al.'s (2009d) article on coaches and mental toughness has, for me, a decidedly psychodynamic feel. Although the role of early childhood experiences and parent–child relationships were not the primary focus of the study, it was refreshing to see those issues get some playing time. Freud is often credited with saying 'The child is father of the man' but he probably got the expression from Wordsworth (*Ode: Intimations of Immortality*). Whatever the source, that statement goes to the core of psychodynamic theory. Childhood experiences, for good and ill, lay a foundation for adolescent and adult development. Children who grow up in nurturing, safe, loving and holding environments with 'good enough' parenting (see Winnicott, 1971) are likely to be resilient and have quite a few characteristics of being mentally tough. The psychodynamic tone of the article continues with the importance of coach–athlete relationships. The authors could easily have interpreted the data from their coaches through the psychodynamic lens of the effects of positive and negative transference and counter-transference. The role of coaching philosophy in developing mental toughness reads like a sport interpretation of the English child psychoanalyst Winnicott's description of the 'good enough' mother. When I finished reading this article, I did not think it was really about mental toughness. On the surface level it looks like it is about the ingredients for developing mental toughness, but at another level it seems to be about something else. I thought that one could replace the various phrases such as 'development of mental toughness' with 'development of a happy athlete' and the paper would read just fine too.

A final note

Andre Agassi was, by almost anyone's measure, one of the great tennis competitors of the last 50 years. Was he mentally tough? Maybe sometimes, but often not. One measure of mental toughness might be a long and successful career near the top of one's field. By that criterion, Agassi would be mentally tough, but his autobiography (Agassi, 2009) tells a different story. He had doubts and slumps and setbacks. He did not overcome *any* obstacle. If he had any insatiable desire, it had more to do with his relationship with his father than it had to do with tennis. He hated tennis for much of his career. His beliefs in himself were shaken repeatedly. He was, and is, a fallible and flawed human being (as we all are), and a great tennis player, and that is why he and his struggles should be studied by tennis players, and not some fantasy of the mentally tough athlete. There is probably no way anyone can live up to the definitions of mental toughness that we have in the literature. By promulgating such fantasies to the sports community of the mentally tough athlete, we communicate a standard that hardly anyone could reach, and we may contribute to the psychological and physical damage of athletes trying and repeatedly failing to reach such standards. If we take the step after our fantasy definitions of the mentally tough athlete and go on to say, 'And we have a mental toughness development programme to help you [become that fantasy]', then what are we doing?

I have often wondered why so many mental toughness researchers embrace fantasy. Most of the researchers in this area are dyed-in-the-wool scientists, or at least would label themselves so (even the qualitative ones). I have not formulated any good answers to that question. I think it may have something to do with sport being an enchanting and seductive realm of fantasies, dreams and myths. Maybe we need to be more grounded in the real lives of athletes.

References

Agassi, A. (2009) *Open: An Autobiography,* London: HarperCollins.

American Psychiatric Association (2000) *Diagnostic and Statistical Manual of Mental Disorders* (4th edn, rev. text), Washington, DC: APA.

American Psychological Association (2002) *Ethical Principles of Psychologists and Code of Conduct,* Washington, DC: APA; http://www.apa.org/ethics/code/code.pdf.

Andersen, M. B., McCullagh, P., and Wilson, G. J. (2007) 'But what do the numbers really tell us? Arbitrary metrics and effect size reporting in sport psychology research', *Journal of Sport & Exercise Psychology,* 29, 664–672.

Blanton, H., and Jaccard, J. (2006) 'Arbitrary metrics in psychology', *American Psychologist,* 61, 27–41.

Boyle, G. J. (1995) 'Myers-Briggs Type Indicator (MBTI): Some psychometric limitations', *Australian Psychologist,* 30, 71–4.

Bull, S. J., Shambrook, C. J., James, W., and Brooks, J. E. (2005) 'Towards an understanding of mental toughness in elite English cricketers', *Journal of Applied Sport Psychology*, 17, 209–27.

Clough, P., Earle, K., and Sewell, D. (2002) 'Mental toughness: The concept and its measurement', in I. Cockerill (ed.), *Solutions in Sport Psychology*, London: Thomson, pp. 32–45.

Connaughton, D., Hanton, S., Jones, G., and Wadey, R. (2008) 'Mental toughness research: Key issues in this area', *International Journal of Sport Psychology*, 39, 192–204.

Coulter, T. J., Mallet, C. J., and Gucciardi, D. F. (2010) 'Understanding mental toughness in Australian soccer: Perceptions of players, parents, and coaches', *Journal of Sports Sciences*, 28, 699–716.

Crust, L. (2008) 'A review and conceptual re-examination of mental toughness: Implications for future researchers', *Personality and Individual Differences*, 45, 576–83.

Crust, L., and Clough, P. J. (2005) 'Relationship between mental toughness and physical endurance', *Perceptual and Motor Skills*, 100, 192–4.

Darwin, C. (1872) *The Expression of Emotion in Man and Animals*, New York: Penguin Classics, 2009 edn.

Epstein, M. (1996) *Thoughts without a Thinker: Psychotherapy from a Buddhist Perspective*, New York: Basic Books.

Gardner, F. L., and Moore, Z. E. (2007) *The Psychology of Enhancing Human Performance: The Mindfulness–Acceptance–Commitment (MAC) Approach*, New York: Springer.

Golby, J., Sheard, M., and van Wersch, A. (2007) 'Evaluating the factor structure of the Psychological Performance Inventory', *Perceptual and Motor Skills*, 105, 309–25.

Goleman, D. (1995) *Emotional Intelligence: Why it can Matter More than IQ*, New York: Bantam Books.

Gordon, S., and Gucciardi, D.F. (in press) 'Mental toughness', in J. Adams (ed.), *Sport Psychology: Theory and Practice*, London: Pearson.

Gucciardi, D. F., and Gordon, S. (2009) 'Development and preliminary validation of the Cricket Mental Toughness Inventory', *Journal of Sports Sciences*, 27, 1293–1310.

Gucciardi, D. F., Gordon, S., and Dimmock, J. A. (2008) 'Towards an understanding of mental toughness in Australian football', *Journal of Applied Sport Psychology*, 20, 261–81.

Gucciardi, D. F., Gordon, S., and Dimmock, J. A. (2009a) 'Advancing mental toughness research and theory using personal construct psychology', *International Review of Sport and Exercise Psychology*, 2, 54–72.

Gucciardi, D. F., Gordon, S., and Dimmock, J. A. (2009b) 'Development and preliminary validation of a mental toughness inventory for Australian football', *Psychology of Sport and Exercise*, 10, 201–9.

Gucciardi, D. F., Gordon, S., and Dimmock, J. A. (2009c) 'Evaluation of a mental toughness training program for youth-aged Australian footballers: I. A quantitative analysis', *Journal of Applied Sport Psychology*, 21, 307–23.

Gucciardi, D. F., Gordon, S., Dimmock, J. A., and Mallett, C. J. (2009d) 'Understanding the coach's role in the development of mental toughness: Perspectives of elite Australian football coaches', *Journal of Sports Sciences*, 27, 1483–96.

Jones, G., Hanton, S., and Connaughton, D. (2002) 'What is this thing called mental toughness? An investigation of elite sport performers', *Journal of Applied Sport Psychology*, 14, 205–18.

Kabat-Zinn, J. (2005) *Coming to our Senses: Healing ourselves and the World through Mindfulness*, New York: Hyperion.

Kazdin, A. E. (2006) 'Arbitrary metrics: Implications for identifying evidence-based treatments', *American Psychologist*, 61, 42–9.

Kelly, G. A. (1991) *The Psychology of Personal Constructs: A Theory of Personality*, vol. 1, London: Routledge; originally publ. 1955.

Leahy, T. (in press) 'Safeguarding child athletes from abuse in elite sports systems: The role of the sport psychologist', in D. Gilbourne and M. B. Andersen (eds), *Critical Essays in Applied Sport Psychology*, Champaign, IL: Human Kinetics.

Levy, A. R., Polman, R. C. J., Clough, P. J., Marchant, D. C., and Earle, K. (2006) 'Mental toughness as a determinant of beliefs, pain, and adherence in sport injury rehabilitation', *Journal of Sports Rehabilitation*, 15, 246–54.

Loehr, J. E. (1982) *Athletic Excellence: Mental Toughness Training for Sports*, New York: Plume.

Loehr, J. E. (1986) *Mental Toughness Training for Sports: Achieving Athletic Excellence*, Lexington, MA: Stephen Greene Press.

Richardson, S. O., Andersen, M. B., and Morris, T. (2008) *Overtraining Athletes: Personal Journeys in Sport*, Champaign, IL: Human Kinetics.

Runyan, W. M. (1984) *Life Histories and Psychobiography: Explorations in Theory and Method*, New York: Oxford University Press.

Salovey, P., and Mayer, J. D. (1990) 'Emotional intelligence', *Imagination, Cognition, and Personality*, 9, 185–211.

Schultz, W. T. (2005) *Handbook of Psychobiography*, New York: Oxford University Press.

Seligman, M. E. P. (1995) 'The effectiveness of psychotherapy: The *Consumer Reports* study', *American Psychologist*, 50, 965–74.

Sexton, T. L., and Whiston, S. C. (1994) 'The status of the counseling relationship: An empirical review, theoretical implications, and research directions', *The Counseling Psychologist*, 22, 6–78.

Shea, A. (2005) *Petria Thomas: Swimming against the Tide*, Ultimo, NSW, Australia: ABC Enterprises.

Sheard, M., and Golby, J. (2006) 'Effect of a psychological skills training program on swimming performance and positive psychological development', *International Journal of Sport and Exercise Psychology*, 4, 149–69.

Sheard, M., Golby, J., and van Wersch, A. (2009) 'Progress toward construct validation of the Sports Mental Toughness Questionnaire (SMTQ)', *European Journal of Psychological Assessment*, 25, 186–93.

Winnicott, D. W. (1971) *Playing and Reality*, London: Routledge.

Zuckerman, M. (ed.) (1983) *Biological Bases of Sensation Seeking, Impulsivity, and Anxiety*, Hillsdale, NJ: Erlbaum.

Part II
Measuring mental toughness

6 Development and validation of the mental toughness inventory (MTI)

A construct validation approach

*S. Cory Middleton, Andrew J. Martin
and Herb W. Marsh*

Introduction

The rise of a champion athlete is a fascinating and complex process. This process is often marked by significant and determining moments or turning points – moments that provide new wisdom and provoke change, growth and learning. Yet, initially these adverse or pressure-filled moments are often unappreciated, recognized only in hindsight. It is suggested here that, once overcome, adversity can provide a significant turning point in an athlete's career pathway. To the extent that this is the case, it is evident that 'success' requires adversity as much as it requires competitive triumph. It is further proposed that the capacity to endure and triumph over adversity is as relevant to athletes preparing for an Olympic Games or World Championships as it is to business people progressing through a global financial crisis, or families living through hardship. Thus, the concept of mental toughness is generalizable to all individuals who must endure and triumph over adversity to perform to their potential. In this chapter we describe key findings from our qualitative and quantitative research into mental toughness and the implications these findings have for mental toughness theorizing, measurement and practice.

Mental toughness

Increased pressure and scrutiny experienced by the modern athlete (e.g. media, sponsorship, public exposure) have led to a greater interest in how to utilize the 'powers' of the mind to achieve superior athletic performance. In attempting to reach true athletic potential, athletes have been complementing physical training with psychological training tools such as goal setting, visualization and relaxation (for a review, see Vealey, 2007). In the last two decades, researchers have become increasingly interested in how psychological factors such as personality, group dynamics and individual cognitions affect sporting performance (for a review, see Tenenbaum and Eklund, 2007). An emerging area of research is the role of mental toughness in human performance. Sport psychologists (researchers and practitioners), coaches, sports commentators, sports fans and athletes acknowledge the importance of mental toughness in sporting performance (see Goldberg, 1998; Hodge, 1994). In early work on the issue, Loehr (1982, 1986) emphasized that athletes and coaches felt that at least 50 per cent of success is due to psychological factors that reflect mental toughness. Goldberg argued that a lack of mental toughness is the reason some athletes suffer from slumps, 'choke' and experience runaway emotions; why they perform better in practice than in competition; and why they underachieve. He claimed that learning about mental toughness will assist coaches to be better motivators, develop winning teams, prepare teams for big games, develop winning concentration, snap losing streaks, end slumps and teach athletes to stay 'cool in the clutch'. Similarly, Gould et al. (1987) emphasized that, while coaches feel that mental toughness is important in achieving success, it is difficult for athletes to achieve.

Despite growing interest, large-scale empirical studies on the makeup of mental toughness are still in their infancy. The last few years have seen some significant developments in mental toughness research. Emerging from this work is some agreement on the multidimensionality of mental toughness (Connaughton et al., 2008; Crust, 2007). Although the factors that constitute the multidimensional models vary from researcher to researcher, there is agreement that multiple factors are relevant. A review of these research efforts is beyond the scope of the present chapter, but Crust (2007) provides one of the most balanced overviews of the field. Connaughton et al. (2008) along with Gucciardi et al. (2009) provide more recent overviews. The lack of a valid understanding about mental toughness undermines any interventions aiming to increase mental toughness in athletes. Thus, there is a need to operationalize the concept of mental toughness and to develop appropriate and valid measurement of it.

In this chapter, we describe recent work we have conducted to build a model of mental toughness and the development of an assessment tool to measure it. This work stems from the first author's doctoral dissertation (Middleton, 2005). First, we identify hypothesized components of mental toughness, integrating them into a model that captures the multidimensionality of the construct. Second, we describe the Mental Toughness Inventory (MTI), the tool that assesses multidimensional mental toughness. Third, from a construct validity perspective we validate the MTI in an athlete sample. As construct validation is an ongoing process (Marsh, 1997), the evidence we detail in this chapter provides a useful foundation upon which to ascertain the robustness of our model and measure.

A construct validation approach

A central element of our mental toughness research is based on well-established construct validation principles. According to Gill et al. (1988), these principles guide the development of models and multidimensional instruments based on theory, item and reliability analysis, exploratory and confirmatory factor analyses, tests of convergent and discriminant validity, validation in relation to external criteria, and application in research and practice. Of the currently available mental toughness measures, no inventory completely fulfils these important principles (see Chapter 7 below).

The present research sought to redress these gaps through two approaches to construct validation: within-network validity and between-network validity (Marsh, 1997). Within-network validity explores the internal structure of a construct. This approach begins with a logical analysis of internal consistency of construct definition, measurement and generation of predictions. This first approach is followed by analyses that employ techniques such as factor analysis to assess the dimensionality of instrumentation (and, by implication, conceptual framework). Between-network validity attempts to establish a logical, theoretically consistent pattern of relations between measures of a construct and other constructs. Between-network research is often based on correlational and regression-like (e.g. structural equation modelling) procedures to determine convergent and discriminant validity.

In psychological research, there is a tendency to move too quickly to between-network studies that seek to relate central constructs to other factors of interest (Marsh, 1996; Marsh and Craven, 1997). In contrast, an important step in our research was to first develop a sound conceptual understanding of the hypothesized construct (i.e. within-network validity). Specifically, we first sought to address the following question: what is mental toughness and what are the characteristics that underlie it?

Consistent with the construct validity approach, our research looked to extend established theory by exploring the within-network properties of mental toughness through an in-depth qualitative study of mental toughness in elite athletes. Through integrating theory with qualitative findings we developed a multidimensional measurement instrument to assess mental toughness. In line with the within-network approach, the internal properties of this instrument were empirically examined and appropriately refined. Following the within-network analyses, the between-network construct validity approach was used to determine how well the mental toughness construct and its component factors related to a selection of established constructs.

Within-network validity: qualitative findings

A first step in our research was to qualitatively develop a model of mental toughness that we would subsequently develop into psychometric instrumentation and validate using quantitative methods. This qualitative component involved interviewing elite athletes and coaches to learn from their experiences and identify core characteristics of mental toughness from those experiences.

Approach

The sample comprised 33 participants ranging between 25 and 70 years of age ($M = 37.68$; $SD = 13.36$). In total, there were 21 males and 12 females. The participants included 19 current and 9 former elite athletes, with 15 of them being gold medallists or world champions in their respective sports (8 being world champions on multiple occasions). The participant sample also included three sport psychologists and five elite coaches.

Data were collected using a semi-structured interview schedule. Consistent with the grounded theory approach, it was important that the interview approach did not 'lead the participant'. Therefore, the interviews started with each participant identifying some of their toughest experiences, before being asked to recount their experiences, elaborating on the thoughts, feelings and behaviours they experienced. The interview transcripts were analysed through a process of coding, categorization and abstraction. This analytical process involved disaggregating text into categories (e.g. text grouped into categories such as task focus, or coping, or self-efficacy), and making informed decisions about those categories. To move beyond the codes and categories to concepts and theories we made informed decisions about the data, thinking, linking and abstracting (Morse and Richards, 2002). Our grounded theoretical approach applied inductive logic to develop concepts and frameworks in concert with the qualitative data (Strauss, 1987). This approach allowed themes to emerge and for us to truly learn from participants in developing our multidimensional mental toughness framework (Miles and Huberman, 1994; Morse and Richards, 2002).

Mental toughness, adversity, and key characteristics

A dominant finding that emerged when interviewing participants, and also later when reviewing and analysing the interview statements, was that mental toughness seems to exist in the presence of or response to adversity. The types of adversity reported ranged greatly and included situations such as: something going awry in a competition, high levels of performance pressure, physical pain associated with high-level physical effort, competing through an injury, falling behind in a competition and performing under bad conditions. These findings are consistent with previous research involving Australian football coaches (Gucciardi et al., 2008) and soccer players, parents and coaches (Coulter et al., 2010). Although the type of adversity took different forms, the common thread in relation to mental toughness was the notion of overcoming the adversity. Mental toughness, according to the participant group, appears to primarily exist in relation to overcoming adversity.

Twelve mental toughness characteristics evolved through the qualitative research. These characteristics were: self-efficacy, mental self-concept, potential, task focus, perseverance, task familiarity, personal bests, task value, goal commitment, positivity, stress minimization and positive comparisons. Table 6.1 presents an overview of each factor – including a definition and quote that represents the central theme of the factor. Mental toughness was thereby defined as 'an unshakable perseverance and conviction towards some goal despite pressure or adversity'. Moreover, achieving mental toughness defined in this way involves the before-mentioned 12 characteristics. The strength of this definition and conceptualization of mental toughness is that it is not limited to what may be

Table 6.1 Mental toughness factors, definitions and quotes

Factor	Definition	Representative quote
Self-efficacy	The athlete's judgment or belief in his or her own ability to succeed in reaching a specific goal	'You believe in your heart that you can go and do it…I was just following my heart, believing in myself that I could do it and come back.'
Mental self-concept	Viewing one's self as being mentally strong in relation to dealing with adversity	'I have the attitude that mentally I am superior, mentally I am stronger and mentally I am capable of hanging in there for longer.'
Potential	Believing that one has the inherent ability or capacity for growth, development or coming into being	'The driving thing for me at the moment is the fact that I haven't achieved everything I think I'm capable of, and I still think I can.'
Task focus	The unshakeable concentration of mental processes on a task whilst excluding other distractions from concentration	'The ability to remain focused in extreme situations… you are constantly trying to redirect your focus back into what you are doing that moment.'
Perseverance	Persisting in or remaining constant to a purpose, idea, or task in the face of obstacles, discouragement or adversity	'When all hell's breaking loose around you, you just keep going… you just knuckle down to what you are doing and you just keep grinding away.'
Task familiarity	Having a good understanding and being well acquainted with the task or adversity	'Being familiar with your environment and with the competition just makes you relaxed.'
Personal bests	An internal motivation or drive to pursue personal best performances	'I enjoy exploring my physical and mental limits… seeing how much pain and adversity I can overcome… seeing what my best is.'
Task value	The quality of importance or the significance the successful completion of the task holds for the individual	'The value of what you are going after is very critical. How significant is that to you? If it's not important, why would you put yourself through it?'
Goal commitment	The act of binding oneself (intellectually and emotionally) to a goal or a course of action	'There was no way I would ever have given up after making that commitment to myself. I had to follow it through, no matter what, just for me.'
Positivity	The process of being positive and remaining positive in the face of adversity or challenge	'I always try to see the positive, no matter what I'm faced with.'
Stress minimization	The process of reducing one's emotional reaction to adversity	'I think he can see and dismiss small failures for what they are, where the others get focused on small failures and blow them out of proportion.'
Positive comparisons	Sensing that one is coping better with adversity and thus has a psychological and competitive advantage over one's opponent	'I remember looking across at her and I could see her eyes widening and I thought— she's shitting herself. So I kept going.'

seen as the outcomes of mental toughness. One accusation that has been levelled at others who have attempted to define mental toughness, is a tendency to confuse what mental toughness allows one to *do* (i.e. outcomes of mental toughness) with what it actually *is* (e.g. Jones et al., 2002). The definition presented here looks not only at what mental toughness is, but also includes the characteristics that help an individual achieve a mentally tough orientation: for example, stress management, perseverance, task focus and commitment.

Integrating the factors into a multidimensional structure

Our proposed multidimensional framework is shown in Figure 6.1. In support of this multidimensional model of mental toughness, one participant (sport psychologist) reported,

> I sort of see it a bit like a pyramid I guess, with mental toughness being the final outcome sitting at the top of the pyramid and at the base a number of quite broad platform factors if you like, and then skills being built upon those to the extent that the outcome at the end of the day is an athlete that's mentally tough under pressure.

This multidimensional view is also supported by recent research (e.g. Coulter et al., 2010; Gucciardi et al., 2008; Jones et al. 2002, 2007). Figure 6.1 shows the proposed structure of mental toughness, warranting quantitative validation.

Within-network validity: quantitative findings

Using the qualitatively derived model of mental toughness as a foundation, a large pool of items ($n = 108$) was developed to assess the 12 characteristics of mental toughness – forming the basis of the Mental Toughness Inventory (MTI). Where possible, items were developed based on participants' statements about mental toughness in the qualitative interviews. The range of items developed for each factor aimed to capture the breadth and depth of that factor. Before progressing to more sophisticated quantitative analyses, the pool of items was then subjected to two preliminary refinement methods, namely q-sort and talk-aloud responses. Q-sort methodology involved research assistants (blind to the project) being asked to take the pile items presented in randomized order and then sort them into 'like' piles. This process resulted in poorer fitting items (i.e. items that continually got sorted into the wrong piles) being culled from the overall item pool. The talk-aloud response method involved a group of experts (i.e. three psychology professors and two leading sport psychologists) talking through the item pool with a focus on refining item wording to accurately capture the intent of the characteristic to be measured. Thus, the design of the instrument – 12 specific subscales and one global mental toughness scale, comprising sets of items intended to measure each scale – provided an a priori model that formed the basis of subsequent quantitative analyses.

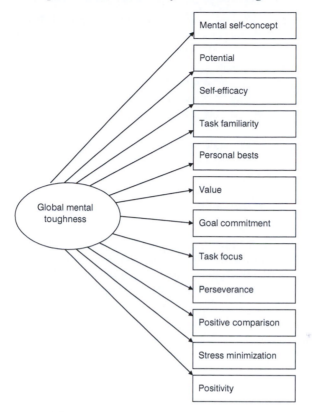

Figure 6.1 Structure of the proposed model of mental toughness

Administering the MTI

The instrument was next administered to groups of athlete participants, with the resulting quantitative data being used to refine and finalize the instrument and assess the validity of our hypothesized model. There were two rounds of administration using the MTI. For consistency, the same administration procedures were used across each round of testing. Anonymity was guaranteed in that participants were assured that the data would be used for research purposes only and not for athlete selection purposes. Each testing session began with a brief set of instructions on how to use the rating scale in the questionnaire. All participants were encouraged to seek assistance from a member of the research group if they were experiencing any difficulties in responding to an item. Participants were then asked to work through the questionnaire and submit the completed form to the researcher when they had finished.

The first was a pilot administration of the MTI intended to refine the number of items in the instrument. The pilot version of the MTI was an 108-item questionnaire – 12 factors each measured by 9 items. The pilot MTI was administered by the research team to 479 athletes from an elite sports high school (age range = 12 to 19 years, M age = 14.29, SD age = 1.54 years, males = 58 per cent, females = 42 per cent). The large sample size needed for such research, and the limited availability of such large numbers of world-class athletes, led us to select competitive athletes of a lower age for this stage of the research. We do however acknowledge the limitations the nature of this sample presents with regards to generalizing these findings to athletes of other age groups. This issue remains an important future direction. Nonetheless, the test results from this sample were used to refine the instrument.

Ensuring that the MTI was brief and concise, yet maintained psychometric soundness, required that an acceptable level of reliability (e.g. at least .80) should be achieved, based on scales having a relatively small number of items. As a guide, the aim was to (a) reduce the length of the MTI; (b) measure and maintain the content of all 12 mental toughness characteristics as well as one global mental toughness scale; (c) maintain reliability estimates of at least .80; and (d) provide a factor structure in which goodness of fit indexes met acceptable standards. These standards were determined following recommendations from Marsh et al. (1988, 1996) where the Non-Normed Fit Index (NNFI; also known as the Tucker-Lewis Index, TLI), the Comparative Fit Index (CFI; also known as the Relative Noncentrality Index, RNI), and root mean square error of approximation (RMSEA) were emphasized to evaluate goodness of fit – as they provide a relatively nonbiased indication of fit for large sample sizes. The NNFI and CFI vary along a 0 to 1 continuum in which values greater than .90 and .95 are typically taken to reflect acceptable and excellent fits to the data, respectively (McDonald and Marsh, 1990). For RMSEAs, values less than .05 indicate good fit and values as high as .08 represent reasonable errors of approximation in the population (Jöreskog and Sörbom, 2005). The CFI contains no penalty for a lack of parsimony so that improved fit due to the introduction of additional parameters may reflect capitalization on chance, whereas the NNFI and RMSEA contain penalties for a lack of parsimony. Whereas tests of statistical significance and indices of fit aid in the evaluation of the fit, ultimately, there is a degree of subjectivity and professional judgement in the selection of a 'best' model.

The first task in data analysis was to work through the MTI subscale-by-subscale with a view to removing items that were not loading particularly well on hypothesized subscales. This process involved examining results from: (a) a series of one-factor congeneric CFA models, (b) a full model CFA, and (c) Cronbach's alpha coefficients, given the removal of each item from the subscale. Item strength was considered in relation to multiple criteria. Items were selected using the following guidelines:

a   Items that best measured the intended construct as inferred on the basis of corrected item-total correlations and the size of standardized factor loadings in CFA

b   Items that had minimal cross-loadings as evidenced by LISREL's modification indexes, indicating the extent to which the fit would be improved if an item were allowed to load on a factor other than the one it was intended to measure and the expected size of the cross-loading

c   Items that had minimal correlated uniquenesses, particularly with other items within the same scale. In the case where two items within the same scale had substantial correlated uniquenesses, only one of the two items was retained

d   The number of times that an item was left blank (although the proportion of missing responses was very small – less than 1 per cent)

e   A subjective evaluation of the content of each item in order to maintain the breadth of content of the original construct

f   Sufficiently parsimonious items in each scale in order to maintain a coefficient alpha estimate of reliability of at least .80.

The above refinement process resulted in a version of the MTI in which each subscale was captured by five items. One sample item for each of the 12 subscales of mental toughness in the model is presented in Table 6.2.

This 60–item questionnaire was subsequently administered by the research team in the second round to a wide sample of sport institute and high school-based athletes (school-based athlete number = 438, age range = 12–18 years, M age = 14.34 years, SD age = 1.5 years, males = 62.6 per cent, females = 37.4 per cent; and institute-based athlete number (including international elite) = 392; age range = 11 to 38 years, M age = 18.55 years, SD age = 4.48, males = 51 per cent, females = 49 per cent). The following tests of within-network validity were used to assess the psychometric properties of the instrument.

Table 6.2 MTI subscales and representative items

Sub Scales	Representative item
Self-efficacy	'No matter what the pressure, I still believe in myself.'
Task value	'This activity is one of the most valuable parts of my life.'
Potential	'I feel my future in this area will be good.'
Task familiarity	'My experience makes me stronger when performing.'
Personal bests	'To have done my best is the most important thing to me.'
Stress minimization	'I am good at minimising the effects of stress.'
Mental self-concept	'I excel because of my mental strength.'
Positivity	'When things are bad I try to turn it around into something positive.'
Perseverance	'I keep working at things until I overcome them.'
Positive comparison	'Seeing the opposition feeling the pressure builds my confidence.'
Task focus	'I get absolutely focused on the task, nothing distracts me.'
Goal commitment	'No matter what, I remain committed to my goals.'

Confirmatory factor and reliability analysis of the MTI

Confirmatory factor analysis (CFA) was used to test the a priori model behind the MTI. CFAs were conducted for school-based athletes and then for institute-based athletes. The structure of the 12-factor MTI was well defined for the school-based athlete sample ($c^2 = 4515.78$ (df = 1644), NNFI = .98, RNI = .98, and RMSEA = .063). Reliabilities (i.e. Cronbach's alpha) for this group were strong and ranged from .83 to .91. Factor loadings ranged from .44 to .89. The factor structure was also well defined for the institute-based athlete sample ($c^2 = 4201.87$ (df = 1644), NNFI = .98, RNI = .98, and RMSEA = .062). Reliabilities for this group were strong and ranged from .85 to .93. Factor loadings ranged from .38 to .93. According to current standards (e.g. Marsh, 2007), the a priori model was able to fit the data extremely well in both samples, providing strong support for design of the MTI.

The next step in validation involved investigating whether the MTI measures the same components of mental toughness with equal validity for school- and institute-based athletes and for males and females. The findings of these analyses hold implications for the generalizability of the factor structure across groups – with invariance across groups suggesting the structure and model are generalizable. Such concerns about factor structure invariance are most appropriately evaluated by using CFA to determine whether – and how – the structure of mental toughness varies according to gender and context (see Byrne and Shavelson, 1987; Hattie, 1992; Marsh, 1993).

The first multigroup CFA examined the factor structure for school- and institute-based athletes and allowed all factor loadings, uniquenesses and correlations to be freely estimated. This model yielded an excellent fit to the data ($c^2 = 9717.65$, df = 3288, NNFI = .98, RNI = .98, RMSEA = .063). Furthermore, results indicated that when successive elements of the factor structure (i.e. factor loadings, uniquenesses and correlations) were held invariant across context, the fit indices remained comparable. Multigroup CFA findings suggest that the factor structure, factor loadings, uniquenesses and factor correlations are parallel for school-based athletes as they are for institute-based athletes. An invariance check between male and female athletes using the same multigroup CFA procedures yielded an excellent fit to the data ($c^2 = 9821.92$, df = 3288, NNFI = .96, RNI = .96, RMSEA = .069). Taken together, these data suggest that, in terms of the underlying characteristics of mental toughness and the relationships amongst those characteristics, school- and sports institute-based athletes, and males and females, are not substantially different.

Relating the MTI model to key correlates

Although within-network validity (e.g. reliability and factor analysis) is a necessary condition in evaluating instrumentation, alone it is not a sufficient condition for establishing construct validity (Marsh, 1997). Demonstrating construct validity also requires the presence of supporting data that shows a logical, theoretically consistent pattern of relationships between the construct being validated and other constructs salient in the substantive domain under focus. These cognate constructs are referred to in the present chapter as 'key correlates'. Herein, between-network validity is assessed by examining associations (i.e. correlations) between MTI factors and a set of hypothesized key correlates.

Three sets of key correlates were utilized for this component of the research: multidimensional athletic self-concept, flow and personal effectiveness. These correlates were measured by the Elite Athlete Self-Description Questionnaire (EASDQ: Marsh et al., 1997), Flow Trait Scale (FLOW: Jackson, 1994; Jackson and Marsh, 1996), and Review of Personal Effectiveness and Locus of Control scale (ROPELOC: Richards et al., 2002) instruments, respectively. These key correlates were selected on the basis of being well established measures and hypothesized to be logical correlates of mental toughness. That is, the relationships between the key correlates and mental toughness were predicted on the basis of their conceptual relatedness to mental toughness, either as correlates or outcomes of individuals' mental toughness. Hence, they were deemed to be feasible constructs with which to validate the MTI structure.

The MTI factors correlated as hypothesized with the specific validating factors. That is, relationships between specific factors were differentially stronger and weaker as expected (i.e. based on content analyses and theory). For example, the MTI factor 'Task Focus' correlated more strongly with the FLOW factor 'Concentration' than with other, less theoretically related factors such as ROPELOC factors 'External Locus of Control' and 'Social Effectiveness'. Overall, correlations indicated that 'like' concepts were more strongly correlated than 'less like' concepts. Thus, results demonstrated convergent and discriminant validity and supported the between-network validity of the scales within the MTI.

Summary of qualitative and quantitative methods

A particular strength of the methodology we employed is the combination of qualitative and quantitative methods to establish and test a hypothesized framework and instrumentation. By employing the qualitative method we were able to learn about mental toughness from those most directly relevant to the construct – elite sportspeople (in many cases, world champions) who display mental toughness. However, to accept this qualitative model at this point would only be to describe mental toughness, not validate it. Accordingly, the quantitative data provided both within-network and between-network validity support for the qualitatively derived conceptual model. The model was found to be internally strong, as demonstrated by internal reliabilities, factor loadings, goodness-of-fit indices and tests of invariance across groups. The model was further found to be valid when located within the context of cognate key correlates.

Hence, to progress the field of mental toughness, qualitative research was a necessary but not sufficient undertaking. Qualitative research captured the quality of mental toughness, but lacked the methodology capable of demonstrating construct validity. On the other hand, quantitative techniques comprise the methods capable of demonstrating construct validity but are less capable of tapping into the qualities underpinning mental toughness. It is proposed, then, that significant advancements in this field will be best achieved when research programmes gain a synergy between qualitative and quantitative techniques.

Implications for measurement and practice

The findings of the present programme of research hold a number of implications for practice. Lessons learnt from this research can be used at an individual level (e.g. athletes, coaches, and sport psychologists) and at an organizational level (e.g. institutes) to enhance the mental toughness qualities of emerging and current athletes.

Implications for mental toughness measurement

Prior to our programme of research, mental toughness measurement was generally unproven from a construct validation perspective. Loehr (1986) offered the Psychological Performance Inventory (PPI) as a test of his heuristically developed seven-factor model of mental toughness. Loehr presented incomplete conceptual rationale for the development of the instrument and offered little validational data supporting the use of the PPI. Other measures have since been developed but none fully satisfy standard criteria based on conceptual, statistical or empirical, and practical grounds (see Chapter 7 below). Because the MTI has emerged from data collected from target stakeholders and undergone preliminary construct validation, we propose it as a research tool that extends the field and adds significant value to researchers wishing to study mental toughness amongst elite athletes. A valid instrument such as the MTI has the potential to address many questions of interest in mental toughness research. Once validated in independent samples of athletes, researchers could look to develop specific normative data for athletes in different circumstances. Such normative data would be useful for athletes, coaches and sport psychologists wanting to better understand their athletes in the context of normative data – thereby aiding the interpretation of results and what they mean for training purposes.

Implications for practice

The evidence detailed in this chapter provides preliminary support for the MTI as a reliable and valid tool that captures the characteristics of mental toughness. The characteristics measured by the MTI align with established research domains, each with recognized training and development methods. For example, the MTI includes characteristics of self-belief and self-concept – research domains that have received extensive interest and yielded a variety of effective intervention frameworks (Martin, 2005, 2008; O'Mara et al., 2006). Following already established training approaches, then, sport psychologists and coaches can develop training regimes to enhance specific characteristics of mental toughness.

By understanding the characteristics of mental toughness and how they develop, coaches are in a better position to structure their training sessions and specific training drills in a way that fosters the development of mental toughness. Underlying the process of mental toughness is a particular motivational style. This style is one of curiosity, a need to learn and develop an interest in personal improvement, and a striving for personal best performances. Coaches can help foster this motivational style. When working with athletes, coaches can be less focused on outcomes and more genuinely interested in personal development towards the ability to execute skills to appropriately high standards under conditions of pressure and adversity. When coaches can create an environment that is more focused on personal excellence in execution as a means to winning, they create the most positive environment conducive to developing mental toughness (Martin, 2005, 2008). Coaches can influence the environment by the way they talk about the challenges ahead, by the things they focus on at training and competition, and by the way they recognize and reward their athletes. The inclusion of a discussion on mental toughness, and factors associated with the development of mental toughness, would therefore be worthy inclusions in practical supervision programmes and in professional texts (e.g. Andersen, 2005; Murphy, 2005).

Future research

Moving forward, we propose three directions for mental toughness research: further theory development, extension to other performance domains and further exploration of the mental toughness process. In regards to theoretical development, we propose that researchers employ research designs that move beyond description of mental toughness towards mental toughness theory enhancement (e.g. more research designs that combine qualitative and quantitative techniques). The risk is that the domain of mental toughness becomes plagued by attempts to apply the concept before adequately understanding it from a theoretical perspective. Given mental toughness research is still in its relative infancy, there is a continued need for conceptual advances in order to better understand the concept and its theoretical parameters.

Mental toughness as a concept has applications that potentially reach beyond the sporting domain. Clearly, there are performance pressures and adversity in the domains of work, performing and creative arts, and even school. There is now a need to test the MTI across a range of performance settings. It is not appropriate to develop instrumentation in a specific population and then generalize the concept and framework beyond the confines of that population without formal tests of that generalization. Rather, the instrument needs to be tested to evaluate its generalizability across different types of performance and adversity contexts. Although the present research evaluated the generalizability of the MTI across males and females and across school- and sports institute-based athletes, the promising findings derived from these analyses now point to the need for expansion to other domains.

Future research is also needed to understand how the process of mental toughness works. Does the nature of mental toughness change as a person moves into and through adversity? Does a person activate all 12 characteristics at once? In related research on cognitive strategies associated with improved endurance, McCaul and Mallott (1984) demonstrated how the use of cognitive strategies changes through the experience of overcoming endurance-related discomfort. They concluded that for higher intensity and discomfort levels, redefinitional (associative type) cognitions are most successful, whereas at lower intensity levels, distraction (dissociative type) cognitions fill attentional space and prevent or reduce the conscious sensation of pain. At higher levels, pain reaches a degree of salience that results in an inevitable invasion of awareness. For mental toughness, the strategies used are likely to change, too, as the athlete moves through adversity (whether that be pain or pressure). As with McCaul and Mallott's findings, changes in cognitive strategy throughout the experience may be related to the intensity of the adverse stimulus (i.e. pain or pressure). Hence, research is needed to understand precisely how these characteristics are used as a person moves through challenging experiences.

Understanding the process of mental toughness has considerable applied value, demonstrating how mental toughness plays out in real time. With such knowledge in hand, trainers are better equipped to teach athletes not only what mental toughness is, but how to achieve it. The multidimensionality of mental toughness points to a potential inherent difficulty in coordinating cognitive, behavioural and emotional skills to counter adversity. Research that details a step-by-step understanding of the hypothesized mental toughness process is likely to add significant value to training and development seeking to promote it.

Summary

The central purpose of the research described in this chapter was to develop mental toughness definition, progress mental toughness conceptualization, and construct and validate a mental toughness measurement tool. Both qualitative and quantitative approaches have been employed to develop a conceptual model and definition of mental toughness. These developments were used as building blocks to construct the MTI. Quantitative methods using a construct validity approach (Marsh, 1997) were then used to establish the MTI as a valid tool (based on multiple psychometric criteria) capable of measuring mental toughness across a range of athlete groups.

Taken together, we conclude that the present programme of research has resulted in several significant yields for research and practice. Specifically, this programme:

- provides confirmatory measurement work on the structure of mental toughness in athletes and clarifies the factors that encapsulate mental toughness;
- supports the body of mental toughness research by identifying a variety of factors proposed to be core mental toughness factors;

- is among the first to explicitly draw together a range of qualitatively derived mental toughness factors under a common conceptual framework and then to validate the derived framework using multivariate quantitative methods;
- provides important insights into patterns of mental toughness across males and females, younger and older athletes, and across institution- and school-based athletes.

In summary, our mental toughness research has provided unique data on mental toughness in the sporting context. Rich qualitative data on mental toughness were gathered through recording the collective experience of over 30 world-class athletes and coaches. Factors described as encapsulating mental toughness were identified and were drawn together into a multidimensional structure of 12 key factors. While this qualitative work was necessary to understand the building blocks of mental toughness, by itself it was not sufficient to demonstrate validity. Accordingly, the MTI was developed and its 12 component factors were validated using quantitative methods. Taken together, the findings emanating from our research hold substantive and methodological implications for researchers studying mental toughness, and are also relevant to sport psychologists and coaches aiming to help athletes in their quest for mental toughness and sporting excellence under diverse and challenging performance domains.

References

Andersen, M. B. (ed.) (2005) *Sport Psychology in Practice,* Champaign, IL: Human Kinetics.

Byrne, B. M., and Shavelson, R. J. (1987) 'Adolescent self-concept: Testing the assumption of equivalent structure across gender', *American Educational Research Journal*, 24, 365–85.

Connaughton, D., Hanton, S., and Jones, G. (2008) 'Mental toughness research: Key issues in this area', *International Journal of Sport Psychology*, 39, 192–204.

Coulter, T. J., Mallett, C. J., and Gucciardi, D. F. (2010) 'Understanding mental toughness in Australian soccer: Perceptions of players, parents, and coaches', *Journal of Sports Sciences,* 28, 699–716.

Crust, L. (2007) 'Mental toughness in sport: A review', *International Journal of Sport and Exercise Science*, 5, 270–90.

Gill, D. L., Dzewaltowski, D. A., and Deeter, T. E. (1988) 'The relationship of competitiveness and achievement orientation to participation in sport and nonsport activities', *Journal of Sport and Exercise Psychology*, 10, 139–50.

Goldberg, A. S. (1998) *Sports Slump Busting: 10 Steps to Mental Toughness and Peak Performance,* Champaign, IL: Human Kinetics.

Gould, D., Hodge, K., Peterson, K., and Petlichkoff, L. (1987) 'Psychological foundations of coaching: Similarities and differences among intercollegiate wrestling coaches', *The Sport Psychologist*, 1, 293–308.

Gucciardi, D. F., and Gordon, S. (2009) 'Revisiting the performance profile technique: Theoretical underpinnings and application', *The Sport Psychologist*, 23, 93–117.

Gucciardi, D. F., Gordon, S., and Dimmock, J. A. (2008) 'Towards an understanding of mental toughness in Australian football', *Journal of Applied Sport Psychology*, 20, 261–81.

Gucciardi, D. F., Gordon, S., and Dimmock, J. A. (2009) 'Advancing mental toughness research and theory using personal construct psychology', *International Review of Sport and Exercise Psychology*, 2(1), 54–72.

Hattie, J. (1992) *Self-Concept*, Hillsdale, NJ: Erlbaum.

Hodge, K. (1994) 'Mental toughness in sport: Lessons for life. The pursuit of personal excellence', *Journal of Physical Education New Zealand*, 27, 12–16.

Jackson, S. A. (1994) 'Athletes in flow: Towards a conceptual understanding of flow state in elite athletes', *Research Quarterly for Exercise and Sport*, 65(3), *122–36*.

Jackson, S. A., and Marsh, H. W. (1996) 'Development and validation of a scale to measure optimal experience: The Flow State Scale', *Journal of Sport and Exercise Psychology*, 18, 17–35.

Jones, G., Hanton, S., and Connaughton, D. (2002) 'What is this thing called mental toughness? An investigation of elite sport performers', *Journal of Applied Sport Psychology*, 14, 205–18.

Jones, G., Hanton, S., and Connaughton, D. (2007) 'A framework of mental toughness in the world's best performers', *The Sport Psychologist*, 21, 243–64.

Jöreskog, K. G., and Sörbom, D. (2005) *LISREL 8.72*, Scientific Software International.

Kaplan, D. (2000) *Structural Equation Modelling: Foundations and Extensions*, Newbury Park, CA: Sage.

Loehr, J. E. (1982) *Athletic Excellence: Mental Toughness Training for Sports*, New York: Plume.

Loehr, J. E. (1986) *Mental Toughness Training for Sports: Achieving Athletic Excellence*, Lexington, MA: Stephen Greene Press.

McCaul, K. D., and Mallott, J. M. (1984) 'Distraction and coping with pain', *Psychological Bulletin*, 95, 247–63.

McDonald, R. P., and Marsh, H. W. (1990) 'Choosing a multivariate model: Noncentrality and goodness-of-fit', *Psychological Bulletin*, 107, 247–55.

Marsh, H. W. (1993) 'Academic self-concept: Theory measurement and research', in J. Suls (ed.), *Psychological Perspectives on the Self*, Hillsdale, NJ: Erlbaum, vol. 4, pp. 59–98.

Marsh, H. W. (1996) 'Construct validity of Physical Self-Description Questionnaire responses: Relations to external criteria', *Journal of Sport and Exercise Psychology*, 18(2), 111–31.

Marsh, H. W. (1997) 'The measurement of physical self-concept: A construct validation approach', in K. Fox (ed.), *The Physical Self-Concept: From Motivation to Well-Being*, Champaign, IL: Human Kinetics, pp. 27–58.

Marsh, H. W., and Craven, R. (1997) 'Academic self-concept: Beyond the dustbowl', in G. Pye (ed.), *Handbook of Classroom Assessment: Learning, Achievement, and Adjustment*, Orlando, FL: Academic Press, pp. 131–98.

Marsh, H. W., Balla, J. R., and Hau, K. T. (1996) 'An evaluation of incremental fit indices: A clarification of mathematical and empirical processes', in G. A. Marcoulides and R. E. Schumacker (ed.), *Advanced Structural Equation Modelling Techniques*, Hillsdale, NJ: Erlbaum, pp. 315–53.

Marsh, H. W., Balla, J. R., and McDonald, R. P. (1988) 'Goodness-of-fit indices in confirmatory factor analysis: The effect of sample size', *Psychological Bulletin*, 102, 391–410.

Marsh, H. W., Hey, J., Johnson, S., and Perry, C. (1997) 'Elite Athlete Self-Description Questionnaire: Hierarchical confirmatory factor analysis of responses by two distinct groups of elite athletes', *International Journal of Sport Psychology*, 28, 237–58.

Martin, A. J. (2005) 'Exploring the effects of a youth enrichment program on academic motivation and engagement', *Social Psychology of Education*, 8, 179–206.

Martin, A.J. (2008) 'Enhancing student motivation and engagement: The effects of a multidimensional intervention', *Contemporary Educational Psychology*, 33, 239–69.

Middleton, S. C. (2005) 'Mental toughness: Conceptualization and measurement', PhD thesis, University of Western Sydney.

Miles, M. B., and Huberman, A. M. (1994) *Qualitative Data Analysis: An Expanded Source Book* (2nd edn), London: Sage.

Moran, A. (1996) *The Psychology of Concentration in Sport Performers: A Cognitive Analysis*, Hove, East Sussex: Psychology Press.

Morse, J. M., and Richards, L. (2002) *Readme First for a User's Guide to Qualitative Methods*, Thousand Oaks, CA: Sage.

Murphy, S. (ed.) (2005) *The Sport Psych Handbook*, Champaign, IL: Human Kinetics.

O'Mara, A. J., Marsh, H. W., Craven, R. G., and Debus, R. L. (2006) 'Do self-concept interventions make a difference? A synergistic blend of construct validation and meta-analysis', *Educational Psychologist*, 41, 181–206.

Richards, G. E., Ellis, L. A., and Neill, J. T. (2002) 'The ROPELOC: Review of personal effectiveness and locus of control. A comprehensive instrument for reviewing life effectiveness', paper presented at the Self-Concept Research Conference: Driving International Agendas, Sydney.

Strauss, A. L. (1987) *Qualitative Analysis for Social Scientists*, New York: Cambridge University Press.

Tenenbaum, G., and Eklund, R.C. (eds) (2007) *Handbook of Sport Psychology* (3rd edn.), Hoboken, NJ: Wiley.

Vealey, R.S. (2007) 'Mental skills training in sport', in G. Tenenbaum and R. C. Eklund (eds), *Handbook of Sport Psychology* (3rd edn), Hoboken, NJ: Wiley, pp. 287–309.

7 Measuring mental toughness in sport

Current status and future directions

Daniel F. Gucciardi, Clifford J. Mallett,
Stephanie J. Hanrahan and Sandy Gordon

Interest in mental toughness among academic circles has proliferated since first making an appearance in the peer-reviewed literature 10 years ago. Beyond peer-reviewed manuscripts and conference presentations, mental toughness has also made its way into popular press and textbooks (e.g. Siebold, 2005; Wakefield, 2009). The escalating interest appears to lie in the commercial appeal of the construct, with most key stakeholders (e.g. athletes, coaches, administrators) acknowledging the central role of mental toughness for getting the best out of one's talent and achieving success. Since the emergence of mental toughness in the academic domain, a number of conceptual models and measures have appeared. Although measures of mental toughness are at a fairly preliminary phase in their development, research using these recently developed measures has not abated. With several reviews of the literature focusing on definitional and conceptual issues emerging in recent years (e.g. Connaughton and Hanton, 2009; Gucciardi et al., 2009a), the purpose of this chapter is to assess the current status of mental toughness measurement. We commence our discussion with a brief overview of mental toughness. Following an overview and critical discussion of the currently available mental toughness measures, we conclude the chapter with some recommendations relating to measurement issues for future research.

Brief history of mental toughness

The roots of mental toughness can be traced back to personality research in the 1950s in which 'tough-minded' (vs. tender-minded) was discussed as one of the most important traits for success (Cattell et al., 1955), although Loehr's (1982, 1986) books appear to have popularized the construct as well as stimulated academic interest and subsequent investigations. The term 'mental toughness' appeared several times in the literature (for a review, see Connaughton and Hanton, 2009) before the first formal empirical examination of its key components (Fourie and Potgieter, 2001). Much of the early work in the area focused on qualitative approaches in which the perspectives of key stakeholders (i.e. athletes, coaches, sport psychologists) were generated and explored to define and conceptualize mental toughness in sport, with subsequent research adopting a quantitative approach using psychometric inventories to explore relationships with hypothesized key correlates (for reviews, see Connaughton and Hanton, 2009; Gucciardi et al., 2009a). More recent inquiries have begun to explore the development of mental toughness through retrospective interviews and evaluation of intervention programmes (for reviews, see Chapters 8 and 10 below). As with research that has sought to understand mental toughness and its development, attempts to develop psychometrically sound inventories have revolved around sport-general (i.e. across all sports) and sport-specific (i.e. within one individual context such as cricket) investigations. Both sport-general and sport-specific measures feature in the current chapter.

Mental toughness measurement

Before reviewing the available mental toughness instruments, it is important to note that we consider several criteria that are commonly used to evaluate the reliability and validity of psychometric tools (e.g. Bryant, 2004; Hagger and Chatzisarantis, 2009; Kaplan and Saccuzzo, 2008). Tables 7.1 and 7.2 provide a brief overview of these criteria as well as the methods employed to generate evidence on these concepts. In considering these traditional indicators of the validity and reliability of a measurement instrument, our discussion focuses on three broad fundamental issues that stem from these considerations (for discussions, see Hagger and Chatzisarantis, 2009; Mallett et al., 2007; Marsh, 1997, 2002). First and foremost is the issue of conceptual underpinning; i.e. is the measurement instrument based on a theory or model that has empirical support? Although there is agreement amongst researchers on the multidimensionality of mental toughness (e.g. Connaughton and Hanton, 2009; Gucciardi et al., 2009a), there does not appear to be any consensus about the number of dimensions or its hierarchical representation (i.e. a general mental toughness factor encompassing several different dimensions). The second issue is largely of a statistical nature, and relates to the procedures employed to develop and examine the psychometric properties of the measure. Finally, we consider the practical utility of each measure in terms of its ability to capture and distinguish between the main facets of mental toughness in a user-friendly manner (i.e. online administration versus hardcopy, number of items) as well as predict or explain important behaviors (e.g. performance). Thus, we assess each mental toughness inventory on conceptual, statistical or empirical, and practical grounds. We focus initially on sport-general measures and then turn our attention to sport-specific inventories.

Psychological Performance Inventory

Much of the early work claiming to explore 'mental toughness' in sport adopted the Psychological Performance Inventory (PPI: Loehr, 1986) as its central measure (e.g. Golby and Sheard, 2004; Golby et al., 2003). The PPI assesses what

Table 7.1 Criteria commonly employed for evaluating the reliability of measurement

Type of reliability	Description
Properties of scores derived from a measure	
Parallel forms reliability	Concept: Assesses the consistency of individuals' scores from two tests covering the same content domain (i.e., two separate forms considered to measure the same attribute), usually completed at two different points in time.
	Assessment: Squared correlation between the two composite scores.
Test-retest reliability	Concept: Assesses the consistency of individuals' score of the same measure at two different points in time.
	Assessment: Correlation analysis using scores at both points in time.
Internal consistency reliability	Concept: Assesses the extent to which items designed to reflect the same construct yield similar results (i.e., consistency across items).
	Assessment: The split-half (i.e. splitting a scale in half and correlating the two summed scores) and Cronbach's alpha (i.e., function of the number of items, mean inter-item covariance, sum of the square variance/covariance matrix) are the two most common approaches (Gignac, 2009). Within factor analytical models, McDonald's (1970) omega is the most popular method (Gignac, 2009).

Loehr claimed as being the seven most essential ingredients of mental toughness: self-confidence, attention control, negative energy, motivation, attitude control, positive energy, and visual and imagery control. Loehr's conceptualization of mental toughness was based on his extensive experience as an applied sport psychologist working with some of the world's most talented athletes and coaches. Although representing an intuitively appealing conceptualization of mental toughness that is somewhat consistent with recent qualitative research, psychometric examinations of the PPI have failed to support its factorial validity (e.g. Golby et al., 2007; Middleton et al., 2004). For example, using responses from 263 young elite athletes aged 12 to 17 ($M = 13.8$), Middleton et al. revealed inadequate fit between the hypothesized seven-factor model and the data as well as an improper solution (i.e. factor correlations > 1) using confirmatory factor analysis (CFA). Failure to support the hypothesized model perhaps reflects the limited information regarding the instrument's conceptual underpinnings and rationale for both selection and inclusion of items. Nevertheless, despite the lack of evidence supporting its factorial validity, some researchers (e.g. Kuan and Roy, 2007) have continued to use the PPI as a measure of mental toughness.

What emerges from the limited research on the PPI is that it does not hold up well with regard to the three guiding criteria. Although the conceptual model underpinning the PPI is intuitively appealing (i.e. face validity) and the seven factors appear to capture some of the main facets of mental toughness (i.e. content validity), the psychometric evidence for the hypothesized measurement model of the PPI is not encouraging (i.e. factorial validity). As a consequence, there is little

Table 7.2 Criteria commonly employed for evaluating the validity of measurement

Type of validity	Description
Properties of a measure	
Face validity	Concept: The extent to which a measure appears (i.e., "on the surface") to assess what it claims to capture.
	Assessment: Experts provide subjective assessments on the appropriateness of the measure for assessing the construct of interest.
Content validity	Concept: The degree to which the items of a measure sufficiently represent all facets (i.e., entire domain) of the construct of interest.
	Assessment: Experts provide subjective assessments on the thoroughness of content coverage (i.e., breadth and depth), which can form the basis for a content validity index (Lynn, 1986). Having a fully defined construct and understanding of the entire spectrum of facets is important.
Properties of scores derived from a measure	
Factorial validity	Concept: The dimensional make-up of a measurement instrument (i.e., number of factors) as well as the nature of those dimensions (i.e., strength and direction).
	Assessment: Statistical techniques including exploratory and confirmatory factor analyses (CFA). According to Gignac (2009, p. 26), "the more impressive factorial validity evidence may be derived from CFA, as simple structure is specified and tested statistically within a restricted factor analytic framework."
Predictive validity	Concept: The extent to which scores obtained from a measure predict another variable or measure in a theoretically justifiable manner.
	Assessment: Statistical techniques (e.g., regression, structural equation modeling) that identify the amount of variance explained in the dependent variable by the measure. Although cross-sectional data can be used to assess predictive validity, collecting a response to the measure (i.e., predictor) at one point and the dependent variable at a later time is more impressive (Gignac, 2009).
Incremental validity	Concept: The extent to which scores obtained from a measure uniquely (i.e., over and above other related measures) predicts another variable in a theoretically justifiable manner.
	Assessment: Statistical techniques (e.g., regression, structural equation modeling) that identify the unique amount of variance explained in the dependent variable by the measure over and above related constructs. Although regression and path analyses can be used to ascertain this type of validity, they do not take into consideration the reliability of measurement (i.e., measure without error) as structural equation modeling does (Gignac, 2009).
Concurrent validity	Concept: A theoretically justifiable relationship between one measure and those of another measure collected at the same time.
	Assessment: Statistical techniques (e.g., correlations, regression) that index the relationship between two or more variables. Although comparisons with other self-report inventories are common place, explorations of relationship with other variables (e.g., age, performance, playing experience) that do not share a common method are preferred (Gignac, 2009).

Continued...

Table 7.2 continued

Type of validity	Description
Discriminant validity	Concept: When a measure does not show a relationship with another measure that it is theoretically postulated to be unrelated to.
	Assessment: Statistical techniques (e.g., correlations, regression, structural equation modeling) that assess the nature of a relationship between two or more variables.
Plausibility of a construct	
Multitrait-multimethod validity	Concept: Concerned with confirming or disconfirming the validity of a construct through an assessment of the pattern of correlations among test measuring a set of traits using different methods.
	Assessment: Statistical techniques (e.g., correlations, confirmatory factor analysis, structural equation modeling) that assess the nature of a relationship between two or more variables. Regardless of method (i.e., there should be no method bias), instruments measuring the same traits should evidence strong correlations (i.e., converge), whereas different traits should show weak correlations (i.e., diverge).

evidence to support the other forms of validity such as predictive, incremental, discriminant or concurrent validity, thereby having limited practical utility in terms of being able to predict or explain behavioral processes or outcomes.

Psychological Performance Inventory-Alternative

With their analyses revealing a lack of support for the hypothesized factor structure of the original PPI (Loehr, 1986), Golby et al. (2007) set out to find some structure in their data using principal components analysis (PCA). PCA is a variable reduction technique, which makes no assumptions about an underlying causal model, applied to reduce a large number of redundant items into a smaller number of factors accounting for most of the variance (Thompson, 2004). Specifically, Golby et al. revealed support for the existence of a 14-item higher-order general mental toughness factor that was subsumed by four components, namely *determination, self-belief, positive cognition,* and *visualization,* and accounted for 55.7 per cent of the variance. Golby et al. termed this revised version the Psychological Performance Inventory-Alternative (PPI-A). Although using the same dataset to generate and test a measurement model is considered a 'dicey business' (Thompson, 2004: 131), Golby et al. subsequently applied a CFA using the original dataset upon which the PCA was performed to further assess the psychometric structure of the 14-item higher-order model and revealed support for the hypothesized structure (i.e. factorial validity). Thus, cross-validation of the hypothesized PPI-A measurement model with independent samples is required to alleviate concerns relating to sample-specific nuances or chance relationships in the original dataset.

The PPI-A (Golby et al., 2007) was recently employed to explore cross-national differences between Australian ($n = 25$) and British ($n = 25$) rugby league players (Sheard, 2009). Analyses of the cross-sectional data revealed that the British players reported higher levels of self-belief than the Australian players, whereas the latter reported higher levels of positive cognition, visualization and total mental toughness than their British counterparts. Correlational analyses also revealed low-to-moderate relationships between PPI-A subscales and hardiness (r = .06 to .55). Support for the internal reliability of the PPI-A subscales was also revealed (Cronbach's α > .75). Although these findings are based on a small sample size, Sheard concluded that these findings provided evidence for the divergent (or discriminant) validity (i.e. does not correlate too much with similar but distinct constructs) of the PPI-A. Meaningful cross-national comparisons of construct means, however, require equality of factor loadings and item intercepts (i.e. scalar invariance) (Meredith, 1993; Vandenberg and Lance, 2000). Without evidence to support scalar invariance, comparing composite scale means across different countries can lead to erroneous conclusions (Meredith, 1993; Vandenberg and Lance, 2000). We return to the issue of measurement invariance later in this chapter.

In summary, the PPI-A appears limited in its ability to satisfy the three guiding criteria. Although there is emerging evidence to support its factorial validity and internal consistency, concerns remain about how well the PPI-A captures the breadth of the mental toughness conceptual space (i.e. content validity) across different cultures (i.e. configural invariance), thereby reducing its practical utility. The use of PCA to 'identify' a structure in the data rather than presenting an a priori conceptual model and testing this conceptualization is also problematic (see Marsh, 1997, 2002). Nevertheless, item brevity is key strength of the PPI-A in terms of practical utility, although the lack of predictive and incremental validity requires further attention. As construct validation is an ongoing process (Marsh, 1997, 2002), further conceptual development and statistical examination of the PPI-A is warranted.

Mental Toughness Questionnaire-48

In what was the first attempt to adopt a scientifically rigorous process to conceptualizing and measuring mental toughness, Clough et al. (2002) integrated the perspectives of sportspeople (e.g. coaches, athletes) with an extensive body of evidence relating to the stress–illness relationship in health psychology. They argued that mental toughness resembled tenets outlined in hardiness theory in which three interrelated attitudes (*commitment, control,* and *challenge*; 3Cs) are said to provide an individual with existential courage and motivation to appraise stressful situations as opportunities for growth (for reviews, see Maddi, 2004, 2006). Stemming from their qualitative interviews, they added the fourth dimension of *confidence* to propose a 4Cs model of mental toughness in which mentally tough individuals are said to (a) view negative experiences (e.g. anxiety and stress) as *challenges* that they can overcome but also natural and essential catalysts for growth and development; (b) believe that they are influential in dealing with and *controlling* negative life experiences; (c) be deeply involved themselves in what they are doing and remain *committed* to achieving their goals; and (d) be *confident* in their abilities to deal with and overcome negative life experiences. Accordingly, the following definition of mental toughness emerged:

> Mentally tough individuals tend to be sociable and outgoing; as they are able to remain calm and relaxed, they are competitive in many situations and have lower anxiety levels than others. With a high sense of self-belief and an unshakeable faith that they can control their own destiny, these individuals can remain relatively unaffected by competition or adversity.
>
> (Clough et al., 2002: 38)

Although this definition of mental toughness is described in relatively highly specific terms, the nature and number of dimensions associated with the construct of interest should be encapsulated by the corresponding model (Bacharach, 1989; Spector, 1992).Thus, Clough et al. (2002) subsequently developed the Mental Toughness Questionnaire-48 (MTQ48) to measure the four components of their model. They developed statements that were designed to tap into one of the 4Cs, with a total of 48 items included in the final item pool. Although Clough et al. failed to report factor analyses supporting their hypothesized four-factor model, an internal consistency estimate of overall mental toughness ($\alpha = .90$) was detailed as supporting the reliability of the MTQ48. Because Cronbach's alpha is sensitive to the number of items in a scale (i.e. a greater number of items will increase internal reliability; Gignac, 2009), it is of no surprise that the internal reliability estimate for total mental toughness was high. Concurrent validity data were offered in terms of positive and moderate correlations with related constructs such as optimism, self-image, life satisfaction, and self-efficacy ($r = .42$ to .68). They also reported two experiments in which they examined relationships between mental toughness and perceived effort and type of feedback (negative or positive). In the first experiment, Clough et al. found that participants high in mental toughness (based on a median split) reported lower levels of perceived exertion when cycling at 70 per cent of the their VO_2max than participants low in mental toughness. In the second experiment, they found that individuals high in mental toughness performed a cognitive planning task consistently no matter the type of feedback, whereas participants low in mental toughness performed significantly worse following negative feedback. Collectively, these findings were put forward as supporting the utility of the MTQ48 as a sport-general measure of mental toughness.

Clough and his colleagues have since produced a technical manual (http://www.aqr.co.uk/html/top_menu/Psychometrics/Products/Downloads), which includes more information on the development of the MTQ48 than what is presented in their original publication (Clough et al., 2002). In constructing the MTQ48, data from a sample of 963 individuals ($n_{students} = 619$; $n_{athletes} = 163$; $n_{adminstrators/managers} = 136$; $n_{engineers} = 42$) were subjected to a PCA with varimax rotation, and revealed six factors with eigenvalues greater than one. Collectively, the six factors explained 62.7 per cent of the variance, and were named challenge, commitment, life control, emotional control, confidence in abilities, and interpersonal confidence. Factor loadings, which were not explicitly detailed for each item for the respective factor and other subscales (i.e. cross-loadings), appear satisfactory (i.e. > .30). These findings provided preliminary evidence for the factorial validity of the MTQ48.

The application of hardiness theory (for reviews, see Maddi, 2004, 2006) to sport contexts is undoubtedly a key strength of Clough et al.'s (2002) approach to conceptualizing and measuring mental toughness. The addition of confidence to the hardiness model has received overwhelming support from subsequent qualitative mental toughness research (e.g. Gucciardi et al., 2008; Jones et al., 2002) thereby facilitating the transposition of the health-based model into sport contexts. Nevertheless, further conceptual justification and empirical work is required to delineate the usefulness of integrating hardiness with confidence as being mental toughness in sport, because hardy individuals have also been found to be more confident than less hardy individuals (Florian et al., 1995). Moreover, with confidence being the only unique contribution to this conceptualization of mental toughness (i.e. 75 per cent of the model is hardiness theory) some researchers (e.g. Chapter 5 above) argue that the 4Cs model is simply hardiness 'repackaged' as something new.

Despite the limited empirical evidence to support the hypothesized four-factor structure of the 4Cs model in the original publication (Clough et al., 2002) and the test manual (i.e. they reported a six-factor model), the MTQ48 has received widespread use as a sport-general measure of mental toughness. For example, researchers have conducted cross-sectional studies to explore relations between mental toughness and coping (see Chapter 3 above), leadership style preferences (Crust and Azadi, 2009), and affect intensity (Crust, 2009), as well as examine demographic differences according to such variables as gender, age, sporting experience, sport type and achievement level (Nicholls et al., 2009). In addition to providing further evidence for the construct validity of the MTQ48, these studies have consistently revealed adequate levels of internal reliability for total mental toughness and its subscales.

Nevertheless, important information regarding the hypothesized measurement structure is limited. As the only evaluation of the hypothesized measurement model to date of which we are aware, researchers employing a non-athlete sample reported conducting psychometric analyses (i.e. exploratory and confirmatory factor analyses) yet provided little detail on the statistical results. Specifically, they stated, 'the four-factor solution provided a better fit to the data than did a single factor … following oblimin rotation, the pattern matrix suggested that the items fit moderately well onto their designated factors' (Horsburgh et al., 2009: 102). Other research has included adequate samples sizes (i.e. > 300), yet none has examined the factorial validity of the MTQ48 before conducting the main analyses (e.g. Kaiseler et al., 2009; Marchant et al., 2009; Nicholls et al., 2008, 2009). Clearly, there is a need to examine the factorial validity of the MTQ48 with athlete-only samples before we can be confident that the measure is a psychometrically robust assessment of mental toughness in sport (cf. Hagger and Chatzisarantis, 2009; Marsh and Hau, 2007).

In summary, it appears that further conceptual and statistical work is required to clarify and add value to the existing evidence base in relation to the three guiding criteria. While the MTQ48 is grounded in hardiness theory from health psychology that has received substantial empirical support, and the statistical procedures (e.g. PCA, internal reliability, correlational analyses) employed to develop the MTQ48 appear sound, subsequent examinations of the hypothesized measurement model are limited. Of particular note is the need to explore the robustness of the measurement model (i.e. factorial validity) using 'state-of-the-art' analytical techniques such as CFA (Hagger and Chatzisarantis, 2009) that test an a priori structure against the data. Factorial validity has implications both for practice (e.g. how an instrument is scored, defining subscales based on item content) and theory (e.g. dimensionality, hierarchical representation), and it is important to ascertain this type of validity before other forms such as predictive and concurrent validity (Gignac, 2009). Concerns also remain about how well the MTQ48 captures the breadth of the mental toughness conceptual space (i.e. content validity).

Sport Mental Toughness Questionnaire

Noting the lack of rigorous research aimed at developing a psychometrically sound measure of mental toughness as the rationale for their work, Sheard et al. (2009) reported two studies in which they described the development of their Sport Mental Toughness Questionnaire (SMTQ). Initially, 10 athletes and 10 coaches provided a dichotomous assessment (applicable vs. inapplicable) of a preliminary pool of 53 items, which were developed using the themes and quotes reported in previous qualitative investigations (i.e. face validity). Mental toughness researchers (number unknown) reviewed the items and retained 18 of the 53 statements.

Using a sample of 633 competitive athletes (226 females), the 18 items retained from the experts' ratings for subsequent statistical analysis were first subjected to a principal axis factoring analysis (PAF) using an oblique rotation, thereby allowing for correlation among subscales. The PAF produced a 14-item, three-factor solution including *confidence, constancy* and *control* dimensions, which explained 40.7 per cent of the variance. The three-factor model was next subjected to a CFA using a second independent sample of 509 athletes (158 females), which revealed good fit between the data and the hypothesized model (i.e. factorial validity). Support for the internal reliability of the SMTQ subscales was also revealed (Cronbach's $\alpha > .72$). Low-to-moderate correlations between the SMTQ and hypothesized key correlates including hardiness ($r = .14$ to $.33$), optimism ($r = .23$ to $.38$), and positive and negative affect ($r = .12$ to $.49$) were put forward as evidence for its divergent (or discriminant) validity. The SMTQ was also found to adequately distinguish athletes based on competitive standard, age, and gender. Collectively, these findings provided preliminary support for the within- and between-network properties of the SMTQ.

A key strength of Sheard et al.'s (2009) methodology is the application of the construct validation approach advocated by prominent education psychology researchers (see Marsh, 1997, 2002). Specifically, within-network analyses involving rigorous statistical techniques (e.g. CFA, distributional properties, internal reliability) to assess the hypothesized model at both the item and factor levels, as well as between-network analyses exploring relationships with key correlates and demographic variables. Sport psychology researchers (Gill et al., 1988) have advocated a similar methodological approach to questionnaire development in which item development is based on theory and evaluated using rigorous analyses (e.g. item and reliability analysis, factor analyses, tests of convergent and divergent validity, validation in relation to external criteria). We return to a discussion on the construct validation process later in this chapter. Nevertheless, there are a number of methodological and conceptual limitations that should be taken into consideration when assessing the utility of the SMTQ as a measure of mental toughness.

Conceptually, the SMTQ is limited in its ability to capture the breadth of mental toughness that has been reported in previous qualitative research (i.e. limited content validity). Key components such as attentional control, success mindset, and context intelligence, for example, which have been reported in at least three qualitative studies (for reviews, see Connaughton and Hanton, 2009; Gucciardi et al., 2009a), are overlooked in the three-factor SMTQ model. The lack of an a priori hypothesized model (i.e. identifying key facets of mental toughness across the available literature and developing items that capture those dimensions) may account for this limitation (cf. Gill et al., 1988). Thus, although the psychometric properties of the measure appear to be strong (i.e. factorial validity, internally reliable), a concern remains about the conceptual coverage of a three-factor model. Conceptual issues are also apparent at the item and factor level. Although the authors provided labels for the emergent factors, their meanings are open to interpretation without clear description of the nature of each facet. One could expect that the control subscale, for example, should be measuring the idea that individuals can manage their internal states for achieving optimal performance (e.g. Jones et al., 2002). The items loading on this factor, however, don't appear to be measuring that type of control, and are conceptually similar to descriptions of anxiety (e.g. 'I worry about performing poorly' and 'I get anxious by events I did not expect or cannot control').

A number of methodological concerns also exist at both the global and item levels. Investigations of age and gender differences in mental toughness are important considerations for theory development in the area; however, demonstrating the appropriateness of the key dimensions (i.e. face validity) and the equivalence of the underlying measurement model (i.e. scalar invariance) for different age groups and for both males and females is a necessary condition for making valid comparison of such group means (Meredith, 1993; Vandenberg and Lance, 2000). Issues at the item level relate to the quality of certain statements. For example, there appear to be a number of double-barrelled items in the SMTQ (e.g. 'I get angry and frustrated when things do not go my way'). One item ('I am able to make decisions with confidence and commitment'), in particular, asks about two distinctly different mental toughness characteristics reported in the literature (i.e. confidence and commitment). Response issues may arise when respondents are committed but lack confidence, or are confident in their abilities but don't care much about the purpose or outcome.

Assessing the available evidence base on the SMTQ against the three guiding criteria indicates that further work is required. Encouragingly, the SMTQ is grounded in the available body of mental toughness evidence, albeit in an atheoretical nature. In other words, it would have been more impressive if Sheard et al. (2009) identified a conceptual model of mental toughness based on the available literature and then applied CFA to test viability of its factorial structure (Gignac, 2009) rather than employing PCA to find some structure in the data. Moreover, in its current format the SMTQ appears limited in its ability to capture the breadth and distinguish between the main facets of mental toughness (i.e. content validity). Nevertheless, item brevity is another key strength of the SMTQ in terms of practical utility, although the lack of predictive and incremental validity requires further attention. As construct validation is an ongoing process (Marsh, 1997, 2002), further conceptual development and statistical examination of the SMTQ is warranted.

Australian football Mental Toughness Inventory

Offering an alternative approach to the aforementioned research, Gucciardi et al. (2009b) set out to develop a measure that captures context-specific dimensions of mental toughness identified in previous qualitative research in Australian football (Gucciardi et al., 2008). They subjected an initial pool of 60 items designed to tap into the 11 key facets of mental toughness in Australian football to a CFA using data from 418 footballers. The hypothesized 11-factor model did not fit the data well. The authors then performed a series of PCA using both varimax and promax rotations to explore the usefulness of three-, four-, and five-factor solutions. These analyses supported a 24-item, four-factor model (*thrive through challenge, sport awareness, desire success, tough attitudes*), which they labelled the Australian football Mental Toughness Inventory (AfMTI). Subsequent between-network analyses provided preliminary support for the construct validity of the AfMTI. For example, Gucciardi et al. observed small and non-significant correlations between the AfMTI and social desirability ($r = -.04$ to .07). As expected, they also revealed low to moderate and positive relationships between mental toughness and resilience ($r = .10$ to .45) and flow ($r = -.10$ to .62). Finally, the AfMTI adequately discriminated participants based on their age, playing level and years of playing experience. Subsequent examinations using the AfMTI support its practical utility in assessing the effectiveness of psychological skills training (Gucciardi et al., 2009c) as well as ascertaining differences between footballers in different developmental phases (Gucciardi, 2009) and identifying mental toughness profiles among adolescent footballers (Gucciardi, 2010).

Despite having an adequate conceptual foundation (Gucciardi et al., 2009b) and being sensitive to changes in multisource ratings (i.e. self, parent, coach) of mental toughness following exposure to an intervention program (Gucciardi et al., 2009c), the AfMTI appears limited in terms of its factorial validity and practical utility. Perhaps most troubling is that both the original (Gucciardi et al., 2008) and revised hypothesized measurement models (Gucciardi et al., 2009b) have not received statistical support beyond the samples used to calibrate the factor structure. For example, the measurement model failed to receive support with an adolescent-only sample of Australian footballers (Gucciardi, 2009). Thus, although the instrument appears to be internally consistent across different populations (i.e. athletes, coaches, parents), concerns remain about the factorial validity of the AfMTI as well as its ability to capture the breadth and distinguish between the main facets of mental toughness (i.e. content validity).

The issue of measurement invariance is another important statistical and methodological consideration when evaluating the psychometric rigour of the AfMTI, because evidence to support the generalization of the model across different raters (i.e. athletes, coaches, parents) is unavailable, thereby questioning the validity of the work that has employed multisource ratings (Gucciardi et al., 2009b, 2009c). Practically, the AfMTI being developed to measure context-specific dimensions of mental toughness in Australian football is both a strength and limitation of this measure. Although being grounded in the narratives and language of the Australian football context strengthens its face validity, the specialized focus limits its practical utility beyond this unique sport.

In summary, the AfMTI does not appear to adequately satisfy all three of the assessment criteria at this stage in its development. Although initially founded on an empirically derived model of mental toughness, statistical analyses failed to support its factorial validity. With only four of a possible 11 mental toughness facets assessed in the final measurement model, there also remain concerns about the practical utility of the AfMTI in assessing the breadth of the construct (i.e. content validity). Further work is required to address these concerns.

Cricket Mental Toughness Inventory

Recognizing the need to capture context-specific dimensions of mental toughness, Gucciardi and Gordon (2009b) conducted a series of studies within a mixed-methods framework to develop their Cricket Mental Toughness Inventory (CMTI). Interviews with Indian (*n* = 11) and Australian (*n* = 5) cricketers, five of whom were still involved in international cricket at the time of the study, provided a foundation upon which to develop a model of mental toughness in this context. Specifically, a six-factor model emerged from the participants' discourse: *affective intelligence, desire to achieve, resilience, attentional control, self-belief* and *cricket smarts*. Items generated to tap into these six dimensions were examined through two independent focus groups involving nine Australian male, first-class cricketers, which resulted in the addition of eight items and some minor modifications to the wording of several statements (i.e. face validity). The authors next administered the preliminary pool of 50 items to a general (i.e. cricketers from the various leagues around the world; *n* = 570) and Australian-only sample of cricketers (*n* = 433). Initially, the authors split the general cricket sample into two equal portions to serve as either a calibration or cross-validation cohort. A series of CFA with the calibration sample provided support for a 15-item, five-factor model of mental toughness (the *cricket smarts* factor was removed). This measurement model received support with the cross-validation and Australian-only samples both in terms of its hypothesized factor structure and internal reliability estimates. Inter-factor correlations corrected for attenuation (cf. Bagozzi and Kimmel, 1995) supported discriminant validity between the five mental toughness components, whereas positive and moderate correlations with resilience (r = .35 to .54), hardiness (r = .05 to .38), and flow r = -.01 to .58) and negative and moderate correlations with burnout (r = -.15 to -.43) supported convergent validity.

When considering the three guiding criteria, there are both strengths and weaknesses of the CMTI. As with research on the development and validation of the SMTQ (Sheard et al., 2009), the adoption of a construct validation framework (see Marsh, 1997) is a key strength of the CMTI. Unlike the SMTQ model, however, Gucciardi and Gordon developed and tested an a priori model of mental toughness. Although the originally proposed six-factor did not receive statistical support, the revised five-factor CMTI model held up across three independent samples of cricketers, thereby adding further confidence in the hypothesized conceptualization of mental toughness in cricket. Nevertheless, the samples comprising largely male cricketers creates some concern regarding the generalizability of the measurement model across genders (i.e. factorial validity). Although item brevity is a key practical strength of the CMTI, there remain concerns about its practical application beyond the cricket context. Thus,

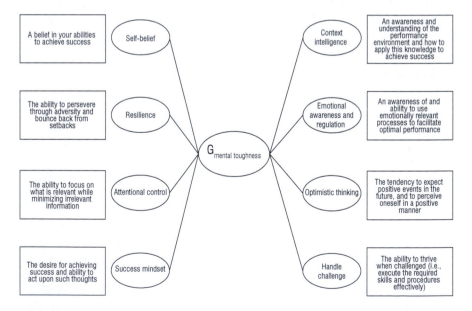

Figure 7.1 Conceptual overview of the hypothesized key components of mental toughness

it appears that further conceptual and statistical work is required to clarify and value-add to the existing evidence base in relation to the three guiding criteria.

Measurement issues in moving forward

What becomes apparent from the aforementioned discussion is that researchers have had differing views on the topic of measuring mental toughness. Whereas some researchers (e.g. Clough et al., 2002; Sheard et al., 2009) have approached this venture from a sport-general viewpoint, others (e.g. Gucciardi and Gordon, 2009b; Gucciardi et al., 2009b) have emphasized the need to capture context-specific dimensions of mental toughness. Differences also exist in the processes involved in developing and validating mental toughness inventories. For example, some researchers display a preference for a strong conceptual underpinning over rigorous factor analytical strategies such as CFA (e.g. Clough et al., 2002) and vice versa (e.g. Sheard et al., 2009). In this final section, we discuss six issues that we believe stand out as being important considerations for future work that attempts to progress the measurement of mental toughness in sport. These recommendations are offered with the inherent recognition that construct validation is an ongoing process (Marsh, 1997, 2002) involving the accumulation of reliability and validity evidence (see Tables 7.1 and 7.2) to support the utility of a measurement instrument.

Construct validation is an ongoing process

Researchers in psychology and education (e.g. Marsh, 1997, 2002) have increasingly emphasized the need to develop and evaluate instruments within a construct validation framework in which the intimate relationship between theory, measurement, empirical research, and practice is emphasized. When adopting this perspective, studies typically involve within- and between-network examinations of the target construct. Of particular importance for within-network validity are the factor structure and its invariance across key subgroups (e.g. age, gender) as well as the distributional (e.g. skew, kurtosis) and descriptive properties of items (e.g. item-level means and variances). Within-network studies explore the internal structure of a construct using techniques such as exploratory factor analysis (EFA), CFA, and reliability analysis, thereby providing evidence for its measurement and psychometric robustness (i.e. factorial validity). In contrast, between-network studies involve an examination of relationships between the target construct and hypothesized key correlates (e.g. predictors, outcomes). Of particular importance for between-network validity is an understanding of the relationships with key demographic (e.g. age, gender, playing experience) and other cognate (e.g. burnout, anxiety interpretation) and behavioral correlates (e.g. performance consistency). Correlational, regression or cluster analyses are typically employed to examine such relationships (i.e. predictive, incremental, concurrent, discriminant validity). Consistent with the construct validation framework, therefore, researchers are encouraged to present a sound theoretical framework and definition of mental toughness before engaging in statistical processes that seek to validate this conceptualization. Empirical evidence gleaned from both within- (e.g. item and reliability analysis, EFA, CFA) and between-network (e.g. convergent, divergent, predictive validity) analytical techniques can then be forwarded to support the conceptualization. It is important to note that establishing the within-network validity of a measurement model is considered a necessary prerequisite to exploring relations between latent constructs (Marsh and Hau, 2007).

Clarification of the key components and hierarchical structure

A central issue relevant to the measurement and conceptualization of mental toughness is how best to operationalize the breadth of this construct. We see this venture as a delicate balance between a parsimonious model and one that attends to the complexity of mental toughness. Recognizing that we cannot likely expect complete consensus regarding the key mental toughness facets (Chapter 2 above), we report on core components that appear in at least three descriptions or models, but exclude peripheral aspects that have received attention in only one conceptualization. The systematic nature of this approach contrasts with the haphazard procedures on which some inventories are predicated (e.g. Gucciardi et al., 2009b; Sheard et al., 2009). The key facets illustrated in Figure 7.1 are designed to provide a comprehensive but not exhaustive coverage of the sampling domain, with the expectation that each component shares a considerable amount of variance with overall mental toughness. Nevertheless, we recognize that as theory and empirical evidence evolve, it is likely that adjustments and amendments to this make-up will be required to reflect such evolutions (Zuckerman, 1996). Alternatively, a useful process might involve a study in which mental toughness researchers assess the importance of all previously reported dimensions. For example, one could create an exhaustive list of the key facets and ask a group of 20 or more researchers to demarcate those dimensions they consider as being central to this construct and others that are not. Regardless of the approach, clarifying the key facets of mental toughness has two important implications. First, agreement on the make-up of mental toughness will facilitate the development of a measurement instrument that incorporates recent empirical and theoretical advances in our understanding of this phenomenon. Second, clarification of the key facets will assist in ascertaining the uniqueness of mental toughness as a latent construct; that is, the extent to which mental toughness differs from related constructs such as resilience and hardiness.

There is also the need to consider the hierarchical nature of mental toughness in future research. Preliminary research (e.g. Gucciardi and Gordon, 2009b; Sheard et al., 2009) supports the notion of a higher-order representation of mental toughness. From a conceptual standpoint, a higher-order representation of mental toughness contains a specific causal logic whereby a latent general-factor represents the common cause of all covariation among the lower-order constructs.

This higher-order model would be useful for researchers who are interested in an overall measure of mental toughness. However, if researchers are interested in examining whether specific components of mental toughness relate with or predict specific outcomes, the lower-order dimensions would provide the appropriate model. Researchers (e.g. Clough et al., 2002; Crust and Azadi, 2009; Crust and Keegan, 2010) employing the MTQ48 have shown a preference for reporting both a global score of mental toughness and its specific components, despite the lack of evidence to support a higher-order factorial structure of this measure. As noted previously, factorial validity is an important precursor to assessing other forms of validity (Gignac, 2009).

Measurement invariance

Insufficient attention is given to analyses of the factor structure and the extent to which a given mental toughness instrument and its components are invariant across different groups (e.g. age, gender, culture); that is, does the measurement model measure the same construct the same way across different groups? The assumption that mental toughness 'looks and behaves' the same across all groups in previous research (e.g. Gucciardi et al., 2009b; Nicholls et al., 2009; Sheard, 2009) is a risky one. Even when one supports the factorial validity of an instrument with a varied sample considered representative of the overall population, inferences about invariant measurement properties for subgroups

"You work hard all week in training, but perform poorly during the competition. How do you respond?"

	Strongly disagree			Neutral			Strongly agree
You believe that you have the ability to achieve success [*self-belief*]	1	2	3	4	5	6	7
You bounce back with a quality performance the next time you compete [*resilience*]	1	2	3	4	5	6	7
The poor performance does not affect your ability to control your attention during your next competition [*attentional control*]	1	2	3	4	5	6	7
You still have the ability to act upon your desire for success [*winning mentality*]	1	2	3	4	5	6	7
Your know what you have to do to perform well next week [*context intelligence*]	1	2	3	4	5	6	7
Your emotions do not get the better of you [*emotional awareness and regulation*]	1	2	3	4	5	6	7
You are optimistic about being able to perform well next time [*optimistic thinking*]	1	2	3	4	5	6	7
You will thrive when next challenged during training or competition [*handle challenge*]	1	2	3	4	5	6	7

Figure 7.2 Example of a scenario-based measure of mental toughness

of the population cannot always be guaranteed (Horn and McArdle, 1992). Measurement invariance has both methodological and conceptual implications for the study of a construct (Cheung and Rensvold, 2002). Methodologically, demonstrations of measurement invariance are a necessary prerequisite for making valid comparisons of group means or pooling data across groups. In other words, if an inventory is found to lack measurement invariance across groups then comparisons between groups may not accurately reflect real group differences and may lead to erroneous conclusions. From a conceptual standpoint, failure to support stable factor structure or interpretations of items can reflect substantive between-group differences that are of theoretical interest. In addition to the conceptual and methodological implications for the study of a construct, support for measurement invariance would also present evidence for a mental toughness measure that has a higher potential applicability for practitioners than one that does not remain invariant across groups. Nevertheless, it is important that convincing evidence supporting the factorial validity of a measurement instrument is revealed prior to conducting invariance analyses.

Nomological validity

Although other forms of validity (e.g. convergent, discriminant, concurrent, predictive) are important in establishing support for the target construct, the system of relations between the latent variable and hypothesized key correlates (i.e. nomological network) is among the most central issues in delineating its substantive impact (Hagger and Chatzisarantis, 2009). To assess nomological validity, a theoretical network of antecedents and consequences of the target construct is developed, and the relationships between them and the central construct are evaluated (Cronbach and Meehl, 1955). Support for a construct's nomological validity is indicated by evidence of distinct conceptual antecedents, consequences, and/or modifying conditions (Iacobucci et al., 1995); that is, the degree to which the construct is associated with other variables in a way that is theoretically meaningful. Validation of mental toughness inventories in a nomological network of relationships has not yet been tested in the literature. Attempts to explore discrete aspects of nomological validity do exist (e.g. Crust, 2009; Nicholls et al., 2008), but are assessed using bivariate correlations. Nevertheless, these empirical data are important for specifying relationships between constructs in the nomological network that can be tested in full at a later stage. In addition to advancing construct conceptualization, definition and measurement, assessments of the nomological network will also assist in determining whether mental toughness is conceptually distinct from related constructs such as resilience and hardiness (cf. Sternthal et al., 1987). If, for example, mental toughness and resilience are found to share all antecedents and consequences within a nomological network, then discussing each variable as anything but an isomorphic construct would be untenable. Thus, evaluations of mental toughness inventories within a broader theory that describes its causes, effects and correlates and how they relate to one another are an important avenue for future research.

Likert Format							
	Strongly Disagree						Strongly Agree
When confronted with an unexpected event, I am able to successfully adapt my behavior	1	2	3	4	5	6	7
My knowledge of the performance context constantly evolves	1	2	3	4	5	6	7
When faced with challenge or adversity, I believe in my ability to perform well	1	2	3	4	5	6	7
I interpret pressure or adversity as a positive challenge	1	2	3	4	5	6	7

Semantic Differential Format									
When confronted with an unexpected event, I am...	able to successfully adapt my behavior	1	2	3	4	5	6	7	unable to adapt my behavior
My knowledge of the performance context...	constantly evolves	1	2	3	4	5	6	7	is mediocre
When faced with challenge or adversity, I...	believe in my ability to perform well	1	2	3	4	5	6	7	have doubts in my ability to perform well
I interpret pressure or adversity...	as a positive challenge	1	2	3	4	5	6	7	in a negative manner

Figure 7.3 Example of a traditional Likert and semantic differential measure of mental toughness

Scenarios and semantic differential

Another consideration that we believe warrants attention in future research concerns alternative methods of assessment in self-report measures of mental toughness. Whereas some researchers (e.g. Gucciardi et al., 2009b, 2009c) have approached this issue from the perspective of obtaining multisource ratings of mental toughness, we believe there is potential for the examination of both scenario-based and semantic differential measures. In terms of theoretical contributions, there is much to gain from exploring the utility of alternative forms of measurement. If, for example, research involving alternative forms of measurement is significantly related to Likert-based scales and to hypothesized related constructs in a similar manner, then there is further evidence for the nomological validity of mental toughness. If these hypothesized links are not significant or in the expected direction then it may be that different constructs are being assessed or the intrusion of method biases or trait method effects exist (Byrne, 1989).

In a scenario-based approach, one would ask individuals to imagine themselves in a series of specific, un/common, day-to-day 'mental toughness' inducing situations or scenarios. Individuals are then asked to indicate the probability or likelihood of various affective, cognitive and behavioral reactions typical of the mentally tough athlete in these scenarios. We provide an example of a scenario-based measure of mental toughness in Figure 7.2. Importantly, scales based only on 'traditional' Likert items tend to hold lower construct (i.e. less accurate descriptions and predictions of behaviors) and cross-cultural validity (i.e. less meaningful comparisons) than scales based on scenarios (Peng et al., 1997). A scenario-based approach to measurement also aligns well with a personal construct psychology (PCP: Kelly, 1991) approach to understanding mental toughness. In other words, whether or not a person will react in a certain way depends on their construal of the situation or scenario. PCP is one of the most popular theoretical frameworks for researching mental toughness (e.g. Coulter et al., 2010; Gucciardi et al., 2008; Jones et al., 2002). Within the context of PCP, situations or scenarios included in the measure might also include anticipations of future events (e.g. 'Your preparation for the competition has been less than satisfactory. What are your expectations?') or reactions to situations that have already occurred (e.g. 'You worked hard in the lead-up to the event, but performed poorly. How do you respond?').

The semantic differential approach (Osgood et al., 1957) has become a popular method for assessing subjective meanings of positive constructs. Whereas 'traditional' Likert scales include declarative statements to which people are required to report the extent which they agree with the item, semantic differential scales consist of evaluative statements to which respondents are required to

	Category labels	Sample items	Category labels
Step 1: Practice block (*n* trials)	Not me		Me
	O	Self	●
	●	Other	O
Step 2: Practice block (*n* trials)	Mentally weak		Mentally tough
	O	Confident	●
	●	Distracted	O
Step 3: Practice block (*n* trials) Critical block (*n* trials)	Not me or Mentally weak		Me or Mentally tough
	O	Confident	●
	●	Distracted	O
	O	Desire success	●
Step 4: Practice block (*n* trials)	Mentally tough		Mentally weak
	●	Confident	O
	O	Distracted	●
Step 5: Practice block (*n* trials) Critical block (*n* trials)	Me or Mentally weak		Not me or Mentally tough
	O	Confident	●
	●	Distracted	O
	O	**Desire success**	●

Figure 7.4 Example of an implicit association test for mental toughness (Note: n = the number of trials)

report their position using bipolar labels (e.g. self-doubt vs. self-belief). As with scenario-based measurement, semantic differentials align well with a PCP (Kelly, 1991) approach to understanding mental toughness (i.e. dichotomy corollary). Thus, researchers can leverage off previous research that has generated bipolar constructs of the key components of mental toughness (e.g. Coulter et al., 2010; Gucciardi et al., 2008) to develop semantic differential scales. We provide an example of a semantic differential measure of mental toughness in Figure 7.3. Particularly with positive constructs such as resilience, researchers have found that the acquiescence bias (i.e. agreeing or responding positively to items regardless of item content) inherent with Likert scales can be reduced when using a semantic differential approach (Friborg et al., 2006). Nevertheless, although providing a better model fit than Likert scales, semantic differentials may increase cognitive demand and random errors in measurement (Friborg et al., 2006). Thus, participant characteristics (e.g. age, experience) need to be considered before deciding to use a semantic differential approach.

Explicit versus implicit measurement

Is it preferable to measure mental toughness directly or explicitly by asking athletes to report their self-perceptions using the aforementioned questionnaires, or is it desirable to assess mental toughness indirectly or implicitly using tasks that rely on unconscious processes? Although direct assessments have the advantage of explicitly targeting the precise construct of interest and being relatively straightforward to implement, there is the disadvantage of individuals knowing what is being assessed that comes with high face validity. Thus, items that are high in face validity are potentially more vulnerable to issues associated with socially desirable responding or faking than are items low in face validity (Schulman et al., 1987). Nevertheless, recognizing that both explicit (i.e. reflective and conscious) and implicit aspects (i.e. impulsive and unconscious) are influential in determining one's behavior (Back et al., 2009), there is a need to consider indirect measurement of mental toughness in the future.

The implicit association test (IAT: Greenwald et al., 1998) was introduced over a decade ago and has since been used in hundreds of studies focusing primarily on various attitudes (e.g. race, sexual orientation, political views) but also personality constructs such as self-esteem and the Big Five (for a review, see Greenwald et al., 2009). The IAT is a performance-based assessment tool in which reaction times taken to sort opposing concepts serve as indices of the target construct. If two concepts are highly associated, the sorting task should be easier (i.e. faster) when the two associated concepts share the same response key than when they are assigned to difference response keys. In contrast to traditional self-report questionnaires, which appear to tap a reflective-reasoning process, the IAT is thought to reflect the strength of automatic or associative representations of the self (Greenwald et al., 1998).

The IAT can be applied to assess aspects of implicit mental toughness by combining the categorization of items into the categories *me* and *other* with the classification of items into two opposing or bipolar key components (see Coulter et al., 2010; Gucciardi et al., 2008) such as *self-belief* vs. *self-doubt*. Thus, words belonging to four categories (e.g. self, other, mentally tough characteristics, mentally weak characteristics) would appear sequentially (see Figure 7.4). The participant then uses key presses to sort the words as quickly as possible into compound categories (e.g. self/mentally tough characteristic vs. self/mentally weak characteristic). The IAT depends on the observation that mentally tough participants, for example, make accurate sorting decisions faster when the category pairing is congruent with their implicit associations (e.g. self/mentally tough characteristic) than when the pairing is incongruent (e.g. self/mentally weak characteristic).

Conclusion

Recent efforts of mental toughness researchers around the world have increased significantly. Nevertheless, the measurement of mental toughness is only now beginning to take shape. Despite this widespread attention to mental toughness and advances in the conceptual evolution of this important construct, much more work is needed to clarify its definition and conceptualization, measurement and universality. In this chapter we have reviewed the available literature that focuses specifically on the measurement of mental toughness with the hope of critically assessing the current status as well as offering suggestions for progressing future research. In assessing the adequacy of each mental toughness inventory on conceptual, statistical or empirical, and practical grounds, we conclude that, at present, no measure sufficiently satisfies all three criteria. Construct validation is an ongoing process (Marsh, 1997, 2002) and further work is required to address the limitations of currently available measures and/or work towards developing a new inventory that is grounded in empirical knowledge. In recommending the potential of other forms of measurement, there is also a need to consider a multi-measurement approach in which mental toughness can conceivably be measured via self-report, other-report, scenarios and implicit tests. Within the context of multitrait-multimethod validity research (Campbell and Fiske, 1959), scores derived from such an array of tests would more likely provide a complete assessment of mental toughness than any one method alone. It is important to note, however, that mental toughness measurement is a relatively new area of research and, despite the recent influx of empirical papers, much work remains to be done. We hope the information reviewed in this chapter will provide a useful foundation upon which to initiate future measurement research.

References

Bacharach, S. B. (1989) 'Organisational theories: Some criteria for evaluation', *Academy of Management Review*, 14, 496–515.

Back, M. D., Schmukle, S. C., and Egloff, B. (2009) 'Predicting behavior from the explicit and implicit self-concept of personality', *Journal of Personality and Social Psychology*, 97, 533–48.

Bagozzi, R. P., and Kimmel, S. K. (1995) 'A comparison of leading theories for the prediction of goal-directed behaviours', *British Journal of Social Psychology*, 34, 437–61.

Bryant, F. B. (2004) 'Assessing the validity of measurement', in L. G. Grimm and P. R. Yarnold (eds), *Reading and Understanding More Multivariate Statistics* (4th edn), Washington, DC: American Psychological Association, pp. 99–146.

Byrne, B. M. (1989) 'Multigroup comparisons and the assumption of equivalent construct validity across groups: Methodological and substantive issues', *Multivariate Behavioral Research*, 24, 503–23.

Campbell, D. T., and Fiske D. W. (1959) 'Convergent and discriminant validation by the multitrait-multimethod matrix', *Psychological Bulletin*, 56, 81–105.

Cattell, R. B., Blewett, D. B., and Beloff, J. R. (1955) 'The inheritance of personality: A multiple variance analysis determination of approximate nature–nurture ratios for primary personality factors in Q data', *American Journal of Human Genetics*, 7, 122–46.

Cheung, G. W., and Rensvold, R. B. (2002) 'Evaluating goodness-of-fit indexes for testing measurement invariance', *Structural Equation Modeling*, 9, 233–55.

Clough, P., Earle, K., and Sewell, D. (2002) 'Mental toughness: The concept and its measurement', in I. Cockerill (ed.), *Solutions in Sport Psychology,* London: Thomson, pp. 32–45.

Connaughton, D., and Hanton, S. (2009) 'Mental toughness in sport: Conceptual and practical issues', in S. D. Mellalieu and S. Hanton (eds), *Advances in Applied Sport Psychology: A Review,* London: Routledge, pp. 317–46.

Coulter, T. J., Mallett, C. J., and Gucciardi, D. F. (2010) 'Understanding mental toughness in Australian soccer: Perceptions of players, parents, and coaches', *Journal of Sports Sciences*, 28, 699–716.

Cronbach, L. J., and Meehl, P. E. (1955) 'Construct validity in psychological tests', *Psychological Bulletin*, 52, 281–302.

Crust, L. (2009) 'The relationship between mental toughness and affect intensity', *Personality and Individual Differences*, 47, 959–63.

Crust, L., and Azadi, K. (2009) 'Leadership preferences of mentally tough athletes', *Personality and Individual Differences*, 47, 326–30.

Crust, L., and Keegan, R. (2010) 'Mental toughness and attitudes to risk-taking', *Personality and Individual Differences*, 49, 164–8.

Florian, V., Mikulincer, M., and Taubman, O. (1995) 'Does hardiness contribute to mental health during a stressful real-life situation? The roles of appraisal and coping', *Journal of Personality and Social Psychology*, 68, 687–95.

Fourie, S., and Potgieter, J. R. (2001) 'The nature of mental toughness in sport', *South African Journal for Research in Sport, Physical Education and Recreation*, 23, 63–72.

Friborg, O., Martinussen, M., and Rosenvinge, J. H. (2006) 'Likert-based vs. semantic differential-based scorings of positive psychological constructs: A psychometric comparison of two versions of a scale measuring resilience', *Personality and Individual Differences*, 40, 873–84.

Gignac, G. E. (2009) 'Psychometrics and the measurement of emotional intelligence', in C. Stough, D. H. Saklofske, and J. D. A. Parker (eds), *Assessing Emotional Intelligence: Theory, Research, and Applications,* New York: Springer, pp. 9–42.

Gill, D. L., Dzewaltowski, D. A., and Deeter, T. E. (1988) 'The relationship of competitiveness and achievement orientation to participation in sport and nonsport activities', *Journal of Sport & Exercise Psychology*, 10, 139–50.

Golby, J., and Sheard, M. (2004) 'Mental toughness and hardiness at different levels of rugby league', *Personality and Individual Differences*, 37, 933–42.

Golby, J., Sheard, M., and Lavallee, D. (2003) 'A cognitive-behavioral analysis of mental toughness in national rugby league football teams', *Perceptual and Motor Skills*, 96, 455–62.

Golby, J., Sheard, M., and van Wersch, A. (2007) 'Evaluating the factor structure of the psychological performance inventory', *Perceptual and Motor Skills*, 105, 309–25.

Greenwald, A. G., McGhee, D. E., and Schwartz, J. L. (1998) 'Measuring individual differences in implicit cognition: The implicit association test', *Journal of Personality and Social Psychology*, 74, 1464–80.

Greenwald, A. G., Poehlman, T. A., Uhlmann, E. L., and Banaji, M. R. (2009) 'Understanding and using the implicit association test: III. Meta-analysis of predictive validity', *Journal of Personality and Social Psychology*, 97, 17–41.

Gucciardi, D. F. (2009) 'Do developmental differences in mental toughness exist between specialized and invested Australian footballers?', *Personality and Individual Differences*, 47, 985–9.

Gucciardi, D. F. (2010) 'Mental toughness profiles and their relations with achievement goals and sport motivation in adolescent Australian footballers', *Journal of Sports Sciences*, 28, 615–25.

Gucciardi, D. F., and Gordon, S. (2009a) 'Construing the athlete and exerciser: Research and applied perspectives from personal construct psychology', *Journal of Applied Sport Psychology*, 21 (suppl.), S17–S33.

Gucciardi, D. F., and Gordon, S. (2009b) 'Development and preliminary validation of the Cricket Mental Toughness Inventory', *Journal of Sports Sciences*, 27, 1293–1310.

Gucciardi, D. F., and Gordon, S. (2009c) 'Revisiting the performance profile technique: Theoretical underpinnings and application', *The Sport Psychologist*, 23, 93–117.

Gucciardi, D. F., Gordon, S., and Dimmock, J. A. (2008) 'Towards an understanding of mental toughness in Australian football', *Journal of Applied Sport Psychology*, 20, 261–81.

Gucciardi, D. F., Gordon, S., and Dimmock, J. A. (2009a) 'Advancing mental toughness research and theory using personal construct psychology', *International Review of Sport and Exercise Psychology*, 2, 54–72.

Gucciardi, D. F., Gordon, S., and Dimmock, J. A. (2009b) 'Development and preliminary validation of a mental toughness inventory for Australian football', *Psychology of Sport and Exercise*, 10, 201–9.

Gucciardi, D. F., Gordon, S., and Dimmock, J. A. (2009c) 'Evaluation of a mental toughness training program for youth-aged Australian footballers: I. A quantitative analysis', *Journal of Applied Sport Psychology*, 21, 307–23.

Hagger, M. S., and Chatzisarantis, N. L. D. (2009) 'Assumptions in research in sport and exercise psychology', *Psychology of Sport and Exercise*, 10, 511–19.

Horn, J. L., and McArdle, J. J. (1992) 'A practical and theoretical guide to measurement invariance in aging research', *Journal of Experimental Aging Research*, 18, 117–44.

Horsburgh, V. A., Schermer, J. A., Veselka, L., and Vernon, P. A. (2009) 'A behavioral genetic study of mental toughness and personality', *Personality and Individual Differences*, 46, 100–5.

Iacobucci, D., Ostrom, A., and Grayson, K. (1995) 'Distinguishing service quality and customer satisfaction: The voice of the consumer', *Journal of Consumer Psychology*, 4, 277–303.

Jones, G., Hanton, S., and Connaughton, D. (2002) 'What is this thing called mental toughness? An investigation of elite sport performers', *Journal of Applied Sport Psychology*, 14, 205–18.

Kaiseler, M. H., Polman, R. C. J., and Nicholls, A. R. (2009) 'Mental toughness, stress, stress appraisal, coping, and coping effectiveness', *Personality and Individual Differences*, 47, 728–33.

Kaplan, R. M., and Saccuzzo, D. P. (2008) *Psychological Testing: Principles, Applications, and Issues* (7th edn), Belmont, CA: Wadsworth.

Kelly, G. A. (1991) *The Psychology of Personal Constructs: A Theory of Personality,* vol 1, London: Routledge; originally publ. 1955.

Kuan, G., and Roy, J. (2007) 'Goal profiles, mental toughness and its influence on performance outcomes among Wushu athletes', *Journal of Sports Science and Medicine*, 6, 28–33.

Loehr, J. E. (1982) *Athletic Excellence: Mental Toughness Training for Sports,* New York: Plume.

Loehr, J. E. (1986) *Mental Toughness Training for Sports: Achieving Athletic Excellence,* Lexington, MA: Stephen Greene Press.

Lynn, M. R. (1986) 'Determination and quantification of content validity', *Nursing Research*, 35, 382–5.

McDonald, R. P. (1970) 'The theoretical foundations of principal factor analysis, canonical factor analysis, and alpha factor analysis', *British Journal of Statistical and Mathematical Psychology,* 23, 1–21.

Maddi, S. R. (2004) 'Hardiness: An operationalization of existential courage', *Journal of Humanistic Psychology*, 44, 279–98.

Maddi, S. R. (2006) 'Hardiness: The courage to grow from stresses', *Journal of Positive Psychology*, 1, 160–8.

Mallett, C. J., Kawabata, M., and Newcombe, P. (2007) 'Progressing measurement in sport motivation: A response to Pelletier, Vallerand, and Sarrazin', *Psychology of Sport and Exercise*, 8, 622–31.

Marchant, D. C., Polman, R. C. J., Clough, P. J., Jackson, J. G., Levy, A. R., and Nicholls, A. R. (2009) 'Mental toughness in the workplace: Managerial and age differences', *Journal of Managerial Psychology*, 24, 428–37.

Marsh, H. W. (1997) 'The measurement of physical self-concept: A construct validation approach', in K. Fox (ed.), *The Physical Self: From Motivation to Well-Being,* Champaign, IL: Human Kinetics, pp. 27–58.

Marsh, H. W. (2002) 'A multidimensional physical self-concept: A construct validity approach to theory, measurement, and research', *Psychology: The Journal of the Hellenic Psychological Society*, 9, 459–93.

Marsh, H. W., and Hau, K.-T. (2007) 'Applications of latent-variable models in educational psychology: The need for methodological-substantive synergies', *Contemporary Educational Psychology*, 32, 151–70.

Meredith, W. (1993) 'Measurement invariance, factor analysis and factorial invariance', *Psychometrika*, 58, 525–43.

Middleton, S. C., Marsh, H. W., Martin, A. J., Richards, J. E., Savis, J., Perry, C., and Brown, R. (2004) 'The Psychological Performance Inventory: Is the mental toughness test enough?', *International Journal of Sport Psychology*, 35, 91–108.

Nicholls, A. R., Polman, R. C. J., Levy, A. R., and Backhouse, S. H. (2008) 'Mental toughness, optimism, pessimism, and coping among athletes', *Personality and Individual Differences*, 44, 1182–92.

Nicholls, A. R., Polman, R. C. J., Levy, A. R., and Backhouse, S. H. (2009) 'Mental toughness in sport: Achievement level, gender, age, experience, and sport type differences', *Personality and Individual Differences*, 47, 73–5.

Osgood, C. E., Suci, G. J., and Tannenbaum, P. H. (1957) *The Measurement of Meaning*, Urbana, IL: University of Illinois Press.

Peng, K., Nisbett, R. E., and Wong, N. Y. C. (1997) 'Validity problems comparing values across cultures and possible solutions', *Psychological Methods*, 2, 329–44.

Schulman, P., Seligman, M. E. P., and Amsterdam, D. (1987) 'The Attributional Style Questionnaire is not transparent', *Behavior Research and Therapy*, 25, 391–5.

Sheard, M. (2009) 'A cross-national analysis of mental toughness and hardiness in elite university rugby league teams', *Perceptual and Motor Skills*, 109, 213–23.

Sheard, M., Golby, J., and van Wersch, A. (2009) 'Progress toward construct validation of the Sports Mental Toughness Questionnaire (SMTQ)', *European Journal of Psychological Assessment*, 25, 186–93.

Siebold, S. (2005) *177 Mental Toughness Secrets of the World Class: The Thought Processes, Habits, and Philosophies of the Great Ones*, London: House Press.

Spector, P. E. (1992) *Summated Rating Scale Construction: An Introduction*, Newbury Park, CA: Sage.

Sternthal, B., Tybout, A. M., and Calder, B. J. (1987) 'Confirmatory versus comparative approaches to judging theory tests', *Journal of Consumer Research*, 14, 114–25.

Thompson, B. (2004) *Exploratory and Confirmatory Factor Analysis: Understanding Concepts and Applications*, Washington, DC: American Psychological Association.

Vandenberg, R. J., and Lance, C. E. (2000) 'A review and synthesis of the measurement invariance literature: Suggestions, practices, and recommendations for organizational research', *Organizational Research Methods*, 3, 4–70.

Wakefield, T. S. (2009) *Developing Mental Toughness: Teaching the Game of Life*, Bloomington, IN: Authorhouse.

Zuckerman, M. (1996) '"Conceptual clarification" or confusion in "The study of sensation seeking"', *Personality and Individual Differences*, 21, 111–14.

Part III

Developing mental toughness

8 Mental toughness development

Issues, practical implications and future directions

Declan Connaughton, Richard Thelwell and Sheldon Hanton

Mental toughness is a term used by numerous athletes, coaches, members of the press and sports commentators to indicate a key psychological characteristic that distinguishes the great from the good, and the victorious from the rest of the field (Gould et al., 1987; Loehr, 1986). The fascination with mental toughness began in the 1950s, with investigators citing and attempting to explain this concept in a variety of manners that included mental toughness as a personality trait (Cattell et al., 1955; Werner and Gottheil, 1966), a defense mechanism against adversity (Alderman, 1974; Favret and Benzel, 1997), a critical asset for athletes to endure the long hours of strenuous training associated with top-level performance (Bull et al., 1996; Goldberg, 1998), and a decisive factor in distinguishing successful and unsuccessful performances (Luszki, 1982; Pankey, 1993). However, prior to 2002, the conceptual underpinnings of the proposed definitions of mental toughness were questionable, the vast literature was based on opinion, coaching and counselling experience, and anecdotal evidence rather than scientific research, and many of the studies investigated mental skills rather than mental toughness *per se* (for reviews, see Connaughton et al., 2008a; Connaughton and Hanton, 2009). This lack of empirical research exacerbated misinterpretation and created confusion regarding a clear understanding of mental toughness.

In 2001, Fourie and Potgeiter stimulated interest in the concept of mental toughness; however, it was not until 2002 that investigators began to develop research programs to facilitate an in-depth understanding of what mental toughness is, what it is made-up of, how it can be measured, and how it is developed and maintained. Two main approaches were adopted in the pursuit of understanding mental toughness. One group of researchers used previous findings and adopted theory from other disciplines of psychology (e.g. health psychology) to develop a conceptual model (4Cs: control, commitment, challenge, confidence) and measure of mental toughness (e.g. MT18 and MT48: Clough et al., 2002). Using this knowledge, hypotheses (e.g. mental toughness will have a significant impact upon beliefs, pain and adherence within a sport injury rehabilitation context) were proposed with regard to levels of mental toughness and various perceptual and behavioural differences (e.g. Crust and Clough, 2005; Levy et al., 2006). The second group of researchers (Bull et al., 2005; Coulter et al., 2010; Gucciardi et al., 2008; Jones et al., 2002, 2007; Thelwell et al., 2005) acknowledged the problems and anecdotal issues surrounding the mental toughness literature (i.e. contradictory explanations of mental toughness, no clear or broadly accepted definition, positive psychological characteristics being incorrectly labelled as mental toughness) and developed research programs, using Personal Construct Theory (Kelly, 1991) as a guiding framework, to qualitatively address mental toughness.

While mental toughness research may be considered to be at a relatively early stage in its development, there is some agreement with regard to a definition and the key characteristics of mental toughness. The aim of this chapter is to review the literature that has investigated mental toughness development, highlighting the associated practical implications and future directions of mental toughness development research. The review is presented in four parts: (1) an evaluation of the anecdotal accounts prior to 2002, with an emphasis on development; (2) a brief appraisal of post-2002 investigations that have attempted to define and identify the essential characteristics of mental toughness. The purpose of these two sections is to present the reader with an overview of the mental toughness literature and provide a base for understanding the direction researchers took in investigating the development of mental toughness. Then (3) there is a review of recent empirical studies that have addressed the development and maintenance of mental toughness; and finally, (4) we highlight the practical implications of these developmental studies, and provide direction with regard to future research, the measurement of mental toughness, and intervention programs.

Anecdotal accounts prior to 2002

Over the years numerous articles and texts have sought to explain the concept of mental toughness and its development (e.g. Bull et al., 1996; Loehr, 1986). Reviewing these sources Connaughton and Hanton (2009) concluded that the vast majority were based on anecdotal evidence and coaching experience rather than scientific research, and focused on developing general mental skills training programs rather than the specific development of mental toughness. This section of the review focuses specifically on developmental issues and the subsequent ambiguity created within the literature prior to 2002.

Initial articles and texts purporting to develop mental toughness proposed mental skills within training programs to enhance performance and linked these training programs as a means of developing what was suggested to be 'mental toughness' (e.g. Goldberg, 1998; Loehr, 1986; Watts, 1978). From this viewpoint, mental toughness was believed to be an acquired skill, developed through 'the fruits of learning, deliberate sometimes but mostly unknown' (Jones, 1982: 30). Tapp suggested that the process through which mental toughness was acquired 'is precisely the same as applies to physical skills: hard work, understanding, and practice' (1991: 48). Others argued that the building blocks of mental toughness were achieved by enduring competitive pressure while remaining focused on mastery goals, hard work, determination and commitment (Hodge, 1994), and implementing extreme physical workouts with minimal rest to dull athletes' awareness of pain so they could rise above that pain in competitions (Watts, 1978). In their applied text, Bull et al. (1996) devoted a full chapter to mental toughness and its development. They identified six attributes that they felt characterized mental toughness in performers (i.e. a strong desire to succeed, staying positive in the face of challenge and pressure, being able to control the 'controllables', demonstrating high commitment with a balanced attitude, having a high level of self-belief and displaying positive body language), and development involved implementing mental skills to improve these six specific aspects of mental toughness. While many useful practical examples were provided in these texts, the authors' explanations were based solely on their experiences and personal observations and not through systematic research programs. Equally, no agreed definition of mental toughness was established, and the specific details of how a performer developed mental toughness were not addressed.

Prior to 2002, two of the most prominent and comprehensive discussions of mental toughness and its development (or training) in sport originated from Jim Loehr's and Alan Goldberg's applied texts. These texts associated the possession of psychological skills as an indicator of mental toughness and proposed mental techniques and skills to develop mental toughness by sustaining an individual's ideal performance state (Loehr, 1982, 1986, 1995), and overcoming slumps in order to achieve peak performance (Goldberg, 1998). Loehr (1982, 1986, 1995) suggested that mentally tough competitors possessed nine characteristics (i.e. being self-motivated and self-directed; positive but realistic; in control of emotions; calm and relaxed under fire; highly energetic and ready for action; determined; mentally alert and focused; doggedly self-confident; and fully responsible), and have learned to respond to situations in a specific manner.

> They think in specific ways (i.e. they have the right attitudes regarding problems, pressure, mistakes, and competition), know how to focus correctly (i.e. their skills in concentration are exceptional), and can increase their flow of positive energy in crisis and adversity ... The athletes who fit this description best dominate the world of sports ... and the world's greatest athletes give testimony to the reality of mental toughness every time they perform.
>
> (Loehr, 1982: 12)

Loehr (1982) devised a measure to profile a performer's mental strengths and weaknesses and regarded this profile as the performer's mental toughness score. The overall score from this profile, the Psychological Performance Inventory (PPI), could be subdivided into seven sub-scales (i.e. self-confidence, negative energy, attention control, visual and imagery control, motivational level, positive energy, and attitude control). Each sub-scale contained six items (scores ranging from 6 to 30), with high scores in all seven sub-scales linked to an individual's Ideal Performance State (IPS). This IPS was perceived to be mental toughness and was purported to exist for every performer and to be fundamentally the same for all athletes, across all sports (Loehr, 1982, 1986, 1995). In order for performers to achieve their IPS (become mentally tough), 12 ideal climate aspects needed to be in place: being physically relaxed, mentally calm, low in anxiety, energized, optimistic, enjoying, effortless, automatic, alert, mentally focused, self-control and in control. Loehr further proposed a six-stage 'Athletic Excellence Training Program' (AET) to develop these 12 aspects and to overcome any sub-scale deficiencies. Each stage of the AET built upon the previous stage, beginning with an increased self-awareness and greater understanding of the IPS (Stages 1–2), which allowed for better control of the IPS and more emotional control during competition (Stages 3–4), thereby increasing performance consistency and mental toughness (Stages 5–6).

In a similar manner, Goldberg (1998) published an applied text which claimed to provide the mental techniques and skills necessary to become mentally tough. He provided many anecdotal accounts of how his ten steps developed and enhanced seven characteristics (i.e. passion and fun, high self-confidence, concentration on the process of the performance, resilience, a sense of challenge, a non-thinking automatic quality and a sense of relaxation during the performance). When performers were considered 'at their best', they possessed all seven characteristics, but these characteristics were 'conspicuously absent when you're caught in the clutches of a slump' (Goldberg, 1998: 4). The ten steps began with ruling out non-mental causes (e.g. physical and technical), establishing self-control by keeping things in perspective, developing a championship focus (e.g. redirect focus to promote peak performance) and dealing with fears by facing up to them and defeating them (steps 1–5). Steps 6–9 included increased expectation of success through the use of positive self-talk and affirmation statements, developing positive images (via vivid, real-time imagery), setting slump-busting goals to increase motivation, and building self-confidence in order to become mentally tough. Mental toughness was described here as a 'psychic resilience or an ability to quickly rebound from setbacks and failures, fuelled by a dogged persistence and refusal to quit until the goal has been achieved' (Goldberg, 1998: 241–2). Finally, being mentally tough ensured that the performer did not experience future slumps (step 10).

These conceptualizations of mental toughness and its development (i.e. Bull et al., Goldberg, Hodge, Loehr, Watts) were all based on applied work with elite athletes and coaches and, while heuristically appealing, were not based on scientific research. The articles and texts omitted to reveal any systematic research programs, or provide any evidence base to describe the methods involved in defining, measuring and developing what they suggested to be mental toughness. In fact, no published research has been carried out to determine whether the methods Watts applied actually developed mental toughness or even contributed to his team's success, if Goldberg's ten steps were effective in developing mental toughness or preventing slumps in sport, and whether Loehr's AET program could develop mental toughness or even allow a performer's IPS to occur. Additionally, psychometric examinations have failed to support the PPI's hypothesized factor structure, reliability and validity (e.g. Golby et al., 2007). Finally, the vast list of psychological skills and techniques proposed to develop mental toughness in the above articles and texts led Jones et al. (2002) to conclude that virtually every desirable positive psychological characteristic has been labelled as mental toughness at one time or another. This multitude of descriptions has created confusion and increased the bewilderment of performers, coaches and practitioners pursuing ways to develop mental toughness (e.g. Goldberg, 1998). On a positive note though, while creating confusion and empirically unsubstantiated, the claims of these texts provided a catalyst for empirical interest into the elusive concept 'mental toughness'. The following section of this chapter reviews how researchers have addressed mental toughness in a scientific manner and sets up the knowledge base which investigations into mental toughness development were based.

Post-2002 mental toughness investigations

Since 2002, two distinct methodological approaches have been adopted in advancing the understanding of mental toughness. One approach integrated previous findings and adopted theories from health psychology to devise measures (e.g. PPI: Loehr, 1982; MT48: Clough et al., 2002) that could be used to investigate mental toughness and individual differences (Clough et al., 2002; Crust and Clough, 2005; Levy et al., 2006; Nicholls et al., 2008). The second approach developed qualitative research programs to overcome the previous ambiguity in the literature and advance the understanding of mental toughness (Bull et al., 2005; Coulter et al., 2010; Gucciardi et al., 2008; Jones et al., 2002, 2007; Thelwell et al., 2005).

Clough et al. (2002) adopted previous explanations of mental toughness (i.e. Loehr's definition), anecdotal evidence gathered from athletes, coaches and sport psychologists, and psychological theory examining hardiness (Kobasa, 1979; Kobasa et al., 1982) to conceptualize mental toughness as a similar construct to hardiness. Clough and colleagues differentiated their conceptualization of mental toughness from hardiness by adding confidence as a component. According to Clough et al. (2002), mentally tough performers are totally committed to achieving their goals, view negative experiences as challenges and natural catalysts for growth and development, and believe in their ability to deal with, control and overcome negative life experiences. Clough et al. (2002) further devised Mental Toughness-48 (MT48) which measures the 4Cs of mental toughness (i.e. commitment, control, challenge and confidence). While adopting a theoretical stance was viewed as a strength, Clough et al.'s (2002) conceptualization of mental toughness has received criticism for lacking scientific rigour, in that no information was presented regarding data collection and analysis of the views of practitioners, players and coaches (Connaughton and Hanton, 2009; Gucciardi et al., 2009a). Additionally, it was developed on existing theoretical frameworks of (hypothesized) related constructs (with no detailed rationale for drawing on hardiness theory), and research in non-sporting populations, raising questions

Table 8.1 General themes of mental toughness characteristics

	Sport General Studies		Sport-specific studies			
	Jones, Hanton, and Connaughton, 2002	Jones, Hanton, and Connaughton, 2007	Bull, Shambrook, James, and Brooks, 2005	Thelwell, Weston, and Greenlees, 2005	Gucciardi, Gordon, and Dimmock, 2008	Coulter and Gucciardi, 2010
	12 attributes identified in a broad mix of sports and gender	30 attributes identified in a broad mix of sports and gender	20 Global themes identified in English cricket (Male only)	10 attributes identified in Soccer (Male only)	32 characteristics identified in Australian-rules football (Male only)	14 characteristics identified in Soccer (Male only)
Belief	Self-belief	Belief	Self-belief Robust and resilient confidence	Total self-belief	Self-belief	Self-belief
Coping / handling pressure	Coping with competition-related pressure and anxiety	Handling pressure	Thriving on competition	Cope with and enjoy pressure	Handling pressure	Coping under pressure
Focus / commitment	Focus (performance and lifestyle)	Focus	Dedication and commitment Self-focus	Remain focused	Concentration and focus	Concentration and focus
Motivation	Desire and motivation	Motivation	Ability to set challenging targets		Motivation	Winning mentality and desire
Control	Controlling thoughts and feelings Controlling the environment	Controlling thoughts and feelings Controlling the environment	Ability to keep perspective	Control over emotions Control outside the performance environment		Control

				Emotional and sport intelligence	Performance
Sporting intelligence / knowledge		Self-reflection, Ability to exploit learning opportunities Good decision making	A sporting knowledge or intelligence	Emotional and sport intelligence	Performance Awareness Sport intelligence Risk taker Emotional intelligence
Tough / resilient attitude	Dealing with hardship Dealing with physical and emotional pain	A never give up determination and attitude Willing to take risks	Ability to react to situations positively Superior self-presentation	Tough attitude Resilience	Tough attitude Resilience
Personal Values		Ability to keep perspective and self-appraise Independence Competitiveness		Personal values Work ethic	Personal values Work ethic Competitive effort
Physical Toughness	Regulating performance Pushing yourself to the limit			Physical toughness	Physical toughness

as to the applicability of their model in sport (Gucciardi et al., 2009a). Other research has used the PPI (Loehr, 1986) to measure relationships between mental toughness and characteristics of performers (e.g. Golby et al., 2003). However, the PPI contains insufficient discriminative power and was found to only measure distinct attributes of mental skills (Golby et al., 2003; Middleton et al., 2004).

Researchers adopting the qualitative approach focused on understanding mental toughness in relation to defining it and identifying the key characteristics that encompass mental toughness, in various sports and from the perspectives of athletes, coaches, parents and sport psychologists (e.g. Bull et al., 2005; Coulter et al., 2010; Gucciardi et al., 2008; Jones et al., 2002, 2007; Thelwell et al., 2005). The majority of these research studies used Personal Construct Theory (Kelly, 1991) as a guiding framework to define and identify the characteristics of mental toughness. Two main definitions of mental toughness have been put forward within these qualitative studies (i.e. Gucciardi et al., 2008; Jones et al., 2002), providing an overall consensus and greater clarity of what mental toughness is (Connaughton and Hanton, 2009). Specifically, Jones et al. (2002: 209) defined mental toughness as:

> Having the natural or developed psychological edge that enables you to: Generally, cope better than your opponents with the many demands (competition, training, lifestyle) that sport places on a performer. Specifically, be more consistent and better than your opponents in remaining determined, focused, confident, and in control under pressure.

In a more recent study, Gucciardi et al. (2008: 218) defined mental toughness as 'a collection of values, attitudes, behaviors, and emotions that enable you to persevere and overcome any obstacle, adversity, or pressure experienced, but also to maintain concentration and motivation when things are going well to consistently achieve your goals'. Interestingly, both these definitions refer to mental toughness as a collection of interrelated protective and enabling factors that result in consistent superior performances, suggesting the construct of mental toughness can be defined in a similar manner, irrespective of sampling methods and sports investigated (Thelwell et al., 2005).

With regard to the make-up of mental toughness, these six studies appear, at first glance, to have identified a multitude of characteristics to explain the make-up of mental toughness (i.e. collectively, 118 characteristics were identified). Upon closer inspection however, the identified characteristics display a consistency in describing the make-up of mental toughness which can be broadly classified under nine major themes or categories: belief, coping/handling pressure, focus/ commitment, motivation, control, sporting intelligence/knowledge, tough/ resilient attitude, personal values, and physical toughness (presented in Table 8.1 on pp 140-1). In addition, despite the limitations and the very different approach to the study of mental toughness, the sub-scales of the MT48 (Clough et al., 2002) resemble many of the attributes identified by the six qualitative studies, particularly in relation to self-belief, pushing oneself to the limits, commitment to goals, and retaining emotional control (Crust, 2008).

While there is some consensus regarding key themes or features of mental toughness, there are many different views and scope for future research. To date research has investigated the key components of mental toughness in broad samples of sports and contexts (e.g. Jones et al., 2002, 2007) or specific to a given sport or context (Bull et al., 2005; Coulter et al., 2010; Gucciardi et al., 2008; Thelwell et al., 2005). Both these approaches are important in furthering the understanding of mental toughness – as Crust (2008: 578) suggested, 'the study of mental toughness is still evolving'. Connaughton and Hanton (2009) concluded that the specific wording of attributes and characteristics may be crucial and fundamental to understanding a performer's state of mental toughness, and it is this specific wording that distinguishes the characteristics of mental toughness from other psychological constructs. For example, Jones et al. (2002) purported that the distinguishing factors for belief and desire in the mental toughness process was the magnitude of these factors (i.e. unshakable and insatiable); while Bull et al. (2005) identified 'resilient confidence', suggesting that confidence alone was not sufficient to ensure mental toughness. Additionally, Bull et al. (2005) indicated that different forms of mental toughness may exist (e.g. pressure mental toughness, endurance mental toughness and mental toughness in circumstances of extreme physical danger), while Crust (2008) suggested that, in practical terms, the mental toughness requirement of a snooker player would not be the same as that of a rower, or a mountaineer. Therefore, questions regarding the situations that demand mental toughness, whether mental toughness may be different in varying circumstances and sports, or whether broadly applicable features of mental toughness are more or less important in specific sports, have yet to be answered.

While these six studies provided some practical assistance for coaches and performers trying to develop mental toughness (e.g. teaching mental skills and strategies to enhance and optimize focus, confidence and control in pressure situations), they provided more in terms of avenues for further investigation (Connaughton and Hanton, 2009). The following section of this chapter details how researchers have attempted to address the development of mental toughness based upon previous peer-reviewed research. Specifically, it discusses the findings of five recent studies that have investigated the development (and maintenance) of mental toughness (i.e. Bull et al., 2005; Connaughton et al., 2008b, 2010; Gucciardi et al., 2009e; Thelwell et al., 2010) and two studies that have proposed and attempted to evaluate the effectiveness of a mental toughness training program (Gucciardi et al., 2009c, 2009d).

Mental toughness development and maintenance

With an increased understanding of what mental toughness is, and findings supporting the contention that mental toughness could be acquired (e.g. Jones et al., 2002, 2007; Thelwell et al., 2005), researchers began to investigate the mechanisms by which mental toughness develops. The five qualitative studies that investigated mental toughness development adopted one of two approaches: a specific sport-context approach (Bull et al., 2005; Gucciardi et al., 2009; Thelwell et al., 2010), and a mixture of sports and contexts (Connaughton et al., 2008b, 2010).

Specific sport-context approach

Bull et al. (2005) was the first study to highlight factors perceived to influence the development of mental toughness. They focused on the single-sport population of cricket in order to gain insight into how mental toughness might be more systematically developed within young male England players, and to provide recommendations for coaches trying to improve performance at international level. Bull and colleagues presented 20 global themes, organized under four category locations, that were suggested as characteristics, as well as factors to aid the development of mental toughness and a 'winning mind'. The interaction of a performer's environment, character, attitudes and thinking (i.e. the four category locations) were proposed as a possible means of developing mental toughness. According to Bull et al. (2005), the environment was an important external variable and provided the foundation for mental toughness to develop. This environmental influence, covering the performer's upbringing and transition into an appropriate cricket environment, was described as impacting directly upon the individual, rather than the individual deliberately exposing themselves to specific environments. Tough character referred to personality characteristics that were believed to be essential components in mental toughness, while tough attitudes played a role in allowing the performer's tough character to be exploited effectively. The final location, tough thinking, represented the pinnacle of the mental toughness pyramid and related directly to desirable thought patterns around the competitive situation. Specifically, it referred to the ability of the player to translate the global character and attitude themes into the competition environment (i.e. players are able to make use of their abilities when it really matters). Finally, the robustness of the thought patterns in 'tough thinking' were suggested to be determined by the presence and stability of the environmental influence, tough character and tough attitude categories (i.e. the broader the base of the pyramid, the more stable tough thinking was).

The identification of such interactions were suggested as reference points for the development of mental toughness (Bull et al., 2005); however, it was not made clear which global themes related to the development of mental toughness. Additionally, no supportive data or explanations were presented as to how mental toughness actually developed (Connaughton and Hanton, 2009; Thelwell et al., 2010). For example, Bull et al. (2005) suggested the need to develop an environment within which players could be given maximum opportunity to benefit in terms of character, attitude and thinking. However, there was no identification or explanation as to what type of environment would develop this 'enduring mental toughness'. Equally, 'parental influence' was cited as an important influence in a performer's upbringing but questions still remain as to what kind of influence was beneficial, how this influence impacted upon mental toughness development or at what stage in a performer's career this influence had maximum impact (Connaughton et al., 2008a; Connaughton and Hanton, 2009).

Still with an emphasis on a specific sport, Thelwell et al. (2010) explored mental toughness development via interviews with elite British (*n* = 5) and American female gymnasts (*n* = 5). Based on the definition and attributes reported by Jones et al. (2002), findings suggested that mental toughness could be developed through a range of mechanisms and experiences. Fourteen mechanisms were identified and categorized under four general dimensions to represent how mental toughness developed in gymnastics: sport process (training, competition and club); sporting personnel (coach, teammates, competitors and sport psychologists); non-sporting personnel (parents, siblings and significant others); and environmental influences (training environment, family environment, modelling and country).

Sport process was perceived as central in the development of mental toughness and contained three categories (training, competition and club) which enabled athletes to experience a positive and motivational training environment, competition type scenarios during training, a determination to succeed, and assisted in overcoming problems with skills and recovering from injury. Additionally, the experience of adversity, pressure, successes and failures in competitions, and learning how to 'bounce back' from performance setbacks, had a positive impact on the development of mental toughness. Sporting personnel contributed to mental toughness development via four key sources (coach, teammates, competitors and sport psychologists). Specifically, the coach instilled hard work and discipline, individual training programs and mental skill development to encourage a mindset for success and enhance the athlete's belief and confidence. Teammates provided emotional support and encouragement, and the appropriate rivalries for a healthy competitive environment in training, whereas competitors provided targets to work towards. Both teammates and competitors were perceived to develop and enhance the appropriate coping and focusing skills necessary for a tough mindset in competition. Finally, sport psychologists provided a mindset for success, the appropriate appraisal of situations and performances through individual attention and support, and instruction on basic and advanced psychological skills and strategies.

Non-sport personnel (i.e. parents, siblings and significant others) encouraged rivalry, an internalized desire for success, and provided support 'with no pressure' in the form of feedback, guidance, motivation, the rationalization of thoughts and feelings and the reinforcement of beliefs (i.e. those held by the gymnasts). Environmental influences comprised four key mechanisms (training environment, family environment, modelling and country) and facilitated mental toughness development through instilling the characteristics necessary to succeed (e.g. hard work, discipline and determination). For example, the training environment instilled perseverance or a 'never give up attitude when faced with difficult situations', while a hard work ethic and an exceptionally high level of self-belief were influenced by the family environment. Modelling (e.g. competing and training with better gymnasts) heightened the gymnasts' determination to succeed, and provided the belief that they could one day progress to their role models' achievements. Finally, country influenced mental toughness development through the performer's perception of their country's expectation, reputation and past success, and the high cultural value placed on success in gymnastics. Country inspired the gymnasts and instilled a belief in their ability to continue the tradition of success.

Thelwell et al. (2010) also suggested that the development of mental toughness was influenced by both negative and positive experiences, and that certain sporting and lifestyle demands or experiences acted as developmental catalysts (e.g. moving home/location, parental separation/divorce, bereavements and school-related difficulties). Finally, some tentative differences emerged between American and British gymnasts in their explanation of mental toughness development. Within their overall training programs, the American gymnasts described the engagement with coaches and sport psychologists in learning basic and advanced psychological skills as a means of developing mental toughness.

This female-only study, examining British and American gymnasts, provided many conceptual and practical implications, and highlighted the importance of examining possible gender and cultural differences in mental toughness development. However, Thelwell et al. (2010) examined the development of mental toughness *en bloc,* and no details were provided as to how specific attributes of mental toughness were developed. Additionally, the question of whether mental toughness needed to be maintained was not addressed.

Gucciardi et al. (2009e) also explored mental toughness development from a single-sport perspective, but uniquely in relation to elite male coaches' perceptions of mental toughness development. They investigated how coaches might facilitate (and impede) the development of mental toughness, based on Gucciardi et al.'s (2008) 11 key mental toughness characteristics (i.e. self-belief, motivation, tough attitude, concentration and focus, resilience, handling pressure, personal values, work ethic, emotional and sport intelligence, and physical toughness). Findings revealed a multitude of strategies and mechanisms by which coaches positively (and negatively) influenced the development of 11 key mental toughness characteristics. Six overarching categories accounted for the perceived strategies, experiences and mechanisms employed by coaches to develop mental toughness: early childhood experiences, football experiences, coach–athlete relationship, coaching philosophy, training environment and specific strategies.

According to these coaches, development began with early childhood experiences, which played an important role in nurturing a 'generalized form' of mental toughness. Strategies and mechanisms employed in this category (early childhood experiences) included emotional support and encouraging the young performer to learn from exposure to a variety of experiences, adversities, challenges and pressures. Parents were perceived to possess the central role here; however, once engaged in youth football (football experiences), coaches replaced parents as the most influential source in developing mental toughness. Within football experiences, coaches aided development through the relationship they formed with the athlete (coach–athlete relationship), and their coaching philosophy, training environment and specific strategies they employed to transform 'generalized forms' of mental toughness into 'sport-specific forms'. A positive and supportive coach–athlete relationship facilitated the development of emotional intelligence (a key mental toughness characteristic), through instructive and socio-emotional components related to the affective and cognitive aspects of performance. Coaching philosophy was perceived to play a pivotal role in the development of seven characteristics: self-belief, personal values, work ethic, self-motivation, emotional and sport intelligence, and physical toughness. Coaches assisted the development of these characteristics by promoting a 'holistic development' of life skills (e.g. the athlete's social and personal development), in addition to the skills necessary for performance excellence (e.g. teaching an understanding of the game, how it is played and the many obstacles, challenges, and pressures facing players). Training environment was perceived as an important means of developing mental toughness through which coaches pushed performers to the limits of physical pain during drills, simulated competition pressure and anxiety, and enabled experiences of tough, adverse situations. Finally, specific strategies for developing three characteristics (i.e. personal values, concentration and focus, and able to handle pressure) involved the coach engaging and communicating with performers regarding the implications of training drills for competitive performances, viewing mistakes as opportunities to learn from, encouraging self-assessment of performances, providing positive reinforcement and exposing players to a variety of pressure simulations.

Gucciardi et al. (2009e) also highlighted the notion that coaches could hinder optimal development of mental toughness in their players. This was perceived to occur by: (a) coaches letting their desire for success overrule the need for individual player development, (b) focusing on and over-emphasizing players' weaknesses, (c) imposing low or unrealistic expectations and (d) fostering an 'easy' training environment by accepting excuses from players and not encouraging them to take personal responsibility for their actions. Coaches explained that these impeding strategies and mechanisms did not expose players to the experiences that were crucial for developing key facets of mental toughness (e.g. self-belief, sport intelligence, physical toughness and ability to handle pressure).

Given the central and influential role coaches possess in the psycho-social development of athletes (Wyllemann and Lavallee, 2004), Gucciardi et al. (2009e) provided several conceptual advances in the understanding of mental toughness development, and recommendations for possible educational and training programs. They identified strategies and mechanisms that coaches use in the mental toughness development process, and proposed that coaches could impact the development of mental toughness in a debilitative as well as a facilitative manner. In addition, the multitude of strategies and mechanisms impacted several key characteristics of mental toughness, rather than being a sole determinant of one key characteristic. However, Gucciardi et al.'s study was specific to mental toughness development in Australian-rules football and, as such, cannot be generalized to all sporting populations or towards a holistic understanding of mental toughness development. Gucciardi et al. (2009e) also investigated development in relation to Gucciardi et al.'s (2008) 11 key mental toughness characteristics, and not each of the 32 specific characteristics. Additionally, while the findings tentatively suggest that mental toughness is developed throughout a performer's career (i.e. a generalized form of mental toughness in early childhood experiences to sport-specific forms of mental toughness in football experiences), Gucciardi et al. did not investigate career-stage development of mental toughness (Bloom, 1985; Côté et al., 2003) or whether, once developed, mental toughness characteristics needed to be maintained. This holistic approach to understanding the development of mental toughness within career stages was adopted by Connaughton and colleagues (e.g. Connaughton et al., 2008b, 2010), and is discussed in the following section.

Mixture of sports and contexts approach

In a similar manner to Jones et al. (2002, 2007), and to provide implications that could be generalized to a variety of sporting populations, Connaughton and colleagues (e.g. Connaughton, et al., 2008b, 2010) addressed the development of mental toughness in broad samples of sports and contexts. Connaughton et al. (2008b) began the process of understanding mental toughness development and maintenance by investigating perceptions of mental toughness development in international performers. Based on Jones et al.'s (2002) definition and 12 attributes of mental toughness, they adopted procedures from previous development research (e.g. Durand-Bush and Salmela, 2002; Gould et al., 2002) and integrated an involvement progression questionnaire (i.e. careers phases: Bloom, 1985; Côté et al., 2003) to examine mental toughness development and maintenance.

Connaughton et al. (2008b) interviewed seven athletes, who possessed an intimate knowledge of the specific meanings of each of Jones et al.'s (2002) 12 attributes, to understand their perceptions of how mental toughness was developed and maintained in elite performers. Findings revealed a multitude of underlying mechanisms that operated in a combined, rather than independent manner, to facilitate the development of mental toughness (e.g. motivational climate, key individuals within an athlete's socialization network, sport-specific and life experiences, and a strong intrinsic motivation to succeed). Additionally, each of the 12 attributes were perceived to initially develop in one of three distinct career phases (early, middle and later years), with development of certain attributes (e.g. thriving on competition pressure) being dependent upon the previous acquisition of other attributes (e.g. an insatiable desire to succeed). During the early years the process of mental toughness development began with the development of three of the 12 attributes (i.e. an unshakable self-belief to achieve goals, unshakable belief that you possess unique qualities and abilities to make you better than opponents and an insatiable desire to succeed). Athletes reported development was influenced through effective leadership, taking advice from parents and coaches, and observing older, elite performers in a training and competitive environment. Parents were perceived as a source of knowledge, inspiration and encouragement that provided a powerful influence in the development of these three attributes. Additionally, effective leadership from coaches assisted in nurturing the correct motivational climate that was challenging, rewarding, enjoyable, and enabled the efficient mastery of relevant skills. Whilst these three attributes were further enhanced during the 'middle years', another five attributes began to develop (e.g. recovering from performance setbacks, overcoming physical and emotional pain, accepting competitive anxiety to be present and using it in a facilitative manner, thriving on competition pressure and regaining control following unexpected events). The middle years were more competitive and brought with them experiences of competitive anxiety, pressure and setbacks. Strategies and mechanisms by which these five attributes developed included: having a heightened determination to succeed (i.e. an attribute developed in the early years), competitive rivalry, rationalization of successes and failures, and receiving guidance and support from significant others (e.g. senior athletes, coaches, parents and non-sporting peers).

In the 'later years' the final four of Jones et al.'s (2002) 12 attributes developed (i.e. switching a sport focus on and off as required, remaining fully focused on the task at hand in the face of competition-specific distractions, not being adversely affected by others' good and bad performances, and remaining fully focused in the face of personal life distractions). The eight attributes developed in the 'early' and 'middle' years were also enhanced in the later years, with strategies and mechanisms involving experience of elite level competition, simulation training and the extraction of positive experiences and rationalization of setbacks, via reflective practice. Connaughton et al. (2008b) reported mental toughness to be at its strongest after competing at the highest level for around three years, and that once acquired, mental toughness needed to be maintained with effort or it would diminish. Three key underlying mechanisms were reported to assist the maintenance of mental toughness, an insatiable desire and motivation to succeed, a strong social support network and the use of basic and advanced psychological skills. Connaughton et al. (2008b) also identified perceived critical incidents (e.g. disruptions at school, loss of a peer, parental divorce) which appeared to act as catalysts in developing mental toughness throughout all three developmental stages of the performer's career.

While Connaughton et al. (2008b) provided a detailed insight into the development of mental toughness over a performer's entire career, their investigation was limited, in that it was based on elite performers' perceptions of Jones et al.'s (2002) definition and 12 attributes of mental toughness, and they did not investigate to what level or extent attributes developed within each career phase. Jones et al. (2007) proposed a more detailed make-up of mental toughness (i.e. a framework containing 30 attributes categorized under 13 subcomponents and 4 overall dimensions), and Connaughton and Hanton (2009) suggested that using this framework, coupled with a super-elite sample of performers, coaches and sport psychologists, could provide a more comprehensive insight into the development and maintenance of mental toughness.

In response to this suggestion, Connaughton et al. (2010) explored the development and maintenance of mental toughness based on (a) Jones et al.'s (2007) framework of mental toughness and outcome component criteria (e.g.

Olympic or world champion or coach/sport psychologist to such performers), and (b) the findings and procedures adopted in Connaughton et al. (2008b). Connaughton et al. (2010) also investigated mental toughness development and maintenance from the separate perspectives of performers, coaches, and sport psychologists. The Olympic/world champions' perceptions addressed the underlying processes involved in the development and maintenance of mental toughness throughout four pre-determined career phases (adapted from Bloom, 1985; Côté et al., 2003), while the second part of the study sought to understand coaches' and sport psychologists' views and strategies on the development and maintenance of mental toughness in performers.

Findings from the performers' perceptions revealed a multitude of experiences, strategies and mechanisms that combined to influence the development and maintenance of mental toughness throughout four distinct career phases: (a) initial involvement to intermediate level, (b) intermediate to elite level, (c) elite to Olympic/world champion status and (d) maintenance. Additionally, transition between each career phase was associated with significant events (e.g. changing clubs, working with a new coach, making the national team or winning a major event). Development began during the initial involvement to intermediate-level career phase, with the acquisition of four of the 13 subcomponents, two within the attitude/mindset dimension (i.e. belief and focus) and two of the three subcomponents within the training dimension (i.e. using long-term goals as the source of motivation and pushing yourself to the limit). Development in this career phase was influenced by the environment, parents and coaches, and included being competitive in training, and engaging in activities for enjoyment, socialization and skill mastery (Connaughton et al., 2008b; Gucciardi et al., 2009e). Specifically, focus and a belief of sporting superiority were developed by performers deriving a sense of achievement from learning skills more quickly and to a higher level than their peers, thus increasing work ethic and motivation to strive to be better in practice.

During the intermediate- to elite-level career phase, ranging in length from three to six years, the remaining nine subcomponents developed: controlling the environment (training dimension); belief, staying focused, regulating performance, controlling the environment, handling pressure, and awareness and control of thoughts and feelings (competition dimension); and handling success, and handling failure (post-competition dimension). Influences included a disciplined and structured training environment, learning from role models, and doing what was necessary in order to achieve success in training. However, Connaughton et al. (2010) suggested that these nine subcomponents did not all develop to their highest perceived levels during this career phase. These 'peak' developments were reported to occur for all 13 subcomponents in the elite to Olympic/world champion status phase which lasted between two and four years. Development was influenced by a variety of mechanisms and experiences, including: experience of international competition, an intense desire to win and upstage world-class performers, a wide-ranging social support network, the use of mental skills, attaining the correct balance in life, gaining knowledge from respected individuals (e.g. coaches, competitors, sport psychologists) and reflective practice. For example, the experience of international competition empowered performers to become self-aware, implement change and cope more positively in future competitions (Ghaye and Ghaye, 1998; Hanton et al., 2007). Interestingly, performance failures in the elite to Olympic/world champion status career phase caused temporary reductions in mental toughness, but were attributed to overall mental toughness development by assisting in creating the awareness, balance and control to 'love the pressure' of high-level competition. Finally, becoming an Olympic or world champion coincided with the end of the elite to Olympic/world champion status phase, and the beginning of the maintenance years.

In support of Connaughton et al. (2008b), Connaughton et al. (2010) suggested that the experience of (perceived) positive and negative critical incidents were found to act as catalysts in cultivating mental toughness throughout all three development phases. Positive critical incidents (e.g. the recognition of talent by respected individuals) were perceived to enhance belief and motivation, by providing the encouragement and inspiration that goals and potential were achievable. Negative critical incidents (e.g. being involved in a car accident) were suggested to result in a reappraisal of priorities and increased focus on performance goals. Finally, Connaughton et al. (2010) suggested that, once acquired, it was necessary to continue to work on maintaining mental toughness or it would diminish. Maintenance was achieved through the use of mental skills and strategies, strong sporting and non-sporting support networks, and preserving the correct balance with life and sport.

The second part of the Connaughton et al.'s (2010) research results presented coaches' and sport psychologists' unique and distinctive insights into how mental toughness developed and was maintained in performers. A combination of several strategies and experiences were believed to develop mental toughness over a number of years. Specifically, experiences, strategies and mechanisms initiated the development of five of the 13 subcomponents, two within the attitude/mindset dimension (i.e. belief and focus) and three within the training dimension (i.e. using long-term goals as the source of motivation, pushing yourself to the limit and controlling the environment). Examples included: trial and error, expert instruction, building a positive training atmosphere, challenging performers and encouraging competitiveness in training, effective communication, achieving successes in training and the use of positive imagery. Once acquired, these five subcomponents were used and adapted in conjunction with specific strategies and mechanisms to influence the development of the remaining eight subcomponents, six in the competition dimension (i.e. belief, controlling the environment, regulating performance, handling pressure, staying focused, and awareness and control of thoughts and feelings) and two in the post-competition dimension (i.e. handling success, and handling failure). Strategies and mechanisms employed included involving the performer in the planning process, educating performers (e.g. how to handle pressure situations), simulating competitive pressures and experiences, actual competitive experience and engaging in post-race or game analysis. According to Connaughton et al. (2010), coaches and sport psychologists viewed positive and negative critical incidents as important factors and catalysts in a performer's development process, and that mental toughness needed to be maintained. Effective communication, the establishment of sporting (e.g. coaches, team mates, sport psychologists) and non-sporting (e.g. friends, parents) support networks, education regarding preserving the correct balance of life and sport, the use of a variety of mental skills and strategies, and the act of winning an Olympic or world title were suggested to protect or maintain high levels of mental toughness.

Overall, Connaughton et al. (2010) revealed that mental toughness developed through three main phases of an athlete's sporting career, with a variety of individuals (parents, coaches, family, friends: Bull et al., 2005; Gucciardi et al., 2009e) and factors (environment, critical incidents: Bull et al., 2005; Connaughton et al., 2008b; Thelwell et al., 2010) influencing this process, directly and indirectly. Parents and coaches appear to have a crucial role in the development of mental toughness in young performers, while coaches, sport psychologists and older, more experienced performers become the most influential source in developing mental toughness in subsequent years (Gucciardi et al., 2009e). Once acquired, high levels of mental toughness can be maintained through the use of mental skills and strategies, including: goal setting, mental imagery, self-talk, cognitive reconstruction, pre-performance and pre-race routines, simulation training and a social support network. Connaughton et al. (2010) also revealed that both development and maintenance of mental toughness occurred in the specific dimensional order of attitude/mindset, training, competition and post-competition. However, similar to Gucciardi et al., Connaughton et al. (2010) only investigated the development and maintenance of mental toughness in relation to Jones et al.'s (2007) 13 subcomponents, and not each of the 30 specific attributes. Finally, the findings of Connaughton et al. (2010) highlight the need to explore whether specific psychological skills training programs can be effective in developing and enhancing mental toughness. The next section of the review focuses on two intervention studies (i.e. Gucciardi et al., 2009c, 2009d) that evaluated the effectiveness of a mental toughness training program.[1]

Mental toughness training program

Based on the findings of Gucciardi et al. (2008), Gucciardi et al. (2009b) set about to develop and validate a measure of mental toughness in Australian-rules football. The resultant inventory, the Australian football Mental Toughness Inventory (AfMTI), contains 24 items measuring four components of mental toughness: thrive through challenge, sport awareness, tough attitude and desire success. Using the AfMTI, Gucciardi et al. (2009c) evaluated a mental toughness training program for youth-aged Australian-rules footballers and followed up this quantitative study with a qualitative investigation to enhance the understanding of the training intervention and its impact on mental toughness development (Gucciardi et al., 2009d).

Gucciardi et al. (2009c) investigated the effectiveness of two different psychological skills training packages in developing and enhancing mental toughness among Australian footballers. Youth-aged footballers (under 15s) categorized within the specializing years (Côté, 1999) were targeted, and put into one of three groups: (a) a mental toughness training group (MTT), (b) a general psychological skills training program group (PST), and (c) a control group. The AfMTI (Gucciardi et al., 2009b) was used to measure four components of mental toughness (i.e. thrive through challenge, sport awareness, tough attitude and desire success) from the multiple source ratings of players, parents and coaches both pre- and post-intervention (approximately six months apart).

The MTT program comprised psycho-educational and experiential activities that directly and indirectly targeted Gucciardi et al.'s (2008) 11 key mental toughness characteristics. The PST incorporated self-regulation, arousal regulation, mental rehearsal, attentional control, self-efficacy and ideal performance state, while the control group did not receive any psychological support during the intervention. Increases in thrive through challenge and tough attitude were significantly greater for both the MTT and PST groups, compared to the control group. However, no significant differences were found between the MTT and PST groups on any of the four components, or for all three groups in relation to sport awareness and desire success. The lack of change in sport awareness and desire success was attributed to the possibility that the MTT intervention needed more time to develop and solidify (e.g. youth-aged footballers were not particularly focused on achieving success at this stage in their sporting careers: Gucciardi et al., 2009c). However, neither program (i.e. MTT or PST) was more effective in enhancing mental toughness, with Gucciardi et al. (2009c) suggesting that common components of both programs (i.e. self-regulation, arousal regulation, mental rehearsal, attentional control, self-efficacy and ideal performance state) may have been responsible for these positive effects in the AfMTI scores.

To provide greater detail on the effectiveness of the MTT program, Gucciardi et al. (2009d) interviewed the MTT participants (10 players, 10 parents, 3 coaches) regarding their thoughts on the goals, procedures and findings of the intervention. Findings revealed that the processes of enhanced self-awareness, techniques for self-monitoring and self-regulation, and multiple-perspective discussions (e.g. influential individuals in a performer's socialization network) contributed to the enhancement of mental toughness. Specifically, the benefits of the MTT intervention enhanced mental toughness by: improving the players' ability to prepare mentally and physically for both training and games; increasing team communication and confidence regarding individual and team goals; enabling greater personal responsibility and accountability; enhancing the facilitation of personal growth through experiences of, and learning from, obstacles and challenges; and finally, enhancing the ability to identify and understand how skills acquired in sport could be transferred and applied to life.

In conclusion, Gucciardi et al. (2009c, 2009d) provided support for the contention that psychological skills training programs assist in developing and enhancing mental toughness (Connaughton et al., 2010; Thelwell et al., 2010). However, despite the valuable findings and practical implications of these studies (i.e. Gucciardi et al., 2009c, 2009d), further research is required to ascertain the most effective content and method of delivering mental toughness training programs. In particular, findings and implications are specific to mental toughness development in youth-aged Australian football. Equally, the duration of the intervention programs (i.e. two weeks), the absence of follow-up assessments, and the multimodal nature of the interventions made it difficult to determine the possible long-term benefits of both programs, and limited the identification of the specific aspects that contributed to mental toughness development. Therefore, Gucciardi et al. (2009c, 2009d) should be viewed as a starting point to understanding how psychological skills and training programs can be implemented to develop and enhance mental toughness in performers.

Practical implications and future research directions

The final section of this chapter discusses the practical implications and future directions that have emerged from these recent development and intervention studies. It also provides the reader with some direction with regard to measurement issues, and intervention strategies to develop, enhance and maintain mental toughness.

Practical implications

Research suggests that mental toughness is a multidimensional construct made up of a number of key components that are perceived to develop over a performer's sporting career (Connaughton et al., 2008b, 2010; Gucciardi et al., 2009e; Thelwell et al., 2010). The recent empirical contributions regarding the understanding, processes and mechanisms of mental toughness development and maintenance offer some evidence-based practical advice to performers, coaches and sport psychologists. This knowledge is important for developing coach education and training programs that can facilitate the development and enhancement of mental toughness in performers (Gucciardi et al., 2009e). To begin with, key stakeholders (i.e. athletes, coaches, parents, sport psychologists) should be educated with regard to what the characteristics of mental toughness are, and what sources and mechanisms influence (facilitate and hinder) its development and maintenance (Connaughton et al., 2010; Gucciardi et al., 2009e).

In the early stages of performers' careers, young athletes should be encouraged to engage in sporting activities as a means of skill mastery, enjoyment, socialization and to develop a sense of discipline and work ethic. Every effort should be made to educate performers (via parents, coaches and sport psychologists) regarding the developmental requirements that are perceived to operate in the mental toughness development process. Additionally, exposure to a variety of situations and environments could assist performers to acquire the experiences necessary to develop mental toughness (Connaughton et al., 2010; Thelwell et al., 2010). Parents and coaches appear to have the central roles in creating motivational environments for a generalized form (Gucciardi et al., 2009e) or foundation attributes of mental toughness to develop (Bull et al., 2005; Connaughton et al., 2008b). Specifically, parents were considered the primary influence in a performer's upbringing, instilling hard work and discipline, providing encouragement and support, and teaching mental skills (Bull et al., 2005; Connaughton et al., 2010). Governing bodies need to consider the performers' early childhood experiences, and the role of parents in influencing mental toughness development when devising national strategies and programs.

Once engaged in a more disciplined and structured training regime (e.g. the middle years: Connaughton et al., 2008b; or intermediate to elite level: Connaughton et al., 2010), coaches appear to assume the major role in developing mental toughness (Gucciardi et al., 2009e). Coaches can facilitate the development of mental toughness by creating training environments that continuously challenge and expose players to pressures and adversities, and provide individual training programs and mental skill development that encourage a mindset for success and build a belief of superiority (Gucciardi et al., 2009e; Thelwell et al., 2010). Performers can benefit from observing and learning from knowledgeable role models, such as older, elite performers (Connaughton et al., 2010). Coaches should also adopt a coaching philosophy that emphasizes a 'holistic' development of sporting and life skills, develop a positive and supportive relationship with their performers, and avoid letting their desire (i.e. coach's desire) for success overrule the needs of the individuals' development (Gucciardi et al., 2009e). In addition, Gucciardi et al. (2009e) suggested that mental toughness education programs (i.e. for coaches) should include mediated (e.g. coaching classes), unmediated (e.g. watching other coaches, mentoring) and internal (e.g. reflecting on their own coaching) learning contexts (Werthner and Trudel, 2006).

In the final developmental years (i.e. later years: Connaughton et al., 2008b; elite to Olympic/world champion status: Connaughton et al., 2010), sport psychology support can facilitate the development of mental toughness to 'its highest perceived levels' through advice and education regarding: strategies to achieve success, the recognition and control of inappropriate thoughts, and strategies to handle competitive pressure (Connaughton et al., 2010). Connaughton et al. (2010) further suggested that gaining knowledge from respected athletes (e.g. mentoring talented youth performers with older elite performers) and the experience of international competition enhanced mental toughness. This mentoring and exposure to elite environments can facilitate the necessary experiences of competitive pressure at world level, allowing performers to become more familiar with and cope more positively in future competitions. Therefore, sporting associations need to recognize the role that vicarious learning plays in the development of mental toughness, and facilitate opportunities for youth performers to compete at international level (Connaughton et al., 2010; Thelwell et al., 2010). Additionally, reflective practice was highlighted as valuable means of enhancing mental toughness (Connaughton et al., 2008b, 2010; Thelwell et al., 2010). Being involved in the process of reflection can enable familiarization of competition-specific symptoms and empower individuals to become self-aware, implement change and cope more positively (Ghaye and Ghaye, 1998; Hanton et al., 2007). Therefore, coaches and performers should include post-performance analysis as part of their structured training programs in order to develop mental toughness.

Once developed, mental toughness must be maintained or it will decrease (Connaughton et al., 2010). Maintenance appears to be influenced by an intense desire to win and upstage world-class performers, strong sporting (e.g. coaches, team mates, sport psychologists) and non-sporting (e.g. friends, parents) support networks, fostering the correct life–sport balance, reflective practice and the use of psychological skills and strategies (Connaughton et al., 2008b; Thelwell et al., 2010). In addition, new, challenging goals need to be set to maintain mental toughness, once specific goals (e.g. Olympic title) have been achieved. Coaches and performers need to be cognizant of sustaining the performer's focus and strong desire to succeed when setting goals for Olympic and world champions (Connaughton et al., 2010). Interestingly, the importance of learning basic and advanced psychological skills was highlighted as important to the enhancement and maintenance of mental toughness (Connaughton et al., 2008b, 2010).

Mental toughness develops over a performer's career and must be continually maintained; therefore, performers should be encouraged to take part in PST programs that can assist in developing, enhancing and maintaining key components of mental toughness. Gucciardi et al. (2009c) found that psychological skills such as self-regulation, arousal regulation, mental rehearsal, attentional control, self-efficacy and ideal performance state were found to have a positive impact on the development and enhancement of mental toughness. As a result, intervention and general mental toughness training programs should target a performer's ability to prepare mentally and physically (training and competition), increase communication and confidence regarding goals, and empower and facilitate personal growth through experiences of obstacles and challenges (Gucciardi et al., 2009c). Connaughton et al. (2010) suggested that general mental toughness training programs should concentrate on skill mastery, enjoyment and socialization, a disciplined and structured training regime, building a belief of superiority, expert coaching and promoting successes in training. Performers should also receive psychological support from an early age (Connaughton et al., 2010; Gucciardi et al., 2009e), as young performers are considered more suited to PST than older athletes (Gould, 1983; Vealey, 1988). Early introduction to PST would also allow for more advanced psychological skills and strategies to be learned in later years. Such early PST exposure would clearly be of benefit to performers developing and maintaining mental toughness (Connaughton et al., 2010; Thelwell et al., 2010). Additionally, Gucciardi et al. (2009c) provided tentative support for the contention that PST programs may assist in making up for the absence of facilitative environments to develop mental toughness during the early and middle years of their sporting careers.

While environmental factors, personnel and PST have a clear role in the development and maintenance of mental toughness, a number of other factors also contribute to this process. The experience of life events or perceived critical incidents (positive and negative) appear to act as catalysts in cultivating mental toughness (Connaughton et al., 2010; Thelwell et al., 2010). Positive critical incidents (e.g. the recognition of talent by respected individuals) enhanced mental toughness by increasing belief and motivation (Connaughton et al., 2010), whereas negative critical incidents (e.g. parental divorce) increased focus and prioritization of goals, and developed the necessary perspective on life and sport (Connaughton et al., 2008b; Thelwell et al., 2010). Although many of these incidents may be outside the control of the coach and sport psychologist (and even the performer), being able to recognize them, and knowing how to handle such experiences (in particular, the negative life experiences) would be of great use to coaches and sport psychologists trying to facilitate the enhancement of mental toughness. Success was also a factor that contributed to the development and maintenance of mental toughness (Connaughton et al., 2008b, 2010). Skill mastery, beating your opponents in training and competitions, and winning competitions or games were highlighted as essential in developing and enhancing mental toughness (Connaughton et al., 2008b, 2010). With regard to maintenance, Connaughton et al. (2010) reported that winning an Olympic or world title protected high levels of mental toughness for up to two years. Coaches should therefore encourage performers to strive to be successful in training (e.g. mastering skills and successful completion of training sets) and competition in order to enhance motivation, work ethic and further strengthen mental toughness components (e.g. belief).

Overall, the findings of the mental toughness development literature provide some guidance on the implementation of training programs to develop and maintain mental toughness. Specifically, educating performers, expert coaching, providing exposure to a variety of situations, experiences and environments, and using basic and advanced psychological skills can assist performers to develop and maintain mental toughness. While these studies have increased the conceptual and practical understanding of mental toughness development and maintenance, there are many issues that require attention for future research.

Future directions

With regard to understanding mental toughness development and maintenance, many of the participants within the current development studies may not have possessed all of the key components (or high levels) of mental toughness; that is, an objective measure of mental toughness was not employed to select participants. The lack of objective sampling may have had a negative impact on the degree to which they were able to comment on mental toughness development. Equally, the five mental toughness development studies reviewed relied on participants' retrospective accounts which could have been influenced by the individual's recall of that past experience (i.e. objective and subjective performance outcomes: Ross and Conway, 1986). Consequently, it is important that future research includes alternative methods of data collection (Gucciardi et al., 2009e). However, the number of common themes, experiences and strategies identified in the mental toughness developmental literature offer preliminary support for the validity of findings in relation to the development and maintenance of mental toughness. Another research concern relates to the lack of focus on the development of specific attributes within mental toughness. Apart from Connaughton et al. (2008b), the developmental studies only investigated mental toughness development *en bloc* (Thelwell et al., 2010) or in relation to 13 subcomponents (i.e. Connaughton et al., 2010) and 11 key characteristics of mental toughness (i.e. Gucciardi et al., 2009e). Future research should explore the development and maintenance of all 32 (Gucciardi et al., 2008) and 30 (Jones et al., 2007) specific attributes of mental toughness.

Overall, there is an overriding need to develop a measure of mental toughness that can be implemented in multi and singular sports contexts (Connaughton and Hanton, 2009). Recent advancements have been made with regard to single sport-specific measures of mental toughness, in Australian football (i.e. AfMTI: Gucciardi et al., 2009b), and cricket (i.e. CMTI: Gucciardi and Gordon, 2009); however, a conceptually accurate and psychometrically valid and reliable measure that is applicable in a broad variety of sports is required. This measure would allow for cross-sectional group comparisons, and to explore mental toughness development and maintenance in performers who could be objectively identified as lacking in mental toughness. Equally, talented but mentally weak performers could be identified to see what subcomponents or attributes require attention, and specific tailored intervention programs could then be designed and implemented to facilitate the development and enhancement of mental toughness. Furthermore, a measure would allow practitioners to assess the effectiveness of their mental toughness interventions and training programs. Finally, the area of perceived critical incidents or life events requires investigation. Future research should explore: what constitutes a critical incident, what different types of critical incidents exist and how they create the psychological climates that are necessary for developing mental toughness (Connaughton and Hanton, 2009).

Conclusion

In this chapter, mental toughness was identified as an important psychological construct and its development and maintenance worthy of investigation. Mental toughness development has been addressed from various perspectives (e.g. performers, coaches and sport psychologists), approaches (e.g. specific sport/ context and a mixture of sports and contexts) and based on the findings of a number of studies (e.g. Gucciardi et al., 2008; Jones et al., 2002, 2007). Despite these differences, common themes, experiences and strategies have emerged.

All five development studies (i.e. Bull et al., 2005; Connaughton et al., 2008b, 2010; Gucciardi et al., 2009e; Thelwell et al., 2010) suggested that a multitude of strategies and mechanisms impacted on the development of mental toughness in a combined, rather than independent manner. Connaughton et al. (2008b and 2010) further reported that mental toughness developed over three stages of a performer's career and, once acquired, needed to be maintained with effort or it would diminish. The environment in which the performer lives, trains and competes was found to affect the development of mental toughness. According to Bull et al. (2005), the environment (e.g. exposure to foreign cricket) provided the foundation for mental toughness to develop, whereas the training environment (e.g.

disciplined and structured) was perceived as an important means of developing specific components of mental toughness (Connaughton et al., 2010; Gucciardi et al., 2009e). Several individuals within an athlete's socialization network were also identified as important sources in the development and maintenance of mental toughness. Gucciardi et al. (2009e) suggested parents as possessing a central role in nurturing a 'generalized form' of mental toughness, whereas Thelwell et al. (2010) identified coaches as contributors to mental toughness development by instilling hard work, discipline and a never-give-up attitude. A positive and supportive coach–athlete relationship was suggested to facilitate the development of emotional intelligence (a key mental toughness characteristic), via affective and cognitive aspects of performance (Gucciardi et al., 2009e). Additionally, receiving guidance and support from significant others (e.g. senior athletes, sporting and non-sporting peers) increased performers' determination to succeed (Connaughton et al., 2010; Thelwell et al., 2010), and was perceived to assist in the development of a number of mental toughness attributes (Connaughton et al., 2008b). Sporting experiences and life events were deemed important in the development of mental toughness. Thelwell et al. (2010) purported that sporting experiences of adversity, pressure, and successes and failures in competitions had a positive impact on the development of mental toughness. Furthermore, negative (e.g. moving home/location, parental separation/divorce, bereavements, and school-related difficulties) and positive (e.g. international selection, the recognition of talent by respected individuals and beating respected opponents) life events acted as catalysts in enhancing mental toughness during all stages of a performer's developmental career (Connaughton et al., 2008b, 2010; Thelwell et al., 2010). Finally, psychological skills and strategies were identified as playing a vital role in developing and maintaining mental toughness. Thelwell et al. (2010) and Connaughton et al. (2010) suggested that performers engaged with coaches and sport psychologists in learning psychological skills and strategies as a means of developing mental toughness, whereas Connaughton et al. (2008b, 2010) reported the use of basic and advanced psychological skills to maintain mental toughness.

The development studies reviewed in this chapter have provided a greater conceptual understanding of mental toughness development, and collectively assist in explaining the processes and mechanisms involved in its development and maintenance. However, many questions regarding mental toughness development remain and it is hoped that this chapter will stimulate further research on the mental toughness development process.

Note

1 Gucciardi et al. (2009c) also addressed resilience and flow; however, this chapter only focuses on findings related to mental toughness.

References

Alderman, R. B. (1974) *Psychological Behavior in Sport,* Toronto: W. B. Saunders Co.

Bloom, B. (1985) *Developing Talent in Young People,* New York: Ballantine.

Bull, S. J., Albinson, J. G., and Shambrook, C. J. (1996) *The Mental Game Plan: Getting Psyched for Sport,* Eastbourne: Sports Dynamics.

Bull, S. J., Shambrook, C. J., James, W., and Brooks, J. E. (2005) 'Towards an understanding of mental toughness in elite English cricketers', *Journal of Applied Sport Psychology,* 17, 209–27.

Cattell, R. B., Blewett, D. B., and Beloff, J. R. (1955) 'The inheritance of personality: a multiple variance analysis determination of approximate nature–nurture ratios for primary personality factors in Q data', *American Journal of Human Genetics,* 7, 122–46.

Clough, P. J., Earle, K., and Sewell, D. (2002) 'Mental toughness: The concept and its measurement', in I. Cockerill (ed.), *Solutions in Sport Psychology,* London: Thomson, pp. 32–43.

Connaughton, D., and Hanton, S. (2009) 'Mental toughness in sport: Conceptual and practical issues', in S. D. Mellalieu and S. Hanton (eds), *Advances in Applied Sport Psychology: A Review,* London: Routledge, pp. 317–46.

Connaughton, D., Hanton, S., Jones, G., and Wadey, R. (2008a) 'Mental toughness research: Key issues in this area', *International Journal of Sport Psychology,* 39, 192–204.

Connaughton, D., Wadey, R., Hanton, S., and Jones, G. (2008b) 'The development and maintenance of mental toughness: Perceptions of elite performers', *Journal of Sports Sciences,* 26, 83–95.

Connaughton, D., Hanton, S., and Jones, G. (2010) 'The development and maintenance of mental toughness in the world's best performers', *The Sport Psychologist,* 24, 168–93.

Côté, J. (1999) 'The influence of the family in the development of talent in sport', *The Sport Psychologist,* 13, 395–417.

Côté, J., Baker, J., and Abernethy, B. (2003) 'From play to practice: A developmental framework for the acquisition of expertise in team sports', in J. L. Starkes and K. A. Ericsson (eds), *Expert Performance in Sports: Advances in Research on Sport Expertise,* Champaign, IL: Human Kinetics, pp. 89–115.

Coulter, T., and Gucciardi, D. F. (2010) 'Understanding mental toughness in Australian soccer: Perceptions of players, parents, and coaches', *Journal of Sports Science,* 28, 699–716.

Crust, L., and Clough, P. J. (2005) 'Relationship between mental toughness and physical endurance', *Perceptual and Motor Skills,* 100, 192–4.

Crust, L. (2008) 'A review and conceptual re-examination of mental toughness: Implications for future researchers', *Personality and Individual Differences,* 45, 576–83.

Durand-Bush, N., and Salmela, J. (2002) 'The development and maintenance of expert athletic performance: Perceptions of world and Olympic champions', *Journal of Applied Sport Psychology,* 14, 154–71.

Favret, B., and Benzel, D. (1997) *Complete Guide to Water Skiing,* Champaign, IL: Human Kinetics.

Fourie, S., and Potgeiter, J. R. (2001) 'The nature of mental toughness in sport', *South African Journal for Research in Sport, Physical Education and Recreation,* 23, 63–72.

Ghaye, A., and Ghaye, K. (1998) *Teaching and Learning through Critical Reflective Practice,* London: David Fulton Publishers.

Gibson, A. (1998) *Mental Toughness,* New York: Vantage Press.

Golby, J., Sheard, M., and Lavallee, D. (2003) 'A cognitive-behavioural analysis of mental toughness in national rugby league football teams', *Perceptual and Motor Skills,* 96, 455–62.

Golby, J., Sheard, M., and van Wersch, A. (2007) 'Evaluating the factor structure of the psychological performance inventory', *Perceptual and Motor Skills*, 105, 309–25.

Goldberg, A. S. (1998) *Sports Slump Busting: 10 Steps to Mental Toughness and Peak Performance,* Champaign, IL: Human Kinetics.

Gould, D. (1983) 'Developing psychological skills in young athletes', *Coaching Science Update*, 4–13.

Gould, D., Dieffenbach, K., and Moffett, A. (2002) 'Psychological characteristics and their development of Olympic champions', *Journal of Applied Sport Psychology*, 14, 172–204.

Gould, D., Hodge, K., Peterson, K., and Petlichkoff, L. (1987) 'Psychological foundations of coaching: similarities and differences among intercollegiate wrestling coaches', *The Sport Psychologist*, 1, 293–308.

Gucciardi, D. F., and Gordon, S. (2009) 'Development and preliminary validation of the Cricket Mental Toughness Inventory', *Journal of Sports Science*, 27, 1293–1310.

Gucciardi, D. F., Gordon, D. F., and Dimmock, J. A (2008) 'Towards an understanding of mental toughness in Australian football', *Journal of Applied Sport Psychology,* 20, 261–81.

Gucciardi, D. F., Gordon, S., and Dimmock, J. A. (2009a) 'Advancing mental toughness research and theory using personal construct psychology', *International Review of Sport and Exercise Psychology*, 2, 54–72.

Gucciardi, D. F., Gordon, D. F., and Dimmock, J. A (2009b) 'Development and preliminary validation of a mental toughness inventory for Australian football', *Psychology of Sport and Exercise,* 20, 261–81.

Gucciardi, D. F., Gordon, S., and Dimmock, J. A. (2009c) 'Evaluation of a mental toughness training program for youth aged Australian footballers: I. A quantitative analysis', *Journal of Applied Sport Psychology*, 21, 307–23.

Gucciardi, D. F., Gordon, S., and Dimmock, J. A. (2009d) 'Evaluation of a mental toughness training program for youth aged Australian footballers: II. A qualitative analysis', *Journal of Applied Sport Psychology*, 21, 324–39.

Gucciardi, D. F., Gordon, S., Dimmock, J. A., and Mallett, C. J. (2009e) 'Understanding the coach's role in the development of mental toughness: Perspectives of elite Australian football coaches', *Journal of Sports Sciences*, 27, 1483–96.

Hanton, S., and Jones, G. (1999) 'The acquisition and development of cognitive skills and strategies I. Making the butterflies fly in formation', *The Sport Psychologist*, 13, 1–21.

Hanton, S., Cropley, B., Miles, A., Mellalieu, S. D., and Neil, R. (2007) 'Experience in sport and its relationship with competitive anxiety', *International Journal of Sport and Exercise Psychology,* 5, 28–53.

Hodge, K. (1994) 'Mental toughness in sport: lessons for life. The pursuit of personal excellence', *Journal of Physical Education New Zealand*, 27, 12–16.

Jones, C. M. (1982) 'Mental toughness', *World Bowls* (Nov.), 30–1.

Jones, G., Hanton, S., and Connaughton, D. (2002) 'What is this thing called mental toughness? An investigation with elite performers', *Journal of Applied Sport Psychology*, 14, 211–24.

Jones, G., Hanton, S., and Connaughton, D. (2007) 'A framework of mental toughness in the world's best performers', *The Sport Psychologist*, 21, 243–64.

Kelly, G. A. (1991) *The Psychology of Personal Constructs: A Theory of Personality,* vol. 1, London: Routledge; originally publ. 1955.

Kobasa, S. C. (1979) 'Stressful life events, personality, and health: An inquiry into hardiness', *Journal of Personality and Social Psychology*, 37, 1–11.

Kobasa, S. C., Maddi, S. R. and Kahn, S. (1982) 'Hardiness and health: A prospective study', *Journal of Personality and Social Psychology*, 42, 168–77.

Levy, A. R., Polman, R. C. J., Clough, P. J., Marchant, D. C., and Earle, K. (2006) 'Mental toughness as a determinant of beliefs, pain, and adherence in sport injury rehabilitation', *Journal of Sports Rehabilitation*, 15, 246–54.

Loehr, J. E. (1982) *Athletic Excellence: Mental Toughness Training for Sports,* New York: Plume.

Loehr, J. E. (1986) *Mental Toughness Training for Sports: Achieving Athletic Excellence,* Lexington, MA: Stephen Greene Press.

Loehr, J. E. (1995) *The New Toughness Training for Sports,* New York: Plume.

Luszki, W. A. (1982) *Winning Tennis through Mental Toughness,* New York: Everest House.

Middleton, S. C., Marsh, H. W., Martin, A. J., Richards, G. E., Savis, J., Perry, C., et al. (2004) 'The Psychological Performance Inventory: Is the mental toughness test tough enough?', *International Journal of Sport Psychology*, 35, 91–108.

Nicholls, A. R., Polman, R. C., Levy, A. R., and Backhouse, S. (2008) 'Mental toughness, optimism, and coping among athletes', *Personality and Individual Differences*, 44, 1182–92.

Pankey, B. (1993) 'Presence of mind: Five ways to lower your class drop-out rate with mental toughness', *American Fitness*, 11, 18–19.

Ross, M., and Conway, M. (1986) 'Remembering one's own past: The construction of personal histories', in R. M. Sorrentino and E. T. Higgins (eds), *Handbook of Motivation and Cognition: Foundations of Social Behaviour,* New York: Guilford Press, pp. 122–44.

Tapp, J. (1991) 'Mental toughness', *Referee*, 16, 44–8.

Thelwell, R., Weston, N., and Greenlees, I. (2005) 'Defining and understanding mental toughness in soccer', *Journal of Applied Sport Psychology*, 17, 326–32.

Thelwell, R., Such, B., Weston, N., Such, J., and Greenlees, I. (2010) 'Developing mental toughness: Perceptions of elite female gymnasts', *International Journal of Sport and Exercise Psychology*, 8, 170–88.

Vealey, R. S. (1988) 'Future directions in psychological skills training', *The Sport Psychologist*, 2, 318–36.

Watts, G. (1978) 'Mental toughness for disadvantaged track teams', *Scholastic Coach*, 47, 100–2.

Werner, A. C., and Gottheil, E. (1966) 'Personality development and participation in collegiate athletics', *Research Quarterly*, 37, 126–31.

Werthner, P., and Trudel, P. (2006) 'A new theoretical perspective for understanding how coaches learn to coach', *The Sport Psychologist*, 20, 198–212.

Williams, R. M. (1988) 'The U.S. open character test: Good strokes help. But the most individualistic of sports is ultimately a mental game', *Psychology-Today*, 22, 60–2.

Woods, R., Hocton, M., and Desmond, R. (1995) *Coaching Tennis Successfully,* Champaign, IL: Human Kinetics.

Wyllemann, P., and Lavallee, D. (2004) 'A developmental perspective on transitions faced by athletes', in M. Weiss (ed.), *Developmental Sport and Exercise Psychology: A Lifespan Perspective,* Morgantown, WV: Fitness Information Technology, pp. 507–27.

9 Mental toughness as a life skill

Daniel Gould, Katherine Griffes
and Sarah Carson

One only needs to listen to televised sports broadcasts or read the sports page to encounter references made to the mental toughness of athletes and teams. It is ironic, then, that until recently so little attention had been paid to the concept of mental toughness in the sport psychology literature. Nevertheless, over the last 10 years sport psychologists have shown considerable interest in the topic. As reflected in this book, an abundance of studies have been conducted on mental toughness in sport psychology in recent years.

A second topic that has been of considerable interest to sport psychology researchers in recent years has been the role sport participation plays in life skills development of athletes. That is, the study of what capabilities, skills and attributes athletes (especially young people) develop through sport participation that transfer to other areas of their lives. Typical life skills discussed in the literature include topics such as goal setting, self-confidence, the development of initiative and effort, stress management and teamwork.

Given that the most recent conceptualization and research on mental toughness focuses on many similar psychological attributes that are often referred to in the sport psychology life skills literature, we wanted to explore the possibilities of linking these two divergent areas of research and discussing how they may augment each other. Our contention is that some components of mental toughness can not only be used to help athletes perform effectively, but also have the potential to help individuals be successful in other areas of their lives. In particular, we begin by first defining life skills and reviewing some of the current life skills literature. Next, we define mental toughness, in general terms, and overview both the 'core' dimensions that appear transferable across sports and life's contexts, as well as those dimensions that appear to be situational (i.e. less transferable). Because other chapters in this volume discuss the literature on mental toughness in great depth, our focus here will be on general conclusions and information needed to link the two areas. We follow this section with a more in depth review of life skills development research. After these two areas are reviewed, we turn our attention to mental toughness as a life skill, focusing on arguments for and against the construct being classified as a life skill and how life skills and mental toughness are developed. Finally, future research directions will be discussed.

Defining and identifying key life skills

Life skills have been defined in a number of ways both in the positive youth development and sport psychology literatures. At the most general level the World Health Organization (WHO, 1999) has defined life skills as those behaviors which enable individuals to effectively cope with the demands of everyday life. Danish and Nellen (1997) further broke life skills down into three categories: (a) behavioral skills like effectively communicating with others; (b) interpersonal or intra personal skills like being assertive or being able to set goals; and (c) cognitive skills like planning and decision-making. An implicit assumption in these definitions is that life skills help a young person not only succeed in the activity in which these skills are developed or refined, but also transfer to other settings in a young person's life (Gould and Carson, 2008), or as Danish and Nellen (1997) have argued, the asset must at least have the potential to transfer. Looking across the various definitions while trying to define life skills more specifically Gould and Carson (2008: 60) suggested that life skills are 'those internal personal assets, characteristics and skills such as goal setting, emotional control, self-esteem, and hard work ethic that can be facilitated or developed in sport and are transferred for use in non-sport settings'. This definition of life skills will guide this chapter.

While any number of life skills could be developed through sports participation, several studies have identified specific skills key stakeholders feel are most important to develop. Gould et al. (2006a), for example, surveyed 154 high school coaches and asked them to rate the life skill areas that their student-athletes most needed to develop. Results revealed that taking personal responsibility for one's self and one's actions, developing a work ethic and motivation, and improving communication and listening skills were three of the areas perceived to be most needed. In another study, Gould et al. (2009) conducted focus group interviews with key constituency groups involved in high school athletics (i.e. coaches, athletic directors, principals, parents of athletes and athletes). Life skills identified as needing development included time and stress management skills, moral development, healthy choice decision-making skills, communication skills and confidence. Finally, Jones and Lavallee (2009) interviewed 19 adolescent athletes, 4 sport psychologists and 10 coaches and asked them to identify life skills developed through sport participation. Results revealed that participants identified two categories of life skills: interpersonal skills (e.g. social skills, leadership, respect, communication and family interaction) and personal skills (e.g. discipline, self-reliance, goal setting, self-organization, motivation, managing performance outcomes). Participants were also asked what life skills were most important for adolescents to learn. Social skills like getting along with others, communication skills and teamwork/responsibility skills were perceived as most important for youth athletes to learn.

Taken together, these results show that life skills most often identified as needing development include personal responsibility, work ethic/motivation, communication skills, confidence, moral development and goal setting.

One of the most interesting questions remaining unresolved in the life skills area focuses on the issue of transferability. If one learns life skills in one sport do they transfer to other sports and, more importantly, non-sport settings? Intuitively, one would logically assume if an athlete develops skills like leadership, goal setting, teamwork and a hard work ethic in one setting that these skills would be available for use in other contexts such as school, work, personal relationships, etc. Coaches certainly believe that this transferability is the case (Gould et al., 2006b). However, Danish et al. (1993) and, more recently, Carson (2009) contend that the transfer of life skills from sport to other contexts is at best haphazard because athletes are often not aware that they have acquired skills that are transferable and may not have the confidence and knowledge to make such transfers take place. They further contend that unless initial life skills learning experiences are structured to facilitate transfer, transfer is less likely to be achieved. This view is best summarized by Petitpas et al. (2005) who indicated that, for life skills learned in sport to transfer to other life contexts, the sport context must be conducive to life skills development, be carried out by caring adults in positive group climates and involve skills and strategies that are highly meaningful and important to the youth involved.

Mental toughness and its components

In early studies on athletes' mental toughness investigators struggled to identify a universal definition of the topic. More recently, researchers have stepped forward to attempt to fill this gap in the literature. Jones et al. (2002) proposed a definition for mental toughness that includes (a) the ability to cope better than an opponent; and (b) a focus on outcome, with mental toughness relating to athletes winning more than an opponent. The resulting definition was that mental toughness is:

> having the natural or developed psychological edge that enables you to, generally, cope better than your opponents with the many demands (competition, training, lifestyle) that sport places on a performer and, specifically, be more consistent and better than your opponent in remaining determined, focused, confident, and in control under pressure.
>
> (Jones et al., 2002: 209)

While other definitions of mental toughness exist, this definition has been widely cited in the literature and will be used to define the term for the purposes of this chapter. What has come from the vast research attempting to define mental toughness is a list of components that make up mental toughness (see Figure 9.1). Looking across studies, the most often identified characteristics include self-belief, intelligence, high motivation/work ethic/commitment, the ability to concentrate, and the ability to cope with and handle pressure.

Another important consideration in defining mental toughness is the sport context. Gucciardi et al. (2008) contend that mental toughness components need to be considered in the context in which the athlete experiences them. That is, mental toughness skills could be behavior-specific, such as recovering from injury, preparing for competition, having a consistent performance and making good decisions. Conversely, situational mental toughness skills focus on the context where these qualities are required, such as dealing with internal and external pressures during competition, rehabilitation and practice preparation.

Each of these contexts could be further subdivided into general practice settings or competition settings. Jones et al. (2007) classified mental toughness components based on when they were used as well. Components specific to training or pre-competition include setting goals and controlling environments. Competition mental toughness skills include handling pressure, belief, focus, regulating performance, controlling the environment and being aware of thoughts and feelings. Mental toughness skills are required post-competition as well, to handle either a success or a failure. Gucciardi and Gordon (2009b) recognized that a variety of mental toughness components may be required in each situation. Thus, while mental toughness may have components that are more universal, it also appears to have situation-specific aspects. Current research suggests that situational elements should be considered when viewing mental toughness as a life skill.

Considering this literature and examining Figure 9.1 it is interesting to note that there are most likely some 'core' components of mental toughness that would not be expected to vary significantly from sport to sport. Self-belief, high levels of motivation and resiliency would be good examples of these core elements. Other elements of mental toughness might be very context-specific, such as sport intelligence, which one would expect to differ greatly between athletes such as a golfer and weight lifter. Others like attentional focus and control may fall in the middle of the continuum, with some aspects like the ability to concentrate and hold one's attention being highly transferable across sports while other aspects like what specific cues to attend to are highly specific to the sport. Others such as one's work ethic might be highly transferable.

This distinction between core and situational specific components of mental toughness raises some interesting questions regarding transferability of mental toughness skills, both between sports and relative to other life contexts. For example, if an athlete develops an unshakable belief in him- or herself, will he or she transfer that confidence from one sport to another? Basketball great Michael Jordan left basketball at the peak of his career to try his hand at baseball and played at a fairly high level (although, arguably, never at the same level as basketball). Yet other athletes have played at high levels in multiple sports (e.g. Rebecca Romero, current Olympic track cycling gold medallist and world champion, who also won Olympic silver in rowing; Dennis Compton who played for England in cricket and association football; and American Bo Jackson who played professional baseball and football at the highest levels). Did the core mental toughness skills these individuals developed in one sport transfer to the other? This question is an interesting one that researchers should pursue in the future.

Fourie & Potgieter (2001)
- Motivational level
- Coping skills
- Confidence maintenance
- Cognitive skill
- Competitiveness
- Prerequisite physical and mental skills
- Team unity
- Preparation skills
- Psychological hardiness
- Religious convictions
- Ethics

Jones et al. (2002)
1. Having an unshakable self-belief in your ability to achieve your competition goals
2. Having an unshakable self-belief that you possess unique qualities and abilities that make you better than your opponents
3. Having an insatiable desire and internalized motives to succeed
4. Bouncing back from performance set-backs as a result of increased determination to succeed
5. Thriving on the pressure of competition
6. Accepting that competition anxiety is inevitable and knowing that you can cope with it
7. Not being adversely affected by others' good and bad performances
8. Remaining fully-focused in the face of personal life distractions
9. Switching a sport focus on and off as required
10. Remaining fully-focused on the task at hand in the face of competition-specific distractions
11. Pushing back the boundaries of physical and emotional pain, while still maintaining technique and effort under distress (in training and competition)
12. Regaining psychological control following unexpected, uncontrollable events (competition-specific)

Jones et al. (2007)
- Belief (attitude/mindset)
- Focus (attitude/mindset)
- Using long-term goals as the source of motivation (training)
- Controlling the environment (training)
- Pushing yourself to the limit (training)
- Handling pressure (competition)
- Belief (competition)
- Regulating performance (competition)
- Staying focused (competition)
- Awareness and control of thoughts and feelings (competition)
- Controlling the environment (competition)
- Handling success (post-competition)
- Handling failure (post-competition)

Bull et al. (2005)
- Exposure to foreign cricket
- Independence
- Self-reflection
- Competitiveness with self and others
- Exploit learning opportunities
- Belief in quality preparation
- Self-set challenging targets
- Needing to "earn" success
- "Never say die" mindset
- "Go the extra mile" mindset
- Determination to make most of ability
- Resilient confidence
- Belief in making the difference
- Robust self-confidence
- Thrive on competition
- Willing to take risks
- Thinking clearly

Thelwell et al. (2005)
1. Having total self-belief at all times that you will achieve success
2. Wanting the ball at all times (when playing well and not so well)
3. Having the ability to react to situations positively
4. Having the ability to hang on and be calm under pressure
5. Knowing what it takes to grind yourself out of trouble
6. Having the ability to ignore distractions and remain focused
7. Controlling emotions throughout performance
8. Having a presence that affects opponents
9. Having everything outside of the game in control
10. Enjoying the pressure associated with performance

Gucciardi et al. (2008)
1. Self-belief
2. Work ethic
3. Personal values
4. Self-motivation
5. Tough attitude
6. Concentration and focus
7. Resilience
8. Handling pressure
9. Emotional resilience
10. Sport intelligence
11. Physical toughness

Gucciardi & Gordon (2009a)
- The ability to regulate one's emotions and moods in any circumstance to facilitate performance
- An internalised, insatiable desire and commitment to consistently improve one's performance levels and achieve success
- The ability to withstand and bounce back from situations in which negative outcomes are experienced (i.e., pressure, adversity, challenge)
- The ability to manage one's attention and focus over extended periods of play involving various distractions
- An unshakeable self-belief in your physical ability to perform in any circumstance
- An awareness and understanding of the game and the processes required to perform well

Figure 9.1 Characteristics identified in qualitative mental toughness research

Jones (personal communication, September 2010) suggests that the transfer of mental toughness across sports might also be dependent on other factors like perceived ability. For example, he suggests that mental toughness itself may manifest itself in sport when an athlete has reached the highest stages of skill development and has high perceived competence which, in turn, allows him or her to appraise challenge over threat. In contrast, when one has not reached the highest stages of skill development and does not have high perceived ability appraising challenges over threat may be much harder to do. Hence, the transfer of mental toughness components may depend on other factors of influence.

Similarly, one might ask if mental toughness components transfer beyond sport. For example, does the self-belief one develops from athletic involvement transfer to self-belief in pursuing achievements in other areas of one's life like business? It would seem that core components of mental toughness might transfer across settings, and may transfer more easily than those assets that are highly tied to the sport context in which they are learned and utilized, but little evidence exists to support this contention.

Mental toughness as a life skill

Over the last decade researchers have paid increased attention to the mental toughness and life skills areas. However, these two areas of research have been developed separately and studied by different investigators and investigative teams. It is our contention that these two areas of research can be integrated and doing so will facilitate development in each area. We will begin our discussion of mental toughness as a life skill by first presenting the case of why the two areas should be integrated.

The case for mental toughness as a life skill

The main appeal to looking at mental toughness as a life skill is that reviews of both sets of literature reveal considerable overlap in the characteristics that have been identified in each. For example, both have identified the importance of learning emotional control, developing a belief in oneself and one's capabilities, giving maximum effort and effectively dealing with failure and adversity. The development of mental toughness and life skills seems to follow a similar process as well. Both phenomena have been found to be developed through an informal socialization process in which significant others and environmental experiences continually shape the characteristics and skills comprising the two phenomena (see Chapter 8 above and Chapters 10 and 11 below). In addition, recent research reveals that formal intervention programmes can be effective in facilitating the development of the skills and attributes comprising each phenomenon (e.g. Gucciardi et al., 2009b; Goudas and Giannoudis, 2010). Finally, mental toughness and life skills areas are very similar in that both assume the skills and attributes developed in one context or situation transfer to other situations and contexts (e.g. Gucciardi et al., 2009c). So, both sets of literature seem to pay considerable attention to transfer issues.

Mental toughness and life skill differences

While there are many similarities between life skills and mental toughness, the research to date has differed in several important ways. First, mental toughness research has been driven by a performance-enhancement emphasis, with researchers focused on why some individuals can achieve consistent peak performance. In contrast, life skills research has focused on personal development, examining how young people develop relative to their own standards, and has not been tied directly to athletic performance. Mental toughness research has also predominately focused on elite adult athletes, often studying some of the world's best performers. Life skill research, in contrast, has almost exclusively focused on children and youth, often studying underserved young people or youth who have demonstrated behavioral problems. Third, the research on life skills tends to avoid highly organized competitive sport environments, suggesting that a focus on competition often results in a decreased emphasis on personal development by adult leaders and the youth involved. Mental toughness research, however, often studies individuals who achieve success in highly competitive environments.

Is mental toughness a life skill?

After reviewing and comparing the mental toughness and life skills literature, it is our contention that many of the components of mental toughness are or have the potential to be life skills. They are attributes that are developed or enhanced through sport, which can be used to help people function effectively in other areas of their lives. Most likely, the core mental toughness skills are those that can also serve as life skills.

What can be learned by integrating these two bodies of knowledge?

When mental toughness is viewed a life skill, a topic of central importance is identifying the degree to which mental toughness transfers from one arena to another. This transfer might involve the identification of what elements of mental toughness are sport-specific (since evidence has shown some elements of mental toughness are sport-specific) and what elements learned in one sport or situation transfer to another. Life skills research is mixed in this regard, showing that transfer can occur with some individuals and settings (Walsh et al., 2010), but has proven to be more difficult with others (Martinek et al., 2001). Interestingly, a recent business study showed that being a competitive athlete did not correlate with business management success later in life (Extejt and Smith, 2009). However, another economics study found that having experience as a sport leader correlated to greater adult success in one's nonsport career (Kuhn and Weinberg, 2005). This discrepancy certainly suggests that investigators should examine if and under what conditions mental toughness elements may transfer from one sport to another and from sport to life. Examining if some characteristics are more amenable to transfer than others is also important.

One life skill benefit associated with sports participation and often identified in the literature is teamwork and the ability to work with others. Given the importance of working in groups in many adult occupations, interpersonal skills are very important. However, the mental toughness research has focused much more attention on the individual performer and little attention on how that individual may interact with or influence the larger team in which they are a member. It is possible that demonstrating mental toughness on a team may be different than demonstrating individual mental toughness because the team performer often has to put the group first rather than the self. This interpretation begs the question of how individual athlete and team mental toughness differ.

One problematic issue that arises when mental toughness is viewed as a life skill is the fact that much of the previous research has tied mental toughness to performance success. If mental toughness is something that is desirable to develop in all performers, what happens when someone demonstrates mental toughness (e.g. does not give up, handles stress) but loses consistently (perhaps because physical criteria needed for athletic success such as strength and power are missing). Does losing imply that an individual is mentally deficient or weak? This issue needs to be examined.

One of the most interesting challenges researchers and practitioners hoping to develop mental toughness as a life skill will need to focus on is the role of competition in the mental toughness developmental process. Most life skills interventions, for example, use sport as a tool for focusing on the development of life skills (the primary goal). Thus, performance success is not focused on and, in fact, the activities are often stopped, manipulated or modified so that life skill lessons can be taught. Most competitive sports programmes, however, do not allow such flexibility and focus on athletic talent development and performance success as important goals. While developing mental toughness as a life skill should appeal to performance-focused coaches and athletes (because of the potential performance enhancement benefits), competitively oriented coaches will need to understand that developing life skills requires time and effort and cannot always play second fiddle to the athletic performance needs of the individual athlete or team. Shields and Bredemeier (2009) have also argued that 'true' competition, where one views the opposition as one's partner in a joint quest for excellence versus his or her enemy, can be used to foster excellence and character (and develop life skills). However, the competitive sport environment often becomes toxic and is characterized by what these authors call decompetition where there is little respect for one's opponent and winning at almost any cost becomes the dominant theme. While some components of life skills could be developed in decompetitive environments, it is unlikely that mental toughness as a life skill could be. If a coach exclusively focuses on winning, he or she will not prioritize personal development and athletes would learn that any means possible is acceptable as long as one wins.

In one recent study of 10 university coaches, Flett et al. (2010) found that competitive coaches highly value athletes with life skills, character and other intangible assets. The coaches were also found to have specific strategies for assessing and identifying players with stronger intangibles, as well as for filtering out recruits who severely lack these positive qualities. Hence, there is some evidence coaches who work with high-level athletes and focus on athletic success feel that life skills contribute to performance.

Related to this issue is the importance of broadening the notion of mental toughness if it is to be viewed as a life skill. Those studying life skills have often talked about the importance of developing character, ethics and values. While not reviewed here, some have argued that the vast literature on moral development and sportspersonship are important life skill components. Shields and Bredemeier (2008), for example, have made an important distinction between instrumental skills (e.g. discipline, persistence) and moral skills (e.g. values, higher moral reasoning stages), citing both as important components of character development. Previous mental toughness research has focused most attention on instrumental skills that can enhance performance. Mental toughness researchers should consider the moral aspects of athlete development as well (today's primary focus) if an inclusive conceptualization of mental toughness as a life skill is to be studied.

The development of life skills and mental toughness through sport

Life skills researchers have been keenly interested in understanding how life skills are developed in athletes, especially in young athletes. Several types of studies have been conducted in this regard, examining if life skills are actually associated with sports participation, how socialization practices influence life skills development and whether interventions are successful at enhancing athletes' life skills. Each of these lines of research will be summarized below.

Studies examining the development of life skills through sport

Life skills and athletic participation relationship studies

Investigators have begun to study if participation in sport is associated with athletes' life skills, and personal and social development. Much of this work is patterned after the positive youth development studies conducted by Reed Larson, David Hansen and their colleagues (Dworkin et al., 2003; Hansen et al., 2003; Hansen and Larson, 2007; Larson et al., 2006) in which young people involved in a wide variety of extracurricular activities have been interviewed and surveyed to examine what relationship exists between participation and psychosocial development.

In the latest studies in this line of research Larson and his colleagues (Hansen and Larson, 2007; Larson et al., 2006) sampled almost 2,300 high school students from a number of different schools. These students completed the YES-2 (see Table 9.1) and an activity participation survey. It was found that students involved in sport and art activities reported experiences related to goal setting and sustaining effort. In contrast to all the other activities, sports participants reported higher levels of stress. In a second article from the same dataset, Hansen and Larson (2007) began to identify variables that might influence these relationships. It was found that the greater the time involved in an activity, the more a young person is motivated by enjoyment and future goals, and having a lead role and a higher adult-to-youth ratio were positively related to higher frequencies of reported positive life skill experiences.

Gould and Carson (2010) have extended the work of Larson and colleagues by conducting studies exclusively in sport, particularly looking at how the coaching environment is related to YES-2 scores. In their first study they found perceptions of coaching actions were related to perceived life skills benefits derived from past high school sport participation. In particular, linkages were found between coaches' helping athletes develop competition strategies and goal setting skills, talking about sport and life lessons, and building positive rapport with their athletes and athletes' perceived development of emotional regulation, cognitive skills, feedback, and prosocial norms. In a follow-up study (Gould and Carson, under review), active high school athletes were investigated. Once again coaching behaviors like positive and negative rapport and emphasis placed on coaching life skills were significant predictors of the positive and negative YES-2 developmental or life skill experiences reported by the athletes (e.g. effort, time management, group process skills and inappropriate adult behaviors). Gender and sport type differences were also found, with females reporting more positive experiences and males more negative.

Table 9.1 YES-2: Three major scales and subscales (Hansen & Larson, 2005)

Personal development subscales	Identity exploration
	Identity reflection
	Goal setting
	Effort
	Problem solving
	Time management
	Emotion regulation
	Cognitive skills
	Physical skills
Interpersonal development subscales	Diverse peer relationships
	Prosocial norms
	Group process skills
	Feedback
	Leadership/responsibility
	Integration with family
	Linkages to community
	Linkages to work/college
Negative experience subscales	Stress
	Negative peer influences
	Social exclusion
	Negative group dynamics
	Inappropriate adult behavior

In the latest study in this line of research Gould et al. (under review-a) assessed what YES-2 outcomes underserved youth baseball and softball players reported from their sports participation and examined the relationships between participant participation and developmental gains. YES-2 scores and perceptions of the psychosocial sports climate (the motivational climate and caring coaching climate) were examined. Results revealed that these youth felt teamwork and social skills, physical skills development and initiative were the outcomes most often derived from their sports experience. Stress was the negative experience most often reported. These results compare favourably with the work of Larsen et al. (2006) who found the positive experiences of initiative, emotional regulation and teamwork and the negative experience of stress were most experienced by sport participants. The results were also consistent with caring coaching climate (Newton et al., 2007) and motivational climate (e.g. Cummings et al., 2007) research.

Finally, Strachan et al. (2009) compared young athletes who specialized in a single sport versus those who were engaged in multiple sports (samplers) using the YES-2 to determine what life skill benefits might result from participation. Results revealed that both types of sports involvement contexts had benefits, but the types of benefits reported were dependent on the participation context. In particular, sport samplers had higher scores on linkages to the community and integration with the family, whereas specializers demonstrated higher scores on diverse peer group relationships.

In summary, the development of life skills through sport research has shown that a number of benefits are derived by young people from sports participation. Sport participation seems to be especially associated with the development of initiative, emotional control and teamwork. However, unlike many other extracurricular activities, sport participation is also associated with negative influences like increased stress and inappropriate adult influences. It is important to note that the designs of these studies do not allow us to derive causal relationships. Thus, we cannot conclude that participation in sport caused these developmental gains. Researchers have also begun to identify factors that influence the effects participation has on young athletes, with some key factors including whether the young person plays a lead role on the team, is more involved and has a lower ratio of adults to students. Coaching behaviors have also been identified as a key influence on the life skills young athletes develop, with the coach–athlete relationship and motivational climate being particularly important.

Life skills socialization through sport studies

Several researchers have begun to examine the general socialization process by which young athletes develop life skills. Wright and Côté (2003) conducted interviews with six male athletes who were leaders on Canadian university ice hockey teams to determine what factors in their youth sport backgrounds were perceived to influence the development of their leadership skills. A focus on skill development, encouragement of a strong work ethic, opportunities to be engaged in the cognitive side of sport and development of cognitive sport knowledge, and the fostering of positive relationships with others were factors identified as influential to leadership development.

Voelker et al. (2010) studied the high school captaincy experience by interviewing young people who had recently held this position. The researchers were surprised to learn how little preparation these young people received from coaches for their leadership roles. In a follow-up study of 10 high school coaches known for developing leadership in their captains (Gould et al., under review-b), it was reported that proactive methods, such as developing ongoing communication with captains, providing them with feedback and reinforcement, holding coach–captain meetings, encouraging or conducting formal leadership training initiatives, and teaching and educating captains on concepts relevant to their leadership role are most effective for developing captains as leaders.

In research examining how coaches develop a number of life skills in their athletes, Gould et al. (2006b, 2007) examined the life skill coaching strategies of high school football coaches who had been recognized for developing life skills and character in their players. Results revealed that these coaches conveyed clear expectations to their players relative to rules, appropriate behavior and team expectations. They also had well-thought-out coaching philosophies that placed the personal and life skills development of their athletes as a top priority. These coaches adhered to their pro life skills coaching philosophy while still being highly motivated to win.

From the interviews it was also clear that the coaches were skilled at building relationships with their players and reported a variety of well-thought-out strategies for teaching the life skills that they viewed as important. Not only did these coaches use specific strategies for teaching life skills, but they also infused the teaching of life skills into their on-the-field coaching. Finally, the respondents recognized environmental factors (e.g. socioeconomic status) and other individuals (e.g. parents) influenced life skills development and took steps (e.g. educated parents about programme goals, adapted expectations based on family economic factors) to adapt to, deal with and/or resolve environmental issues that influenced player life skills development. Thus, these coaches did not view the teaching of life skills as a separate activity from their general coaching duties.

In a case study of a high school soccer team, Holt et al. (2008) not only conducted interviews with athletes and coaches, but also examined organizational documents and policies and made numerous fieldwork observations across an entire season to examine how youth learned life skills via sports participation. It was found that the coach of the team embraced a philosophy that focused on building relationships and involving the players in decision-making and worked hard to make sure these things happened. However, the investigative team witnessed little direct teaching of life skills. Instead, life skills like taking responsibility, goal setting and time management seemed to be associated with athletes' general participation in the sport and may have been a prerequisite for involvement. The athletes felt what they learned about leadership and teamwork transferred to other areas of their life, but there was no evidence that this transfer resulted from direct instructional strategies of the coach. Rather, the investigators felt that the athletes produced their own experiences in this respect. It was concluded that the programme structure provided by the coach created opportunities for the student-athletes to learn these life skills.

While only a few studies have been conducted in this area, the initial results are encouraging. Additional longitudinal investigations are needed, especially ones that use multiple data sources like interviewing coaches, players and parents and making numerous field observations as well as examining larger programmatic policies and guidelines. Taking more theoretical approaches, such as those used to study family socialization, is recommended as well.

Life skills intervention effectiveness studies

Steven Danish from the Life Skills Center at Virginia Commonwealth University has developed several life skills education outreach programmes with goal setting as the basis (Danish, 1996, 2002; Danish et al., 1998). Their 'Sports United to Promote Education and Recreation' (SUPER) programme, for instance, is a 25-hour, 10-session programme that is run like a sport clinic with a focus on having young people learn about and participate in a particular sport(s) and, by doing so, become more aware of and practice several life skills (e.g. communicating with others, managing anger, problem-solving, and setting and attaining goals). It is a sport-adapted version of the 'Going for the Goal' programme (Danish, 1996), which uses sport metaphors to help develop confidence and a sense of control in young people. The programme is typically conducted by college or high school student-athlete mentors who serve as role models for the young participants. Since its development, others have successfully implemented the SUPER programme and its premises with groups such as young New Zealand rugby players and youth golfers (Danish et al., 2004).

Over the last decade, a line of studies has been conducted to evaluate the effectiveness of SUPER and related programmes (Brunelle et al., 2007; Goudas et al., 2006; Goudas and Giannoudis, 2008; Papacharisis et al., 2005). For example, Goudas and Giannoudis (2008) assigned physical education students engaged in a team sports programme to either an experimental or control group, and had the experimental group take part in an abbreviated SUPER programme focused on goal setting, positive thinking and problem solving. Knowledge, self-beliefs relative to goal setting, positive thinking, problem solving and sports skills were assessed. Results were consistent with other studies on the programme and revealed that experimental group participants differed from controls on two of four skills tests and their knowledge and beliefs about the effective use of the life skills taught. Thus, the effectiveness of a team sports based life skills programme was demonstrated.

Personal responsibility has been considered an important life skill for youth to develop and is often lacking in many underserved young people. Spearheaded by the groundbreaking work of Don Hellison, a number of researchers have examined how personal responsibility might be developed through physical activity programmes. In particular, based on his experience running out-of-school sports clubs with underserved youth in Chicago, Hellison (1995) developed his teaching personal and social responsibility model. Through his model he contends that youth develop responsibility in physical activity situations by moving through stages of (a) self-control and respecting the rights and feelings of others; (b) giving good effort and participating; (c) being self-directed; (d) demonstrating leadership and helping others; and (e) transferring the previous levels outside of the sport context. Participants move through these stages with the help of mentors who share power and discuss responsibility with them and help the youth engage in considerable reflection.

In a review of studies examining the effectiveness of programmes that implement the personal and social responsibility model with youth, Hellison and Walsh (2002) concluded that there is clear support for the effectiveness of teaching responsibility in the form of self-direction and goal setting, respect for the rights of others, effort and leadership and teamwork. However, they also noted that most studies did not include design characteristics that permitted broad generalizations to be made. Lastly, it is important to note that these programmes were not typical extracurricular competitive sports. In contrast, most involved small numbers of youth who took part in out-of-school informal sports clubs for underserved youth with the majority of club activities being specifically designed to enhance personal and social development through means like awareness talks, group meetings and reflection time.

Studies examining the development of mental toughness in athletes

In addition to defining mental toughness, identifying its key components and examining factors correlated with it (all discussed in other parts of this text), researchers have begun to learn how mental toughness develops in athletes (for reviews, see Connaught et al; Mallett and Coulter; Weinberg and Butt, this volume). Several researchers recognize that mental toughness development in athletes begins early in childhood. Gucciardi et al. (2009d) identified the role of the parents, before children even enter the sporting field, in developing general mental toughness. Creating an atmosphere where children experience challenges and adversity, and being taught a 'can do attitude', can instill the skills behind mental toughness in children. As children grow older and get more involved in sport, the parents have less influence in the development of mental toughness, and more influence falls on the shoulders of the coach to develop these more sport-specific skills in the athletes. Along with coaches, but not as significant, are the influences of family, friends and teammates in the development of mental toughness (Gucciardi et al, 2009b).

The environment an athlete practices and competes in can also influence the amount of mental toughness the athlete develops. Athletes need to have a strong, trusting relationship with the coach, open lines of communication with topics of discussion stretching outside the realm of sport, and a focus on maintaining a long-term relationship. A coaching philosophy geared towards the development of mental toughness is also key. Coaches should put personal and athletic development as a priority over team success to best instill mental toughness skills, particularly self-belief, work ethic, personal values, self-motivation, emotional and sport intelligence, and physical toughness. Creating a challenging environment, where players are pushed both on and off the field is also important in the development of mental toughness. Negative environments or experiences in early sport can deter the development of mental toughness, highlighting the importance of these positive characteristics (Gucciardi et al, 2009a). More recently, Gucciardi et al. (2009b) identified exposure to experiences, challenges and adversity in the environment as important factors to mental toughness development, using a personal construct psychology model which includes values, attitudes and cognitions in the conceptualization of mental toughness.

In their assessment or mental toughness training programmes, Gucciardi et al. (2009c) identified characteristics that mental toughness programmes should teach to be successful. These characteristics are very similar to the list of mental toughness components, including preparation, work ethic, receptiveness to criticism, tough attitudes, transferable skills, self-awareness and monitoring, and multi-perspective discussions. Furthermore, mental toughness development may be hindered by overloading athletes with information in too short a period of time – the programme evaluated here was only a two-week course.

Gucciardi et al. (2009b) took another approach to programme evaluation, and compared the development of mental toughness skills in a general psychological skills training programme with a programme specifically designed to develop mental toughness, as well as a control group with no relevant training. Both the psychological skills and mental toughness programmes increased scores in areas such as thriving through challenges and tough attitudes. No gains were seen in desiring success or sport awareness in comparison with the control group. Overall, there was no significant difference in the development between the two programmes; both were successful at developing mental toughness skills.

This emerging research, then, shows that mental toughness is developed in several ways. First, through an informal socialization process where individuals (e.g. parents, coaches) and institutions (e.g. the family, sporting environment) influence the acquisition and development of mental toughness skills, most likely through some type of social learning process. Second, formal mental toughness training programmes are being developed and their effectiveness in enhancing mental toughness assessed. Initial results in this area are encouraging.

Studies examining life skills transfer

The issue of transfer may be the most important one to examine in both literatures on life skills and mental toughness as a life skill. One programme that has been found to be successful at facilitating the development of life skills in its participants as well as the transfer of these skills to other life arenas is First Tee (First Tee, 2005), a developmental programme that utilizes the sport of golf as a means of providing participants with lessons for and opportunities to practice and develop skills in the areas of honesty, integrity, sportsmanship, respect, courtesy, judgement, confidence, responsibility and perseverance. In an evaluation study of the First Tee programme, Weiss (2006) interviewed youth athletes, parents of participating athletes and First Tee coaches as to the knowledge pertaining to and implementation of behaviors related to the programme goals at home, in school, in various social situations and at the workplace. The interviews revealed promising results that included citations from all 95 participants of instances when they had transferred the 'meet and greet' skills and were able to manage negative thoughts, emotions and behaviors in other contexts (e.g. school, home, other sports, or with siblings, peers, and parents). In addition, 94 per cent of the youth cited examples of when they had transferred respect to others and 95 per cent demonstrated controlling negative emotions in other life contexts. Finally, over 90 per cent of all interviewed youth could clearly define and apply the concept of wellness and recounted experiences of how their participation in the First Tee programme led them to adopt a greater appreciation and understanding of diversity.

Unfortunately, even well-designed and carefully implemented programmes often find difficulty in aiding the transfer of the lessons and skills acquired during activity time to life outside of the programme's immediate context. For example, Martinek et al. (2001) not only evaluated the effectiveness of their Project Effort programme for developing social responsibility within its elementary-aged participants, but also assessed whether or not the youth were transferring these skills to their academic lives (a central goal of the programme). Transfer was evaluated by the degree to which the four central objectives (i.e. effort, self-direction, self-control and caring) were applied in the classroom setting according to information gathered from programme mentors, classroom teachers and exit interviews with each participant. Analyses of the data indicated that of the 16 participants involved in the programme, 10 (or 62 per cent) were rated as having demonstrated medium to high levels of skill transfer, while six (37 per cent) youth exhibited only low levels of transference. Furthermore some behaviors were more successfully transferred to the school setting than others (e.g. effort was more easily and frequently applied in the classroom than behaviors such as setting personal goals and showing care and concern for others). One caveat that must be considered, however, is that the transfer of these skills and attitudes is not a quick process. Although the evaluation of Project Effort was carried out over a six-month period, perhaps greater levels of transfer would have been observed if the youth had been tracked over a longer period of time.

While research on the transferability of life skills is only now beginning, it is fortunate that professional practice literature from other disciplines has provided strategies that can be adopted in sport settings to increase the likelihood of the application of the life skills acquired through participation in athletics to life outside of sport. For example, the conditions outlined by Gass (1985) for the transfer of skills gained through experiential education can be easily modified for use with youth coaches and their athletes. A central objective of any programme aimed at promoting positive development should be to structure activities and lessons so that participants are 'aware' from the beginning of their involvement that the skills they are developing can be utilized in other contexts. Furthermore, the instructions for skill transfer should be consistently reinforced throughout the duration of their involvement, and opportunities for follow-up should be provided. Another factor that enhances the likelihood of successful skill transfer is if the learning environment and other applicable contexts share similar aspects. In other words, the positive attribute of initiative, if learned in sport, may easily transfer to another activity that requires physical discipline such as participation in physical education classes or doing chores when asked, but may not transfer to a cognitive activity such as doing one's homework on time. Clear similarities between contexts may not always exist or may not be obvious to the young learner, so an important task of a programme leader is to engage the youth in discussions during which parallels that exist between the contexts are highlighted.

Other suggestions proposed by Gass (1985) to facilitate skill transfer are to provide ample opportunities for individuals to practice adapting the skills to different activities and between different contexts. The learner should not be expected to only engage in this practice on his or her own time, but should be given the opportunity to test out this transfer in situations during which he or she can receive guidance and feedback. Additionally, the participants should be encouraged to reflect on their practice and experiences of transferring skills so that their awareness is increased and their learning is more thoroughly solidified. Finally, if possible, having new learners interact with peers who have previously practiced and implemented the skills in other contexts provides the young learners with vicarious experiences of the desired transfer.

When implementing life skills training in their youth developmental programmes, Danish et al. (2003) adopted several of the strategies outlined by Gass (1985). In their various programmes, these researchers and practitioners facilitated the development and transfer of life skills outside of athletics within the physically skill based lessons by: (a) having discussions with participants about the importance of physical and 'mental skills' (or life skills) to sport performance; (b) providing examples and demonstrations of how these mental skills are practiced and cultivated both inside and outside of sport; (c) creating opportunities for athletes to practice these skills within the sport setting; (d) helping athletes develop a plan for and carry out the plan to utilize the skills outside of sport; and (e) debriefing with athletes the successes and failures of using the skills in the sport and other life contexts. These strategies have been deemed useful in terms of involving life skill lessons within an athletic context, while still distancing the skills enough from the sport environment so that participants can appreciate how the assets are useful beyond their sporting experiences.

Future research directions

There are a number of future research directions that should be pursued by investigators interested in studying mental toughness as a life skill. First and foremost is the need to demonstrate that mental toughness and its components learned in sport transfer across sports and to other life situations. Only when such transfer is demonstrated can mental toughness be considered a life skill.

A second important question that must be addressed is whether mental toughness as a life skill can be taught in programmes that place a great deal of emphasis on winning and athletic talent developed. While many argue such environments would not be conducive to doing so, Gould and his colleagues (2007) found that high school football coaches recognized for their ability to foster character and life skills in their players were able to embrace a double goal approach, engaging their athletes in highly competitive environments while simultaneously emphasizing life skills development. Yet, in most cases, moral development researchers have found clear links between the adaptation of ego goal-oriented approaches and lower levels of moral development. Research is needed to better understand this situation. It is highly likely that the motivational climate created and attitudes fostered by coaches and significant others has much to do with whether life skills are developed, the type of life skills developed and whether they transfer beyond sport.

Third, researchers should not only examine the instrumental components of mental toughness, but the moral components as well. An interesting question to pose is whether mental toughness can be viewed as a life skill if the skills are used in unethical and immoral ways. For example, if an athlete learns how to set and achieve goals in sport but then transfers these instrumental skills to negative life situations (e.g. uses goal setting as a member of a criminal organization), can this attribute then be called a life skill?

The role that failure and other forms of adversity play in the development of mental toughness as a life skill is another important topic in need of future research. Youth sport research has shown that taking positive approach to coaching young athletes leads to a number of desirable outcomes like enhanced self-esteem, lower anxiety and higher levels of motivation (Smoll and Smith, 2010). However, it is doubtful that athletes can become mentally tough if they have not faced adversity as evidenced by recent research by Gucciardi et al. (2009a). The dosage and timing of experiencing adversity is likely an important issue. Martens (1978), for example, suggested that young athletes best learn to deal with adversity by experiencing small dosages that they can successfully handle – in essence akin to inoculations given to prevent diseases. Although this idea was put forward almost 30 years ago, little research has examined this issue.

It is also important to begin to identify the characteristics that allow athletes to develop mental toughness skills and the ability of mental toughness components to transfer to other life situations. It is likely that being aware of the skills being taught and reflecting on one's experiences are especially important in this regard (Danish et al., 2003).

Taking a developmental approach to the mental toughness as a life skill concept would be important for future investigators. For example, are there critical times in one's development that are best to develop mental toughness? Is it less effective to develop mental toughness in adulthood? Are there different ways to develop mental toughness at different ages? These are important questions in need of additional study.

Theoretical explanations

One weakness of the current life skills development through sport research is the lack of theoretical explanations; this claim applies to the few studies that have examined the development of mental toughness via sport. In particular, few studies have worked from a theoretical base, and those that have tended to use broader explanations like Bronfenbrenner's (1977, 2005) ecological systems theory where it is contended that people interact and develop within several levels of a human ecological system (e.g. macro system, micro system) or Lerner et al.'s (2005) 5Cs (competence, confidence, connection, character and caring) view of positive youth development. Petitpas et al. (2005) have also outlined a framework for explaining psychosocial development through sport, which focuses on the interaction of context, external asset, internal asset and evaluation. While all three of these approaches are useful in a general sense, they may not offer the level of precise predictions and explanations needed to advance the field.

In a recent review, Gould and Carson (2008) discussed the need to take a more theoretical approach and suggested two general sets of explanations to explain the life skills–sport participation link. Based on the work of Eccles et al. (2003) the first set of explanations focused on how social environment influences might affect young athletes via positive identity changes, membership in a desirable peer group and forming attachments with positive adults. The work of Certo and colleagues (2003) was also discussed, which suggests that participating in sport facilitates a needed sense of belonging for youth. Lastly, they suggested that positive social norms can emerge from team membership as well as changes in locus of control, self-worth, perceived competence and autonomy.

Gould and Carson's (2008) second category of explanations was centred on the usefulness of the life skill strategies themselves. It was suggested that many life skills like goal setting, stress management and learning to communicate prove effective and are readily adopted in the sport setting and can be directly transferred to other settings and used throughout life as well. It was also suggested that life skills may also influence the development of dispositional characteristics such as self-confidence and self-esteem.

Perhaps the most cited explanation for the life skill–sport participation link is Hellison's (1995) model of personal and social responsibility. As previously discussed, this view holds that five developmental levels must occur for youth to develop personal and social responsibility and movement through the five stages is facilitated by a number of power sharing, awareness and reflection experiences. The model's predictions have good support. However, it only explains responsibility-related life skills and could be improved by better containing more in-depth explanations for why predictions are made.

Gaps in the life skills research

A decade of research examining life skills development through sport has been productive. We now have a good idea of the life skills that are most desired by sport stakeholders and better understand the association between life skills reported and sports participation. Research is also beginning to help us understand how life skills develop over one's lifetime and factors which influence their development. Finally, evidence shows that interventions can be designed to facilitate life skills development in athletes.

With the above being said, significant gaps exist in our knowledge of life skills development through sport. We need more experimental and longitudinal studies that establish cause and effect and true developmental relationships between sport participation and life skills. It is also important that we better understand what particular experiences lead to the development of specific life skills. Studies examining the transfer issue are badly needed as well. How valid is the assumption that life skills that are fostered via sport participation transfer to other life situations? Are some skills more amenable to transfer than others? What factors influence this transfer? In discussing this issue, Carson (2009) has suggested that a lack of intentional intervention on the part of coaches may inhibit the ability of the athletes to gain full use of the life skills learned in sport, because the transfer of any skill to another domain often requires a great deal of cognitive work that adolescents may not be able to do on their own. This point was further reinforced by the work of Jones and Lavallee (2009) who conducted a single case study with a female tennis player who when asked about transferring life skills outside of sport explained that no systematic intervention was necessary and her own process of transferring life lessons outside of tennis happened somewhat automatically. Finally, the life skills development via sport research lacks detailed theoretical explanations for the development and transfer of life skills and how they influence behavior.

Conclusion

This chapter integrates two important areas of contemporary sport psychological research: studies on mental toughness in athletes and the development of life skills through sport involvement. Based on logic and the previous research in the two areas we argue that mental toughness can be viewed as a life skill. However, before this contention can be verified, studies that examine mental toughness as a life skill must be conducted. It is our hope that this chapter facilitates that process.

Author note

The authors would like to acknowledge Martin Jones and Steve Danish for their excellent suggestions for improving the quality of this chapter as external reviews.

References

Bronfenbrenner, U. (1977) 'Toward an experimental ecology of human development', *American Psychologist*, 32, 513–31.
Bronfenbrenner, U. (ed.) (2005) *Making Human Beings Human: Bioecological Perspectives on Human Development,* Thousand Oaks, CA: Sage Publications.

Brunelle, J., Danish, S. J., and Forneris, T. (2007) 'The impact of a sport-based life skill program for adolescent prosocial values', *Applied Development Science*, 11, 43–55.

Bull, S. J., Shambrook, C. J., James, W., and Brooks, J. E. (2005) 'Towards an understanding of mental toughness in elite English cricketers', *Journal of Applied Sport Psychology*, 17, 209–27.

Carson, S. A. (2009) 'Life skills development and transfer through high school sport participation: How life lessons are taught and brought to life', unpublished doctoral dissertation,. Michigan State University, East Lansing, MI.

Certo, J., Cauley, K., and Chafin, C. (2003) 'Students' perspectives on their high school experience', *Adolescence*, 38, 705–24.

Cummings, S. P., Smoll, F. L., Smith, R. E., and Grossbard, J. R. (2007) 'Is winning everything? The relative contributions of motivational climate and won–lost percentage in youth sports', *Journal of Applied Sport Psychology*, 19, 322–36.

Danish, S. J. (1996) 'Interventions for enhancing adolescents' life skills', *Humanistic Psychologist*, 24, 365–81.

Danish, S. J. (2002) 'Teaching life skills through sport', in M. J. Gatz, M. A. Messner, and S. J. Ball-Rokeach (eds), *Paradoxes of Youth and Sport*, Albany, NY: State University of New York Press, pp. 49–60.

Danish, S. J., and Nellen, V. C. (1997) 'New roles for sport psychologists: Teaching life skills through sport to at risk youth', *Quest*, 49, 100–13.

Danish, S. J., Petitpas, A. J., and Hale, B. D. (1993) 'Life development intervention for athletes: Life skills through sports', *The Counseling Psychologist*, 21(3), 35–386.

Danish, S. J., Meyer, A., Mash, J., Howard, C., Curl, S. Brunelle, J., and Owens, S. (1998) *Going for the Goal: Student Activity Book* (2nd edn), Richmond, VA: Department of Psychology, Virginia Commonwealth University.

Danish, S. J., Fazio, R., Nellen, V. C., and Owens, S. (2002) 'Teaching life skills through sport: community programmes to enhance adolescent development', in J. Van Raalte and B. W. Brewer (eds), *Exploring Sport and Exercise Psychology*, Washington, DC: American Psychological Association, pp. 269–88.

Danish, S. J., Forneris, T., Hodge, K., and Heke, I. (2004) 'Enhancing youth development through sport', *World Leisure*, 46, 38–49.

Danish, S. J., Taylor, T. E., and Fazio, R. J. (2003) 'Enhancing adolescent development through sports and leisure', in G. R. Adams and M. D. Berznsley (eds), *Blackwell Handbook of Adolescence*, Malden, MA: Blackwell Publishing, pp. 92–108.

DeBusk, M., and Hellison, D. (1989) 'Implementing a physical education self-responsibility model for delinquency-prone youth', *Journal of Teaching Physical Education*, 8, 104–13.

Dworkin, J. B., Larson, R., and Hansen, D. (2003) 'Adolescents' accounts of growth experiences in youth activities', *Journal of Youth and Adolescents*, 32, 17–26.

Eccles, J. S., Barber, B. L., Stone, M., and Hunt, J. (2003) 'Extracurricular activities and adolescent development', *Journal of Social Issues*, 59, 865–89.

Extejt, M. M., and Smith, H. E. (2009) 'Leadership development through sports participation', *Journal of Leadership Education*, 8, 224–37.

First Tee (2005) *Longitudinal Effects of The First The Life Skills Education Programs on Positive Youth Development*, Charlottesville, VA: University of Virginia, M. Weiss.

Flett, M. R., Gould, D., Pauley, A., and Schneider, R. P. (2010) 'How and why university coaches define, identify, and recruit intangibles', *International Journal of Coaching Science*, 4, 15–21.

Fourie, S., and Potgieter, J. R. (2001) 'The nature of mental toughness in sport', *South African Journal for Research in Sport, Physical Education and Recreation*, 23, 63–72.

Gass, M. (1985) 'Programming the transfer of learning in adventure education', *Journal of Experiential Education*, 8(3), 18–24.

Goudas, M., and Giannoudis, G. (2008) 'A team-sports-based life-skills program in a physical education context', *Learning and Instruction*, 18, 528–36.

Goudas, M., and Giannoudis, G. (2010) 'A qualitative evaluation of a life-skills program in a physical education context', *Hellenic Journal of Psychology*, 7, 298–314.

Goudas, M., Dermitzaki, I., Leondari, A., and Danish, S. (2006) 'The effectiveness of teaching life skills program in a physical education context', *European Journal of Psychology of Education*, 21, 429–38.

Gould, D., and Carson, S. (2008) 'Life skills development through sport: Current status and future directions', *Sport and Exercise Psychology Reviews*, 1, 58–78.

Gould, D., and Carson, S. (2010) 'The relationship between perceived coaching behavior and developmental benefits of high school sports participation', *Hellenic Journal of Psychology,* 7, 298–314.

Gould, D., and Carson, S. (under review) 'The relationship between perceived coaching behaviors and developmental experiences of young athletes'.

Gould, D., Carson, S., Fifer, A., Lauer, L., and Benham, R. (2009) 'Social-emotional and life skill development issues characterizing today's high school sport experience', *Journal of Coaching Education*, 2, 1–25.

Gould, D., Chung, Y., Smith, P., and White, J. (2006a) 'Future directions in coaching life skills: Understanding coaches' views and needs', *Athletic Insight*, 8(3). Available at http://www.athleticinsight.com/Vol8Iss3/CoachingPDF.pdf (accessed 23 May 2011).

Gould, D., Collins, K., Lauer, L., and Chung, Y. (2006b) 'Coaching life skills: A working model', *Sport and Exercise Psychology Review*, 2, 10–18.

Gould, D., Collins, K., Lauer, L., and Chung, Y. (2007) 'Coaching life skills through football: A study of award winning high school coaches', *Journal of Applied Sport Psychology*, 19, 16–37.

Gould, D., Flett, M. R., and Lauer, L. (under review-a) 'The relationship between psychosocial development and the sports climate experienced by underserved youth'.

Gould, D., Voelker, D. K., and Griffes, K. (under review-b) 'Best coaching practices for developing team captains'.

Graham, J., Hanton, S., and Connaughton, D. (2007) 'A framework of mental toughness in the world's best performers', *The Sport Psychologist*, 21, 243–64.

Gucciardi, D. F., and Gordon, S. (2009a) 'Development and preliminary validation of the Cricket Mental Toughness Inventory', *Journal of Sports Sciences*, 27, 1293–1310.

Gucciardi, D. F., and Gordon, S. (2009b) 'Revisiting the performance profile technique: Theoretical underpinnings and application', *The Sport Psychologist*, 23, 93–117.

Gucciardi, D. F., Gordon, S., and Dimmock, J. A. (2008) 'Towards an understanding of mental toughness in Australian Football', *Journal of Applied Sport Psychology*, 20, 261–81.

Gucciardi, D. F., Gordon, S., and Dimmock, J. A. (2009a) 'Development and preliminary validation of a mental toughness inventory for Australian football', *Psychology of Sport and Exercise*, 10, 201–9.

Gucciardi, D. F., Gordon, S., and Dimmock, J. A. (2009b) 'Evaluation of a mental toughness training program for youth-aged Australian footballers: A quantitative analysis', *Journal of Applied Sport Psychology*, 21, 307–23.

Gucciardi, D. F., Gordon, S., and Dimmock, J. A. (2009c) 'Evaluation of a mental toughness program for youth-aged Australian footballers II. A qualitative analysis', *Journal of Applied Sport Psychology*, 21, 324–39.

Gucciardi, D. F., Gordon, S., Dimmock, J. A., and Mallett, C. J. (2009d) 'Understanding the coach's role in the development of mental toughness: Perspective of elite Australian football coaches', *Journal of Sports Sciences*, 27, 1483–96.

Hansen, D. M., and Larson, R. (2005) 'The Youth Experience Survey', University of Illinois at Urbana-Champaign. Retrieved May 2006, from: http://web.aces.uiuc.edu/youthdev/.yesinstrument.html.

Hansen, D. M., and Larson, R. (2007) 'Amplifiers of developmental and negative experiences in organized activities: Dosage, motivation, lead roles, and adult–youth ratios', *Journal of Applied Developmental Psychology*, 28, 360–74.

Hansen, D. M., Larson, R. W., and Dworkin, J. B. (2003) 'What adolescents learn in organized youth activities: A survey of self-reported developmental experiences', *Journal of Research on Adolescence*, 13, 25–55.

Hellison, D. (1995) *Teaching Responsibility through Physical Activity,* Champaign, IL: Human Kinetics.

Hellison, D., and Walsh, D. (2002) 'Responsibility-based youth program evaluation: Investigating the investigators', *Quest*, 54, 292–307.

Hodge, K., Creswell, S., Sherburn, D., and Dugdale, J. (1999) 'Physical-activity based life skills programmes: Part II – Example programmes', *Physical Education New Zealand Journal*, 32, 12–15.

Holt, N. L., Tink, L. N., Mandigo, J. L., and Fox, K. R. (2008) 'Do youth learn life skills through their involvement in high school sport? A case study', *Canadian Journal of Education*, 31, 281–304.

Jones, G., Hanton, S., and Connaughton, D. (2002) 'What is this thing called mental toughness? An investigation of elite sport performers', *Journal of Applied Sport Psychology*, 14, 205–18.

Jones, G., Hanton, S., and Connaughton, D. (2007) 'A framework of mental toughness in the world's best performers', *The Sport Psychologist*, 21, 243–64.

Jones, M. (2010) Reviewer feedback letter to D. Gould, Sept.

Jones, M. I., and Lavallee, D. (2009) 'Exploring the life skills needs of British adolescent athletes', *Psychology of Sport and Exercise*, 10, 159–67.

Kuhn, P., and Weinberg, C. (2005) 'Leadership skills and wages', *Journal of Labor Economics*, 23, 395–436.

Larson, R. (2000) 'Toward psychology of positive youth development', *American Psychologist*, 55, 170–83.

Larsen, R. W., Hansen, D. M., and Moneta, G. (2006) 'Differing profiles of developmental experiences across types of organized youth activities', *Developmental Psychology*, 42, 849–63.

Lerner, R. M., Lerner, J. V., Almerigi, J. B., Theokas, C., Phelps, E., et al. (2005) 'Positive youth development. Participation in community youth development programs, and community contributions of fifth-grade adolescents: Findings from the first wave of the 4-H study of positive youth development', *Journal of Early Adolescence*, 25, 17–71.

Martens, R. (1978) *Joy and Sadness in Children's Sports,* Champaign, IL: Human Kinetics.

Martinek, T., Schilling, T., and Johnson, D. (2001) 'Transferring personal and social responsibility of underserved youth to the classroom', *Urban Review*, 33, 29–45.

Newton, M., Watson, D. L., Gano-Overway, L., Fry, M., Kim, M., and Magyar, M. (2007) 'The role of a caring-based intervention in a physical activity setting', *Urban Review*, 39, 281–99.

Papacharisis, V., Goudas, M., Danish, S. J., and Theodorakis, Y. (2005) 'The effectiveness of teaching a life skills program in a sport context', *Journal of Applied Sport Psychology*, 17, 247–54.

Petitpas, A. J., Cornelius, A. E., Van Raalte, J. L., and Jones, T. (2005) 'A framework for planning youth sport programs that foster psychosocial development', *The Sport Psychologist*, 19, 63–80.

Shields, D. L., and Bredemeier, B. J. L. (2008) 'Sport and the development of character', in L. Nucci and D. Navaez (eds), *Handbook of Moral and Character Education,* New York: Routledge, pp. 500–19.

Shields, D. L., and Bredemeier, B. L. (2009) *True Competition: A Guide to Pursuing Excellence in Sport and Society,* Champaign, IL: Human Kinetics.

Smith, R. E., Smoll, F. L., and Cumming, S. P. (2007) 'Effects of a motivational climate intervention for coaches on young athletes' sport performance anxiety', *Journal of Sport and Exercise Psychology*, 29, 39–59.

Smoll, F. L., and Smith, R. E. (2010) 'Conducting sport psychology training programs for coaches: Cognitive-behavioral principles and techniques', in J. M. Williams (ed.), *Applied Sport Psychology: Personal Growth to Peak Performance* (6th edn), Mountain View, CA: Mayfield, pp. 392–416.

Strachan, L., Côté, J., and Deakin, J. (2009) '"Specializers" versus "samplers" in youth sport: Comparing experiences and outcomes', *The Sport Psychologist*, 23, 77–92.

Thelwell, R., Weston, N., and Greenlees, I. (2005) 'Defining and understanding mental toughness in soccer', *Journal of Applied Sport Psychology*, 17, 326–32.

Voelker, D. K., Gould, D., and Crawford, M. J. (2010) 'Understanding the experience of high school sport captains', *The Sport Psychologist,* 25(1), 47–66.

Walsh, D. S., Ozaeta, J., and Wright, P. M. (2010) 'Transference of the responsibility model goals to the school environment: Exploring the impact of a coaching club program', *Physical Education and Sport Pedagogy*, 15, 15–29.

Weiss, M. R. (2006) *The First Tee 2005 Research Summary: Longitudinal Effects of the First Tee Life Skills Educational Program on Positive Youth Development,* St Augustine, FL: First Tee.

World Health Organization (1999) *Partners in Life Skills Education,* Geneva: World Health Organization, Department of Mental Health.

Wright, A., and Côté, J. (2003) 'A retrospective analysis of leadership development through sport', *The Sport Psychologist*, 17, 268–91.

10 Understanding and developing the will to win in sport

Perceptions of parents, coaches and athletes

Clifford J. Mallett and Tristan J. Coulter

Sporting contexts provide ample opportunities for participants to undertake challenges that require a steely determination and commitment in the pursuit of excellence. The highly competitive athlete's obvious desire to win a race or match often exemplifies this determination and commitment. Some athletes, compared to others, seem to be more committed and determined in the pursuit of success, that is, they demonstrate a range of behaviors that reflect an immense desire to win. What makes some athletes so much more determined to win? Of particular interest to athletes, coaches and psychologists are the associated cognitions and emotions that underpin those determined and focused behaviors.

Although there may be differential contributions of innate personality characteristics and the environment to the development of mental toughness (Jones et al., 2002), the evidence to date supports the notion that the context can play an essential role. It is therefore the purpose of this chapter to foreground what research has contributed to our understanding of the how mental toughness is developed. Specifically, the research has sought the perceptions of multiple data sources; namely, parents, coaches and athletes. Some researchers have sought multi-source perceptions (e.g. Coulter et al., 2010) whilst others have sought a single perspective (e.g. Bull et al., 2005; Connaughton et al., 2008b; Gucciardi et al., 2009d). In this chapter, the research that has examined the influences of key actors in the lives of mentally tough athletes – namely, parents, coaches and the athletes themselves – will be reviewed.

Recent research has underscored the will to win in those athletes identified as being mentally tough (e.g. Connaughton et al., 2008b; Jones et al., 2002). This strong desire to succeed is evidenced in the following quotation:

> You've got to have that winning mentality and desire to be considered a mentally tough sportsman. It's that hunger to win and desire to continuously chase the game in the pursuit of success that separates mentally tough players from the rest. Regardless of their performance at the time or the final end result, players with this mindset do not fear defeat, but rather pride themselves

on the principle to achieve and, most importantly, their need to consistently apply oneself to this cause regardless of the situation.

(Coulter et al., 2010: 703)

Although several important attributes (e.g. self-belief, physical toughness, attentional control, work ethic/motivation and resilience) associated with mental toughness have been identified in the literature, a winning mentality and desire was identified as the key attribute of mentally tough soccer players (Coulter et al., 2010). Key cognitions reported by mentally tough soccer players enabled them to remain focused and competitive during training and matches and highlighted the adoption of several forms of self-talk in dealing with challenging situations. It is important to stress that these players' hunger for winning was in the 'chase'; that is, it was the actual pursuit itself that provided more pride and satisfaction rather than performance outcomes. This hunger and passion in wanting to win was central to their understanding of mental toughness and differs from pursuing victory as an end in itself (Gucciardi et al., 2009a; Harwood et al., 2008). This 'will to win' is distinguished from an understanding of the various forms of motivation (e.g. intrinsic motivation) in that it highlights the intensity of the desire to compete to the best of their ability. It is our contention that mental toughness is not always associated with successful performance outcomes and, therefore, not all successful performers can be considered mentally tough; rather it is the process undertaken by mentally tough individuals in the pursuit of success regardless of the outcome itself. Hence, it is proposed that the 'will to win' is central to understanding and developing mental toughness.

In this chapter we argue that mental toughness can be differentially developed and present research supporting this contention. Furthermore, we underscore the significant role of key actors (e.g. coaches, parents) in the lives of athletes in developing mental toughness, especially through early childhood and adolescence. Specifically, we examine the means through which coaches and parents uniquely and collectively contribute to the athletes' development of mental toughness in sport. Finally, we contend that central to the development of mental toughness are the athletes themselves and their adaptive responses to many life experiences that facilitate mental toughness.

What is mental toughness?

Various groups of scholars have conceptualized mental toughness in different ways. We adopted a conceptual understanding of mental toughness that is, in the main, consistent with several other groups such as Jones, Connaughton and colleagues, Gucciardi and colleagues, and Thelwell and colleagues. The aforementioned research groups have used first principles (i.e. interpretivist methodologies, such as phenomenological studies) to examine the notion of mental toughness to derive their understanding of the construct. Other groups (e.g. Clough and colleagues) have used sport-specific adaptations of related constructs (e.g. hardiness and confidence) in their conceptualization of mental toughness, despite the lack of empirical evidence based in first principles supporting that understanding. Whilst these adaptations of constructs have guided measurement in some studies, it is important to clarify our understanding of mental toughness and its subsequent development. Hence, in defining mental toughness for the purpose of this chapter, we consider research that has specifically examined those players/athletes identified as mentally tough within their respective sports. As discussed earlier, successful performers are not necessarily mentally tough. Nevertheless, research (e.g. Connaughton et al., 2008b; Coulter et al., 2010; Gucciardi et al., 2009d) that has examined multi-source ratings from key actors (e.g. players, coaches, parents) associated with mentally tough sportspeople adds to the rigour of a clearer conceptualization of mental toughness.

We adopt the following conceptualization: mental toughness is associated with the pursuit of goals in achievement contexts, and in that quest, particular values, attitudes, emotions, cognitions, and behaviors seem to influence the way in which an individual approaches, responds to and appraises both negatively and positively construed pressures, challenges, and adversities (Coulter et al., 2010). That is, mentally tough athletes seem to possess a consistent pattern of adaptive cognitions, emotions, and behaviors that encapsulate mental toughness in a broad sense. Therefore, mental toughness seems to buffer players against (perceived) adversity as well as maintaining and promoting a clear focus on a full commitment to the performance. The literature on mental toughness suggests that it is multidimensional and there is increasing evidence that hardiness or resilience is only one (albeit important) aspect (Coulter et al., 2010; Gucciardi, et al., 2008). Other key qualities associated with mental toughness include: winning mindset, self-belief/confidence, attentional control, self-motivation, positive and tough attitude, enjoying and handling pressure, and quality preparation (Coulter et al., 2010).

The saliency of context

A key question within the research on the development of mental toughness is the contribution of genetic and environmental influences. Specifically, is mental toughness an inherited, innate personality characteristic (Golby and Sheard, 2006; Horsburgh et al., 2009), or is it developed through the socialization process – either through specific training (e.g. psychological skills or coach-mediated training; e.g. Bull, et al., 2005; Connaughton et al., 2008b; Gucciardi et al., 2009c) or 'caught' through life experiences (Bull et al., 2005; Connaughton et al., 2008; Jones et al., 2007; Thelwell et al., 2010)?

Golby and Sheard (2006) argued that mental toughness is partly genetically determined. They examined the relationship between genotype (serotonin transporter 5-HHT gene) and positive psychological development (e.g. mental toughness using the PPI) in national-level British swimmers but found no relationship between the presence of the gene and scores on measures of positive psychological development. They argued that the serotonin transporter 5-HHT gene might provide a buffer against stress; however, other genes may also provide such buffering against stress. Horsburgh et al. (2009), who examined individual differences in mental toughness scores (using the MTQ48) from monozygotic and dizygotic twins, reported that although there was significant variance attributed to genetic and non-shared environments, there was much unexplained variance, partially supporting the view that mental toughness is both inherited and developed. Neither the PPI nor the MTQ48 measures a conception of mental toughness that is consistent with our understanding; therefore, further examination of the genetic contribution to mental toughness as conceptualized by us is necessary before progressing that debate. Nevertheless, it is proposed that consideration be given to individual variation in the contribution of both nature and nurture.

It is likely that many contexts provide opportunities for the development of mental toughness, including family, sport and school. Key actors such as parents and coaches are responsible for shaping the environments in which athletes are nurtured (Mallett, 2005). What is less clear is the type of climate that is best suited to developing mental toughness in aspiring athletes (Crust, 2008). Nevertheless, there is sufficient evidence supporting the view that mental toughness can be developed. Several studies have reported that mental toughness is partially 'caught' through environmental influences (Bull et al., 2005; Connaughton et al., 2008b; Coulter et al., 2010; Gucciardi et al., 2009d) and 'taught' through training (Gucciardi et al., 2009b, 2009c). Moreover, there is evidence from the research on talent development (e.g. Côté, 1999; Gagné, 2004; Martindale et al., 2005) that supports the view that components of mental toughness are largely 'caught' through engagement in youth sporting contexts; however, caution is urged when extrapolating the findings of talent development research as they do not focus specifically on the mental toughness construct. Nevertheless, not all sporting environments provide the same opportunities for developing mental toughness. What is less known is the capacity of sportspeople to be taught mental toughness through interventions such as mental skills training or specific mental toughness programmes. Several recent studies have examined the effects of interventions aimed at developing mental toughness, which will be discussed later in this section.

Research that has examined the conceptualization of mental toughness within specific sports, and subsequently investigated those situations in which key qualities were required, provides sport psychologists, coaches and players with some insight into how mental toughness might be developed. Several studies in specific sports such as Australian football (e.g. Gucciardi et al., 2008), soccer (Coulter et al., 2010), cricket (Bull et al., 2005), and gymnastics (Thelwell et al., 2010) have contributed to our understanding of mental toughness in those sports and how it can be developed. Understanding those situations that require mental toughness in specific sports allows for the identification and development of specific strategies fostering players' 'situated' learning (Gucciardi et al., 2008). The identification of those situations that require a high degree of mental toughness enables sports participants to recall how they felt, what they were thinking and how they behaved in such situations. Consequently, we can understand how key mental toughness characteristics influence how (identified) mentally tough athletes appraise and approach these situations and the subsequent behaviors they demonstrate.

Caught through life experiences

Key persons within the athletes' network (e.g. parents, coaches) seem to play a central role in creating environments that facilitate the development and maintenance of values, attitudes, emotions and cognitions that underpin mental toughness (Bull et al., 2005; Connaughton et al., 2008a; Coulter et al., 2010) in many life domains (e.g. family, sport). Although life events are inherently neutral the athlete interprets those experiences in particular ways. In some cases it appears that athletes may be adaptive in their interpretations of those events. Nevertheless, the mediational role of significant others in the adaptive interpretation of those life events seems to be central to the development of mental toughness. In making sense of life events (e.g. non-selection) there seem to be differential contributions by athletes, parents and coaches. Research that has examined the perceptions of key social agents such as parents, coaches and athletes in how mental toughness is implicitly and explicitly developed is central to making sense of these differential contributions to its development.

Based upon the data analysed from interviews with 12 cricketers (identified by coaches as mentally tough) Bull et al. (2005) developed a mental toughness pyramid that underscored the significant influence of environmental influences in the development of mental toughness. Key factors such as childhood experiences (parental influences, early cricket playing experiences) lay the foundations for tough character, attitudes and cognitions. The creation of tough environments (family, sport, school) was reported as providing opportunities or experiences to build tough character, attitudes and thinking, which underpinned the development of mental toughness. Tough character was reported as primarily influenced by environmental factors and contributed to the development of such qualities as independence, self-reflection and resilient confidence. The pyramid infers a bottom–up approach to the development of mental toughness; however, a top–down approach, which emphasizes the development of tough thinking (and consistent with a cognitive approach to behavior change), may also be possible albeit considered to be less influential. Nevertheless, the model has not been empirically examined. Moreover, it is noteworthy that Bull et al. did not reject the contribution of inherited mental toughness characteristics.

Connaughton et al. (2008b) reported the importance of environmental influences on the development of mental toughness; specifically, parents, coaches, siblings, senior athletes, sport psychologists and others were reported as making contributions to its development. Moreover, they reported the influence of broader social networks to the development of mental toughness through vicarious learning (e.g. observations, role modelling). Nonetheless, it is unclear to what degree other actors deliberately contribute to the mental toughness of athletes. Although there was recognition of the mediating role of others in developing mental toughness, the authors did not report the processes involved in its development.

Taught through interventions and training

The contribution of mental skills training to the development of mental toughness is scarcely reported in the literature (Crust, 2007), probably due to the fact there remains some conceptual ambiguity about what is mental toughness, and the subsequent lack of psychometrically sound measures. Nevertheless, in recent years, a couple of studies using sport-specific and psychometrically supported measures of mental toughness have been reported (e.g. Gucciardi et al., 2009b, 2009c).

Recent research has examined the ability to develop mental toughness in youth athletes. For example, Gucciardi et al. (2009b, 2009c) examined the usefulness of psychological skills training (PST) and mental toughness training (MTT) in facilitating mental toughness in youth-aged Australian football players. Three teams were randomly assigned one of three conditions: a traditional PST programme, a programme of psycho-educational and experiential activities consistent with the research on mental toughness, and a control group. Both interventions showed improvement in mental toughness compared with the control group as measured by the Australian football Mental Toughness Inventory (AfMTI: Gucciardi et al., 2009b) post-intervention. The inclusion of qualitative data from parents and coaches (Gucciardi et al., 2009c) corroborated the self-report findings. Nevertheless, the research project did not include a follow-up study that considered medium- to long-term effects of the interventions, nor did they link self-reported data with objective performance or behavioral indices.

Although not an intervention study *per se*, Connaughton et al. (2008a) found that elite athletes reported the importance of psychological skills in maintaining mental toughness. Specifically, they reported that goal setting and positive self-talk can contribute to the development of mental toughness. Vicarious experience and appropriate role models were also found to contribute to its development.

The use of psychometrically sound measures of mental toughness, such as the AfMTI (Gucciardi et al., 2009b) and the Cricket Mental Toughness Inventory (CMTI: Gucciardi and Gordon, 2009), and other psychological constructs (e.g. optimism, self-efficacy), is pivotal to the evaluation of environmental and specific training packages. Measurement in mental toughness is a major issue and attempts to progress these tools should be valued and encouraged. Construct validation is an ongoing process (Marsh and Jackson, 1999) and requires rigorous examination of measures on conceptual, statistical, and practical grounds (Mallett et al., 2007). Mental toughness measurement issues are beyond the scope of the current chapter but are discussed elsewhere in this volume (Chapters 6 and 7 above). Due to the paucity of rigorous research on interventions such as psychological skills training on the development of mental toughness it is not possible at this time to draw firm conclusions about the utility of such interventions.

In the following sections we review the literature on the unique perspectives of parents, coaches and athletes in how they perceive mental toughness is developed. First, the research highlights that these stakeholders reported that mental toughness could be developed; and secondly, they reported how this development was achieved.

Parents' perceptions of developing mental toughness

Gould et al. (2002) found three key psychological qualities of Olympic champions, namely, self-motivation, self-confidence and mental toughness. Moreover, they reported the influence of the family environment in developing these qualities, which underpinned the development of talent. Several recent studies (e.g. Bull et al., 2005; Connaughton et al., 2008a; Coulter et al., under review) have also reported the importance of early childhood experiences in the development of mental toughness and in particular the influence of parents and siblings. Bull et al. (2005) argued for a significant role of the environment in developing mental toughness. Primary environmental influences, identified by Bull and colleagues, included the familial milieu such as parenting and childhood background as being a foundation upon which key mental toughness characteristics are developed. Nevertheless, Bull et al. were rather unclear as to how specific global themes in the aforementioned research related to the development of mental toughness, while no supportive data or explanation were forwarded as to how mental toughness actually develops (Connaughton and Hanton, 2009). For example, Bull et al. reported parental influence as an important mechanism at various stages in the performer's upbringing; however, there is no clarification by Bull and colleagues as to what kind of influence this was, how this influence impacted on mental toughness development or at what stages in the performer's career this influence actually takes place (Connaughton and Hanton, 2009).

While these findings initiated the process of understanding the role both parents and siblings have within the family environment and recognized that socio-cultural and personal conditions during athletes' upbringing can impact the development of mental toughness characteristics, the literature to date has merely speculated on the perceived role parents (in particular) play within this process. Furthermore, while several studies (e.g. Bull et al., 2005; Connaughton et al., 2008b; Gucciardi et al., 2009d; Thelwell et al., 2010) recognize that parents and the family environment have an influential role in developing mental toughness attributes, it is surprising that few studies have examined the personal experiences of parents of mentally tough athletes as to their insight into their own role (if any) in developing specific and/or general mental toughness characteristics. This methodological limitation is particularly pertinent given that parents possess knowledge that directly relates to their children's character and individuality throughout their development, in addition to having an understanding of the environments within which children grow and the experiences one's children were subjected to throughout their upbringing and playing career (Coulter et al., 2010). Within the mental toughness literature, Coulter et al. (under review) acknowledged the perceptions of parents regarding their views in identifying their own role in fostering a home environment that encouraged the development and maintenance of those values, attitudes, emotions and cognitions encompassing the construct. The parents were purposively sampled from players who were consistently identified by several coaches as mentally tough. Coulter et al. (under review) found that parents (three mothers and two fathers) believed that the important periods within which the development of mental toughness occurs are early childhood and adolescence. Parents also recognized that mental toughness can be developed or maintained following this time, for instance, during the early phase as a professional (approximately 19–23 years old) and later years throughout one's career, respectively. Nevertheless, the important period for developmental influence was believed to occur during a child/athlete's upbringing. The parents perceived mental toughness development being influenced from multiple sources (i.e. environmental, parental, coach, player) where both direct mechanisms, such as teaching or emphasizing certain psychological lessons (e.g. coping skills, sport intelligence) and motivational climates (e.g. emphasizing enjoyment or competitive rivalry), and indirect mechanisms, involving modelling or unknowingly creating certain dominant environments (e.g. emphasizing family values at home) or via uncontrollable events (e.g. critical incidents) are at work. Specifically, parent participants in Coulter et al.'s study acknowledged their essential role in supporting their sons to develop a generalized (consistent with Gucciardi et al., 2009d) *and* sport-specific form of mental toughness to cope with challenge, pressure and adversity both in and outside of the game. In particular, higher-order themes from the findings suggested that parents of identified mentally tough players believed they created home environments that (a) promoted and encouraged learning, (b) created positive psychological experiences and (c) provided ongoing support.

The promotion and encouragement of learning was characterized by developing coping skills and strategies (e.g. optimistic thinking, long-term goals, rationalizing adversity, encouraging perseverance), which sought to develop the will to win, strong work ethic, resilience and tough attitude (i.e. their conception of mental toughness) both in and outside of sport. Parents in this sample viewed themselves as key role models for their sons. The parents deliberately sought to instill particular core values into their sons, which were related to creating a positive psychological home environment: for example, the type and amount of praise and criticism a young athlete receives from parents, and the self-belief parents provided their children (i.e. other-efficacy). Family values played a fundamental role not only in developing a mentally tough soccer player, but also strong, resilient and respectful people. It was perceived that these values must be enforced to create strict ground rules for acceptable and consistent behaviors (i.e. standards to live by in the family environment) regardless of the occasion. The parents of mentally tough soccer players also underscored the importance of providing ongoing support to their sons. In particular, parents in this study perceived that children must be supported at all times during their entire developmental years as young players. Moreover, they reported the need to sustain this support throughout their future career as a player. The specific types of parental support were acknowledged (and prioritized) as emotional (e.g. wanting to win and perform well; develop coping strategies in challenging situations), informational (e.g. honest debriefing post matches and focusing on mastery and accomplishment) and tangible (e.g. transportation, financial support, attendance at matches/training).

The parents interviewed in Coulter et al. (under review) perceived the limited influence of the coach in fostering the mental toughness of a soccer player during a player's early developmental years (i.e. 0–7 years of age). The only qualification to this limited influence was that parents thought coaches should emphasize a motivational training climate of fun and enjoyment (rather than performance outcome), incorporating the basic skills of the game, which was believed to impact how players are 'grabbed' by the game. Nonetheless, once young players start to enter organized forms of soccer (i.e. from approximately 8 years of age), the influence of coaching staff was considered key, especially in developing the soccer-specific form of mental toughness and in creating a motivational climate that influences a player's generalized character outside of the game (consistent with Gucciardi et al., 2009d). In particular, parents identified that coaches have a responsibility to develop the mental toughness of young players by teaching them about the attitude required to develop and succeed as a professional player (e.g. self-responsibility/autonomy, strict personal values, sacrifice, discipline and commitment). Coaches were viewed as having a key instructive role in teaching young players how to understand the game (e.g. formations, role responsibility, team tactics, sport intelligence), while also reinforcing those behaviors that highlight mental toughness qualities (high work ethic). Finally, these parents viewed coaches as providing transitional emotional support for developing players. A key period for coaches to emotionally support young players was recognized during the transition to the senior level where players had to adjust to their new 'apprentice' role within a squad. Parents identified this transition as a potentially difficult time, which might negatively impact a young player's self-belief and dedication to achieve success.

To summarize the perceptions of parents (in accordance with both coach and player views) in understanding the perceived role parents play in developing mentally tough individuals, Coulter et al. (under review) illustrated the apparent bidirectional ways parents, the family, and child(ren) relate to and influence one another in developing the components (e.g. beliefs, values, morals, perspective) of mental toughness (see Figure 10.1). Leveraged from the model in Fredricks and Eccles (2004) of parents' influence upon child motivation and achievement, their model accounts for the perceived interdependent relationships between parent and child, the role of demographic and individual difference factors (e.g. culture, education, knowledge of elite sport, parenting style) that appear to have influence within the development process, the impact of family structure, history, social systems and values, and the consideration that each child actively contributes to its own mental toughness development during upbringing. Essentially, in constructing the family environment, and in managing one's own actions as a parent in response to each child's behavior in both a general and domain-specific context (based upon parental expectations and perceptions of that child within and across each context), parents act as a filter upon which child adaptive responses are shaped when experiencing, becoming aware of and learning from those circumstances that require mental toughness. As such, the aforementioned findings and illustration provide preliminary information that identifies parents, and the role of the family environment, as prominent figures and mechanisms with which mentally tough individuals are raised.

Although preliminary and requiring replication and extension, it appears that parents of mentally tough athletes believe mental toughness can be developed. Moreover, parents viewed themselves as key sources in the development of mental toughness in both childhood and adolescence but acknowledged the increasing role of coaches during youth. Central to the development of mental toughness seemed to be the creation of a home environment that was structured, characterized by core values and challenging. The promotion of learning, interpreting life experiences in a positive way and providing ongoing support to their children was central to the development of adaptive coping styles and a winning mentality. Parents have the capacity to instil key attitudes associated with mental toughness, such as the importance of pursuing excellence. This pursuit of excellence characterizes the will to win and includes a strong work ethic, discipline and a limited fear of tackling challenging tasks. Parental overprotective behaviors were also reported as potentially hindering the development of mental toughness by creating a fear of failure and promoting external motivation. Nevertheless, further studies of the perceptions of parents are necessary before more definitive conclusions can be drawn.

Coaches' perceptions of developing mental toughness

In acknowledging some common mental toughness characteristics in sport, several researchers (e.g. Connaughton et al., 2008a; Coulter et al., 2010; Gucciardi, et al., 2008) have argued the importance of context in understanding and developing mental toughness. The importance of context underscores the ability to better predict behavior and for the provision of guidelines for the development of mental toughness characteristics. Connaughton et al. (2008a) reported the importance of an adaptive motivational climate that focused on mastery and enjoyment and acknowledging that coaches as the architects of the motivational climate (Mallett, 2005; Mallett and Hanrahan, 2004) are therefore the significant actors responsible for the facilitation and inhibition of mental toughness within the sport domain. As such, gaining a comprehensive understanding of how coaches develop performance excellence, and specifically, through recognizing how they understand and view mental toughness to be developed (in their own practice, in addition to the perceived role of significant others) has warranted investigation. Interestingly, however, past qualitative research involving wrestling coaches (Gould et al., 1987) found that while 82 per cent of coaches rated mental toughness as the most important psychological attribute in performance success, only 9 per cent of coaches felt they were successful in developing the construct in their athletes. Consistent with a family systems approach to psycho-social development (Hellstedt, 1995) coaches seem to increase their influence as sportspeople reach adolescence. With the prominence of the coach in mind, and

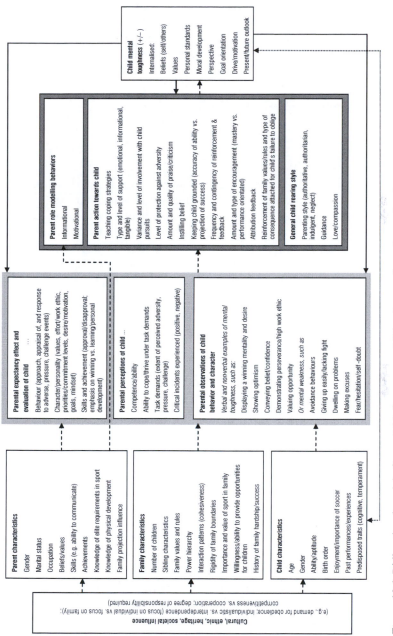

Figure 10.1 Bidirectional model of parental influences on children's mental toughness development

in acknowledging recent developments within the literature in gaining a greater sense of understanding mental toughness conceptualization, this section presents research that examines the perceptions of coaches' understanding of mental toughness and their views about its development.

Coulter et al. (under review) investigated the views of parents, coaches and players on how mental toughness characteristics are acquired and developed in the context of Australian soccer. The influence of coaches and support staff in fostering the mental toughness of a soccer player was reported to have a prominent influence once young players enter organized forms of soccer (i.e. from approximately 8 years of age). This influence was considered key, especially in developing the soccer-specific form of mental toughness, and also in creating a climate that influences a player's generalized character outside of the game (i.e. promoting high work ethic, responsibility, resilience, tough attitudes, emotional intelligence, focus, winning mentality and personal standards in emphasizing life skills that are transferable from within the soccer environment to one's everyday experience).

Within the soccer-related environment, coaches reported that they can shape the development of a sport-specific form of mental toughness through a variety of behaviors, strategies, and an emphasis on preparing players to be professional soccer players. In essence, coaches saw themselves as key individuals in creating a positive psychological environment for young players, while also providing ample learning opportunities throughout their development in teaching the qualities of the mentally tough player. Specifically, providing these opportunities was thought to be achieved through strategies such as instructing junior players to understand the intricacies of the game (i.e. sport intelligence); supporting young players through the transitions of the elite ranks; providing a sounding board of support to discuss personal and soccer-related issues (i.e. developing a strong coach–player relationship); utilizing experience of reputable professionals to convey the attitude that must be adopted to achieve this status; learning how to focus on one's strengths in becoming a dominating player; providing junior players with a sharp reminder of their opportunities if their attitude does not live up to accepted and agreed standards; emphasizing personal responsibility; support in evaluating and coping with adversity; and ensuring that players remain grounded with their soccer-related ability and achievements.

The importance of developing a tough performance-based climate, which emphasized the pursuit of winning, was also recognized as being essential in developing a vigorous mental toughness in Coulter et al. (under review). That tough performance-based climate, which was demanded at all times, allowed junior players to appreciate the value of winning, while also understanding that hard work focused on continuous improvement regardless of ability. The creation of this climate was identified as an important strategy in 'hardening' young players to become determined and persevering individuals with a thirst for success in achieving personal goals. In addition, creating a training environment that pushed players physically (e.g. intense physical drills) and mentally (e.g. simulated pressure scenarios, intra-squad competition) was thought to establish an improved self-awareness of one's capacity to withstand high levels of stress (physical and mental) during challenging competition situations. Within this testing environment it was also recognized how coaches debriefed and reinforced player behavior and reactions to such challenges were pivotal to developing the will to win. Finally, several other strategies such as teaching psychological skills, providing encouragement and support, modelling positive behaviors and attitudes, setting clear standards and expectations, and advocating a philosophy of winning but, at the same time, emphasizing learning, effort and improvement were also perceived by coaches as important mechanisms to developing core mental toughness qualities.

It is noteworthy that coaches also acknowledged family influences upon the development of mental toughness attributes (Coulter et al., under review). In particular, the role of parents in establishing a home environment with strong family values, providing satisfactory support (emotional, informational, tangible), exhibiting appropriate role modelling behaviors, promoting the learning of positive coping skills, and ensuring that children learn the value of opportunity and are praised on their effort (not outcomes) were deemed as being influential to nurturing mental toughness qualities away from the sports field. Importantly, coaches recognized that the messages being reinforced at home greatly influenced the attitude and behavior young players brought to the sport environment. Naturally, coaches perceived this familial influence as an important factor as to whether players embraced the performance climate set by coaches and how they dealt with perceived sporting challenges/adversity off the pitch.

Gucciardi et al. (2009d) examined the perceptions of elite Australian football coaches about the strategies they used to develop mental toughness. They interviewed 11 male coaches who were successful and experienced as players and coaches. In a previous study (Gucciardi et al., 2008) the same coaches identified 11 key mental toughness characteristics: self-belief, work ethic, personal values, self-motivation, tough attitude, concentration and focus, resilience, able to handle pressure, emotional intelligence, sport intelligence and physical toughness. From the follow-up interviews four themes central to the role of the coach in the development of contextualized mental toughness emerged: (a) coach–athlete relationship, (b) coaching philosophy, (c) training environment and specific strategies, (d) negative experiences and influences (impediments). The importance of early childhood experiences also emerged as a central theme. The sport of Australian football provided players with a range of experiences throughout their playing careers, which were considered as opportunities for transforming the generalized forms of mental toughness developed through childhood into a more 'sport-specific' form of mental toughness. Trust and respect were the key to an adaptive coach–athlete relationship that fostered mental toughness. A high level of trust and respect facilitated open and authentic communication between actors. A commitment from both actors to maintaining a healthy relationship was also underscored by the participant coaches. A strong philosophy that emphasized a holistic approach to development rather than emphasizing performance outcomes (e.g. winning) created an environment in which failure was inevitable and necessary for learning to occur. Diligence and thorough preparation underpinned the view that talent must work hard for success and instilled a sense of accomplishment, which facilitated several mental toughness qualities: self-belief, personal values, work ethic, self-motivation and emotional and sport intelligence.

In the design of a training environment that consistently challenged players, the importance of hard work, internal motivation and physical toughness was developed. The capacity to complete physically demanding training was likely to promote a perception of competence (self-belief) and accomplishment (self-motivation). Pushing players to their physical and mental limits provided them with opportunities to learn how to deal with such challenges, preparing them to effectively deal and thrive in the conditions consistently experienced in the cauldron of elite sport. The coaches reported several strategies aimed at developing mental toughness, including 'Socratic' questioning to challenge players' thinking and promote discussion of training activities. 'Understanding breeds compliance' and the importance of understanding the rationale for tasks undertaken is likely to promote autonomy and subsequently internal motivation (Mageau and Vallerand, 2003; Mallett, 2005). The use of training diaries, simulated game situations, positive reinforcement and encouragement for effort, public praise, viewing mistakes as opportunities for learning, and valuing all players in the team, all contributed to the development of self-belief and a strong work ethic.

Coaches influence players' attitudes and beliefs through the implicit and explicit 'messages' they send; for example, an overemphasis on winning and the importance of the outcome in preference to pursuing winning with passion and hunger implies the importance of the outcome as the only criterion for evaluating success. Coaches play an important role in sending consistent messages about what is important – is it winning at all costs, or wanting to win and putting in 100 per cent effort and determination in that pursuit? Negative experiences and influences (e.g. a coach's overemphasis on winning) were reported as impediments to the development of mental toughness. The participants in the study expressed the important role of childhood experiences in nurturing a 'generalized form' of mental toughness. Parents were considered the key people in nurturing mental toughness through childhood experiences. Specifically, the importance of role modelling was reported: 'We are the products of our parents. If they display discipline, a "never give up" or "can do" attitude, then we as their child generally adopt the same attitude' (Gucciardi et al., 2009d: 1488). Parents seemed to influence the development of mental toughness through promoting adaptive interpretations of various situations; providing variety of experience, challenge, and some autonomy; and importantly providing informational, tangible and emotional support. The coaches acknowledged that, although adaptive childhood experiences built a general foundation of mental toughness, there was a declining influence of parents in developing a specific form of mental toughness.

Weinberg et al. (in press) who examined coaches' perceptions of mental toughness (based on Jones et al.'s conception) and its development purposively sampled coaches based on a clear criterion that they were proactive in developing mental toughness in their athletes; that is, coaches were asked at the recruitment stage to provide some details about how they developed mental toughness in their sport. Moreover, their sample of 10 successful (winning) coaches (five female) was from a variety of sports. The content analysis of the interview data revealed that the coaches believed they played an important role in developing mental toughness in their athletes. Moreover, they considered participation in varsity sport in the USA (around 19–23 years) to be a critical period for developing mental toughness. Positive changes in salient behaviors (e.g. an increased ability to handle difficult situations; act more confidently; increased self-motivation to improve skills) were considered signs of developing mental toughness in players. Key qualities were sought in the athletes, including practice intensity, work ethic and game attitude as indicators of mental toughness. Nevertheless, the three higher-order themes to emerge from the data were: psychological skills (focus, confidence, knowledge and mental planning), motivation to succeed (work hard, persistence) and resilience (rebound from setbacks, perform under pressure). In terms of developing mental toughness the coach participants in this study identified three central themes: tough physical practice environment, positive mental environment and providing awareness learning opportunities.

In the development of mental toughness the coaches reported the importance of creating a tough physical practice environment, which included intense training practices that simulated competition, which is consistent with the notion of developing a winning mentality. Time was needed to develop mental toughness and the training environment provided an appropriate forum to simulate situations requiring mental toughness (game-like pressure situations). The high intensity of practice, which included tough physical conditioning, promoted a sense of accomplishment and confidence in their preparation and contributed to the resiliency of the athletes. The importance of facilitating athletes' confidence and perceptions of competence was achieved through the creation of a positive mental environment, which was characterized by constructive, informational feedback and opportunities for enjoyment within a tough physical training environment. The importance of clear expectations (e.g. effort required) of what coaches sought in training and competition was also foregrounded in the development of persistence. Consistent with Bandura's (1997) self-efficacy theory, the coaches reported the deliberate promotion of vicarious learning through the observation of others (e.g. video, imagery). The provision of these opportunities for developing awareness of mental toughness in action was considered part of the strategic approach taken to develop mental toughness.

Some recent research (e.g. Coulter et al., 2010) has focused on identifying the situations within a specific sport (i.e. soccer) that requires mental toughness. The coaches in Weinberg et al.'s (in press) study also took the opportunity to identify situations requiring mental toughness and highlight the qualities required to be mentally tough in those situations. Furthermore, the coaches reported the importance of role modelling relevant mental toughness behaviors such as being organized and prepared. The participant coaches were also concerned about the adverse effects of mental toughness (excessive risk-taking, ignoring pain) in recognizing the need for coaches to monitor athletes training and performance (e.g.

over-training, competing with an injury). In this study the coaches were identified as deliberately attempting to develop mental toughness in their athletes, which assumes a reasonably clear conceptualization of what mental toughness is and how coaches can contribute to its development through their coaching behaviors. Although this research does not highlight specific situations of mental toughness in respective sports, it does support the view that some coaches believe they understand what mental toughness represents within their sport and importantly that they can play an important role in the development of it.

Overall, sports coaches, who were interviewed in the aforementioned studies, have reported the importance of early childhood influences (parents, siblings) in the development of a generalized form of mental toughness and the development of a more specific form of mental toughness within the context of sport. Specifically, coaches reported that the development of mental toughness was deliberate and situated rather than serendipitous. That is, coaches believed they proactively sought to develop mental toughness, suggesting that they (a) had relatively clear conceptions of what mental toughness is, (b) valued this quality and (c) that it could be developed. Nevertheless, Gould et al. (1987) found that less than 10 per cent of Olympic coaches interviewed believed they were successful in developing mental toughness in their athletes. Perhaps some coaches lack the knowledge and/or skills to develop mental toughness in athletes. Alternatively, some coaches might believe that mental toughness is innate. Coaches are not only responsible for the design of an adaptive motivational climate but are important role models for athletes. An adaptive motivational climate as reported by these coaches seems to be characterized by mastery (reflecting a tough but fair training environment that mirrors the performance environment and promotes a hunger for wanting to be the best), enjoyment, autonomy, effective and authentic communication, and informational feedback, which is consistent with that approach argued by several sport psychology and coaching science scholars (e.g. Gucciardi and Mallett, 2010; Mageau and Vallerand, 2003; Mallett, 2005). Within this adaptive and autonomy-supportive motivational climate the central role of the coach in providing athletes with a holistic approach to development includes the promotion of the need to engage in hard physical training, mastery of skills and tactics, and simulated competitive situations in training. This adaptive motivational climate should facilitate a passion and hunger for pursuing excellence and an attitude of wanting to win and not giving up until the referee signals the end of the game.

Athletes' perceptions of developing mental toughness

To date, recent investigations have sought to conceptualize mental toughness and these studies have resulted collectively in a greater understanding of the construct, regarding its definition, the identification of its attributes, and the development of a working framework (e.g. Jones et al., 2007). Naturally, within this process, athletes' perspectives have played a dominant role in helping us understand the mindset, emotions and behaviors of the mentally tough individual. Without question, central to the development of mental toughness are the athletes themselves and their adaptive responses to many life experiences that have the potential to facilitate mental toughness. Taking the centrality of players' experiences into account, it would appear that personal insights into the pathways and influences that facilitate the development of the mentally tough athlete would provide a depth of data targeting the motives, experiences, climates and influential personnel that encourage the growth of mental toughness and its characteristics.

When considering the perceptions of athletes regarding mental toughness development a key issue to consider is how do we know that the personal accounts of athletes accurately represent those experiences that facilitate its development (naturally, this is a challenge facing researchers regardless of participant grouping – athletes, parents, coaches, sport psychologists, etc.)? In other words, should we solely target the opinions and experiences of those 'great', not 'good', athletes given that some scholars (e.g. Gucciardi et al., 2008) suggest that mental toughness acts as the ingredient that separates these cohorts and views the outcome component of mental toughness as being better than opponents (Jones et al., 2002), or do we focus attention on those individuals who consistently, year-after-year, compete at the very top of their profession without always reaching the level of success (i.e. wins) of other, potentially more physically talented athletes? The likelihood is that recognizing the circumstances of both would be useful and insightful as to understanding the developmental pathways and global experiences of the mentally tough athlete. Nonetheless, a key point is that it is important to consider the perceptions of the individual, whether or not they are considered to be mentally tough (certainly in comprehending the developmental differences of mentally tough individuals), and to be careful to avoid confusing the outcome of career success (and the developmental reasons underlying such outcomes) with those mechanisms considered to impact mental toughness development *per se*. The reality is that all athletes will have (to some degree) experienced those mechanisms that impact the facilitation of mental toughness and outcome success and one might argue that one impacts the facilitation of the other (and vice versa). A key distinction from a research perspective, however, is to elicit how athletes attribute those underlying mechanisms (e.g. training climate, personnel influence, motives/ drives) to their career success, and how these compare and contrast with their development of specific mental toughness characteristics. Research may identify a natural crossover with such comparisons. Nevertheless, gaining an appreciation for the athletes' understanding of what mental toughness conceptually is (cf. attributes important to performance outcome) may be worthy of discussion prior to any investigation of how the construct characteristics themselves may have been developed on a personal level. With this in mind, three recent investigations by Connaughton et al. (2008a), Thelwell et al. (2010) and Coulter et al. (under review) have investigated the perceptions of athletes about the development of mental toughness. Here, the former two investigations examine the perceptions of highly successful athletes based on the premise that, having reached the elite level in their respective sport, these individuals are therefore best placed to comment on the mechanisms that facilitate mental toughness development. On the other hand, the examination by Coulter et al. inspects the perceptions of those athletes identified as being mentally tough based on the perceptions of elite coaches.

First, data from seven athletes interviewed by Connaughton et al. (2008a) revealed a multitude of underlying mechanisms that were described as operating in a 'combined, rather than independent manner' to facilitate the development of 12 mental toughness characteristics (Jones et al., 2002) over three distinct career phases (namely, those developmental phases, which they aligned with Bloom's (1985) early, middle and later years of elite-performer development). During the early years, three developmental attributes were considered to act as the foundation for mental toughness development. Specifically, these included acquiring an unshakable self-belief (in their ability to achieve one's goals, and that one possesses the ability to be better than opponents), and an insatiable desire and internalized motives to succeed in one's goals, which seems similar to developing the desire to succeed. Underlying mechanisms perceived as impacting upon the development of these characteristics were acknowledged as gaining advice from significant others (e.g. parents, coaches), and observing older, elite performers in training and competition in providing a source of knowledge, inspiration and encouragement that imparted a powerful influence enabling the efficient mastery of relevant skills during this period. Furthermore, the athletes reported that effective leadership from coaches assisted in nurturing an adaptive motivational climate, which was challenging, rewarding and enjoyable. The ongoing development of these attributes was perceived as continuing into the middle years, complementing the development of five additional characteristics, namely, being able to bounce back from setbacks, regaining psychological control, pushing back the boundaries of pain, accepting and coping with competitive anxiety and thriving on pressure. The facilitation of these attributes was perceived by the elite athletes to be most influenced by having a competitive rivalry in training and competition, rationalization of success and failures, and receiving guidance from an understanding social support network. The athletes also reported that reflective practice about the experience of elite-level competition, simulation training, the extraction of positive experiences and rationalization of setbacks contributed to the development of the remaining four attributes during the later phase. These qualities included having the ability to switch a sport focus on and off as required, remaining fully focused on the task at hand in the face of competition-specific distractions, not being adversely affected by other athletes' good and bad performances, and remaining fully focused in the face of personal-life distractions.

It is worth acknowledging that throughout these developmental phases, Connaughton et al. (2008a) also reported that athletes perceived the influence and experience of critical incidents in one's life (e.g. disruptions at school, loss of a peer/parent, family break up) as having an important role in cultivating mental toughness (e.g. internalized desire and motive to succeed, desire for a better life). Additionally, once mental toughness had been developed, athletes perceived that several mechanisms were required to underlie the maintenance of this construct.

For example, the use of a variety of mental skills and strategies, simulation training and the establishment of a trustworthy and dependable social support network underpinned the maintenance of mental toughness.

Thelwell et al. (2010) examined the views of 10 international female gymnasts from the USA and UK (five from each country), who were asked if they believed mental toughness was a natural or developed phenomenon, and what (if any) processes were involved that may be influential in its development. All gymnasts agreed that mental toughness was something that they had been able to develop, especially as the result of negative experiences (e.g. injuries, falls, failures) that made them mentally stronger and enhanced their motivation to succeed. Positive experiences such as gaining confidence from performing well were also highlighted as an underlying mechanism. Importantly, life experiences were also viewed as a catalyst for mental toughness development. For instance, these included incidents such as moving home/location, parental issues (separation/divorce, bereavements) and school-related difficulties (bullying, struggling with work). Together, such experiences outside of sport were perceived to enable mental toughness to develop both in and out of sport and to enhance the focus and drive for gymnasts to achieve success.

Thelwell et al. (2010) also reported that elite international gymnasts recognized the influence of specific processes, personnel and environmental mechanisms to be important in the development of mental toughness. Thelwell and colleagues identified four dimensions athletes perceived as important within this domain. First, sporting processes comprised training, competition and club mechanisms. Training processes included such influences as having goals that motivate and provide focus, utilizing pressured simulation experiences, thorough preparation, learning new skills, and training while injured, as cultivating mental toughness characteristics. Competition processes were predominantly identified as allowing gymnasts to have success and failure experiences within competition in order to assist the learning process to deal with nerves, remain in control, stay focused, and deal with competition adversity (e.g. learning to lose with grace, being determined and learning the ability to bounce back from setbacks). Although perceived as less influential, club gymnastics was identified as providing a positive environment which enabled the opportunity for developing key mental toughness characteristics (e.g. self-belief, positive attitude, motivation).

Similar to Connaughton et al. (2008a), Thelwell et al. (2010) also suggested the important influence of particular personnel (sporting and non-sporting) on the development of athlete mental toughness characteristics. Sporting personnel comprise coaches, teammates, other competitors and sport psychologists. The gymnasts perceived coaching influences to take their form by influencing mental toughness development directly by promoting individual training programmes and mental skills development, and indirectly by instilling hard work and discipline in athletes. Encouragement and emotional support, motivation (instilling determination, high expectations), and the development of challenging situations were recognized as key mechanisms that the coach brings to the developmental process. Interestingly, only USA gymnasts reported their coaches' belief in them to be a key factor and that their coaches taught specific psychological skills, thus suggesting possible cultural differences in development within the participant sample. Teammates and competitors were perceived as helping provide a competitive environment during training and competition that encouraged rivalry, motivation to push oneself, focus and the application of appropriate coping strategies, while sport psychologists (only mentioned by USA gymnasts) helped gymnasts cope with competition anxiety, increasing belief in ability and providing a mindset for success. Consistent with previous research (Connaughton et al., 2008a; Gucciardi et al., 2009c), parents appear a significant contributor to the development of mental toughness. The mechanisms through which athletes perceived parents to contribute to mental toughness included providing feedback, guidance, motivation and involvement through coaching. Being 'positively pushed', with unconditional love and support with no pressure, was most frequently cited, which according to the authors allowed for an internalized desire for success and motivation to be developed. Parents also offered encouragement and emotional support, allowing gymnasts to change how they reacted to various situations by rationalizing their thoughts and feelings. Alternatively, sibling influences developed mental toughness through encouragement, support and rivalry (most frequently cited), where there was a desire to emulate and surpass sibling achievements both inside/outside of sport (consistent with Coulter et al., under review), while significant others impacted characteristic development by providing motivation, emotional support and belief.

Finally, environmental influences were perceived by gymnasts to act as an important contributor to the development of key mental toughness characteristics (Thelwell et al., 2010). Specifically, these mechanisms took shape in the form of the training environment (instilling the characteristics necessary to succeed – hard work, discipline, determination, competitive attitude), family environment (instilling characteristics such as hard work, positive attitude and valuing competition via particular family values, family lifestyle and family dynamics), modelling (having role models who were successful and were excellent trainers to heighten gymnasts' determination to succeed, and provided the belief that one day they might progress to the role model's level), and country (national expectations, past successes and reputation) influences. The interesting identification of 'country influences' and its perceived impact upon mental toughness development once again raises the question of cultural nuances within this process and, specifically, how the mental toughness mindset might be influenced by such potential differences. Thelwell and colleagues suggested that these differences could result from disparities in sports ideology, where factors such as interest in sport and previous success on a national level might be acting mechanisms that impact on the psychological development and mental toughness of athletes (e.g. via promoting positive achievement and a regular competitive environment).

More recently, Coulter et al. (under review) investigated perceptions of six professional A-League soccer players who were identified as being mentally tough by coaches in this Australian league. Together with the views of parents and coaches within a triangulation data capture design, the authors were able to provide a unique perspective from those individuals identified as being mentally tough in their own right as to how they perceived their upbringing and developmental experiences, both in and out of soccer, that were believed to contribute to the development of their tough-natured personality. The reported findings mirrored several of those mechanisms previously reported (Connaughton et al., 2008a; Thelwell et al., 2010) in that the influence of the family environment (e.g. parents, siblings), sporting environment (coaches, motivational climate) and the impact of critical incidents all appear to facilitate the development of mental toughness characteristics.

In addition to the aforementioned investigations, Coulter et al. also identified that players themselves recognize their own role in developing these desirable characteristics. That is, players identified specific areas that they focused on to develop their own mental toughness during their junior athletic development. These areas included educating oneself on the lives of elite and successful individuals in learning about how these individuals coped with adversity throughout their careers, applied hard work, dedication and sacrifice to achieve personal goals, and how they believed in themselves regardless of setbacks both in and out of sport; choosing and surrounding oneself with an encouraging peer/social group that comprehends the commitment being undertaken by talented individuals, who do not add pressure to conform to debilitating adolescent activities and who act as an emotional outlet for players; and establishing a focus on prioritizing one's own self-interests in achieving personal targets. In essence, these findings acknowledge that athletes themselves also appear to play an important role in their own mental toughness development. In particular, parents, coaches, and practitioners may emphasize to players their responsibility in becoming mentally tougher individuals and educating oneself about the mindset, attitude and expectations demanded at the professional level.

In corroborating the findings of the above investigations of athletes' perceptions of mental toughness development, several comments can be made. First, the studies support the contention that mental toughness can be developed. Second, the research reinforces the influence of mechanisms relating to experiences (in and out of sport), to sporting (coaches, teammates, opponents, athletes themselves) and non-sporting (e.g. parents, siblings) personnel, and to the environment on the development of mental toughness. Armed with this knowledge, several practical implications emerge from this body of research (e.g. creating appropriate home/family and training environments, educational programmes for parents and coaches, exposing young athletes to elite environments), which might be considered in designing environments that promote the development of mental toughness.

Summary

The reported research suggests that mental toughness is valued in achievement contexts such as sport. Moreover, the research supports the view that mental toughness can be differentially developed. Several contexts (e.g. home, sport) provide many opportunities for the development of mental toughness in its various forms. Key actors provide emotional, informational and tangible support that facilitates the development of athletes' mental toughness. The key actors are family (especially parents) and coaches who not only create environments that facilitate its development but can mediate athletes' mental toughness through deliberate interventions aimed at rationalizing critical and challenging life events in and out of sport. It would appear that parents play a key role through early childhood, which is achieved through an environment that has clearly understood core values, boundaries for acceptable and unacceptable behaviors, and a positive learning setting. Parents' role in the development of a generalized form of mental toughness seems to provide the foundation for the development of sport-specific mental toughness, which is facilitated by coaches especially during late childhood, adolescence and in the transition into adult sport. Coaches can instill a winning mentality through the creation of a training and competition environment that is adaptive and focused. This adaptive motivational but tough training environment that mirrors the performance context (i.e. competition) seems to be characterized by several features including mastery learning, enjoyment, autonomy, effective and authentic communication, and informational feedback.

Despite the views of parents, coaches and athletes that coaches can influence the development of mental toughness, Gould et al. (1987) found that coaches report their lack of their success in its development, which might suggest the need to assist and guide coaches in how they can mediate the development of this valued quality. Alternatively, some of the coaches in the Gould et al. study may not have had a clear conception of mental toughness, but perhaps a broad understanding. Nevertheless, the athletes are probably the most important actors in the development of their own mental toughness. Mentally tough athletes appear to possess particular attitudes, cognitions, values and emotions. The development of these attitudes and values seem, in part, to be the product of how athletes respond to and learn through their interaction with critical incidents; however, in many instances, parents and coaches can mediate that learning, in their respective environments. Nonetheless, the research presented suggests that mental toughness seems to be mainly 'caught' through life experiences more than it is taught. We argue that parents, for example, implicitly and explicitly teach their children the values and beliefs of being mentally tough. Parents might not realize this as they bring up their children in a way that they believe matches their expectations and perceptions of how children should lead their lives (based on the cultural, personal, family and child characteristics in Figure 10.1).

The authors suggest that it would be advisable for performers to receive support and mental toughness training from an early age rather than in the later stages of their sporting careers. Also, practitioners and coaches should also be aware of the developmental stages/requirements that are perceived to operate within each specific career stage (e.g. early, middle and later years). For example, in the early years, young performers should be encouraged to engage in activities as a means of skills accomplishment, socialization, enjoyment and to develop a sense of discipline and work ethic, while parents and coaches could assist in creating the correct motivational environment for these attributes to be acquired. In the middle years, performers may benefit most from observing and learning from knowledgeable role models (expert coaches/elite performers) to develop a number of positive psychological qualities. Finally, in the later years and during the maintenance years, sources such as experience of international competitions, the use of psychological skills and strategies, and a wide social support network, are alleged to assist in the enhancement and maintenance of mental toughness. Nevertheless, there is an assumption that these development stages are similar across all sports. We would argue that other factors may come into play here (e.g. age, gender) that might impact the type of activities performers are exposed to within each stage and also that the time individuals spend in each stage may be variable dependent upon individual factors and the demands required to become technically elite within a specific sport (e.g. gymnast vs. shooter/archer). Overall, informal learning opportunities, such as providing exposure to a variety of situations and environments, seem to assist performers in acquiring the experience necessary to develop into athletes with a strong will to win.

References

Bandura, A. (1997) *Self-efficacy: The exercise of control*. New York: W. H. Freeman.

Bloom, B. (1985) *Developing Talent in Young People*, New York: Ballantine.

Bull, S. J., Shambrook, C. J., James, W., and Brooks, J. E. (2005) 'Towards an understanding of mental toughness in elite English cricketers', *Journal of Applied Sport Psychology*, 17, 209–27.

Connaughton, D., and Hanton, S. (2009) 'Mental toughness in sport: Conceptual and practical issues', in S. D. Mellalieu and S. Hanton (eds), *Advances in Applied Sport Psychology: A Review*, London: Routledge, pp. 317–46.

Connaughton, D., Hanton, S., Jones, G., and Wadey, R. (2008a) 'Mental toughness research: Key issues in this area', *International Journal of Sport Psychology*, 39, 192–204.

Connaughton, D., Wadey, R., Hanton, S., and Jones, G. (2008b) 'The development and maintenance of mental toughness: Perceptions of elite performers', *Journal of Sports Sciences*, 26, 83–95.

Côté, J. (1999) 'The influence of the family in the development of talent in sport', *The Sport Psychologist*, 13, 395–417.

Coulter, T. J., Mallett, C. J., and Gucciardi, D. F. (2010) 'Understanding mental toughness in Australian soccer: Perceptions of players, parents, and coaches', *Journal of Sports Sciences,* 28, 699–716.

Coulter, T. J., Mallett, C. J., and Gucciardi, D. F. (under review) 'Developing mental toughness in Australian soccer: Perceptions of players, parents, and coaches'.

Crust, L. (2007) 'Mental toughness in sport: A review', *International Journal of Sport and Exercise Psychology*, 5, 270–90.

Crust, L. (2008) 'A review and conceptual re-examination of mental toughness: Implications for future researchers', *Personality and Individual Differences*, 45, 576–83.

Fredricks, J. A., and Eccles, J. S. (2004) 'Parental influences on youth involvement in sports', in M. R. Weiss (ed.), *Developmental Sport and Exercise Psychology: A Lifespan Perspective,* Morgantown, WV: Fitness Information Technology, pp.145–64.

Gagné, F. (2004) 'Transforming gifts into talents: The DMGT as a developmental theory', *High Ability Studies*, 15, 119–47.

Golby, J., and Sheard, M. (2006) 'The relationship between genotype and positive psychological development in national-level swimmers', *European Psychologist*, 11, 143–8.

Gould, D., Hodge, K., Peterson, K., and Petlichkoff, L. (1987) 'Psychological foundations of coaching: Similarities and differences among intercollegiate wrestling coaches', *The Sport Psychologist*, 1, 293–308.

Gould, D., Dieffenach, K., and Moffett, A. (2002) 'Psychological characteristics and development of Olympic champions', *Journal of Applied Sport Psychology*, 14, 172–204.

Gucciardi, D. F., and Gordon, S. (2009) 'Development and preliminary validation of the Cricket Mental Toughness Inventory', *Journal of Sports Sciences*, 27, 1293–1310.

Gucciardi, D. F., and Mallett, C. J. (2010) 'Understanding mental toughness and its development in sport', in S. J. Hanrahan and M. B. Andersen, *Routledge Handbook of Applied Sport Psychology,* London: Routledge, pp. 547–56.

Gucciardi, D. F., Gordon, S., and Dimmock, J. A. (2008) 'Towards an understanding of mental toughness in Australian football', *Journal of Applied Sport Psychology*, 20, 261–81.

Gucciardi, D. F., Gordon, S., and Dimmock, J. A. (2009a) 'Development and preliminary validation of a mental toughness inventory for Australian football', *Psychology of Sport and Exercise,* 10, 201–9.

Gucciardi, D. F., Gordon, S., and Dimmock, J. A. (2009b) 'Evaluation of a mental toughness training program for youth-aged Australian footballers: I. A quantitative analysis', *Journal of Applied Sport Psychology*, 21, 307–23.

Gucciardi, D. F., Gordon, S., and Dimmock, J. A. (2009c) 'Evaluation of a mental toughness training program for youth-aged Australian footballers: II. A qualitative analysis', *Journal of Applied Sport Psychology*, 21, 324–39.

Gucciardi, D. F., Gordon, S., Dimmock, J. A., and Mallett, C. J. (2009d) 'Understanding the coach's role in the development of mental toughness: Perspectives of elite Australian football coaches', *Journal of Sports Sciences*, 27, 1483–96.

Harwood, C., Spray, C. M., and Keegan, R. (2008). Achievement goal theories in sport. In T. S. Horn (Ed.), *Advances in sport psychology* (3rd edn., pp. 157–186). Champaign, IL: Human Kinetics.

Hellstedt, J. C. (1995) 'Invisible players: A family systems model', in S. H. Murphy (ed.), *Sport Psychology Interventions,* Champaign, IL: Human Kinetics, pp. 117–46.

Horsburgh, V. A., Schermer, J. A., Veselka, L., and Vernon, P. A. (2009) 'A behavioural genetic study of mental toughness and personality', *Personality and Individual Differences*, 46, 100–5.

Jones, G., Hanton, S., and Connaughton, D. (2002) 'What is this thing called mental toughness? An investigation of elite sport performers', *Journal of Applied Sport Psychology*, 14, 205–18.

Jones, G., Hanton, S., and Connaughton, D. (2007) 'A framework of mental toughness in the world's best performers', *The Sport Psychologist*, 21, 243–64.

Mageau, G. A., and Vallerand, R. J. (2003) 'The coach–athlete relationship: A motivational model', *Journal of Sport Sciences*, 21, 883–904.

Mallett, C. J. (2005) 'Self-determination theory: A case study of evidence-based coaching', *The Sport Psychologist*, 19, 417–29.

Mallett, C. J., and Hanrahan, S. J. (2004) 'Elite athletes: What makes the "fire" burn so brightly?', *Psychology of Sport and Exercise*, 5, 183–200.

Mallett, C. J., Kawabata, M., and Newcombe, P. (2007) 'Progressing measurement in sport motivation: A response to Pelletier, Vallerand, and Sarrazin', *Psychology of Sport and Exercise*, 8, 622–31.

Martindale, R. J. J., Collins, D., and Daubney, J. (2005) 'Talent development: A guide for practice and research within sport', *Quest*, 57, 353–75.

Marsh, H. W., and Jackson, S. A. (1999) 'Flow experience in sport: Construct validation of multidimensional hierarchical state and trait responses', *Structural Equation Modeling*, 6, 343–71.

Sheard, M., and Golby, J. (2006) 'Effect of a psychological skills training program on swimming performance and positive psychological development', *International Journal of Sport and Exercise Psychology*, 4, 149–69.

Thelwell, R., Weston, N., and Greenlees, I. (2005) 'Defining and understanding mental toughness in soccer', *Journal of Applied Sport Psychology*, 17, 326–32.

Thelwell, R. C., Such, B. A., Weston, N. J. V., Such, J. D., and Greenlees, I. A. (2010) 'Developing mental toughness: Perceptions of elite female gymnasts', *International Journal of Sport and Exercise Psychology*, 8, 170–88.

Weinberg, R., Butt, J., and Culp, B. (in press) 'Coaches' views of mental toughness and how it is built', *International Journal of Sport and Exercise Psychology*.

11 Building mental toughness

Robert Weinberg and Joanne Butt

In the world of competitive sports one often hears of athletes who did not reach their potential. What this statement usually means is that the athlete had great physical skills (e.g. speed, quickness, jumping ability, strength, timing) but somehow lacked the mental application necessary to be successful. Conversely, there are athletes who do not seem to have outstanding physical talent, but yet manage to be successful at the collegiate, professional or international level. Researchers and practitioners have concluded that it is likely the mental game that really distinguishes elite performers from their less elite counterparts (Orlick and Partington, 1988). For example, mental skills have been shown to discriminate those athletes 'who get there' and those 'who stay there' (Kreiner-Phillips and Orlick, 1993), those who perform on the big stage and those who do not (Gould et al., 1993), and those who successfully develop through times of change/transition and those who do not (Sinclair and Orlick, 1993).

Coaches and others involved in developing talent have come to realize that in order to be successful (especially at the highest levels of competition) one needs both physical and mental skills. Coaches have been teaching mental skills and techniques for years but it is only relatively recently that they have started to focus on and teach mental skills. The lack of focus is unfortunate, in that over 20 years ago Gould et al. (1987) found that 82 per cent of coaches rated mental toughness as the most important psychological attribute in determining wrestling success, although only 9 per cent of them felt that they were successful in developing or changing this desirable construct in the performers with whom they had worked. However, there has been an increase in mental toughness research during the past several years that has tended to focus on the conceptualization of mental toughness in order to establish a clearer definition of the construct and its characteristics.

Defining mental toughness

Mental toughness research has tended to focus on elite performers from various sports (e.g. Jones et al., 2002, 2007) as well as within specific sports such as elite cricket (Bull et al., 2005; Gucciardi and Gordon, 2009), soccer (Coulter et al., 2010; Thelwell et al., 2005), and Australian football (Gucciardi et al., 2008). Collectively, findings from these studies demonstrated a fair amount of consistency on what constitutes mental toughness (e.g. coping with pressure, self-belief, dedication and commitment, personal responsibility). It is also important to note that self-belief appears to be one of the most consistent attributes of mental toughness (Jones et al., 2007; Gucciardi et al., 2008).

Research has enhanced mental toughness knowledge from a conceptual perspective. Emerging from the discipline of health psychology, hardiness (Kobasa, 1979) combines the three dimensions of control, commitment and challenge, and is considered to be a personality trait that can be influential in buffering the harmful effects of stress. Clough and his colleagues (2002) used hardiness as a theoretical framework to develop a definition and model of mental toughness (i.e. the 4Cs model). Specifically, these authors combined the components of hardiness (i.e. control, commitment, challenge) with confidence. In addition to the 4Cs model being more applicable than hardiness to the sporting environment, Clough et al. also suggested that confidence (i.e. confidence in one's own ability and interpersonal confidence) distinguishes mental toughness from hardiness. Nonetheless, it is apparent that hardiness and mental toughness share the common thread of mediating how individuals perceive and handle stressful situations. Similarly, others (Gucciardi et al., 2009a) have indicated that, although resilience is considered to be one part of mental toughness, the two constructs can be differentiated. Typically, researchers have considered resilience to be influential in 'dealing with setbacks' and 'bouncing back', and thus a response to more negative outcome situations. An emerging finding is that mental toughness is seen as important whether the outcome of a situation is viewed as positive or negative (e.g. Gucciardi et al., 2009a; Weinberg et al., in press), and therefore, helps to distinguish it from other constructs such as resilience and hardiness.

Although research findings to date have provided further conceptual clarity in understanding what constitutes mental toughness (i.e. the essential attributes), the important implications of this knowledge have been used to spur our investigations into exploring how mental toughness is developed. Indeed, at this time, it has been considered important for the growing body of knowledge in mental toughness to be theoretically driven, whereby findings can facilitate applied practice. This line of inquiry has been aided by the development of theoretical models and frameworks (e.g. Gucciardi et al., 2008; Jones et al., 2007). For example, Jones et al. (2007) reported 30 attributes of mental toughness and proposed a framework on how these attributes can be used. Specifically, the framework consists of four separate dimensions (i.e. attitude/mindset, training, competition and post-competition) and offers insights into which of the attributes are necessary in the different settings. This framework has recently been extended (Connaughton et al., 2010) to offer an insight into the development and maintenance of mental toughness across athletes' various career stages.

Gucciardi et al. (2008) adopted Personal Construct Psychology (PCP: Kelly, 1991) as a framework to create a grounded theory of mental toughness. A key principle of PCP is that individuals strive to make sense of themselves and their environment by devising theories about their world. Further, PCP emphasizes that individuals differ in how they perceive situations and interpret them, what is considered important and what is implied by individuals' particular construing of events (Kelly, 1991). Thus, the interviews conducted by Gucciardi et al. involving elite Australian football coaches were guided by a PCP framework. The mental toughness model encompassed the interaction of three components that were considered central to the conceptualization of mental toughness specific to Australian football. The three components were characteristics (11 ranked bipolar constructs such as self-belief vs. self-doubt; work ethic vs. lazy), situations (i.e. internal and external situations that demand mental toughness), and behaviours (i.e. behaviours displayed in the situations requiring mental toughness). The conceptual model (see Gucciardi et al., 2009a) offers a framework to guide future research as well as serving as a guide to practitioners when exploring athletes' development of mental toughness in their sport. For example, Gucciardi et al. (2009b) successfully implemented a mental toughness training programme for adolescent Australian footballers that contained elements derived from their theoretical conceptualization of mental toughness.

From a theoretical and empirical point of view it is extremely important to understand and define mental toughness (see other chapters in this volume). Nevertheless, from practical and applied perspectives it is important for coaches, athletes and significant others to understand how to build and develop mental toughness. The development of mental toughness is the general focus of the remainder of this chapter.

Pillars of mental toughness

Various models and frameworks of mental toughness have been developed that can provide a guide for how mental toughness can be developed. Conceptualized as a constellation of psychological attributes, Jones and Moorehouse (2007) provided a useful framework based on the attributes of mental toughness research that categorizes the various attributes into the four pillars of mental toughness (i.e. motivation, self-confidence, attentional focus, coping with pressure). Therefore, although mental toughness varies somewhat from sport to sport and across different levels of competition, there appears to be consistency regarding its definition and main characteristics, which broadly fall into these four categories. From a practical perspective, the pillars of mental toughness can provide a structured framework by which to identify strategies to teach and build mental toughness. The four pillars are described below and are later used in this chapter to offer practical strategies on how to build mental toughness by either teaching mental skills or creating a suitable environment (e.g. physical, mental emotional, social).

Motivation

Recognizing that certain types of motivation and motivational strategies are more conducive than others for optimal performance, this pillar is centred on the optimal levels and types of motivation required to achieve your goals. Motivation for the mentally tough athlete would encompass a strong desire for success; willingness to push oneself, persist and work hard; setting difficult but attainable goals; and bouncing back from performance setbacks (e.g. Jones et al., 2002; Weinberg et al., in press).

Self-confidence

Considered one of the most important mental toughness characteristics (Gucciardi et al., 2008; Jones et al., 2002), this pillar encapsulates mentally tough athletes' belief that they have the abilities to achieve their goals. According to Jones and Moorhouse (2007), this strong belief in oneself enables the mentally tough athlete to take educated risks, learn from criticism, control unwanted thoughts and feelings, and expect that good things will happen in the future.

Attentional focus

Being able to focus their attention on the relevant cues in the environment and maintain that focus despite distractions, as well as not allow their attention to be distracted from their priorities, is a hallmark of mentally tough athletes (e.g. Jones et al., 2002, 2007; Gucciardi et al., 2008). Mentally tough athletes maintain such attentional focus by focusing on controlling the controllables; staying in the moment; focusing on the positives; and focusing on the process (Jones and Moorhouse, 2007).

Coping with pressure

This pillar relates to being able to perform under pressure by controlling the amount and nature of stress experienced (Jones and Moorhouse, 2007). The different aspects of pressure as it relates to mental toughness include coping effectively with adversity; staying calm under pressure; accepting that anxiety is inevitable and enjoying it; thriving on pressure; and interpreting anxiety as facilitative for performance (e.g. Gucciardi et al., 2008; Jones et al., 2002, 2007; Weinberg et al., in press).

Developing mental toughness

Despite not dealing specifically with mental toughness, the literature on the development of talent and expertise offers some clues on how this desirable construct may be developed and learned. Research on the development of world-class performers in sport and non-sport domains (e.g. artists, academicians, musicians, mathematicians, swimmers and tennis players), for example, identified that talented individuals will progress through three developmental career stages (i.e. early, middle and late years), and that the focus of why individuals engaged in a particular activity and how they developed their skill differed in each stage (Bloom, 1985; Csikszentmihalyi et al., 1993). In addition, research on the development of expertise (see Ericsson et al., 2006, for a review) has focused on the amount of training an athlete does in the form of what they called deliberate practice. In this approach, practice conditions and the amount of practice are central to building expertise, with most experts having trained for at least 10 years and done 10,000 hours of deliberate practice.

Besides discussing the importance of environmental influences like the type, frequency and intensity of practices, these literatures on expertise and talent development also underscore the importance of significant others in the development of high performers. For example, researchers (Côté, 1999; Gould et al., 2002) have found that significant others including coaches, parents, teammates, friends, and other family members play important roles in the development of talent and mental skills. Although Gould et al. (2002) focused on the development of psychological talent, one of the psychological attributes that was highlighted by the Olympic medallists as being developed was mental toughness. Overall, findings indicated that psychological talent can be developed and this development typically occurs over a long period of time and is influenced by a variety of factors (e.g. coaches, parents, competitive environments, life experiences).

Although there is ongoing research and debate as to exactly how mental toughness is developed, from existing research (e.g. Connaughton et al., 2008; Gucciardi et al., 2009c; Weinberg et al., in press) it appears that mental toughness is both 'caught' via environmental influences and 'taught' through training. The degree to which mental toughness is caught or taught is yet to be determined (Crust, 2008). Nonetheless, it appears that the more salient question in the future for mental toughness development is not whether the caught or taught aspect is more important but rather how the two can combine to influence development.

Following a similar line of inquiry to talent development, mental toughness researchers have used the reflective accounts of elite athletes to provide important information on how they developed their mental toughness during earlier stages of their careers (e.g. Bull et al., 2005; Connaughton et al., 2008). Findings from these studies highlight that mental toughness can be developed (i.e. caught) through certain environmental influences. For example, Bull et al. (2005) reported that environmental influences provided the foundation for the development of tough character (e.g. competitiveness), tough attitudes (e.g. go-the-extra-mile mindset), and tough thinking (e.g. robust self-confidence) in elite cricketers. The cricketers reported that surviving early setbacks and being exposed to foreign cricket (i.e. helping to develop the right mindset as an outsider) were considered influential in developing their mental toughness. Similarly, elite athletes in Connaughton et al.'s (2008) study recalled a variety of experiences including critical life events, performance setbacks, sibling rivalry and having supportive parents.

When referring to environmental influences, athletes who are retrospectively recalling their development are not referring to situations that they have deliberately placed themselves in to specifically develop their mental toughness, but rather they are recalling how the environment has impacted on them (e.g. Bull et al., 2005; Connaughton et al., 2008). This distinction is important because it has implications for the development of mental toughness. Specifically, it will require practitioners to educate athletes and coaches on how to use this information (i.e. the caught element of mental toughness) to manipulate coaching practice environments (as well as educating parents on creating the desired home environment) to create the most effective climate for developing mental toughness in younger athletes. Nonetheless, this focus is where the 'caught' and 'taught' elements of mental toughness knowledge can be combined together to educate significant others regarding their roles in developing mentally tough athletes (i.e. use the information to help create the most effective climate in which to develop mental toughness).

Creating an effective environment to develop mental toughness: the roles of parents and coaches

Coaches and parents have important roles to play in developing mental toughness (whether 'caught' or 'taught'). In a study focusing on National Collegiate Athletics Association (NCAA) athletes, for example, coaches were reported as having the most influence in developing their mental toughness (Butt et al., 2010). Themes that emerged from this study included coaches' practices (e.g. creating a challenging practice environment), coaches' attributes (e.g. role modelling mental toughness qualities such as confidence), and coaches' support (e.g. being positive). Similarly, in a study involving athletes' mental toughness development across career stages (i.e. Bloom's talent development stages of the early, middle, later years: Connaughton et al., 2008), coaches were mentioned as being important in the development of mental toughness, specifically referring multiple times to the coaches' leadership styles. In the early years, athletes reported that the coaches' leadership skills were nurturing and supportive to assist them with successful progressions in their sport. During the middle and later years, athletes desired leadership qualities from their coaches and also perceived the coaches' leadership to assist them in pushing through demanding practices. Thus, coaches were seen as directly (mentoring, planned teaching) or indirectly (fostering/nurturing/ instilling important skills) teaching mental skills.

The importance of coaches in the psychological development of athletes has long been discussed, but only recently been consolidated in the coaching literature. A special issue of *The Sport Psychologist* (Gilbert, 2006) focused on coaching education from both research and applied perspectives. In particular, the role of coaches as facilitators for young athletes learning mental skills and enhancing psychological development and well-being was highlighted in articles in this special issue. These roles and strategies included the type and quality of feedback provided, encouragement and support offered, reinforcement given, and coaching style. Although not specific to the development of mental toughness, these studies underscore the point that coaches appear central to mentoring young athletes and assisting them in developing mental skills both on and off the field.

Given the important roles that coaches appear to play in developing mental toughness, it is surprising that there is limited knowledge on coaches' views on building mental toughness and strategies used to develop it. One study that focused on coaches' views of mental toughness and how it is developed was conducted by Weinberg and colleagues (in press). In this study coaches discussed mental toughness as a key component at the NCAA level and perceived themselves as playing an important role in developing mentally tough athletes. Findings also indicated that coaches tended to recruit athletes for their 'mental character' in addition to their physical skills, thereby highlighting the importance that coaches placed on the role of mental toughness at this stage of athletes' careers. Some key strategies were reported by coaches as ways to build mental toughness in NCAA athletes. These strategies included creating a tough physical practice environment (e.g. intense competitive practices, tough physical conditioning), a positive mental environment (e.g. confidence building/positive atmosphere, high expectations), and providing awareness/learning opportunities (e.g. observing others being mentally tough). Similar findings were reported in a study involving elite Australian football coaches (Gucciardi et al., 2009c). That coaches create a tough practice environment appears to be consistent with athletes' recalled experiences relating to environmental influences (e.g. Bull et al., 2005), reflecting harsh and difficult athletic experiences such as surviving performance setbacks and being in situations where they knew that earning the right to be successful was important.

Implementing tough physical conditioning is emerging in the literature as one way to build a tough practice environment. For example, NCAA coaches reported using tough physical conditioning to build the mental toughness attributes of performing under pressure and self-belief (Weinberg et al., in press). Similarly, NCAA athletes discussed the importance of fitness in that it allowed them to push harder and cope with adversity during stressful situations, as well as providing a robust mental edge (Butt et al., 2010). The extent to which mental toughness has a physical component is not fully understood, although a consistent finding is that being physically prepared is linked to displaying high levels of self-belief (e.g. Bull et al., 2005; Butt et al., 2010; Gucciardi et al., 2008). Thus, it does appear that being in good physical condition is considered a prerequisite for displaying mental toughness. From a practical perspective, this connection between the physical and mental aspects should be emphasized when building mental toughness and designing training sessions.

Manipulating practice environments to create competitive, difficult and pressure-inducing situations is an important strategy for building mentally tough athletes. However, these environments should be positive and confidence-building as opposed to negative and punishment-oriented (e.g. Butt et al., 2010; Connaughton et al., 2008; Weinberg et al., in press). For example, elite athletes have reported that being in a rewarding (e.g. opportunity to demonstrate ability) and enjoyable (e.g. opportunity to master skills) environment has influenced their mental toughness development, and appears to be particularly salient in developing motivational attributes (Connaughton et al., 2008). Similarly, NCAA athletes perceived their coaches to create an encouraging practice environment (e.g. varying direct instruction-oriented drills and problem solving-oriented drills) while still upholding high expectations for them to learn skills central to the development of mental toughness (Butt et al., 2010). These findings are consistent with the talent development literature (e.g. Gould et al., 2002) and with much of the recent sport psychology research on reinforcement and feedback, which emphasizes a positive approach to the learning and performance of skills and competition (Smith, 2006). From an applied perspective, creating a positive motivational climate is just as important as creating a competitive and tough environment for building mental toughness. To help create this positive climate, coaches should consider providing reinforcement and feedback which emphasizes a positive approach to the learning and performance of skills and competition (e.g. provide encouragement, give positive and instructional feedback, set up practices that are fun and enjoyable, consider individual differences).

To develop mental toughness, an athlete being exposed to encouraging environments (both inside and outside of the sport setting) is not only linked to the roles of coaches but also to the roles of athletes' parents (e.g. Butt et al., 2010; Connaughton et al., 2008). A consistent finding in youth-sport literature is that parents play a central role in their child's sporting experience in general and can also influence their motivation to participate in sport, and their enjoyment (e.g. Brustad et al., 2001). Talent development literature supports the idea that parents are important in helping aspiring young athletes to fulfil their potential (Bloom, 1985; Côté, 1999; Gould et al., 2002) and progress through the various stages of their careers. One of the first studies to acknowledge parental influences in developing mental toughness was conducted by Bull et al. (2005). They found that during cricketers' formative years parents were seen to play a supportive role through 'pushing' them to be successful, combined with 'backing' them up through difficult cricket situations. Parents also influenced the cricketers' attitudes towards participation by emphasizing the importance of the game and that 'every inning played was important'. The role of parents influencing an appropriate attitude towards sport participation was also found in a study involving NCAA Division 1 athletes (Butt et al., 2010). The recurring theme among these research findings is that parents encouraged an 'if it's worth doing, it's worth doing right' mindset.

Collectively, these findings indicate that, with the appropriate support and encouragement, parents can influence the development of mental toughness, particularly the motivational attributes of mental toughness. It is important to note that existing sport psychology literature in these areas (e.g. mental toughness, psychological talent development, youth sport) typically acknowledges that parents should adopt an appropriate level of involvement in their child's sport development to be supportive (Connaughton et al., 2008; Gould et al., 2002, 2008). Specifically, parents maintaining an appropriate perspective on their child's sporting involvement, encouraging ownership and responsibility, as well as being part of a supportive social support network, are considered important parent behaviours for developing elite athletes' psychological characteristics (e.g. Gould et al., 2002) and mental toughness (e.g. Connaughton et al., 2008). These behaviours would provide the foundations for educational workshops designed for parents of athletes with potential, to help create an effective mental toughness development environment.

Training to be mentally tough: combining 'taught' and 'caught' strategies

In addition to manipulating the training environment to develop mental toughness as previously discussed (i.e. the caught element), mental skills appear to have an important role to play in training athletes to be mentally tough. In support of this view, elite athletes have reported the successful use of mental skills (e.g. mental preparation, imagery, goal setting, self-talk) in helping them not only to develop their mental toughness but also as a strategy to maintain it (Connaughton et al., 2008). Intervention research has provided preliminary support for the usefulness of mental skills training targeting specific mental toughness attributes for its enhancement with youth footballers (Gucciardi et al., 2009b). Collectively, emerging research (e.g. Connaughton et al., 2008; Gucciardi et al., 2009b; Weinberg et al., in press) indicates that both physical and mental strategies can be used to develop mental toughness. We argue that, when implementing strategies to develop mental toughness, both knowledge from environmental influences and specific mental skills can be combined for optimal effectiveness in developing mental toughness. Using the four pillars of mental toughness model as a framework (Jones and Moorhouse, 2007), the next section draws upon the development of mental toughness literature to provide an overview of some strategies to build mental toughness.

Motivation

Having a desire to succeed and sustaining this internal motivation over long periods of time are often noted as being essential characteristics of mental toughness (e.g. Jones et al., 2002, 2007). This desire can be fuelled by both intrinsic and extrinsic motivation (Gucciardi, 2010), although research has indicated that individuals with high intrinsic motivation exhibited more interest, excitement, confidence and persistence than individuals motivated largely by external demands and rewards (for a review, see Vallerand, 2007).

Creating an effective environment

Coaches can create a practice environment whereby athletes are exposed to successful experiences. Along these lines, they can focus not only on outcome but also on enjoyment, and they can be involved in some decision-making to provide a feeling of ownership. In terms of practice environments, although it appears that a positive motivational climate is appropriate for enhancing intrinsic motivation, using competitive rivalry to develop the motivational properties of mental toughness has received some support in the literature (e.g. Bull et al., 2005; Connaughton et al., 2008). In our research with NCAA head coaches (Weinberg et al., in press; see also Gucciardi et al., 2009c), creating a tough environment by setting up intense competitive practices was mentioned by all interviewed coaches as a strategy to build mentally tough athletes. Specifically, coaches designed drills 'to put athletes in difficult situations to encourage them to hang in there'. In essence, creating competitive and challenging practices that simulate competition are important for providing athletes with opportunities to develop the motivational attributes of mental toughness (e.g. pushing themselves to the limit, go-the-extra-mile, hang-in-there under difficulty). Besides the practice environment, it is also important to note that the behaviours coaches adopt can play important roles in developing athletes' intrinsic motivation. For example, coaches can focus on giving athletes rewards that are contingent on their performance, using verbal and non-verbal praise, and being able to vary the content and sequence of practice drills.

Training motivation

The mental strategy of goal setting can be used to enhance the motivational attributes of mental toughness. For example, the elite athletes in Connaughton et al.'s (2008) study reported goal setting to be a key skill used in their mental preparation and one that helped them to further develop their desire and internalized motives to succeed. In general, research has demonstrated that goals direct attention and action and help players focus on what they need to do in both the short term and the long term (Locke and Latham, 1990). Without specific goals, players' minds will tend to wander (especially in practice) or they will not be sure exactly what to do when they get into a competition. Thus, having specific goals to reach desired outcomes is considered more effective than setting 'do your best' goals or simply knowing what you want (e.g. winning a championship). Indeed, results from goal-setting research consistently demonstrate that specific and hard goals produce better performance than easy goals, 'do your best' goals or no goals at all (Locke and Latham, 1990). Although in the scientific literature a goal is usually defined as an objective, a standard, an aim or a level of performance or proficiency, there are three major types of goals, namely outcome, performance, and process goals.

Setting each type of goal can improve sports performance, although research with elite athletes (Filby et al., 1999) has shown that setting these three types of goals in combination is related to top performance. It is important to remember that elite athletes not only want to perform well but they also want to win. Thus, setting performance and outcome goals appears to be important for elite athletes. Nonetheless, when considering the types of goals to set an athlete, the important point is that, for every outcome goal, there should be several performance and process goals set that ultimately lead to achieving that outcome. Existing literature highlights that mentally tough athletes not only have a clear focus on their long-term goals but are also able to control their focus at important times during competition (Jones et al., 2007). Setting appropriate performance and process goals can help athletes with learning to have control over their focus. In addition to the types of goals, there are some key principles involved in setting effective goals. A good tip for helping athletes remember effective goal principles is SMARTS (see Figure 11.1).

☐ SPECIFIC
   ○ Be precise
☐ MEASURABLE
   ○ Quantify the goal
☐ ACTION-ORIENTED
   ○ How are you going get there?
☐ REALISTIC
   ○ Set your goals to be challenging and attainable
☐ TIMELY
   ○ Set your goals within a reasonable time frame
☐ SELF-DETERMINED
   ○ Athlete input

Figure 11.1 Principles of goal-setting

Self-belief

Existing literature consistently supports self-belief as a key attribute of mental toughness (e.g. Gucciardi et al., 2008; Weinberg et al., in press), with some ranking this facet as the most important (e.g. Jones et al., 2007). Self-belief relates to an athlete's confidence and numerous studies have revealed that confidence has a positive impact on sport performance (see Vealey, 2001, for a review). Accordingly, confidence is considered one of the most important attributes an athlete can possess, yet it is also considered to be one of the most fragile attributes. Therefore, finding ways to build and maintain confidence is important for mental toughness development and for successful performance.

Creating an effective environment

The importance of creating a mastery and positive motivational climate has emerged in the mental toughness development literature (e.g. Connaughton et al., 2008). In shedding some light on developmental considerations, athletes' recollections of developing mental toughness attributes such as self-belief, desire, and motives to succeed throughout varying career stages (i.e. early, middle, later) included mastery, enjoyment, exposure to friendly rivalries, and social support. In a more recent study (Weinberg et al., in press), coaches emphasized that building confidence in athletes required a positive environment and lots of support (e.g. encouragement, positive and instructional feedback). These findings are consistent with recent sport psychology research on reinforcement and feedback, which promotes a positive approach to the learning and performance of skills and competition (Smith, 2006).

Research has also highlighted the role that physical preparation can play when developing the confidence aspect of mental toughness (e.g. Connaughton et al., 2008; Weinberg et al., in press). Specifically, quality physical preparation is often linked with positive psychological characteristics such as confidence (e.g. Hays et al., 2007; Vealey et al., 1998). That is, athletes consistently report gaining their confidence in sport from being physically prepared. Thus, with self-belief being reported as the most important attribute of mental toughness in various studies (e.g. Gucciardi et al., 2008; Jones et al., 2007), it is not surprising that being fully prepared physically has emerged in the literature as a possible prerequisite to demonstrating specific attributes of mental toughness such as confidence and performing under pressure (e.g. Weinberg et al., in press). In essence, coaches should consider the important role that physical conditioning plays in developing mentally tough athletes and, in particular, a robust self-belief.

Training self-belief

Based on current mental toughness research, enhancing self-belief appears to be linked with strategies such as modelling/watching others (Connaughton et al., 2008; Weinberg et al., in press), and recalling previous successful actions (Gucciardi et al., 2009b). There is a long history of research in both imagery (for a review, see Weinberg, 2008) and modelling (McCullagh and Weiss, 2002) attesting to its positive impact in not only improving performance, but also enhancing mental skills. So far in the mental toughness literature, athletes have reported using imagery for a variety of reasons including to stay focused, build self-belief, and increase desire to achieve goals. It is not uncommon to hear great athletes recall how they learned skills (both physical and mental) from watching others and formed images in their minds that they had seen being performed. For example, in a recent mental toughness study (Connaughton et al., 2008) athletes recalled that watching elite athletes and seeing how they trained and completed skills provided them with the belief that they could also achieve this level of performance. When developing the self-belief properties of mental toughness, it is important for coaches to recognize the value in providing athletes with opportunities to observe their own performances and recent accomplishments but also to watch other successful athletes. The use of video clips and performance analysis can be incorporated into athletes' practice schedules to facilitate this development.

Coaches can also incorporate imagery into their practice environments to help athletes mentally prepare for competition. For example, coaches can call out different plays to their respective units whereby the players are then asked to imagine what they would do in specific situations. Another strategy might be for coaches to ask their players to visualize their events the night before competition and see themselves carrying out the movements and strategies as required. Probably one of the most important uses of imagery would be imaging positive performances as a way to build a robust self-belief. Recalling a positive performance (sometimes known as best performance imagery) can help athletes maintain confidence to perform specific skills during competition. In essence, using imagery to see one's self perform well can make athletes feel that they can perform regardless of the circumstances or when faced with adverse situations. Indeed, research conducted in the area of imagery and sport confidence provides evidence for the use of motivational imagery (i.e. motivational general-mastery) to enhance confidence (e.g. Callow et al., 2001).

Attentional control

Concentration is the ability to remain focused on the task at hand, and maintain that focus over a period of time. Being able to remain fully focused especially when faced with adversity is consistently reported as an important mental toughness attribute (e.g. Jones et al., 2002, 2007; Gucciardi et al., 2008). In addition to elite athletes recognizing the importance of focus for mental toughness, coaches also consider it to be an important attribute (e.g. Weinberg et al., in press). The central theme is that, regardless of what is going in the environment, mentally tough athletes have strong attentional control skills and are able to focus on the task at hand.

Creating an effective environment

The practice environment when learning psychological skills is just as important as the learning of physical skills. To improve concentration in competition, it is important that attentional control is self-monitored (e.g. monitoring how much time was spent on a given task, or identifying situations when you had good focus versus losing focus) and that competition is simulated during practice (i.e. making the practice environment more like the competition environment). The importance of practice to achieve expert performance has been emphasized by Ericsson and his colleagues (for a review, see Ericsson et al., 2006). Such research has focused on the amount of deliberate practice athletes engage in, which involves a well-defined task with appropriate difficulty levels, informative feedback and opportunities for repetition and corrections of errors. Approximately 10 years and 10,000 hours of deliberate practice is associated with attaining expertise in a discipline. Thus, in this approach, practice conditions and the amount of practice is central to building expertise. With regard to the development of concentration, setting up practices that encourage athletes to make quick decisions is one way to train concentration. In addition, over-learning skills in practice can enable athletes to make complicated decisions quickly during competition. Finally, a coach can 'stop' or 'freeze play' during practice to ask players what they were focusing on while performing a specific task. By doing this training exercise, players can receive immediate feedback about what they were focusing on to perform a specific task, and if they can improve upon it.

Training attentional control

Although many strategies have been identified to enhance attention control (e.g. competition plans and established routines, negative thought-stopping), recent research supports the utility of self-talk statements (Coulter et al., 2010). Two common causes of attentional problems tend to be in the form of internal distracters such as attending to past events (e.g. dwelling on what just happened) or attending to future events (e.g. thinking about the outcome). Therefore, developing a set of specific verbal and positive cues can help athletes to keep their mind focused on a given task. Verbal cues tend to be broken down into either motivational (e.g. I can do it) or instructional (e.g. keep your eye on the ball) and both can be appropriate depending upon the situation. For mental toughness development, instructional self-talk provides specific information on how to perform a skill or persist in performing a skill, whereas motivational self-talk can help athletes achieve their optimal ready state for competition or help them to hang-in-there during a tough competition. Within existing literature, 'persistence', 'focus despite distraction' and 'hanging in there when the going gets tough' are all common phrases used to describe a mentally tough athlete (e.g. Bull et al., 2005; Jones et al., 2002, 2007). Thus, the use of specific verbal and positive cues for attentional control can be considered central to developing mental toughness.

Dealing with pressure

A consistent theme when investigating mental toughness is players' ability to manage their emotions and cope with pressure. What is emerging in recent literature is that mentally tough athletes do not merely deal with pressure but they thrive on it and can produce an exceptional performance at important moments (Jones et al., 2007; Weinberg et al., in press). It is important that athletes develop a range of coping strategies because they will undoubtedly experience a variety of stressors throughout their sporting careers. Accordingly, it is important that athletes are able to accept and cope with the anxiety and pressures associated with competitive sport.

Creating an effective environment

Recent research on mental toughness development (Connaughton et al., 2008) provides insight into how elite athletes learned to cope with their anxiety and thrive on externally derived pressures. Specifically, athletes felt that they learned to cope with anxiety and pressure due to increased competitive experience. It is important then for mental toughness development that athletes are exposed to competitive stressors in the practice environment (i.e. simulating the competitive environment) so they can learn to enjoy pressure. When considering the best practice environment for mental toughness development and the need for simulating intense and tough competitive experiences within it, research suggests that physical conditioning should be part of it (e.g. Gucciardi et al, 2008). As noted earlier, when discussing the attribute of self-belief, physical conditioning has also been linked to athletes being able to perform under pressure.

Various techniques to cope with pressure can be used and integrated into athletes' physical practice environments. For example, coaches can create pressure situations in various ways and will often involve manipulating time, space and levels of opposition (e.g. overload situations) within the drills that echo a game-related situation. In addition, coaches can choose to hold a physical conditioning session at the start of practice so that players will be prepared to perform skills when they feel fatigued. This approach would lend itself to how some athletes and coaches in the literature reflect on the role of fitness and being able to demonstrate the mental toughness attribute of performing well under pressure. That is, athletes would probably only be able to perform something 'spectacular' under pressure towards the end of the game if they were physically fit.

Training to deal with pressure

With regard to athletes learning to accept anxiety as part of competition, it is important that they are equipped with some strategies to help them view anxiety as having more of a positive than a negative influence on performance. One important coping mechanism to facilitate a positive interpretation of cognitive anxiety that is supported in the literature is cognitive restructuring (e.g. Thomas et al., 2007). Cognitive restructuring can help athletes counter negative thoughts and expectations and turn them into positive thoughts and expectations through a process of rationalization. Typically, 'countering' involves the following three phases: (a) identifying negative thoughts and situations that trigger them through self monitoring procedures (e.g. keeping a thought diary), (b) developing a thought-stopping cue to help stop the negative thoughts before they become harmful to performance (e.g. saying 'stop' to yourself) and (c) replacing the negative thoughts with positive thoughts that can direct your focus back to the task at hand (e.g. I've been in this situation before, play one point at a time). Some other helpful tips to deal with cognitive and somatic anxiety are outlined in Figure 11.2.

Future research

From the emerging research, it appears that creating a positive and tough competitive environment is important for mental toughness development, although the balance between the two environments and at what career stage each one should be emphasized needs to be further explored. Along these lines, although support has been found for creating a tough competitive environment in various stages of athletes' careers, such as the middle and later stages of development (e.g. Connaughton et al., 2008), in NCAA athletes, and also in elite athletes (e.g. Bull et al., 2005; Weinberg et al., in press), relatively little is known about mental toughness development in athletes during earlier stages of their careers. For

---

Learn Relaxation Strategies
☐ Progressive relaxation
    ○ Focuses on physical relaxation through tensing and relaxation of muscles.
☐ Relaxation response
    ○ Focuses on mental relaxation through repetition of a word (mental device).
☐ Slow down
    ○ Individuals under pressure tend to rush their actions.
☐ Use breath control

Figure 11.2 Strategies to deal with anxiety

example, the elite athletes upon recalling their mental toughness development in Connaughton et al.'s (2008) study referred to coaches' leadership, social support, mastery, enjoyment and demonstration of ability as important factors. Thus, competitive rivalry did not emerge until later stages of development (i.e. middle and later years). Second, consistent with talent development research (e.g. Bloom, 1985; Gould et al., 2002), there are some findings indicating that coaches also play important roles in developing athletes' mental toughness (Connaughton et al., 2008). Thus, the psychological skills of athletes and the role that coaches may play in developing and nurturing these skills at various stages of development may be an important avenue for future research. Finally, we provided some mental strategies that can be targeted to develop mental toughness relative to specific attributes. However, empirical intervention research is warranted to investigate the effectiveness of mental toughness interventions. Gucciardi and his colleagues (2009b) have done some initial intervention studies with youth participating in Australian football, which can be used as a benchmark to spur future research in this area. To date, most information regarding building mental toughness has come from athletes' recollections, which, although important, might be questioned due to the long time period in their reflections. Collecting empirical data across different age groups attempting to build mental toughness attributes will provide much needed information regarding the learning of skills necessary to become mentally tough. Furthermore, when considering intervention research, individual differences such as competitiveness and intrinsic motivation (as well as other personality attributes) should be examined to understand how they might influence and relate to the development of mental toughness.

References

Bloom, B. (1985) *Developing Talent in Young People,* New York: Ballantine.

Brustad, R. J., Babkes, M., and Smith, A. (2001) 'Youth in sport: Psychological considerations', in R. Singer, H. Hausenblas, and C. Janelle (eds), *Handbook of Sport Psychology,* NewYork: Wiley, pp. 604–35.

Bull, S., Shambrook, C., James, W., and Brooks, E. (2005) 'Towards an understanding of mental toughness in elite English cricketers', *Journal of Applied Sport Psychology*, 17, 209–27.

Butt, J., Weinberg, R., and Culp, B. (2010) 'Exploring mental toughness in NCAA athletes', *Journal of Intercollegiate Sport*, 3, 316–32.

Callow, N., Hardy, L., and Hall, C. R. (2001) 'The effect of a motivational general mastery imagery intervention on the sport confidence of four high level junior badminton players', *Research Quarterly for Sport and Exercise Psychology*, 72, 389–400.

Clough, P., Earle, K., and Sewell, D. (2002) 'Mental toughness: The concept and its measurement', in I. Cockerill (ed.), *Solutions in Sport Psychology*, London: Thomson, pp. 32–45.

Connaughton, D., Wadey, R., Hanton, S., and Jones, G. (2008) 'The development and maintenance of mental toughness: Perceptions of elite performers', *Journal of Sports Sciences*, 26, 83–95.

Connaughton, D., Hanton, S., and Jones, G. (2010) 'The development and maintenance of mental toughness in the world's best performers', *The Sport Psychologist*, 24, 168–93.

Côté, J. (1999) 'The influence of the family in the development of talent in sport', *The Sport Psychologist*, 13, 395–417.

Coulter, T. J., Mallett, C. J., and Gucciardi, D. F. (2010) 'Understanding and developing mental toughness in Australian soccer: Perceptions of players, parents, and coaches', *Journal of Sports Sciences*, 28, 699–716.

Crust, L. (2008) 'A review and conceptual re-examination of mental toughness: Implications for future researchers', *Personality and Individual Differences*, 45, 576–83.

Csikszentmihalyi, M., Rathunde, K., Whalen, S., and Wong, M. (1993) *Talented Teenagers: The Roots of Success and Failure*, New York: Cambridge University Press.

Ericsson, K. A., Charness, N., Feltovich, P. J., and Hoffman, R. (eds) (2006) *The Cambridge Handbook on Expertise and Expert Performance,* Cambridge: Cambridge University Press.

Filby, W. C. D., Maynard, I. W., and Graydon, J. K. (1999) 'The effect of multiple-goal strategies on performance outcomes in training and competition', *Journal of Applied Sport Psychology*, 11, 230–46.

Gilbert, W. (2006) 'Introduction to Special Issue: Coach education', *The Sport Psychologist*, 20, 123–5.

Gould, D., Hodge, K., Peterson, K., and Petlichkoff, L. (1987) 'Psychological foundations of coaching: Similarities and differences among intercollegiate wrestling coaches', *The Sport Psychologist*, 1, 293–308.

Gould, D., Jackson, S. A., and Finch, L. M. (1993) 'Sources of stress in national champion figure skaters', *Journal of Sport and Exercise Psychology*, 15, 134–59.

Gould, D., Dieffenach, K., and Moffett, A. (2002) 'Psychological characteristics and development of Olympic champions', *Journal of Applied Sport Psychology*, 14, 172–204.

Gould, D., Lauer, L., Rolo, C., Jannes, C., and Pennisi, N. (2008) 'The role of parents in tennis success: Focus group interviews with junior coaches', *The Sport Psychologist*, 22, 18–37.

Gucciardi, D. F. (2010) 'Mental toughness profiles and their relations with achievement goals and sport motivation in adolescent Australian footballers', *Journal of Sports Sciences*, 28, 615–25.

Gucciardi, D. F., and Gordon, S. (2009) 'Development and preliminary validation of the Cricket Mental Toughness Inventory (CMTI)', *Journal of Sports Sciences*, 27, 1293–1310.

Gucciardi, D. F., Gordon, S., and Dimmock, J. A. (2008) 'Towards an understanding of mental toughness in Australian football', *Journal of Applied Sport Psychology*, 20, 261–81.

Gucciardi, D. F., Gordon, S., and Dimmock, J. A. (2009a) 'Advancing mental toughness research and theory using personal construct psychology', *International Review of Sport and Exercise Psychology*, 2, 54–72.

Gucciardi, D. F., Gordon, S., and Dimmock, J. A. (2009b) 'Evaluation of a mental toughness training program for youth-aged Australian footballers: I. A quantitative analysis', *Journal of Applied Sport Psychology*, 21, 307–23.

Gucciardi, D. F., Gordon, S., Dimmock, J. A., and Mallett, C. J. (2009c) 'Understanding the coach's role in the development of mental toughness: Perspectives of elite Australian football coaches', *Journal of Sports Sciences*, 27, 1483–96.

Hays, K., Maynard, I., Thomas, O., and Bawden, M. (2007) 'Sources and types of confidence identified by world class sport performers', *Journal of Applied Sport Psychology*, 19, 434–56.

Jones, G., and Moorehouse, A. (2007) *Developing Mental Toughness: Gold Medal Strategies for Transforming your Business Performance*, Oxford: Spring Hill.

Jones, G., Hanton, S., and Connaughton, D. (2002) 'What is this thing called mental toughness? An investigation of elite sport performers', *Journal of Applied Sport Psychology*, 14, 205–18.

Jones, G., Hanton, S., and Connaughton, D. (2007) 'A framework of mental toughness in the world's best performers', *The Sport Psychologist*, 21, 243–64.

Kelly, G. A. (1991) *The Psychology of Personal Constructs: A Theory of Personality*, vol. 1, London: Routledge, originally published 1955.

Kobasa, S. C. (1979) 'Stressful life events, personality and health: An enquiry into hardiness', *Journal of Personality and Social Psychology*, 37, 1–11.

Kreiner-Phillips, K. and Orlick, T. (1993) 'Winning after winning: The psychology of ongoing excellence', *The Sport Psychologist*, 7, 31–48.

Locke, L., and Latham, G. (1990) *A Theory of Goal-Setting and Task Performance*, Englewood Cliffs, NJ: Prentice Hall.

McCullagh, P., and Weiss, M. (2002) 'Observational learning: The forgotten psychological method in sport psychology', in J. L. Van Raalte and B.W. Brewer (eds), *Exploring Sport and Exercise Psychology*, Washington, DC: American Psychological Association, pp. 131–49.

Orlick, T., and Partington, J. (1988) 'Mental links to excellence', *The Sport Psychologist*, 2, 105–30.

Sinclair, D., and Orlick, T. (1993) 'Positive transitions from high performance sport', *The Sport Psychologist*, 7, 138–50.

Smith, R. (2006) 'Positive reinforcement, performance feedback and performance', in J. M. Williams (ed.), *Applied Sport Psychology: Personal Growth to Peak Performance* (5th edn), NewYork: McGraw-Hill, pp. 40–56.

Thelwell, R., Weston, N., and Greenlees, I. (2005) 'Defining and understanding mental toughness within soccer', *Journal of Applied Sport Psychology*, 17, 326–32.

Thomas, O., Hanton, S., and Maynard, I. W. (2007) 'Anxiety responses and psychological skill use during the time leading up to competition: theory to practice 1', *Journal of Applied Sport Psychology*, 19, 379–97.

Vallerand, R. J. (2007) 'Intrinsic and extrinsic motivation in sport and physical activity', in G. Tenenbaum and R. C. Eklund (eds), *Handbook of Sport Psychology* (3rd edn), New York: Wiley, pp. 59–83.

Vealey, R. S., Hayashi, S. W., Garner-Holman, M., and Giaccobi, P. (1998) 'Sources of sport-confidence: Conceptualization and instrument development', *Journal of Sport and Exercise Psychology*, 21, 54–80.

Vealey, R. S. (2001) 'Understanding and enhancing self-confidence in athletes', in R. Singer, H. Hausenblas, and C. Janelle (eds), *Handbook of Sport Psychology* (2nd edn,), New York: Wiley, pp. 550–65.

Weinberg, R. S. (2008) 'Does imagery work? Effects on performance and mental skills', *Journal of Imagery Research in Sport and Physical Activity*, 3, 1–21.

Weinberg, R.S., Butt, J., and Culp, B. (in press) 'Coaches' views of mental toughness and how it is built', *International Journal of Sport and Exercise Psychology*.

Conclusion

12 Mental toughness in sport

Past, present, and future

Daniel F. Gucciardi and Sandy Gordon

In this concluding chapter, our objectives are to draw together some of the key findings and issues that arise for us from contributions in this book, as well as offer some suggestions for future avenues of research. As there have been some fairly recent and comprehensive reviews of the literature on mental toughness in sport (e.g. Connaughton and Hanton, 2009; Gordon and Gucciardi, in press), the aim in this chapter is not to resynthesize this material, but to highlight existing shortcomings in our understanding and examination of this construct. We begin the chapter by focusing on the past, move our attention to the present and then finish by offering some thoughts for the future. We present ideas for future research and theorizing not as answers to the many pertinent questions but rather hold them up for scrutiny and consideration by others. By considering some of these fundamental issues, we hope that mental toughness researchers will be able to proceed from a solid theoretical and empirical foundation.

The past

Looking back at the state of mental toughness research, it is interesting to note that almost 20 years passed before the construct was given empirical attention following the publication of Jim Loehr's (1982) popular textbook on the topic. Despite the lack of empirical attention between Loehr's publication and the first empirical examination of mental toughness (Fourie and Potgieter, 2001), a number of authors wrote books and articles on the topic (for a review, see Connaughton and Hanton, 2009). Recognizing that these contributions were based on professional experiences and anecdotal evidence, and often focused on mental skills rather than mental toughness per se (Connaughton and Hanton, 2009), it is of no surprise that the last decade has witnessed something of an explosion of empirical interest in understanding this construct and its development in academic circles (for an overview, see Figure 12.1). For us, this renewed interest in going beyond anecdote and professional experience is the major hallmark of the past 10 years. Much of this interest can be attributed to Jones, Hanton, and Connaughton's (2002) seminal paper which, at the time of writing this chapter (December 2010), has since received 42 ISI and 107 Google Scholar citations. In contrast, Loehr's (1982, 1986) books have received 17 and 68 Google Scholar citations, respectively.

Publications in peer-reviewed outlets represent an important source of information about mental toughness research endeavours. Although these publications may not yield a totally comprehensive picture of research conducted, it is reasonable to assume that they reflect important research topics in the field. Figure 12.1 displays the frequency with which various topic areas (i.e. understanding or developing mental toughness) were researched using various methodological approaches (i.e. qualitative or quantitative) over the last decade. An inspection of these topic areas and methodological approaches reveals some interesting trends.

One clear trend over the past 10 years has been the adoption of both qualitative and quantitative methodologies to understand mental toughness and its development in sport contexts. While qualitative methodologies have remained a constant method of choice, an increasing incidence of quantitative approaches is evident and most clearly demonstrated in the emergence of mental toughness questionnaires (for a review, see Chapter 7 above). Indeed, the majority of published, peer-reviewed research (n = 22) has involved some sort of quantitative examination of the relationship between mental toughness and hypothesized key correlates such as coping, psychological strategies, burnout and flow. Attempts to understand mental toughness using qualitative methodologies such as one-to-one interviews and focus groups are the next most prevalent form of peer-review publications (n = 8), followed by quantitative (n = 6) and qualitative (n = 4) examinations of its development. Of interest are four relatively recent reviews of the mental toughness literature.

A closer inspection of both the qualitative and quantitative studies reveals another interesting trend. Within qualitative studies (e.g. Bull et al., 2005; Jones et al., 2002, 2007), the focus has been on seeking the views of people who have been successful or key stakeholders (e.g. coaches, sport psychologists) involved

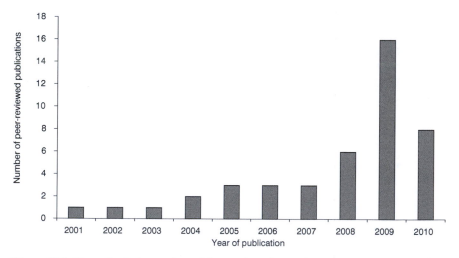

Figure 12.1 Chronological overview of the number of mental toughness papers published in peer-reviewed outlets

in helping such individuals attain success. Researched in this way one may be led to believe that mental toughness is present only in 'winners'. In contrast to the qualitative approach, researchers employing quantitative methods have sampled a greater representation of the athlete population including adolescents (e.g. Gucciardi, 2010) as well as recreational, sub-elite and elite athletes (e.g. Gucciardi and Gordon, 2009).

One final trend relates to the location of mental toughness research. Since the first empirical examination of mental toughness in South Africa (Fourie and Potgieter, 2001), British and Australian researchers have conducted the majority of research on the construct. Nevertheless, North American researchers (e.g. Veselka et al., 2009; see also Chapters 11 and 4 above) have recently weighed in with some important contributions. Domination of Western researchers also exists in data disseminations that do not involve a rigorous peer-review process (e.g. conference presentations, dissertations).

The present

To examine where we are going, we next consider where we are now. For almost a decade, researchers have recognized the need to empirically examine mental toughness and its development. As reflected in the chapters in this volume, increased attention within the academic community has resulted in efforts focused on identifying the key components of mental toughness and understanding how these facets are developed, as well as developing and validating measurement instruments. A comprehensive review of the literature on each of these three issues is beyond the scope of the current chapter but can nevertheless be found elsewhere both within this volume (e.g. Chapters 8, 7 and 10 above) and beyond (e.g. Connaughton and Hanton, 2009; Gordon and Gucciardi, in press). Rather, we focus on highlighting some of the key conclusions from available research.

On the construct definition of mental toughness

As with many new research areas, construct clarity persists as a major problem for the field of mental toughness because its definition remains ambiguous; that is, there is no clear consensus as to what this construct really is and what it is not. Nevertheless, three models of mental toughness currently dominate the field, with the majority of research falling under one of these frameworks. For the purposes of the current chapter, we focus on the construct definition of mental toughness within each of these models (for a critique of the models, see Gordon and Gucciardi, in press).

The most dominant framework in terms of peer-reviewed activity is the 4Cs model of mental toughness where Clough and colleagues (2002) leveraged heavily off hardiness theory (Kobasa, 1979) and their applied experiences to conceptualize their construct. According to the 4Cs model, mentally tough individuals (a) view negative experiences (e.g. anxiety and stress) as a challenge that they can overcome but also a natural and essential catalyst for growth and development; (b) believe that they are influential in dealing with and controlling negative life experiences; (c) are deeply involved in what they are doing and committed to achieving their goals; and (d) are confident in their ability to deal with and overcome negative life experiences. Clough and colleagues subsequently defined mental toughness by looking at these four different aspects:

Mentally tough individuals tend to be sociable and outgoing; as they are able to remain calm and relaxed, they are competitive in many situations and have lower anxiety levels than others. With a high sense of self-belief and an unshakeable faith that they control their own destiny, these individuals can remain relatively unaffected by competition or adversity (Clough et al., 2002: 38).

Another dominant framework is based on the work of Jones and colleagues (2002, 2007) with elite and 'super-elite' (i.e. Olympic medallist) athletes. Their framework consists of four dimensions (attitude/mindset, training, competition and post-competition) and 10 overlapping subcomponents (belief, focus, using long-term goals as the source of motivation, controlling the environment, pushing yourself to the limit, regulating performance, handling pressure, awareness and control of thoughts and feelings, handling failure and handling success). Overall, 30 key mental toughness attributes are assigned and ranked under these four broad dimensions (see Jones et al., 2007). Jones and colleagues proposed the following construct definition:

> Mental toughness is having the natural or developed psychological edge that enables you to: Generally, cope better than your opponents with the many demands (competition, training, lifestyle) that sport places on a performer. Specifically, be more consistent and better than your opponents in remaining determined, focused, confident, and in control under pressure. (Jones et al., 2002: 209)

The most recent model to emerge is that of Gucciardi and colleagues (2009a). Coming to the topic with an interest in integrating theory (i.e. Personal Construct Psychology: Kelly, 1991) and research, they developed a 'process model' in which they sought to encapsulate the experiential processes of mental toughness. Within this model, the key components of mental toughness are said to influence the way in which an individual covertly and overtly approaches, appraises and responds to events demanding varying degrees of challenge, adversity and pressure. Subsequently, self-reflection and feedback from others provides information that an individual may use to evaluate their investment in their experiences and outcomes. In integrating research with their process model, Gucciardi and colleagues proposed a definition of mental toughness that has subsequently been amended:

> Mental toughness is the presence of some or the entire collection of experientially developed and inherent values, attitudes, emotions, cognitions, and behaviors that influence the way in which an individual approaches,

responds to, and appraises both negatively and positively construed pressures, challenges, and adversities to consistently achieve his or her goals.

(Coulter et al., 2010: 715)

The strengths and weaknesses of each of these definitions (and models) have been debated elsewhere (e.g. Gordon and Gucciardi, in press) and are not reiterated here, other than to highlight that each of these definitions differs in their specificity (i.e. broad versus narrow) and focus (i.e. outcomes versus processes). For example, the Clough et al. (2002) definition is highly specific in detailing the attributes of mental toughness, whereas Coulter et al. (2010) is more general in nature. Nevertheless, as with most definitions of psychological constructs, we should be cautious not to accept all mental toughness definitions as equally valid or as representing the same thing. Thus, although research on this construct has proliferated in recent years, the area suffers from a lack of construct clarity. Needless to say, the widely discrepant views of mental toughness pose a problem for the legitimacy of scientific inquiry and progress in the field.

On the dimensionality of mental toughness

Regardless of the approach taken to research this construct, mental toughness is often considered a multidimensional construct that reflects diverse attributes and capacities, some of which are manifested as cognitions, emotions, attitudes and behaviours. In other words, mental toughness represents a higher-order latent construct that integrates (i.e. represents the common variance between components) several distinct but related dimensions (i.e. lower-order factors) into a single theoretical concept (cf. Law et al., 1998). Although much of the support for a multidimensional view of mental toughness stems from qualitative evidence, recent psychometric analyses of measurement instruments also support the existence of a higher-order construct that explains a significant amount of variance between the specific dimensions (e.g. Gucciardi and Gordon, 2009; Sheard et al., 2009). Nevertheless, the specific components housed under the mental toughness construct vary both in terms of their content and breadth across the three dominant models (Clough et al., 2002; Gucciardi et al., 2009a; Jones et al., 2007). Interested readers are referred elsewhere (Connaughton and Hanton, 2009; Chapter 7 above) for comprehensive overviews of the key components identified in previous research.

On the situational relevance of mental toughness

An important finding regarding the conceptualization of mental toughness relates to its perceived utility across the various challenges, pressures and adversities athletes may face during the course of their careers. Some conceptualizations of mental toughness (e.g. Clough et al., 2002; Chapter 6 above) draw heavily on negative life experiences in which an individual is exposed to a serious risk, stressor or adversity that poses a threat to positive outcomes. Conceptualized in this manner, there appears to be considerable conceptual overlap between mental toughness and related constructs such as resilience. However, there is evidence to suggest that mental toughness pertains to the successful navigation of both negative and positive life experiences in which an individual perceives some kind of pressure, adversity or challenge (e.g. Coulter et al., 2010; Gucciardi et al., 2008; Jones et al., 2007). Thus, although mental toughness appears useful in helping an athlete rebound from serious injury or deselection from the team (i.e. negatively construed situations), it may also provide the impetus for assisting transitions into an elite competition and/or maintaining consistent levels of performance when the expectation is for one to perform well (i.e. positively construed situations). Clearly, that this evidence is based on retrospective recall and not on well-controlled experimental designs requires substantiation.

The future

While this book is clear evidence of the advances the field of mental toughness in sport has experienced over the past decade, several challenges remain. Having reflected on the past and assessed the present, we next consider the future of mental toughness research in sport. Specifically, we will focus our attention on conceptual, methodological and practical issues that we believe have the greatest potential for furthering research in this area.

Conceptual considerations

Despite consensus among both academics (i.e. researchers) and professionals (i.e. psychologists, coaches, athletes) on the centrality of mental toughness for performance excellence, there remains considerable disagreement over how to conceptualize and operationalize this construct. As is evident throughout the contributions to this book and elsewhere (e.g. Gordon and Gucciardi, in press), a number of conceptual models of mental toughness exist. Some models are grounded within the socio-cultural boundaries of sport (e.g. Jones et al., 2007), whereas others are founded in research (e.g. Clough et al., 2002) and theory (e.g. Gucciardi et al., 2009a) from non-sport contexts. Regardless of their conceptual and empirical underpinnings, these models have important implications for the subsequent measurement and development of mental toughness. Confusion over how to conceptualize and operationalize mental toughness has discouraged a common language among researchers, thereby the construct has a different meaning to different people. Consequently, the conceptual and practical implications of mental toughness differ as a function of the operationalization used.

Jingle and jangle

As with many other areas of psychology (e.g. Gignac, 2009; Marsh et al., 2003), the mental toughness literature appears to suffer from both the jingle (Thorndike, 1904) and jangle (Kelley, 1927) fallacies (for discussions, see Block, 1996, 2000).

A jingle fallacy refers to the use of common terms for different conceptions, whereas a jangle fallacy refers to the use of different terms for common underlying conceptions. The jingle and jangle fallacies seem especially malicious in the mental toughness literature as we are only beginning to lay the empirical and conceptual foundations of this construct. With the emergence of recent sport-general and sport-specific measures of mental toughness in the last decade, we believe the time is ripe for researchers to consider the jingle-jangle fallacy in future research and theorizing. In other words, how 'jingly' (i.e. different measures of mental toughness are in fact measuring different constructs) and 'jangly' (i.e. measures of resilience or hardiness actually assess a construct that is essentially equivalent to mental toughness) is the mental toughness literature? Indeed, there are critics of mental toughness (Chapter 5 above) who argue the case of a jangle fallacy; that is, mental toughness is simply a new label for an old construct (i.e. resilience). Without any future consideration of these important 'languaging' issues, we believe the plethora of definitions and conceptualizations will work against cumulative knowledge on mental toughness in sport. Having a common definition of mental toughness, in particular, may serve to unite a field that appears fragmented based on preference for a particular model.

Multidimensionality

The large number and variety of facets housed under the mental toughness umbrella has the potential to create theoretical confusion about the boundaries of this construct, as well as complicate which components can be appropriately included in empirical investigations. For example, conceptualizations of mental toughness differ somewhat between sports such as cricket (Gucciardi and Gordon, 2009) and Australian football (Gucciardi et al., 2009b). Differences also exist within sports such as cricket (Bull et al., 2005; Gucciardi and Gordon, 2009) and soccer (Coulter et al., 2010; Thelwell et al., 2005) across different groups of researchers. Both qualitative and quantitative research support the notion that mental toughness is a complex multidimensional construct that encompasses a variety of values, cognitions, attitudes, emotions and behaviours. Nevertheless, researchers are encouraged to 'clearly define the relations between a multidimensional construct and its dimensions. Without specifying these relations, the various dimensions are simply a collection of related variables, and there is no need to label them as components of a multidimensional construct' (Law et al., 1998: 742).

The utility of the higher-order representation is 'generality, breadth, and simplicity', whereas that of first-order representation is 'specificity, precision and accuracy' (Edwards, 2001: 152). In addition to acknowledging the dis/advantages of both higher- and lower-order representations of mental toughness for their relative usefulness, Edwards (2001) recommended that researchers estimate and evaluate models in terms of five key issues: theoretical utility (i.e. usefulness of the multidimensional construct and its dimensions for theory), level of abstraction (i.e. interpretability of the higher-order, general construct versus lower-order dimensions), reliability (i.e. influences of heterogeneity of dimensions and number of items), construct validity (i.e. validity of the interpretation of dimension specificity and the general construct), and criterion-related validity (i.e. ability of the higher-order construct in explaining the variance between lower-order dimensions and external criterion). It is imperative that mental toughness researchers address these dimensionality issues in future research.

Beyond performance excellence

An inherent theme in the available mental toughness research, particularly qualitative investigations that have sampled elite athletes and coaches, is that of an optimal performance perspective. In other words, the motivation behind much of the mental toughness research to date appears to stem from the desire to understand the psychological makeup that differentiates those athletes 'who get there', 'who stay there' and who 'perform to their potential' and those who don't. Currently, there is little evidence to support a link between mental toughness and performance; however, if this expectation turns out to be the case there will be important implications for talent development programmes and coach training. The strong likelihood is that there may be much more to this thing called mental toughness than achieving performance excellence in the sport context.

Reflecting on several attributes that have been discussed in the life skills literature (Chapter 9 above), the majority of the key mental toughness assets (e.g. self-belief, personal values, work ethic, positive and tough attitudes, self-motivation, resilience, attentional control, and enjoying and thriving through pressure, challenge and adversity) appear analogous to accepted indicators of positive youth development (e.g. Lerner et al., 2006). That mental toughness appears to allow one to regain normal levels of psychological and physical functioning following exposure to a highly disruptive event as well as sustain high levels of functioning when faced with a positive event is an important feature of this construct. Both regaining and sustaining optimal levels of functioning are important for youth attempting to thrive in various performance settings (e.g. the classroom, job interview). In addition to these commonalities, mental toughness encompasses a number of other important personal qualities (e.g. emotional intelligence, physical toughness, context intelligence, hard work ethic) that are not commonly reported as accepted indicators of positive youth development. Thus, we argue that the development of mental toughness represents an innovative process by which positive youth development can be achieved in youth sport contexts. In addition, if mental toughness does facilitate positive youth development, the opportunity to develop mentally tough youth sport participants affords a practical significance in which mental toughness represents an attractive 'hook' to encourage key stakeholders to invest their time and energy in engaging in endeavours that also promote the positive development of young people.

Methodological considerations

One of the things that became clear to us in editing the chapters in this book, as well as reflecting upon the available peer-reviewed literature, was the lack of methodological diversity from which researchers have opted to examine mental toughness in sport. Thus, there is a need to consider alternative methodological approaches in future research. These issues are not new to sport psychology, or ground-breaking in any sense, but rather remain relatively uncharted in the mental toughness domain.

Person- vs. variable-centred approaches

The 'variable' and 'person' nomenclature can be traced to Block (1971: 13):

> Variable-centered analyses are useful for understanding the differences between people and what characteristics go with what characteristics in a group of individuals. But as well, and ultimately, psychology will need to seek understanding of the configuration and systematic connection of personality variables as these dynamically operate within a particular person.

Whereas variable-centred approaches focus on examining relations among variables, person-centred approaches identify subgroups of people based on their similarities on a set of variables (Bergman and Trost, 2006). An inherent assumption within variable-centred analytical models is that the population is homogeneous with respect to the variable(s) of interest. In contrast, person-centred analytical models reject the assumption that the entire population is homogeneous but rather are heterogeneous with regard to the variable(s) of interest. Prototypical statistical techniques for variable- and person-centred analyses include, respectively, correlations, regressions and structural equation models and profile, class and cluster analyses.

To date, mental toughness research can be characterized by variable-centred approaches, although exceptions involving person-centred analyses do exist (e.g. Gucciardi, 2010). There is a need, therefore, for researchers to complement the findings of variable-centred research with evidence derived from person-centred analyses such that statements are more accurate and valid, and explain more variance than when assuming a homogeneous population. For example, groups with similar mental toughness profiles identified using person-centred analyses (e.g. cluster analysis) can be compared using a second set of variables such as motivational and achievement goal preferences (see e.g. Gucciardi, 2010) to ascertain whether the clusters are discriminable in theoretically relevant ways. Alternatively, one could utilize latent class growth modelling analyses to discover the number and shape of the developmental trajectories of mental toughness by creating unobservable subgroups or latent classes of individuals with different patterns of change and stability (Nagin, 1999; see also Nagin and Odgers, 2010, for a comprehensive review).

Longitudinal designs

Although the term 'longitudinal' is rather broad and imprecise, longitudinal studies essentially involve the collection and analysis of a variety of variables on the same people over two or more distinct time periods (Menard, 2002). This approach contrasts with cross-sectional research in which data collection occurs at only one point in time for each person. Asking the same individuals the same sequence of questions at regular intervals is considered one of the most reliable and rigorous means of assessing developmental changes in psycho-social constructs because the data are collected while the subjective states actually exist (Menard, 2002; Ruspini, 2008). Some of the benefits associated with longitudinal designs include being able to analyse the duration of phenomena, highlight and identify patterns of intra- and inter-individual differences and changes over time, and identify indications of the direction and magnitude of causality (Menard, 2002; Ruspini, 2008). Cross-lagged panel analyses, for example, could be implemented to ascertain the causal predominance between key mental toughness facets over time. The findings of such analyses would also shed light on which key facets are most influential on other key mental toughness characteristics. Cross-lagged analyses might also include additional variables assessing hypothesized key contributors to the development of mental toughness such as the motivational climate created by coaches and/or peer, and other important developmental experiences (e.g. initiative experiences, critical incidents).

Links with objective indicators of behaviour or performance

Researchers, coaches and athletes all recognize the importance of mental toughness for achieving performance excellence (Connaughton and Hanton, 2009), yet this important issue has not appeared on the radar of most researchers. In his critique of the available research, Andersen (Chapter 5 above) highlighted the lack of empirical evidence supporting a link between mental toughness and objective indicators of behaviour or performance as one of the overarching concerns with the area. In tennis, for example, we might expect that mentally tough athletes are more effective at coming from behind in a game (e.g. down 15:40 on serve) or a set (e.g. down 2 games to 5) than less mentally tough players. Alternatively, it may be that mentally tough tennis players are less likely to let a lead slip away during a game or set than less mentally tough players. We might also expect higher free-throw percentages over the course of a competitive season for mentally tough basketballers when compared with less mentally tough players. Until the question of how mental toughness relates to objective indicators of performance or behaviour is addressed, doubts will remain about the conceptual and applied value of this construct.

Experimental designs

Although we have identified the need for longitudinal examinations of mental toughness to ascertain the temporality of mental toughness within its nomological network, such analyses do not truly establish a causal relationship (Ruspini, 2008). As with the broader field of sport and exercise psychology (Hagger and Chatzisarantis, 2009; Williams et al., 2008), much of the available mental toughness research is characterized by simple, correlational designs exploring relationships with hypothesized key correlates. Although these studies are important for generating theory and hypotheses, they lack the power to provide rigorous information about causal mechanisms. Rather than passively waiting to observe some important phenomenon, therefore, we believe there is a need for mental toughness researchers to proactively produce well-formulated and testable hypotheses under experimental conditions. Nevertheless, we agree that experimental designs should not be considered the 'holy grail' of causal evidence (Hagger and Chatzisarantis, 2009: 515) but rather as an important part of multiple research strategies and methods aimed at understanding these issues (Rutter, 2001).

As mentally tough athletes are characterized by the ability to thrive when under pressure (Gucciardi et al., 2008; Jones et al., 2002, 2007), experimental designs that involve some form of objective performance under low and high anxiety (i.e. pressure-induced) in a 'laboratory setting' represents an excellent starting point. For example, after controlling for potential covariates such as skill level and playing experience (i.e. recruit participants that are closely matched), one could have participants perform a series of perceptual-cognitive (e.g. decision-making, anticipation; Coulter et al., 2010; Gucciardi et al., 2008) or physical tasks (e.g. free-throws, golf putts) in both conditions. Self-reported mental toughness would be obtained prior to participation in the experimental conditions. A mediation analysis could then be performed to ascertain if self-reported mental toughness mediates the relationship between performance in the low (i.e. predictor variable) and high anxiety (i.e. outcome variable) conditions. Alternatively, one could assess the relationship between consistency of performance (cf. Coulter et al., 2010; Gucciardi et al., 2008) in the high anxiety condition and mental toughness, after controlling for low anxiety performance.

Cross-cultural research

Previously, we noted the domination of Western researchers, particularly individuals from the UK and Australia, in generating knowledge and evidence on mental toughness in sport. Notwithstanding these efforts, an implication of this Western dominance is that mental toughness might best be considered a culture-specific construct (emic) as opposed to one that is universal (etic). Cross-cultural research is clearly needed to assess the generality of current conceptualizations, as well as to discover and understand variations which are not present across different cultures (Hui and Triandis, 1985). Testing comparability and equivalence of measurement instruments across cultures, for example, is an important endeavour for future research. In particular, there is a need for cross-cultural research that simultaneously evaluates models of mental toughness from at least three different countries (Bond and Smith, 1996). Failure to support the generality of the measurement instrument can mean that mental toughness is construed differently in different cultures, or that the psychometric properties of the items are non-invariant, thereby requiring amendments so that statements are culturally and contextually sensitive.

In working towards understanding the generality of our knowledge and the novel variations of the phenomenon within different cultures, we can assemble and integrate this information into a nearly universal conceptualization that takes into account unique variations that will be valid for a broader range of cultures. As evidenced in recent conference proceedings, researchers from the Middle East (Shamoun, and Elgamal, 2008) and Asia (Kuo et al., 2010) are indeed interested in the potential value of mental toughness. Thus, we encourage mental toughness researchers to seek out collaborations with non-Western colleagues in exploring the cross-cultural relevance of mental toughness.

Practical considerations

All four chapters in this book that focused on the development of mental toughness have expressed several excellent techniques, strategies and approaches that practitioners should definitely consider applying. We fully encourage and support further research into the application and evaluation of interventions using any of these suggestions. In this section, we would like to offer two other macro-level approaches when attempts are being considered to help athletes develop their mental toughness. First, we briefly describe Carol Dweck's (2006) research on changing 'mindsets'; and, second, we summarize the strengths-based strategies being proposed by Alex Linley and his colleagues (2008, 2010) at the Centre of Applied Positive Psychology (CAPP).

Changing mindsets

Dweck's (2006) research suggests that athletes have a choice between two different mindsets when it comes to developing mental toughness. Those with a fixed mindset might say to themselves 'I'm not mentally tough – never have been, and never will be – so what's the point of trying to develop it?' Growth mindset athletes on the other hand, would say 'I'm not mentally tough, yet – I expect mental toughness to take time and so if I work hard at it I'll improve and I'll get there eventually.' Dweck points out that these two different mindsets are just different beliefs – albeit powerful beliefs – that are susceptible to change in the same way that much of our personalities, beliefs and habits can also be changed. Lots of our innate qualities, such as temperament, have stability over time if you leave them alone. However, according to Dweck, if you work hard at developing anything you can improve. In other words, the environment we choose to expose ourselves to can actually 'over-ride' natural and predispositional tendencies.

Dweck's (2006) strategies for fostering growth mindsets (GMS) in education, business, relationships, and sport involve teaching individuals how to keep learning. She quotes Benjamin Barber, an eminent sociologist, as saying 'I don't divide the world into the weak and the strong, or the successes and the failures … I divide the world into the learners and nonlearners' (Dweck, 2006: 16). To avoid fixed mindsets (FMS) therefore, and to prevent athletes from becoming nonlearners, there needs to be constant provision of opportunities to learn.

Promoting GMS opportunities allows individuals to embrace learning from both failure and success, understand the importance of hard work and effort – talent is a job, not a gift – and to welcome challenges. For example, we believe the following line of GMS questioning would foster the development of a mental toughness mindset: When recently did you struggle with failure or pressure, yet persisted despite the setback and adversity? Besides your attitude and hard work, what else were you proud of in your efforts to learn more about yourself? Such questioning conveys a 'new value system' that involves choices and strategies when dealing with tough situations.

Strengths-based approaches

Alex Linley and his colleagues' recent contributions (Linley, 2008; Linley and Joseph, 2004; Linley et al., 2010) and others (e.g. Ben-Shahar, 2010, Cooperrider et al., 2008; Fredrickson, 2009; Lyubomirsky, 2008; Seligman, 2002) we believe represent the zeitgeist of positive psychology applications to sport and exercise psychology. For example, in relation to Dweck's (2006) GMS 'learn to fail or fail to learn', Ben-Shahar claims we can only learn to deal with mentally tough situations such as failure by actually experiencing it, by living through it. In addition, the earlier we face difficulties and setbacks the better prepared we will be to deal with the inevitabilities that lie ahead on life's path. In talking about the positive value of failure he quotes J. K. Rowling, author of the 'Harry Potter' books:

> Failure taught me things about myself that I could have learned no other way. … The knowledge that you have emerged wiser and stronger from setbacks means that you are, ever after, secure in your ability to survive. You will never truly know yourself, or the strength of your relationships until both have been tested by adversity.
>
> (Ben-Shahar, 2010: 42)

While focusing on solutions, what works and what is strong characterizes most principles and applications of positive psychology, folks at the Centre of Applied Positive Psychology (CAPP) also accommodate problems and weaknesses, and in fact deal with them head on. Recently, we reported an application of the CAPP Realise2 model (Linley, 2008; Linley et al., 2010) in an attempt to develop mental toughness among male professional cricketers (Gordon, 2010). Briefly, the Realise2 model considers strengths as things that we do in sport that we are good at and that energize us. These things can be Realized Strengths that we get to do regularly, or Unrealized Strengths that we don't get as much opportunity to use so much and yet are our greatest areas for development. Learned Behaviours are things we are good at but drain us of energy and, if we use them excessively over time, will burn us out. Weaknesses are things we are not good at and also drain us. Subsequently, the best advice is to marshal realized strengths, by using them to best effect but not too much; maximize unrealized strengths, by finding opportunities to use them more; moderate learned behaviours, by not using them too much; and minimize weaknesses, by finding ways to stop having to focus on them at all. However, if you can't find ways to ignore weaknesses, the model provides five ideas on how to minimize their relevance and impact on performance, which we adapted to our cricket sample. First, we asked players if they could reshape their role on the team so that they could play in their 'element' more rather than have to bat, bowl or field at times and in positions that they felt vulnerable; second, we asked them to consider using their strengths to compensate for their weaknesses such as being more decisive about shot selection with both short and full length quick deliveries, being more disciplined using a pre-delivery routine with both tail-end and top-order batsmen; third, we asked them to find a complementary partner, someone who was strong in areas they were weak so they could buddy up at training or during games and learn vicariously from watching strengths in action; fourth, we grouped players according to their strengths and weaknesses so we could chunk up a level from complementary partner and adopt strengths-based teamwork off-field as well as during training and games; and finally, when none of the above strategies was possible players were invited to undertake specific training and development sessions, with the aim of becoming as good as they needed to be or good enough, but not excellent. While the latter idea – psychological skills training – would traditionally be the first, and perhaps only, strategy adopted by most sport psychology practitioners, the players in our sample reported great benefits from using the other techniques. On the overall value of a strengths-based approach one senior player remarked 'I can't believe how many years I've wasted working on my weaknesses'.

We believe changing mindsets and strengths-based approaches have considerable potential in developing mental toughness, and in the future we encourage experimental evaluation of interventions using each procedure separately or in combination, with athletes of all age and ability levels. Importantly, as well as other strategies previously identified by other contributors in this book, we believe that both methodologies are consistent with the basic tenets of personal construct   psychology (PCP: Kelly, 1991), which we have described elsewhere (e.g. Gucciardi and Gordon, 2009; Gucciardi et al., 2009a). Specifically, guided questioning associated with changing mindsets and strengths-based processes elicits learning and understanding of an individual's personal construct system.

Conclusion

By understanding the past, assessing the present and considering the future we have attempted to highlight existing shortcomings in our understanding and examination of mental toughness in sport. Our intention in this chapter has been to share with the reader some of our ideas that may provide food for discussion and debate among current and future mental toughness researchers. In so doing, we hope to have provided readers with a platform from which to conduct original and rigorous research that will contribute to the conceptual evolution of mental toughness while at the same time raising the standard of research in the area.

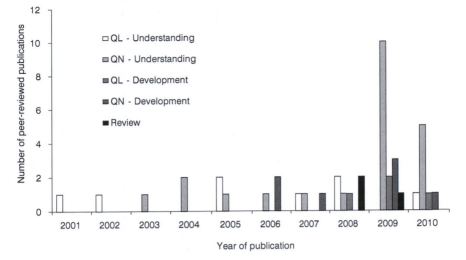

Figure 12.2 Chronological overview of the type of mental toughness papers published in peer-reviewed outlets

References

References marked with an asterisk indicate papers included in the assessment of the 'past' of mental toughness (see Figures 12.1 and 12.2).

Ben-Shahar, T. (2010) *Even Happier: A Gratitude Journal for Daily Joy and Lasting Fulfillment,* Sydney: McGraw-Hill.

Bergman, L.R., and Trost, K. (2006) 'The person-oriented versus the variable-oriented approach: Are they complementary, opposites, or exploring different worlds?', *Merrill-Palmer Quarterly, 52,* 601–32.

Block, J. (1971) *Lives through Time,* Berkeley, CA: Bancroft Books.

Block, J. (1996) 'Some jangly remarks on Baumeister and Heatherton', *Psychological Inquiry,* 7, 28–32.

Block, J. (2000) 'Three tasks for personality psychology', in L.R. Bergman, R.B. Cairns, L.G. Nilsson and L. Nystedt (eds), *Developmental Science and the Holistic Approach,* Mahwah, NJ: Lawrence Erlbaum, pp. 155–64.

Bond, M. H., and Smith, P. B. (1996) 'Cross-cultural social and organizational psychology', *Annual Reviews of Psychology,* 47, 205–35.

*Bull, S. J., Shambrook, C. J., James, W., and Brooks, J. E. (2005) 'Towards an understanding of mental toughness in elite English cricketers', *Journal of Applied Sport Psychology,* 17, 209–27.

Clough, P., Earle, K., and Sewell, D. (2002) 'Mental toughness: The concept and its measurement', in I. Cockerill (ed.), *Solutions in Sport Psychology,* London: Thomson, pp. 32–45.

Connaughton, D., and Hanton, S. (2009) 'Mental toughness in sport: Conceptual and practical issues', in S. D. Mellalieu and S. Hanton (eds), *Advances in Applied Sport Psychology: A Review,* London: Routledge, pp. 317–46.

*Connaughton, D., Hanton, S., Jones, G., and Wadey, R. (2008a) 'Mental toughness research: Key issues in this area', *International Journal of Sport Psychology*, 39, 192–204.

*Connaughton, D., Wadey, R., Hanton, S., and Jones, G. (2008b) 'The development and maintenance of mental toughness: Perceptions of elite performers', *Journal of Sports Sciences*, 26, 83–95.

*Connaughton, D., Hanton, S., and Jones, G. (2010) 'The development and maintenance of mental toughness in the world's best performers', *The Sport Psychologist*, 24, 168–93.

Cooperrider, D. L., Whitney, D., and Stavros, J. M. (2008) *Appreciative Inquiry Handbook: For Leaders of Change* (2nd edn), Brunswick, OH: Crown Custom.

*Coulter, T., Mallett, C. J., and Gucciardi, D. F. (2010) 'Understanding mental toughness in Australian soccer: Perceptions of players, parents, and coaches', *Journal of Sports Sciences*, 28, 699–716.

*Crust, L. (2007) 'Mental toughness in sport: A review', *International Journal of Sport and Exercise Psychology*, 5, 270–90.

*Crust, L. (2008) 'A review and conceptual re-examination of mental toughness: Implications for future researchers', *Personality and Individual Differences*, 45, 576–83.

*Crust, L. (2009) 'The relationship between mental toughness and affect intensity', *Personality and Individual Differences*, 47, 959–63.

*Crust, L., and Azadi, K. (2009) 'Leadership preferences of mentally tough athletes', *Personality and Individual Differences*, 47, 326–30.

*Crust, L., and Azadi, K. (2010) 'Mental toughness and athletes' use of psychological strategies', *European Journal of Sport Sciences*, 10, 43–51.

*Crust, L., and Clough, P. J. (2005) 'Relationship between mental toughness and physical endurance', *Perceptual and Motor Skills*, 100, 192–4.

*Crust, L., and Keegan, R. (2010) 'Mental toughness and attitudes to risk-taking', *Personality and Individual Differences*, 49, 164–8.

*Crust, L., Nesti, M., and Littlewood, M. (2010a) 'A cross-sectional analysis of mental toughness in a professional football academy', *Athletic Insight: The Online Journal of Sport Psychology*, 2(2).

*Crust, L., Nesti, M., and Littlewood, M. (2010b) 'Player and coach ratings of mental toughness in an elite association football academy', *Athletic Insight: The Online Journal of Sport Psychology*, 2(3).

Dweck, C. S. (2006) *Mindset: The New Psychology of Success,* New York: Random House.

Edwards, J. R. (2001) 'Multidimensional constructs in organizational behavior research: An integrative analytical framework', *Organizational Research Methods*, 4, 144–92.

*Fourie, S., and Potgieter, J. R. (2001) 'The nature of mental toughness in sport', *South African Journal for Research in Sport, Physical Education and Recreation*, 23, 63–72.

Fredrickson, B. L. (2009) *Positivity,* New York: Crown.

Gignac, G. E. (2009) 'Psychometrics and the measurement of emotional intelligence', in C. Stough, D. H. Saklofske, and J. D. A. Parker (eds), *Assessing Emotional Intelligence: Theory, Research, and Applications,* London: Springer, pp. 9–40.

*Golby, J., and Sheard, M. (2004) 'Mental toughness and hardiness at different levels of rugby league', *Personality and Individual Differences*, 37, 933–42.

*Golby, J., and Sheard, M. (2006) 'The relationship between genotype and positive psychological development in national-level swimmers', *European Psychologist*, 11, 143–8.

*Golby, J., Sheard, M., and Lavallee, D. (2003) 'A cognitive-behavioral analysis of mental toughness in national rugby league football teams', *Perceptual and Motor Skills*, 96, 455–62.

*Golby, J., Sheard, M., and Van Wersch, A. (2007) 'Evaluating the factor structure of the Psychological Performance Inventory', *Perceptual and Motor Skills*, 105, 309–25.

Gordon, S. (2010) 'Strengths-based coaching of mental toughness in sport: Case study of a professional cricket team', paper presented at the International Congress of Applied Psychology, 11–16 July, Melbourne.

Gordon, S., and Gucciardi, D. F. (in press) 'Mental toughness', in J. Adams (ed.), *Sport Psychology: Theory and Practice*, London: Pearson.

*Gucciardi, D. F. (2009) 'Do developmental differences in mental toughness exist between specialised and invested Australian footballers?', *Personality and Individual Differences*, 47, 985–9.

*Gucciardi, D. F. (2010) 'Mental toughness profiles and their relations with achievement goals and sport motivation in adolescent Australian footballers', *Journal of Sports Sciences*, 28, 615–25.

*Gucciardi, D. F., and Gordon, S. (2008) 'Personal construct psychology and the research interview: The example of mental toughness in sport', *Personal Construct Theory and Practice*, 5, 118–29.

*Gucciardi, D. F., and Gordon, S. (2009) 'Development and preliminary validation of the Cricket Mental Toughness Inventory', *Journal of Sports Sciences*, 27, 1293–1310.

*Gucciardi, D. F., Gordon, S., and Dimmock, J. A. (2008) 'Towards an understanding of mental toughness in Australian football', *Journal of Applied Sport Psychology*, 20, 261–81.

*Gucciardi, D. F., Gordon, S., and Dimmock, J. A. (2009a) 'Advancing mental toughness research and theory using personal construct psychology', *International Review of Sport and Exercise Psychology*, 2, 54–72.

*Gucciardi, D. F., Gordon, S., and Dimmock, J. A. (2009b) 'Development and preliminary validation of a mental toughness inventory for Australian football', *Psychology of Sport and Exercise*, 10, 201–9.

*Gucciardi, D. F., Gordon, S., and Dimmock, J. A. (2009c) 'Evaluation of a mental toughness training program for youth-aged Australian footballers: I. A quantitative analysis', *Journal of Applied Sport Psychology*, 21, 307–23.

*Gucciardi, D. F., Gordon, S., and Dimmock, J. A. (2009d) 'Evaluation of a mental toughness training program for youth-aged Australian footballers: II. A qualitative analysis', *Journal of Applied Sport Psychology*, 21, 324–39.

*Gucciardi, D. F., Gordon, S., Dimmock, J. A., and Mallett, C. J. (2009e) 'Understanding the coach's role in the development of mental toughness: Perspectives of elite Australian football coaches', *Journal of Sports Sciences*, 27, 1483–96.

Hagger, M. S., and Chatzisarantis, N. L. D. (2009) 'Assumptions in research in sport and exercise psychology', *Psychology of Sport and Exercise*, 10, 511–19.

*Horsburgh, V. A., Schermer, J. A., Veselka, L., and Vernon, P. A. (2009) 'A behavioural genetic study of mental toughness and personality', *Personality and Individual Differences*, 46, 100–5.

Hui, C. H., and Triandis, H. C. (1985). Measurement in cross-cultural psychology: A review and comparison of strategies. *Journal of Cross-Cultural Psychology*, 16, 131–152.

*Jones, G., Hanton, S., and Connaughton, D. (2002) 'What is this thing called mental toughness? An investigation of elite sport performers', *Journal of Applied Sport Psychology*, 14, 205–18.

*Jones, G., Hanton, S., and Connaughton, D. (2007) 'A framework of mental toughness in the world's best performers', *The Sport Psychologist*, 21, 243–64.

*Kaiseler, M. K., Polman, R. C. J., and Nicholls, A. R. (2009) 'Mental toughness, stress, stress appraisal, coping, and coping effectiveness', *Personality and Individual Differences*, 47, 728–33.

Kelly, G. A. (1991) *The Psychology of Personal Constructs: A Theory of Personality,* vol. 1, London: Routledge; originally publ. 1955.

Kelley, T. L. (1927) *Interpretation of Educational Measurements,* Oxford: World Book Co.

Kobasa, S. C. (1979) Stressful life events, personality, and health: An inquiry into hardiness, *Journal of Personality and Social Psychology*, 37, 1–11.

Kuo, T. H., Chang, Y. K., Yen, S. H., and Chin, M. C. (2010) 'The relationship between coping strategies and mental toughness among soccer players', *Journal of Sport and Exercise Psychology*, 32, S186–S187.

Law, K. S., Wong, C. S., and Mobley, W. H. (1998) 'Toward a taxonomy of multidimensional constructs', *Academy of Management Review*, 23, 741–55.

Lerner, R. M., Lerner, J. V., Almerigi, J., Theokas, C., Phelps, E., Naudeau, S., et al. (2006) 'Toward a new vision and vocabulary about adolescence: Theoretical and empirical bases of a "positive youth development" perspective', in L. Balter and C. S. Tamis-LeMonda (eds), *Child Psychology: A Handbook of Contemporary Issues,* New York: Taylor & Francis, pp. 445–69.

*Levy, A. R., Polman, R. C. J., Clough, P. J., Marchant, D. C., and Earle, K. (2006) 'Mental toughness as a determinant of beliefs, pain, and adherence in sport injury rehabilitation', *Journal of Sport Rehabilitation*, 15, 246–54.

Linley, A. (2008) *Average to A+: Realising Strengths in Yourself and Others,* Coventry: CAPP.

Linley, A., and Joseph, S. (eds) (2004) *Positive Psychology in Practice,* Hoboken, NJ: John Wiley.

Linley, A., Willars, J., and Biswas-Diener, R. (2010) *The Strengths Book,* Coventry: CAPP.

Loehr, J. E. (1982) *Athletic Excellence: Mental Toughness Training for Sports,* New York: Plume.

Loehr, J. E. (1986) *Mental Toughness Training for Sports: Achieving Athletic Excellence,* Lexington, MA: Stephen Greene Press.

Lyubomirsky, S. (2008) *The How of Happiness: A Scientific Approach to Getting the Life you Want,* New York: Penguin.

*Marchant, D. C., Polman, R. C. J., Clough, P. J., Jackson, J. G., Levy, A. R., and Nicholls, A. R. (2009) 'Mental toughness in the workplace: Managerial and age differences', *Journal of Managerial Psychology*, 24, 428–37.

Marsh, H. W., Craven, R. G., Hinkley, J. W., and Debus, R. L. (2003) 'Evaluation of the Big-Two-Factor Theory of academic motivation orientations: An evaluation of jingle-jangle fallacies', *Multivariate Behavioral Research*, 38, 189–224.

Menard, S. (2002) *Longitudinal Research* (2nd edn), Newbury Park, CA: Sage.

*Middleton, S. C., Marsh, H. W., Martin, A. J., Richards, J. E., Savis, J., Perry, C., and Brown, R. (2004) 'The Psychological Performance Inventory: Is the mental toughness test enough?', *International Journal of Sport Psychology*, 35, 91–108.

Nagin, D. S. (1999) 'Analyzing developmental trajectories: A semiparametric, group-based approach', *Psychological Methods*, 4, 139–57.

Nagin, D. S., and Odgers, C. L. (2010) 'Group-based trajectory modeling in clinical research', *Annual Review of Clinical Psychology*, 6, 109–38.

*Nicholls, A. R., Polman, R. C. J., Levy, A. R., and Backhouse, S. H. (2008) 'Mental toughness, optimism, pessimism, and coping among athletes', *Personality and Individual Differences*, 44, 1182–92.

*Nicholls, A. R., Polman, R. C. J., Levy, A. R., and Backhouse, S. H. (2009) 'Mental toughness in sport: Achievement level, gender, age, experience, and sport type differences', *Personality and Individual Differences*, 47, 73–5.

Ruspini, E. (2008) 'Longitudinal research: An emergent method in the social sciences', in S. Hesse-Biber and P. Leavy (eds), *Handbook of Emergent Methods,* New York: Guilford Press, pp. 437–60.

Rutter, M. (2001) 'Testing hypotheses on specific environmental causal effects on behavior', *Psychological Bulletin*, 121, 291–324.

Seligman, M. E. P. (2002) *Authentic Happiness,* Sydney: Free Press.

Shamoun, M. A., and Elgamal, A. K. (2008) 'Mental toughness and flow state for women elite swimmers', in L. J. Yu, Y. Jiang, and Q. Z. Sun (eds), *Proceedings of First Joint International Pre-Olympic Conference of Sports Science and Sports Engineering*, vol. 3, *Statistics and Management in Sports,* Liverpool: World Academic Press, pp. 448–9.

*Sheard, M. (2009) 'A cross-national analysis of mental toughness and hardiness in elite university rugby league teams', *Perceptual and Motor Skills*, 109, 213–23.

*Sheard, M., and Golby, J. (2006) 'Effect of a psychological skills training program on swimming performance and positive psychological development', *International Journal of Sport and Exercise Psychology*, 4, 149–69.

*Sheard, M., Golby, J., and van Wersch, A. (2009) 'Progress toward construct validation of the Sports Mental Toughness Questionnaire', *European Journal of Psychological Assessment*, 25, 186–93.

*Thelwell, R., Weston, N., and Greenlees, I. (2005) 'Defining and understanding mental toughness in soccer', *Journal of Applied Sport Psychology*, 17, 326–32.

*Thelwell, R. C., Such, B. A., Weston, N. J. V., Such, J. D., and Greenlees, I. A. (2010) 'Developing mental toughness: Perceptions of elite female gymnasts', *International Journal of Sport and Exercise Psychology*, 8, 170–88.

Thorndike, E. L. (1904) *An Introduction to the Theory of Mental and Social Measurements,* Oxford: Science Press.

*Veselka, L., Schermer, J. A., Petrides, K. V., and Vernon, P. A. (2009) 'Evidence for a heritable general factor of personality in twin studies', *Twin Research and Human Genetics*, 12, 254–60.

Williams, A. M., Hardy, L., and Mutrie, N. (2008) 'Twenty-five years of psychology in the *Journal of Sports Sciences*: A historical overview', *Journal of Sports Sciences*, 26, 401–12.

Index